PENGUIN BOOKS

SPANISH JOURNEYS

Adam Hopkins is a journalist and writer. After spending some years in Spain he joined the *Sunday Times* in London, covering Spanish politics as occasion demanded. More recently, as a freelance, he has contributed extensively on Spanish culture and travel to a variety of national newspapers in Britain.

His previous travel books include *Holland*, a study of its history and painting, and *Crete: Its Past, Present and People*. He is also the author of *The School Debate* (Penguin 1978), which deals with education policy.

Adam Hopkins is married to a fellow journalist and has two grown-up children by a previous marriage and three younger step-children.

ADAM HOPKINS

SPANISH JOURNEYS

A PORTRAIT OF SPAIN

PENGUIN BOOKS

PENGUIN BOOKS

Published by the Penguin Group
Penguin Books Ltd, 27 Wrights Lane, London W8 5TZ, England
Penguin Putnam Inc., 375 Hudson Street, New York, New York 10014, USA
Penguin Books Australia Ltd, Ringwood, Victoria, Australia
Penguin Books Canada Ltd, 10 Alcorn Avenue, Toronto, Ontario, Canada M4V 3B2
Penguin Books (NZ) Ltd, 182–190 Wairau Road, Auckland 10, New Zealand

Penguin Books Ltd, Registered Offices: Harmondsworth, Middlesex, England

First published by Viking 1992
Published in Penguin Books 1993
5 7 9 10 8 6 4

Printed in England by Clays Ltd, St Ives plc

This book is dedicated to my friends pictured within, whether or not with speaking parts, to my son Benjamin, born Madrid, 3 May 1965, and to my godson, Carlos Gervás, born Madrid, 7 December 1970.

Contents

List of illustrations ix
Preface xi
Maps of Spain xiv–xvii

1 Where East Meets West: *Hispania, Al-Andalus* 1

2 Moors and Christians: *Goodbye to Universalism* 41

3 Isabel and Fernando: *Catholic Kings, Catholic Conquests* 88

4 Imperial Might: *Dark Deeds in a Brilliant Land* 127

5 'Golden Age': *Art Ascendant in a Time of Trouble* 166

6 Enlightenment and Black Reaction: *Goya's Inheritance* 210

7 Art and Politics: *Nineteenth-Century Madrid and Barcelona* 243

8 Days of Death and Dictatorship: *Spain 1923–1982* 285

9 From Coast to Coast: *Travels in Spain Today* 328

Select bibliography 379
Index 389

List of illustrations

1 Santa María del Naranco, Asturias
2 San Salvador de Valdedíos, Asturias
3 Asturian winter scene
4 The Virgin of Covadonga
5 Sanctuary at Covadonga
6, 7 Madìnat al-Zahra, Córdoba
8 The Aljafería, Zaragoza
9 Inner courtyard, the Aljafería
10 Valencia, a view from the Miguelete tower
11 Sculptural detail, Santa María la Real, Sangüesa
12 The bridge at Puente la Reina, on the Pilgrims' Way
13 Graffito in Puente la Reina
14 The beach at Tazones, Asturias
15, 16, 17 Details, cloister of Las Dueñas, Salamanca
18 Cloister of the College of San Gregorio, Valladolid
19 Sculpted doorway, College of San Gregorio, Valladolid
20 Tordesillas on the Río Duero
21 Shrine to St Teresa, outside Avila
22 Cloister at monastery of Guadalupe
23 Monk at Guadalupe
24 Pottery kilns, Seville
25 Detail from doorway, Seville town hall
26 Seville street scene
27 Ceramic detail, Plaza de España, Seville

28 Lone horseman at El Rocio, Huelva
29 Buildings in Cádiz
30 Nesting stork
31 Coca Castle, Old Castile
32 The bridge of San Martín, Toledo
33 Rockscape on the Costa Brava
34 Modernista roofscape, Manzana de la Discòrdia, Barcelona
35, 36 Ironwork by Gaudí, Palau Guëll, Barcelona
37 Gaudí balcony, Casa Milà (La Pedrera), Barcelona
38 The Miró Foundation, Barcelona
39 Sitges parish church
40 Francoist memorial outside the *alcázar*, Toledo
41 Sculpture and cross at the Valley of the Fallen
42 The ruins of Belchite, Aragón
43 Fountain at Aranjuez
44 Glimpse of the monastery, El Escorial
45 Plaza Mayor, Madrid
46 Brown bear and arbutus, Puerta del Sol, Madrid
47 Horse and carriage in Seville
48 Goatherd near Isla Cristina

All photographs taken by the author

Preface

T HE IDEA FOR a book of this kind has been in my mind for
many years. The extensive travelling involved, and the time
borrowed from other work, have been made possible by the Eleni
Nakou Foundation, a newly established body devoted to the promotion of better understanding between northern and southern
Europe. Brittany Ferries have generously helped me with travel on
their Plymouth–Santander route, the most convenient way of arriving in Spain with a car. My thanks also to the Spanish paradors, a
chain of state-run hotels occupying some of Spain's most prominent
historic sites and buildings and for this reason inevitably entering
my story from time to time. For those who wish to stay in comfort
and some stateliness, not always my own objectives, the paradors
make an outstanding movable base.

Aside from this, my personal debts are almost innumerable.
The greatest thanks of all must go to Agustín Gervás, who has
watched over the project from Madrid with continuous encouragement and patience, suggesting ideas and suffering over early drafts,
endlessly generous with time and knowledge. Javier Coy, then in
Salamanca, now in Valencia, has also been unstinting with his help.
Tim Bozman of Zaragoza has shared with me some of his deepest
insights into Spain, as also has Luisa Asensio of Oviedo. Amidst the
difficulties and dangers of the Basque Country, Pablo Sorozábal
agreed to the proposition that he should be used as a case study, an
act of kindness demanding special thanks.

It is not possible to cite the names of all who have helped me, but I should like in particular to acknowledge the generosity of the following (some of whom are also mentioned in the text): in Barcelona, Xavier Domingo and María José Ania; in Burgos, Daniel de la Iglesia; in Córdoba, José Salinas; in Copenhagen, Denmark, Erik Holm; in León, César Alvarez and Diego Alvarez; in Lanzarote, César Manrique and Enrique Suárez; in London, Vivien Ashley and Richard Gott, Bernice Davison, David Wickers, Charlotte Fenn; in Madrid, in addition to Agustín Gervás, María José Gomez-Navarro, Pablo Gervás, Tom Burns, Susana Moreno and Pablo Sorazábal (hijo); in Oviedo, Paco Mori and Mari Carmen Rodriguez, Juan Benito Argüelles and Loli Lucio, Gerardo Turiel, María Luisa Telenti; in Seville, Antonio Coy, Pilar Marín and Jerry Johnson; in Tampere, Finland, Markku Huotari; in Torremolinos, José García-Rojo; in Valencia, Carmen Aranegui and Antonia Sánchez; in Zaragoza, in addition to Tim Bozman, Julián Casanova. To those many others whose names are not given here, my no less heart-felt thanks.

Many of the journeys in this book were made alone, but whenever opportunity offered I was joined by my wife, Gabrielle Macphedran. Her pleasure in Spanish travelling is quite as keen as mine and I owe much to her observation and insight, as also to her support at home. Thanks also to my agent, Michael Motley.

A NOTE ON PLACE-NAMES

The question of Spanish place-names has grown more complicated recently, with increasing recognition, and use, of the minority languages of Basque, Catalan and Galician, alongside the majority Castilian. In general, I have preferred Castilian place-names for ease of recognition, usually mentioning the fact when departing from this practice, as is from time to time inevitable and proper. In some cases, English versions are so well established that I have used them instead – Catalonia and the Canary Islands, for example, Seville for Sevilla, the River Tagus for the Castilian Río Tajo and so forth. Just occasionally I have declined an English version, even if well established. The reasons are partly personal – I far prefer Spanish Andalucía, for example, to English Andalusia with its false quantities. In other instances, the reasons are more practical. In the case of Saragossa (Castilian Zaragoza), the version used in English is borrowed from the Catalan, reflecting past patterns of trade and politics. But nowadays Zaragoza is a Castilian-speaking city, making the Catalan name seem inappropriate in English.

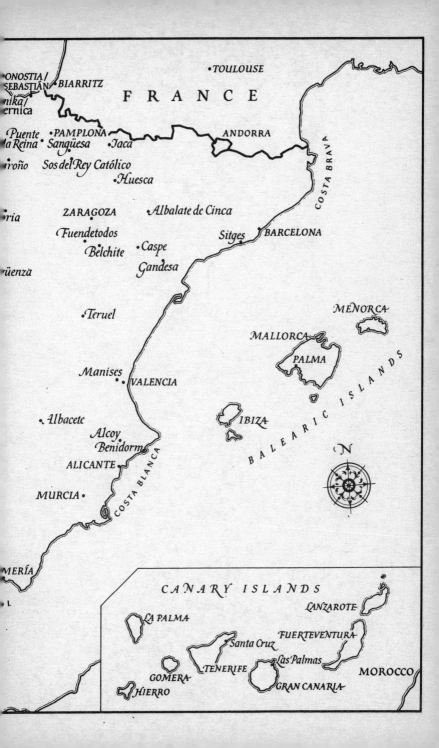

1 Where East Meets West

Hispania, Al-Andalus

I CAME INTO ASTURIAS again on a January evening. Full moon, climbing over the long swell of Biscay, began to finger its way across a bluff coast edged with cliffs. The coming night had drained away the greenness of the countryside but left the pungent smell of cattle everywhere. Down to my right, the Atlantic surge rammed itself purposefully into fissures. Spray leapt in the moonlight, live as an animal, high over stubs of cape.

What made me gasp, though, was the view that suddenly appeared inland, a view that closed, rather than opened, consisting of a wall of rock as clear as any cardboard cut-out, black and without perspective in the gathering darkness but topped, the length of its ragged crest, with fire. It was too much, almost an absurdity, when the evening star began to glimmer just above the red.

The Picos de Europa, perched on the northern edge of Spain, are mountains famous for their mists and driving rain. Often enough this view had been denied me by the weather. Tonight it was revealed just as it had been thirty years ago as I travelled to my first job, heart in mouth, typewriter on my knee, in a crowded bus along the winding northern coast. I fell in love with Asturias, needless to say, its mists and hills and mountains, its dreary mining valleys and grimy industrial towns, nor have I seen any reason since to renounce those first affections. All the while, though, two aspects of this northern principality have stayed with me as symbols for the whole of Spain – the jagged, saw-blade sharpness of the mountain crest,

1

magnificent but most uncomfortable, and on the other hand the soft Asturian mists, their sinuous beauty concealing the asperity of rock.

You can be fooled very easily by surfaces in Spain, all is so rich in appearance, so intensely dramatic. Gypsy faces in the south, the sober Catalans of the north-east, the table-pounding Basques not far back along the coast that I was driving, cork oaks and olives, cities and villages, the sense of suffering and human dignity across the whole of the *meseta*, that high inland plain which occupies by far the larger part of Spain – the images flow so fast they often inundate analysis, making it all too easy to receive this extraordinary country not as a place and people, open to understanding, but as a collection of moods. Such, I fear, has often been the case with me. Tomorrow, though, I start again with my Spanish journeys, this time through art and history and hoping for better understanding of what may lie within those vivid and compelling moodscapes.

Covadonga, green valley under green mountains in the Picos de Europa, is famous for a battle that did or did not take place sometime in the year 718 AD – or it might have happened or not happened in 722 AD or any of the four years in between or even as late as 726. It was a battle, or of course it wasn't, between the Moors and Christians, that much is certain. The evidence lies in untrustworthy Christian chronicles and passing references in Arabic texts.

The background to the story is simple, if, inevitably, dramatic. In the days after the Romans, the Visigoths ruled in Hispania, the land eventually comprising Spain and Portugal. Though often reckoned a rough lot, the Visigoths, quite on the contrary, believed themselves to be the true heirs of the classical world, devoted to its values. They brought a keen if aristocratic sense of honour and established a Christian kingdom, heretical at first but ultimately Catholic, somewhat ineffectively administered yet supple enough to endure for centuries. Its greatest weakness lay in the ceaseless power struggles surrounding the elective leadership.

Matters were at a low ebb in 711. Roderic, king of the Visigoths, was campaigning in the Basque Country (País Vasco in Castilian, Euskadi in Basque) when he heard the shocking news: Islamic troops, some 7,000 of them, had landed in the south of the peninsula. They seem to have come in loose alliance with a Visigothic power block opposed to Roderic – a clear example, often repeated in Spanish history, of inviting the wolf into the sheep pen to help out with some entirely local matter. Roderic now hurried southwards with his army, met the invaders frontally, was, so it seems, betrayed in battle, lost everything and left no further trace in chronicle or song. The Islamic forces, made up of Arabs from far off and Berber soldiers from North Africa, known communally and satisfactorily as the Moors, swept up through Córdoba to winter in Toledo, till then the Visigothic capital. Four years more and it was over – the whole of the peninsula was either paying hefty tribute or was actually in Moorish hands.

All, that is, except for a few deep valleys and steep mountainsides in the Picos de Europa. To reach them on this January morning, I drive under cold blue skies with mountains climbing higher and higher on all sides, crackling with cold, throwing down fierce shadows. The line where shadows end and sun begins is absolute, sharp as a blow. Firewood stands crisp in stacks. I have, of course, been lucky with the weather. More often, all in the valleys is a squelch of mud. Here, thirteen centuries ago, in a situation foreshadowing that of Asterix and friends in Gaul, a pocket of resistance was developing around a leader named Pelayo, perhaps a Visigoth in retreat, perhaps an unconquered Asturian. The shrine of Covadonga – consisting of a shallow cave in the mountain wall, a turn-of-century basilica on a shoulder of hill, a choir school, a museum and a barracks for the Civil Guard, or *Guardia Civil*, that famous paramilitary police force – is entirely devoted to giving an account of the events that now ensued; or did not, as the case may be.

'You see,' said the tall priest on the steps on the huge basilica, gesturing aloft to a grassy mountain scattered with white rocks, 'the Christians were on the top, just there. Ten thousand Moors were approaching from this side' – he pointed below him to the valley – 'and another 20,000 from behind. But the Christians had the image of Mary to protect them, the Queen of Battles we call her, and Pelayo was holding up the cross . . .'

'Yes?' he interrupts himself rather testily as a middle-aged woman approaches, 'Yes, what is it?' She meekly offers a little silver necklace, just purchased, for his blessing. He waves his hand across it with a rapid mumble. Despite the signals, she tries to converse with him, to join in the little lecture I'm receiving. *'Basta,'* he says, 'enough, enough,' driving her away with a peremptory wave, then turns again to me, a foreigner engaged in the important quest for information. I was, as it happens, sufficiently prepared, having already inspected the vast car-parks and tourist shops on entry to the shrine and climbed the steps to the cave that was Pelayo's refuge and now holds both his tomb and the little eighteenth-century image of the Virgin, placed there when the original was burned. Nuns were photographing one another in the cave and old people praying in a ceaseless patter, leaving no doubt at all about the importance of the place.

'Now,' said my priestly informant, 'you will understand that given the power of the cross and then the miraculous appearance of the Virgin herself, right there on the field of battle ...' and off he goes, with what is actually a rather modest version, compared to Christian chronicles, of the first chapter of that orotund, self-deceiving tale in which, from the moment Pelayo first held up the wooden cross and raised his sword in the other hand, the fate of Islam in Spain was irrevocably determined. The great eighth-century Reconquista, or Reconquest, unparalleled in world history, had begun and would be carried on unswervingly till the fall of Granada to Isabel and Fernando, 'the Catholic Kings', in 1492. It was to be a triumph of Church and royalty and feudal lieges, in fervent crusade against the infidel. No matter that the end was far beyond conjecture, that for much of the long period, despite their mutual hostility, Christianity and Islam were deeply interlaced in economic, political and artistic interchange; no matter that the very notion of crusading was still four centuries away from its invention; the Spanish Church and the whole of Spanish tradition still proclaim that it was here, in 718, or 722, or even perhaps in 726, that their great crusade began. It is precisely in the story told me by the priest that Christian Spain has recognized its own reflection.

4

Writers and missionaries, cardinals and generals – notable among them one General Francisco Franco, whose own activities in Spain's Civil War were dubbed a crusade by the Church – have been more than happy to equate their country with a militant, militaristic Christianity. You can see the evidence right there in the church porch, where the framed and printed 'Decalogue of Covadonga' offers quotations propounding just this view. Leopoldo Alas, Spain's great novelist of the nineteenth century, is typical. 'Covadonga,' he declared, 'whether or not the negative rationalist [himself, that is to say] is pleased about the fact, represents two great things – a Spanish patriotism and a great faith, the Catholic faith of the Spaniards who fought in Covadonga for their faith and fatherland.' The historian Menéndez Pidal, apparently arguing from some concept of manifest destiny, asserts that the victory had to happen for the preservation of the West and to prevent Spain from becoming another Syria or Egypt. Only the non-Spaniard, Pope John XXIII, takes a milder view. 'Covadonga is one of nature's smiles,' he says in the Decalogue. 'I love the Madonna of Covadonga as you Asturians love her yourselves. I have her image in my sleeping chamber and it is for her that I make my first prayer of the day.'

Whatever actually happened in Covadonga, there are several independent certainties. A man named Pelayo was at about this time indeed proclaimed king of what became a tiny independent territory. It was briefly centred just nearby in the little town of Cangas de Onís, and then moved on to what has now become the considerable city of Oviedo.

Pausing only to lunch in a noisy teenage dive in Cangas, in error but agreeably enough, I followed the kings and courtiers of Asturias out of the mountains and down to their new capital.

Ah, Oviedo, scene of my first pay packet. Few spots have ever pleased me more than this grey, gritty town, gathered around the park of San Francisco, where mothers watched over their toddlers, lovers cooed with caution – you could be arrested then for kissing in a public place – and folk on business strode determinedly through. The city was still so small in those days that nobody would think of driving. I lived on the Calle Fruela, named for one of the Asturian kings, in the caretaker's flat above the Banco Herrero. It was a surprise to me at first to find that Spaniards waged a systematic war against the daylight, even in the rainy north, pulling down vast, clanking roller-blinds named *persianas* and pursuing their domestic lives in deep obscurity. Thus it was above the Banco Herrero, warm and dark and full of kindness and cockroaches. I slept beneath a twisted wooden crucifix and looked out, when I got the *persianas* open, on heavy Roman tiling, gleaming in the rain.

From here it was only a stone's throw to the cathedral, with its solitary, off-balance, open stonework tower and an interior of flamboyant Gothic from the later Middle Ages. Leopoldo Alas opened his fine Oviedo novel, *La Regenta*, in the cathedral tower and it stands over the old town still with tatty tenderness. Deep inside the cathedral, hidden away behind one of the transepts, is an early memorial of the Asturian kingdom, dating from the time of Alfonso the Chaste. This careful monarch reigned for more than fifty years at the start of the ninth century and, unusually, the name of his architect, Tioda, still survives. Tioda built Alfonso a solemn, barrel-vaulted church above a massive crypt and this, in due course, was enveloped by the cathedral. Today, a building buried within a building, it hides itself inside the cathedral, acting as treasury. The collection it holds includes a great array of saintly relics and two astonishingly sumptuous, bejewelled crosses. The tenth-century Cross of Victory is supposed to contain within its golden casing the wooden original borne by Pelayo at Covadonga. The other, smaller and a century older, is even more gorgeous and goes by the name of the Cross of the Angels. The Victory Cross is the symbol of the principality of Asturias and the Cross of the Angels the symbol of Oviedo, capital of the principality, so it is easy to imagine the dismay that swept across the region when both were stolen in 1977, only to be recovered, some months later, in Portugal, stripped of their jewels.

I go, since it is my evident duty, to pay my respects to the two crosses, now well-restored, and to the stunning little agate casket stolen at the same time and similarly recovered. This morning's guide to the treasury, an old man in a long overcoat, sniffing multitudinously, tells me, with near-miraculous certainty, the provenance of every single item among the treasury's innumerable relics. At length, he leads me down through the cloister, and into a tiny corner of open graveyard, burial place of pilgrims who died before they could reach their holy goal of Santiago de Compostela. From this sad spot, you look up to the heavy external masonry of Tioda's original church, exposed just at this point, blackened by soot, assailed by acid rain, surviving somehow at the heart of Oviedo.

Tioda built another church nearby, known as Santullano or San Julián de los Prados. It stands within ten metres of a local motorway, seemingly larger inside than out – a curious feature of early Asturian buildings – with three stout naves and all the proper appurtenances. As I enter, a group of young people playing wistful, electronic rock look up with smiles of welcome. Beyond them, at the head of the main nave, is a crucifix with lolling head, known locally as Tom Dooley, while all around, more interesting than the fabric of the church, there still exists an almost complete set of murals contemporary with the building. Some of the painting is abstract and decorative, mainly rectangles and circles with petal patterns, looking curiously like Byzantine art of the iconoclastic period. Much of it, though, is representational and offers a glimpse of what the early Asturians evidently admired – fine sturdy palaces of classical style complete with capitals and pediments and even sets of curtains. It is a neat reminder that King Alfonso the Chaste and his tiny following were conscious spiritual heirs of the honourably minded, classically inclined Visigoths, the people who believed they were really Romans underneath the skin. Visigothic blood, if one should be lucky enough to possess some, was a badge of highest nobility; in future days it was to be a standard claim that the Spanish kings were directly descended from the Visigoths.

More, and different – though it should be said that the vast majority of surviving monuments of this period are ecclesiastical – soon follows on the Monte del Naranco. This is a steep hill rather than a mountain, sitting just north-west of Oviedo, and guarding on its flanks still more accomplished memorials of the Asturian kingdom. I am about to visit them in appropriate company.

Paco Mori had been my employer in the days when I lived on the Calle Fruela. The son of the house, he was already married and living out with his own young family but often, on a Sunday morning, he would abandon wife and baby for vigorous excursions on Naranco. As often as I could, I tagged along with him. I loved his energy, his swiftness on the hill, his great, gusty pronouncements on this or that affair of politics or personal relations, followed by a punishing uphill burst, or even worse, a downhill run that left me clasping knees and thighs. More recently, since the death of Franco and the coming of democracy, I knew that Paco had been drawn into Asturian nationalist politics. Indeed, the last time I had seen him was on an election poster near the cathedral, beaming away with his fellow-candidates above the slogan 'Only Asturians will defend Asturias'. Today, it being Sunday once again, I have a date with Paco to retrace our steps of thirty years ago.

We go, to my surprise, by car, two middle-aged men a good deal heavier than we were, wrapped in overcoats and toting serious cameras. I have brought my walking boots along but think it better not to mention them as we begin the well-remembered climb behind the railway station, up by the sanatorium for the tubercular and on past newly constructed restaurants, bars with look-out balconies and a growing number of private houses. There are plenty of other cars on the little road, aiming for a sports club higher up, another novelty. It all seems very different from those earlier slogs on foot. But soon we come to a spot that makes us forget, for a while at least, the encroachments of the city.

Santa María del Naranco, tenderest of buildings made in stone, began its long career in the 840s, in the brief reign of Ramiro I, Alfonso the Chaste's successor. It was originally a place for audiences and royal dinners, perhaps with a wooden palace just beside it and with a still-surviving stone-built church a hundred yards or so along the mountainside. Santa María, too, is now officially designated a church but it remains entirely secular in feeling. Two storeys high, rectangular, with pitched roof and a little, triple-arched balcony at either end, it seems at first extremely simple as it sits in its little meadow just below the road. In fact, the longer you look the more there is to admire: the beautifully balanced tiers of arch and window at the ends of the building; long loops like sunken ropes engraved into the buttresses, giving them height and grace beyond their real proportions; the sweetly carved, shallow medallions inside and out, often with little animals, horses, perhaps, and deer, or pairs of opposed birds; columns with a spiral pattern, looking as if millepedes were swarming up them; capitals with curling leaves like rounded donkeys' ears or human tongues with thick whorls underneath; and best of all, to my taste, the little Greek cross of Alfonso the Chaste with 'alpha' and 'omega' suspended left and right, a motif embracing birth and death and the divinity.

Southwards from Santa María on this January day, looking down towards the main bulk of the peninsula, the view takes in the tall, snow-covered mountains blocking off easy access to the central tableland of Spain. In the middle distance, with mist in green valleys and humped backs of hills like shoals of dolphins, the Monte Sagrado lies. Here Christian images were buried during the Moorish advance. Closer again is the spire of the cathedral, rising above the old grey town of Oviedo and the winter trees of the park, flat-looking from this viewpoint, a dark-coloured handkerchief laid out to dry. Out to the sides, the city is spreading in huge assertions of apartment blocks. From the spot where we are standing, the Asturian kings and their retinue must also have looked out. Perhaps the view was why they chose the site.

Paco and I take photographs of one another and of Santa María. Its elegance contrasts with the solidity of the countryside all round, habitat of peasant farmers who probably have a job in town as well but still cut hay with scythes and sickles. In rainy weather they clomp out to the byre in three-legged wooden clogs, suspended perilously above the mud. They are hearty and voluble, affable and energetic.

The conventional image of the early Asturians is of a people rather in the same mould, except that they probably had beards and helmets too and lacked the three-legged clogs to keep their feet dry. As always though, in the presence of Santa María del Naranco,

Paco and I question this image of the Asturian forefathers; and we have no trouble in agreeing that at the heart of their little kingdom, struggling first for survival and then to enlarge itself, there lay a capacity for great artistic achievement. What does not seem so happy, though, is Paco's estimate of the Asturian present.

Frankly, I had been expecting otherwise. One aspect of the new, post-Franco democracy has been the unleashing almost everywhere of separatist or fiercely regional sentiment. This is strongest, of course, in Catalonia and the Basque Country, supported in the latter case by active, bitter terrorism. Trying vainly for accommodation during the late 1970s and early 1980s, the central government evolved a system of partial autonomy for all Spain's various component parts, from Andalucía to the Canary Islands, from Galicia and La Rioja to the Balearics. The Catalans and Basques got rather more self-government than the rest, but Asturias was right there as one of the autonomies and I had imagined that Paco, loyal son of the principality, would be bubbling with excitement and a sense of possibilities.

'Look,' he said when we reached the summit of Naranco to encounter a wasteland of litter and broken vegetation, 'just look at that scene of public abandonment. If this were Catalonia, there would be no hanging back. A place like this would soon be sorted out. But in Asturias nobody seems to care. We have lost our pride, we have lost our will to keep the things that should be ours. Here, in a country of a million people, no more than would be living in a single suburb of Paris, we are blessed with almost everything that we need for sustenance and pleasure. We have the Picos de Europa for our Alps, fish in the sea and salmon in the rivers, apples for cider and milk enough for almost all of Spain. We have coal and zinc and glass and a steel industry. Yet nobody believes in doing anything. We are willing to abandon ourselves to a world-wide uniformity, a bland universalism, believing in the goodwill of the central state and looking for rescue to outsiders. Our industry is owned by Madrid, our civil servants come from Madrid. In reality, we are a colonized people.'

That night, at dinner among schoolteachers, I recapitulate the argument and nobody takes it seriously – except for the claim that Asturian industry is controlled from elsewhere. This, my friends say, is not only true but contrasts sharply with the Basque Country, where industry is more often than not locally owned – a powerful impulse towards separatism. For the rest, they say that Asturian nationalism has really not got off the mark. Nor is there hope in the new autonomies, a toothless tier of new bureaucracy. The group has extra griefs to add to those of Paco, though, starting with the Bourbon monarchy, restored in the 1970s and comporting itself, as all agree, with almost Scandinavian modesty and probity. But one person after another, going round the room, provides some instance or other of the fragility of the institution, its lack of public support if it should ever come into question. Seamlessly the conversation now moves on to politicians and their supposed cupidity. 'The whole of the political classes, without respect of party, is hopelessly corrupt,' says one of the teachers, anger in his voice. All round the room, men and women nod in agreement.

Was nothing going right, I asked despairingly, my visit having begun so well with the early Asturians? Surely Oviedo was at least enjoying a new prosperity? And back at once came the consensus. Spain was in the grip of a new, contagious materialism which all of them hated uniformly: *'copas y ropas'* – fine clothes and drinks in expensive places.

José Capdevila Orozco, standing in his customary corner in a bar in Córdoba, takes a more sanguine view. In all directions the tangled little streets of the old Jewish quarter wind in and out and round about, offering glimpses of little white patios, sweet and discreet, soon to be hung with an abundance of geraniums. Horsemen in wide-brimmed Cordoban hats are nowhere to be seen, but they too are seasonal, coming with the tourists and good-weather festivals. Señor Capdevila loves it all. 'My theory,' he says, quoting a maxim I will hear more than once during my travels, 'is that God created Andalucía so he would have somewhere to go if he ever got thrown out of heaven.' I rather agree with him, imagining as he speaks those river courses with early almond blossom, the mountains whose lower slopes are planted out with olives, neat and ordered as the buttons on a waistcoat, with wild and leonine sierra rising up above. Most of all, I imagine the little white towns with narrow, floral streets and black steel grilles across the windows.

Erect in posture, correct and rather formal in address, Capdevila lives and breathes Andalucía, gives talks on the region if he travels outside it, and has, indeed, just published a volume containing the purported autobiographies of thirty remarkable Andalusians. Like many in Córdoba, he is a firm believer in history. 'A city which doesn't live with its past is decadent, nothing,' he says, and begins to list a few of the town's great sons: the two Senecas, the poet Lucan, and then, coming closer to the modern, the Arab philosopher Averroes, the poet Ibn-Hazm and the great Jewish polymath Maimonides. 'What counts,' he says, speaking of Moor and Jew and Christian, 'is the universalism of Córdoba, *la convivencia*, the living together of three cultures.'

After the Christian redoubt of Oviedo, Córdoba, the Moorish capital, was clearly my next stop. Travelling top to bottom across Spain, you cannot help but notice how the peninsula is divided into two by the great range of coastal mountains, so that the tiny strip along the north seems like one country and the whole of the rest, consisting mainly of the wide plains of the *meseta*, quite another. It was this other that the Moors occupied by preference, with its three great rivers, the Duero (often known as the Douro in English), Tagus and Guadalquivir, draining away westwards into the Atlantic, and the long Ebro carrying its waters down to the Mediterranean by way of the Levant, the fertile eastern coast of the peninsula. The Moors gave the name al-Andalus to the whole of this considerable country, not just the southern part; but it was in the south, on the banks of the Guadalquivir, that they pitched their camp and created the greatest city in Europe.

It took two centuries and lasted, at its zenith, barely another hundred, but the rise and cultural achievement of Córdoba, together with al-Andalus in general, was by far the most remarkable phenomenon of early medieval Spain. Like the Reconquista, it was by no means inevitable from the start.

The difficulties were mainly ethnic, for the Arabs among the Moors were of two distinct groups, Kalbites and Yemeni Qaysites, often at odds with one another, and both in a state of tension with the Berbers. While the Arabs occupied the fat lands of the southern rivers and the Levant, the Berbers were treated as an underclass and settled in mountainous and less fertile districts. Within thirty years of the invasion, the Berbers were in bitter and prolonged rebellion. Soon after, their settlements in the northern part of the *meseta* were hit by a murderous drought and famine. Many returned to Africa, leaving the plains and valley of the Duero partly denuded of occupants – an event that was to have momentous consequences for the Christians, who little by little filtered across the coastal range and into the open spaces further south. The other great problem was geographical, for the *meseta*, though essentially a plain, has many internal mountain ranges. Given the progressive collapse of the old Roman roads, communications had become extremely difficult, and there was an almost irresistible tendency for isolated regions to assert their independence, sometimes quite close to Córdoba but more often in the 'marches' adjacent to the Christian north. The maintenance of order and unity in al-Andalus was a brutal, bloody business.

Tension between the Moors and the subject peoples of their realm was probably less acute than among the Moors themselves, even though Córdoba embraced one of the more conservative of the several theological and juridical systems then evolving in Islam. As 'people of the book', worshipping a single God and putting their faith in texts that were also sacred to the Muslims, Jews and Christians were subjected to little if any persecution. The Jews, who had suffered greatly under the Visigoths, actually welcomed the Moors as liberators, garrisoning the towns for them during their lightning conquest; some specialists consider the generations that lived under Cordoban rule as the least troubled in the history of the diaspora. Christians were regarded as somewhat inferior but, being a 'protected people' like the Jews, they paid a useful sum in poll tax and were allowed to practise their religion. They came under little or no pressure to convert, though more and more eventually did so, providing a growing power base for the Moorish rulers. There were a handful of Christian martyrdoms in Córdoba, of great propaganda value to the Christians – the bones of the saints who perished somehow made their way to Oviedo – but all appear to have been deliberately sought, through open challenge to Islam, perhaps as a demonstration of faith in reaction to increasing numbers of conversions.

Still expansive in mood after conquering the peninsula, the early Moors made several attempts to break out to the north-east and push on into what is now southern and even central France. They were eventually turned back by Charles Martel. It was Charlemagne, his grandson, on a later expedition into Spain, whose retreating rearguard under Roland was cut to pieces by the Basques at Roncesvalles.

From the Moorish point of view, the next major event was the arrival in Córdoba, after extraordinary adventures, of the last surviving member of the Umayyad dynasty of Damascus. The Umayyads had long provided the caliphs – or 'successors' – who ruled the whole of Islam. Now the entire clan was hunted down and killed by the usurping Abbasids, who at the same time transferred the capital eastwards to Baghdad.

The name of the Umayyad refugee who came to Córdoba was Abd al-Rahman. His mother had been a Berber and he first sheltered among the Berber tribes in North Africa. Finally, through adroit diplomacy, he found a welcome as emir of Córdoba. Theoretically the emirate was a dependency of Baghdad, in political reality deeply opposed. It continued, though, to draw from the oriental mainstream for its cultural development.

Abd al-Rahman governed as a semi-independent sovereign. One of his undertakings was the construction of a large mosque, started in 785. Up to that time, the Moors had worshipped in the same building as the Christians, separated only by a partition wall. Now Abd al-Rahman bought the site from the Christian community and started what became, certainly at the time that it was finished and arguably even today, the most astonishing building in all Spain. The Great Mosque or Mezquita still survives in its final form – except, that is, for one small alteration. A sixteenth-century Christian cathedral has been plonked down right in the middle of it. Señor Capdevila, local biographer, asserts that the mosque has survived only because the site was Christianized, a thought that may indeed be true.

At all events, the Christian bells were pealing lustily as I crossed the Patio de los Naranjos, not for the first time, to visit Abd al-Rahman's handiwork. The mosque we see today is an enormous building, penned in by vast stone walls pierced here and there by highly ornamental gates. It is low in comparison with its acreage and aerial photos show its roof rising in stiff little waves like that of any factory, except where the cathedral bludgeons its way up in disregard of the surrounding structure. The principal entrance to the Patio de los Naranjos, that is to say the Courtyard of the Orange Trees, is through the much later, Christian-built but Moorish-style Puerta del Perdón, the Gate of Absolution. This has a tower above, housing the belfry; alas, poor Moors, there was no sound that set their teeth on edge so much as Christian bells. The ancient pools and fountains of the Patio, perhaps designed for coolness as well as for ablutions, are much reduced in size but the Patio as a whole remains extremely pleasant. Considerable numbers of Cordobans were lounging and chatting among the orange trees, giving the courtyard the relaxed and populous look so often seen in architectural prints of the eighteenth and nineteenth centuries.

Picking my way over the moss-covered cobbles and among the windfall oranges, I enter the mosque itself through the doorspace directly opposite the Puerta del Perdón. This takes you straight into Abd al-Rahman's first construction – and directly to an indrawn breath of astonishment. The familiar photographs are no preparation for the endless, shady groves of columns, the horseshoe arches rising above them, the spokes in each wheel of stone above each horseshoe alternating in blazons of red and white, a second tier of rounded arches rising above the first, also in red and white, the whole receding in each direction in long cool lanes of arch and column, built for prayer but apt for meditation, breathing at least the concept of the infinite. It is necessary first, before so much as consulting a ground-plan, to wander here and there in the orderly forest, exploring vistas and perhaps one's own reaction, encountering suddenly a group of fantastically elaborated, multi-lobed, multi-foliate arches, or marble putti from the cathedral spilling over into an aisle of the mosque, or a great vaulted ceiling like a circular scallop shell, or a series of archways of unbelievable mosaic brilliance, instantly recognizable as the spiritual centre, set into the back wall of the building and partially concealing a yet more sacred inner sanctum. These are some of the great glories of the mosque, built over time and open to all kinds of explication. You start best simply by wandering – and grumbling at the way the cathedral, gross in comparison with the mosque, breaks up the vistas that must in earlier days have seemed almost endless.

Abd al-Rahman's original construction, big enough for the city in his day, occupies one corner of the present mosque, accounting for about a quarter of the whole. Many of his columns are from other sites, Roman and Visigothic, and so are the capitals above them on which the double tier of arches rest. Few of the columns are an exact match in height so they have been placed on bases of differing sizes to bring them up to the same level. It is a simple, almost comical solution.

It is hard not to smile, even harder not to be struck by the originality of the building. Islamic art has always achieved its best effects through uniformity and strict convention, varied over time and place in detail rather than in concept. Yet here is an Islamic building that simply looks quite different from any other, conjured up on the soil of al-Andalus in a style that was new and is now sometimes described as Hispano–Mauresque. Certainly, there are traditional elements, even in the later parts of the building, but much of what pleases most appears completely different, particularly the double tiers of arch. Some writers have suggested, very reasonably, that the idea may have come from Roman aqueducts, pointing to the superb structure at Segovia and the handsome example much nearer at Mérida. The horseshoe arches are a greater puzzle. Art historians seem to have settled on the notion that they are a borrowing from the Visigoths; others may feel, as I do, that the evidence is unconvincing, and that the arches in the courtyard of the Great Mosque of Damascus, dating from 715, look suspiciously like the lightly indented horseshoes of Abd al-Rahman's original construction.

Whatever the answer, the Mezquita requires more than a single visit, as much in this account of Córdoba as in the practical reality of getting to know it well. For the moment, we have just Abd al-Rahman's corner, and Abd al-Rahman himself, the first Umayyad emir, dying before it could be finished and leaving the task to his successor.

For the emirs who came after him, order and unity remained a major problem. It was Abd al-Rahman's grandson, al-Hakam I, who earned himself a name among the chroniclers as the butcher of al-Andalus. The Day of the Fosse (or Ditch) is cited as the great example of duplicity. The emir had sent his son to celebrate the completion of a new citadel in Toledo. A number of local dignitaries, suspected of dissidence, were invited to an official feast. Instead of banqueting, they were decapitated and tossed into a ditch in the construction works. A few years later, across the old Roman bridge in the southern suburbs of Córdoba, a conspiracy developed to overthrow al-Hakam. It was led by disgruntled jurists, a class of intellectual of great importance in Islam and the only countervailing force in a system which relied on the otherwise absolute autocracy of the emir. Apprehended, more than seventy of the leaders were executed. When this and high taxation provoked open revolt, al-Hakam, in a foreshadowing of the more famous Spanish Fury in Antwerp in 1576, set about the frenzied destruction of the suburb. Hundreds were crucified before he was restrained and 20,000 fled to North Africa. But even with such fearful acts, the fissiparous tendencies of al-Andalus could not be checked. Zaragoza, for example, had become effectively an independent state, referring to itself as the 'third kingdom' – third, that is, after Córdoba and little Asturias.

Little Asturias, meanwhile, was coming along very nicely, having possessed itself of all Galicia and some of northern Portugal, not yet differentiated from other parts of Christian Hispania, and with small settlements across the coastal mountains in León; in other words, the whole of the territory in which the Moors had hitherto shown little interest or that which they had actually abandoned. The growth of Christian territory, from a Moorish point of view, was probably more an irritation than a substantial threat. But at about this time an event occurred in Galicia that was little by little to change almost everything. This was the discovery of what seems to have been a late Roman tomb and the immediate conclusion, priestly and popular, that it was none other than the tomb of the Apostle James – in Spanish, Santiago.

It was now accepted as an article of faith – whether inspired by craft or credulity – that following the death of Christ, James had spent a long ministry in Spain, had returned to Jerusalem and been beheaded there, and that his body had then been brought by boat, right through the Mediterranean and up round the Atlantic coast of Hispania, for burial at the place which soon acquired the name of Santiago de Compostela – Compostela being probably a corruption of the Latin for Field of Stars. This strange and unlikely tale, as is well known, became the focus of the greatest of Christian pilgrimages in Europe. It also ushered in French influence, incalculably important, all along its route and ultimately provided, in the person of St James, an ideological rallying point for Christian Spain.

Not yet, though. For the emirate was now enjoying its first real period of success and little in the peninsula seemed more attractive than Arab culture and Moorish luxury.

The luxury was founded above all on agriculture. Out on the plains, there was pasturing of animals and typical dry-country farming. In the valleys, surviving accounts suggest a rural idyll, though a very hard-working one, with densely cultivated fruits and crops, both Mediterranean and semi-tropical, in a carefully irrigated countryside. There were olives and vines; Spanish Muslims were often partial to wine. There were beans, peas, saffron and aubergines, soft wheat and hard (now used respectively for bread and pasta). The Moors had brought not just the orange, which flourished round

Valencia in the Levant, but limes and lemons, rice and cotton, dates and sugar cane, water melons and the coconut palm. Spinach had come, along with the artichoke. The pomegranate flourished.

Irrigation, the essential pre-condition and companion for this plenty, was widespread in the river basins and the Levant. Huge vertical water-wheels called *noria* – one still to be seen in Córdoba – picked up water in scoops, to deposit it in gravity-feed channels. There were smaller, donkey-powered wheels, made of more than 200 separate parts, and others, still more complicated, that emptied their endless ring of buckets into the scoops of a second wheel, set horizontally. It was impressive and extensive and even incorporated elements of the old Roman irrigation system. Perhaps it is for skill with water that the Arab civilization of al-Andalus has been most admired by posterity.

Mining was also briskly pursued, especially round the Río Tinto in the south-west. Silk was produced in many places. Most manufacture, in practice, was concerned with what we would today call luxury items: elaborate and gorgeous textiles (just a few, like the well-known 'Tapestry of the Witches', have survived), equally elaborate metalware, top-quality ceramics, including lustreware, and, of course, the leather of Córdoba.

Elegance is at least implicit in this list of Moorish manufacture and it comes as no surprise to find that Córdoba, now swelling into a very large town indeed, was wide open to the possibilities of fashion. During the reign of Abd al-Rahman II, from 822 to 852, the court gave welcome to a prominent poet from Baghdad. His name was Ziryab and this one man is credited with the introduction of up-to-the-minute haircuts, the choice of special colours for summer and winter clothing and the division of meals into a series of formally served courses. All these innovations, so many that perhaps the name of Ziryab is invoked as a kind of shorthand for the oriental influences pouring in, were eventually adopted by Europe at large. Then there is the fact that Ziryab's primary calling was that of poet.

If anything is clear about al-Andalus, it is that this was a land of poetry – of odes, laments and eulogies, courtly rather than popular, shaped in forms that were as traditional as most Islamic art and winning their writers not only a living but sometimes very high positions. According to one often-quoted witness, Arabic writing had a huge impact on the Christian community.

Our Christian young men, with their elegant airs and fluent speech, are showy in their dress and carriage, and are famed for the learning of the gentiles; intoxicated with Arab eloquence they greedily handle, eagerly devour and zealously discuss the books of the Chaldeans (i.e. Muhammadans), and make them known by praising every flourish of rhetoric, knowing nothing of the Church's literature . . . they can even make poems, every line ending with the same letter, which display high flights of beauty and more skill in handling metre than the gentiles themselves possess.

(Taken from *The Preaching of Islam*, by T. W. Arnold)

Such was the temper of the times under Abd al-Rahman II. He extended the Great Mosque, though not enormously, and left behind a host of political complications that had to be resolved before the city of Córdoba could move on to greater things.

The troubles were mainly local rebellions but so severe that they threatened to tear al-Andalus apart. Through several reigns and more than half a century, the emirate was always close to chaos. It was only from 912, when the third of the Abd al-Rahmans came to power, that the Moorish state was once again consolidated. The new ruler, only twenty-one years old on his accession, briskly mopped up a fifty-year-old separatist pocket in the mountains by Málaga and little by little imposed himself on almost the whole of the former territory of the emirs. His other problem was the rise of a rival dynasty, the Fatimid, too close for comfort in Egypt. Partly to assert al-Andalus against the Fatimids, partly because the Umayyads, his own family, believed in their unique claim to authority, Abd al-Rahman in 929 proclaimed al-Andalus an independent caliphate.

Córdoba had now attained its apogee. It was by European standards an enormous city, with a population of at least 100,000 and perhaps considerably more, many times greater than London or Paris and half the size of Baghdad, the largest city in the world.

There is a tendency to think of Islam as the religion of a desert people, but great urban conglomerations had in fact been a feature of Islamic life since the earliest days in Mecca and Medina. Now Europe was host to just such a city and perhaps, as one tries to tot up the account of Cordoban contributions to the future, one should recognize urbanization itself along with magnificent architecture and fine poetry, agricultural skill and highly advanced irrigation.

One less attractive aspect of the great city, as of the small Christian towns to the north, was the presence of considerable numbers of slaves. It has been suggested that the slave trade was the largest single strand of commerce in early medieval Europe; the Moors were most emphatically a part of it, preferring, when they could find them, fair-haired slaves from Scandinavia and the north-east, known to them as Slavs. Some were emasculated and became eunuchs (part of the tradition in which women lived in the protected circle of the harem, guarded by eunuchs), and many of the young women, free or captive, became the mothers of Moorish children. Intermarriage and simple interbreeding meant that racial lines were now becoming considerably blurred. Abd al-Rahman III, like many of his Umayyad forebears, was the son of a European mother, either Basque or Frank. He had blue eyes and red hair – which he apparently died black for political purposes – and spoke Romance, the degenerate form of Latin that later turned into Castilian. He relied for his military success, as did his successors, on bringing in many fresh contingents of Berbers and northern European mercenaries. This new and unassimilated group was ultimately to undo al-Andalus.

Soon after proclaiming the caliphate, Abd al-Rahman began to build a palace appropriate to his dignity. The very first of the Abd al-Rahmans, the Umayyad prince who had arrived as a refugee and founded the emirate, had built himself a summer retreat a short way out of Córdoba, at the point where the slopes of the sierra rise above the valley, offering a broad view of the fertile plain and city. He called it al-Rusafa after his family's summer retreat in Baghdad and there he wrote melancholy verses of exile, with a good deal of reference to palm trees. The site is now occupied by a modern parador, one of Spain's chain of state-run hotels, and local people flock to its balcony-bar at the weekend to enjoy a drink and look out over the modern city.

Abd al-Rahman III chose a similar site, but about three miles down river from the city. Together with the Great Mosque, his palace is the great place of pilgrimage for those in search of Moorish Córdoba. Here, though, the impression is entirely different, for this great building was destroyed and levelled – by Berbers in rebellion – at the close of the caliphate. During the present century, its principal areas have been excavated and restored, perhaps a little imaginatively, but in a way that certainly appears to give a flavour of the times, suggesting mass and dignity, sumptuousness and style.

The ruins flow downhill at the base of the sierra, arranged in massive terraces. Women in blue smocks sweep busily along the pathways, bougainvillea raises its bright head among the tumbling masonry. There is a wide and moderately pleasing view over the valley, still agricultural but with pylons and workshops dotted across the winter green and summer brown, then hills rising again to the south, beyond the Guadalquivir. Away to the east lies Córdoba itself, seen over the top of a pair of gasholders and a stand of eucalyptus. The edge of town – as is always the case with modern Spanish cities – is a cliff-fall of apartment blocks, startling and depressing in its abruptness. It is hard to imagine the delicate prettiness of the old town within.

Descending now through the Madinat al-Zahra, the name of Abd al-Rahman's palace-city, you pass large roofless buildings with horseshoe arches once used by the Moorish military. There is an eastern entrance under even larger arches and a ramp leading up from it, suitable for clattering cavalry. Down at the bottom, the foundations of a mosque have been revealed. But the unmistakable centre, lodged on a wide terrace once splendidly gardened and ornamented with pavilions, is the large re-erected building containing the royal chambers. This has been credited with a wealth of horseshoe arches, in the same red and white segmenting as the Great Mosque. To its great advantage, the arcade on to the terrace has been left open (the many wide doorways of the Great Mosque have been blocked up by Christian hands, making it much darker than intended).

Like the monastery-palace of El Escorial, built 600 years later by Felipe II of Spain, Madinat al-Zahra is a building that provokes statistics. An account of its construction has survived; we know, for instance, that 6,000 ashlar blocks were brought each day by 1,500 pack animals and 400 camels, together with prodigious quantities of cement. Even the workers' wages have come down to us, along with the numbers of loaves of bread consumed daily by a population that included, when it was finished, almost 4,000 slaves and a women's quarter of over 6,000. And then there was the support system on which it all rested, stud-farms and standing army and a munitions factory turning out, apparently, 20,000 arrows a month.

Which is all well and good for those who like that kind of thing. For me, the horseshoe arches of the royal chambers, however conjectural, speak more eloquently. Nor should one miss the stone wall-cladding, carved in cursive vegetal and geometric patterns, considered Hellenistic in inspiration and unparalleled, up to that time, in the Islamic world. All round on the terrace, among cypresses and low box hedges, lie fragments of this stonework, waiting for reassembly and looking like some kind of crazy gardening. Inside the building, original fragments have been fastened to the wall and the patterns projected out beyond them, making the royal rooms seem wonderfully elaborate.

Everything here was intended to impress. There are tales – unverified by archaeology – of a quicksilver pool stirred into motion by slaves to give off flashes of light quite terrifying to visitors. What we do know for certain is that Abd al-Rahman III and after him his son al-Hakam II were wedded to diplomacy and received a constant succession of embassies and delegations. Descriptions in chronicles, by visitors as well as by the Arab side, yield snapshots of caliphal splendour and behaviour.

Ambassadors from Byzantium brought precious treatises on medicine and pharmacology. Visiting bishops from the Christian north were led past a series of majestically robed figures before each of whom they abased themselves, believing they were in the presence of the caliph, only to be told each time that this was but a slave of the slaves of the caliph. The great man, when they met him, was of course dressed in the utmost simplicity.

One of the most intriguing, and apparently authentic, chronicles (included in *Moors and Christians in Spain*, by Colin Smith) tells of the visit of the monk John of Görz, sent by the Holy Roman Emperor Otto I with a message intended to insult. Three years of diplomatic wrangling ensued during which Monk John, quite possibly in pursuit of martyrdom, declined to water down his message despite pressure from a Christian bishop, anxious to avoid trouble for his own community, and the conciliatory efforts of the caliph's own Jewish physician. Finally Otto wrote again in a more friendly tone and John was received by Abd al-Rahman who 'reclined upon a most richly ornate couch', legs crossed and proffering his hand to kiss. Since most were invited to prostrate themselves this was a mark of favour. John met the caliph twice and there is some account of the discussion. Even more fascinating is the presence in the saga of the Christian bishop and the Jewish physician, proof if any were needed of the universalism of Córdoba.

The Jewish physician, Hasdai ibn Shaprut by name, was a most interesting figure linking the reigns of Abd al-Rahman III and al-Hakam II. Because of his wide knowledge of languages, Hasdai was in constant demand as embassies arrived and made a practice, when the caliph despatched his own ambassadors, of sending letters with them to establish contact with Jewish communities as far distant as the Volga. As a physician, he was called upon to cure the Christian king of Asturias–León, Sancho the Fat, of his obesity. He gave his protection to poets and was a key figure in what became a brilliant revival of Hebrew lyricism.

His second master, al-Hakam II, was almost equally learned, assembling a library of 40,000 volumes and sponsoring studies of astronomy and medicine, a new development in a city that had concentrated up until now on poetry and the intricacies of Islamic law.

It is to the same al-Hakam that Córdoba owes the most splendid part of its Great Mosque, the *mihrab* or inner sanctum, the mosaic-laden arches that protect it, the six-leaved arches that stand in the approach and the final readying of the great mosaic dome in the centre, shaped like an unfolded scallop shell. The dome, supported on intersecting ribs of some architectural importance, is gaudily impressive. Even more so is the mosaic decoration around the arches on the rear wall. This, supposedly, was done by craftsmen from Byzantium; what one actually notices is the glistening of greens and blues and gilt and the elaborate motifs from the Koran. As David Talbot Rice has pointed out in his study of Islamic art, the use of Arabic scripts from India to Spain was one of the great unifying principles of Islamic decoration. As to the *mihrab* itself, the visitor must rely on pictures, since it is roped off and closed to visitors. The cupola of this holy of holies is made from a single piece of stone, pure and beautiful amid the festivity of the surrounding decorations.

There was only one more addition to the mosque to bring it to its final form – barring of course the arrival of the Christian cathedral. This was a fresh series of seven aisles and arches to the east, built to accommodate the ever-swelling congregation. Its author was al-Mansur, 'He whom God has helped to victory', and known in Spanish as Almanzor. A brilliant, self-serving jurist from an estate near Algeciras, al-Mansur rose to be chamberlain of the caliphate and effectively the captor of al-Hakam's son and successor, the young and helpless Hisham, whose mother – angry now but equally helpless – had probably been his mistress during his ascent. Confining Hisham to Madinat al-Zahra, al-Mansur built a palace-city of his own, now vanished, and moved into it the whole of the caliphal bureaucracy. From here he ruled fiercely and indomitably, his very name becoming a terror to the Christians of the north.

Throughout the centuries of Umayyad rule, it had been a habit of the Moors when not excessively preoccupied by troubles of their own to sally out on summer expeditions into Christian territories. Warriors were recruited by appeals to the Jihad, or Holy War, but often the Moors struck up temporary alliances with Christian leaders, recruiting especially among tribute-paying Christian groups. This being so, it would be wrong to think the primary motive of the summer campaigns religious. Nor were they territorial, since territory was seldom if ever formally retained. Far more probably, these were old-fashioned *razzias*, or raids, of the kind which nomadic tribes had traditionally used to bolster numbers of women and cattle. The motives of emirate and caliphate appear to have been similar, concerned with slaves and plunder and intended to keep Christian neighbours on the defensive.

Al-Mansur was the grand master of the *razzia*. In 985 he plundered Barcelona (it had been won back from the Moors by Franks, that is to say, the Carolingians, more than a century before). In 997, aided by a Christian contingent whom he paid in silk and probably in gold as well, al-Mansur devastated almost the whole of Galicia, sacking and burning, seizing the bells of the shrine of Santiago and bringing them back to the Córdoba Mezquita for service, upside down, as outsize oil lamps. For reasons best known to himself, however, he spared the holy tomb of Santiago. The following year he swept through northern Portugal and along the Duero, seizing Zamora and León. This last was perhaps the unkindest cut of all, for as Asturias expanded, its kings had finally moved their main base to León, establishing in effect the kingdom of Asturias–León. Now their principal city, tiny as it was, lay ruined.

Travelling in the province of León, up in the north where winter plains are dominated by the white of mountains, I pick up a young hitchhiker returning to his village at the end of the college day. He is an apprentice electrician, bright and lively, one of seven children. Two of his brothers are policemen in San Sebastián, capital of the vexed Basque Country, doing as dangerous a job as any. My passenger will be moving in with them as soon as he has finished studying. The remaining brothers and sisters all plan to leave when they finish school or college. The reasons become obvious as we reach the village. Most of the houses are of mud-brick, some in partial ruin, with gaps in walls and grey, tumbledown yards. A group of old men standing in the street appear to have few teeth between them. There is no shop, no bar, no place for communal gathering of any kind. Nowadays, says my passenger, the tractors till the land and labour needs are minimal. There is nothing, absolutely nothing, for young people to do. He expresses no grief at the thought of leaving his parents behind.

Later, in León, I hear a little more of the story. It is true, says my informant, an academic with a village background, that the young must almost inevitably take the long road to the cities. But as for the toothless old men and the decaying houses, that is appearance rather than substance. There is a tradition here of hiding wealth and spending as little as possible on anything personal, teeth or underwear for instance. But if a piece of land comes on the market, each of those old men will probably have the wherewithal to buy it. What counts in rural León is canniness.

The city and its countryside are closely, visibly linked. In the ancient part of town just up from the main square – known here and almost everywhere as the Plaza Mayor – old-fashioned shops are full of diaphanous, well-scrubbed guts blown up like long balloons to show their quality for sausage-making. Ground chilli – *pimentón* – lies beneath the sausage skin in small volcanic cones of muted scarlet. Balls of string nestle among the heaps of *pimentón*. In the bars you are served blood sausage, hot and black and peppery, or thin slices of *cecina*, raw, air-cured beef, made only where the mornings are very cold and dry. In restaurant windows, skinned and decapitated lambs hang by the hoof; whole pigs are suspended naked by the trotter.

The city lives off its province, offering services and local administration. I have struck up an acquaintance with Miguel García, a hall porter at San Marcos, the León parador. San Marcos is an extraordinary building, begun by a knightly order in the twelfth century to protect the pilgrims flooding along the way to Santiago. Since then it has acquired all sorts of lordly extras. These include one of the most extravagant and splendid of all Spain's sixteenth-century façades, a large but graceful cloister and a huge barn of a church, lacking a tower but plastered all over with pilgrims' scallop shells. San Marcos has served not just as knightly hospital but also as knightly prison – the baroque writer Quevedo was held here under the orders of a royal minister – as military barracks, and even, in the days after the Civil War, as stabling for the army's stallions.

Miguel García pilots me about the building. He is a true

autodidact, well-read in many subjects and with a memory to match. He quotes Quevedo by the yard, citing the mournful verses of his imprisonment. He takes me to the church for instruction – via the medium of carved choir stalls – in the battle of styles as the communal austerity of Gothic gave way to the more profuse and personalized work of the Renaissance. His knowledge of sculpture shames me as much as his knowledge of history and literature. And on the way he gives me his own view of León. It is, he says, an elegant and dignified city, no accident at all that most of the men wear suits. 'But the real key,' says Miguel García, 'is our dry character.' He points to a desperately uncomfortable-looking wooden sofa, with handsome rough wool cushions. 'Even our furniture expresses that character.

'When I was young and doing military service, I remember we had some leave saved up. My great friend of that time was an Andalusian and when we met again he told me what he had been up to – this, that and the other, of course, and a great deal of dancing. He danced all the time, even with his grandmother. It made me think how I had spent my leave. Do you know, I sat in silence with my own grandmother, holding her hand. Not a word passed, though perhaps a small tear ran down her cheek.'

I leave San Marcos somewhat meditatively, heading for the great Gothic cathedral, the city's other best-known landmark. All inside is dark and heavy. Then, when the midday sun strikes through the windows, stained glass blares bright as orchid house or tropical aquarium – spirituality made manifest in colour. Miguel García is right up to a point, I think, about the dignity of León. The people I pass in this more bourgeois part of town are generally well-dressed and proper. Old men in winter sunlight, playing their game of bowls beside the river, create a tranquil, settled scene. In early evening in the cafés, fur coats piled high behind them, middle-aged women may be glimpsed in sedate card-schools. As in many of the more conservative towns of Spain, the streets still bear the names of the Franco dictatorship – Generalísimo, General Sanjurjo and so forth. But there are cracks in the would-be dignity of the conservatives and visible resistance on the part of what one might call the opposition.

Scenes from a springtime visit, less than a year before, run through my mind. I happened then to be in the cathedral with my wife when we were buttonholed by an aged sacristan, anxious to let us know that he had been a Civil Guard up to retirement age. As if to prove the proposition, he dropped to one knee in machine-gunner's posture and rattled out the sound of bullets like any playground warrior. It came as a real surprise in the cathedral nave. Just at that moment a group of visitors appeared in the cathedral. We had seen them previously and knew them to be members of the British Houses of Parliament. 'Lords, lords,' cried the sacristan, *'lores, lores,'* dashing off to welcome them instead, and a good deal more obsequiously than he had done us. A slip in dignity for the conservatives, we thought.

Outside, as we strolled through the town, we saw young men get out of cars to piss against church walls, without a hint of modesty in any phase of the operation. It seemed the essence of disrespect. Were these the bored young people of the workless villages? we wondered. We sat beside a park, named after Cervantes, where almost a score of drunks and beggars were lying in the sun, and listened willy-nilly to an elderly couple conducting a beastly, rambling row only a little short of violence. The woman, presumably a wife and battered, had cuts about the mouth and half-closed, beaten eyes.

When the bells rang out for morning mass, the beggars rose and hurried to the church door, angrily demanding donations from all who entered and railing at the nuns who gave them nothing – who had, perhaps, nothing to give but certainly looked both discomposed and disapproving. Entering was much as one imagines the crossing of a picket line at the height of an industrial dispute. And there inside, for his Corpus Christi sermon, the priest was gently reminding his tight-packed congregation, including women in jeans as well as those with covered heads, that there was more to life than the everyday, that we should all be mindful of an eternity we would inevitably encounter. Outside, once more in sunlight after recrossing the picket line, we happened upon a cheery old man on the balcony of a decayed stone house, complete with heraldic shield. He held up the insignia of one of the splinter communist parties of the 1930s and a placard reading: 'Put nuns and priests to work'. From here it was only a step to the main street and right-wing representations: a graffito signed by 'The Squadron of Death'. 'Long live the Civil Guard,' it said, 'members of the CNT [National Workers' Confederation] will die.'

Travellers, perhaps, are all voyeurs, as naked in their pleasures as the young men urinating on church walls. I like León, with its teeming contradictions, enjoy San Marcos and come close to venerating the cathedral. I am here on this occasion, though, hot from the caliphate of Córdoba, to practise my voyeurism on the remains of the ancient kingdom of Asturias–León. These are patchy, as it happens, but include, towards the end of the kingdom's epoch of importance, great masterpieces of Spain's Middle Ages. Several are in León, much older than either the cathedral or San Marcos.

It is easiest to pick up the story in the unconquered territory down by the north coast. During the later ninth century, while the Moors were putting up some of the grander parts of the Mezquita, the Asturians continued to build their own little churches in pastoral countryside. One, at Valdedíos, not far from the sea, sits beside a later monastery in a valley burgeoning with luscious meadow, gorse and eucalyptus. Here, when I set off in pursuit of the key, I encounter an old, old lady with a soot smut on her nose and a long stick in her hand. She knew who had the key, she said, she wanted to come with me to find her, yes, she certainly did. But what could she do? The family had all gone out and left her alone to mind the cow. And there it was, ambling up the lane in front of her, contentedly grazing at the banks. Santa Cristina de Leña, another late Asturian church and on the way up towards León from Oviedo, was shown to me, in contrast, by a smart young local woman in a scarlet knitted suit. Tiniest of all the ancient Asturian survivals, it is once again surprisingly sizeable-seeming within. Though it sits on a high knoll above the railway and the road there is no difficulty at all in imagining it in the pristine countryside of its creation. By the time they built it, the Christians, like the modern road and railway, were on their way up to the high mountains and beyond, striking towards the south.

León was convenient as a base for controlling the frontier, which by now lay somewhat further south again. As its name suggests, it had been the encampment of a Roman legion, and much of the layout for a city still survived. There were Roman walls and an area within bisected, as was customary, by Roman roads. It was, however, virtually deserted except for some monasteries in the area which appear to have survived continuously from the Visigothic period, through the years of Berber domination and on through the later depopulation of the countryside.

The frontier itself, as numerous writers have explained, was a dangerous, open place, a no-man's land traversed by many – armies and traders with goods from al-Andalus and then a flow of Christians moving from Moorish rule into the increasingly promising kingdom of Asturias–León. These last are referred to as Mozarabs, meaning arabized Christians. Their home language was probably Romance but most found it convenient to be bilingual in Arabic; their dress was generally Arabic as well. They brought with them, along with considerable culture, all the main elements of Hispano–Mauresque architecture.

There is a fine example of a church in this style at San Miguel de Escalada near León and another at Lebeña, in a site of the greatest beauty deep in the Picos de Europa. I had been there on another icy winter's day to check it out, driving, as one must, along the gorge of Hermida. The steep cleft is defined by folds of limestone hanging like gaunt curtains across the way, the road zigzagging fiercely, rounding them one after the other in an unending succession. There was a view of needle peaks behind and far above. They shone brilliant in the sunlight, the vertical rock exposed but with snow clinging wherever it found a grip. At one point, looking up, I saw apparently hundreds of huge birds of prey, vultures perhaps, eagles to my eye, for this, after all, is a countryside where the brown bear still endures.

The village of Lebeña lies where the valley widens to form an elbow of arable land, the dog-tooth peak behind lit up by morning sun as I arrived. Smoke rose softly from the honey-coloured houses of the village, half a mile or so back from the valley road. The church itself is close to road and river, rising in a Byzantine hump of heavily tiled and differing roof levels, all stacked together. It has a free-standing bell tower with horseshoe arches, the top in pink and white like the Córdoba Mezquita. With graveyard, vegetable patch, an orchard and the river down below as loud as any lorry, it makes a powerfully Arcadian impression. What it is like inside, however, I never discover. A chalk scrawl on a blackboard in the porch advises the visitor to seek out the key in the village. But when I get there, all is deathly still, no movement, no people, no indication which house has the key, nothing but washing on the lines and a small cat playing with a scrap of chicken wire. I knock on the door of one of the closed-up houses, 'Ave María' inscribed in blue on a white plaque above the door, and though there is smoke, nobody answers me. Suddenly, there in the mountains, the stillness seems so precious I cannot bear to knock again. All is perfect, just as it should be, without the intrusion of a traveller.

In the city of León itself there were also, probably, a scattering of other Mozarabic churches. Certainly there was a growing movement and activity, with clerics, monks, peasants and more than a fair share of nobles. Readers familiar with Spanish will find a lively, part-imaginary account – worked up from contemporary sources and scrupulously annotated – in a small but fascinating book by the medievalist Claudio Sánchez-Albornoz.

One striking aspect of the kingdom, reflecting the initial Visigothic imprint, was the dominance of the aristocracy. So great was the gulf between the ruling families and their underlings that there had been a serfs' rebellion in Asturias as early as the eighth century with another soon to follow in Galicia. One somehow thinks of the Spanish aristocracy as having dwelt for ever among the stone-built towns of the *meseta*, the hot sun ranging over dusty streets and throwing deep shadows on their carved escutcheons. This image is fair enough for later days, but it is undoubtedly the case that the group described by the American historian S. G. Payne as 'the historic Spanish master class' evolved at a very early date, in Asturias–

León and along the northern coast – those parts of Spain that had been least Romanized and initially least Christianized, despite their admiration for the Visigoths, and which were in these two senses least obviously Hispanic. This aristocracy, growing and swelling, and ultimately achieving quite outrageous privileges, will play at least as great a part in all that follows as either Church or king.

León, that busy market town and administrative centre so dominated by its aristocracy, was totally destroyed in 998 by al-Mansur, known in these parts as Almanzor. The Moors pulled down the Roman walls to make the site indefensible and left behind a desert. The Christians soon returned, however, and started to rebuild. At much the same time, the royal family of Asturias–León began to construct a mausoleum or pantheon. For those who have seen it – not by any means all visitors to the city – it ranks in the same league as the cathedral and San Marcos.

The pantheon acquired the remarkable shape we see today round about 1060. But in order to grasp its full significance, it is necessary first to look more broadly at affairs among the Christians as a population. Over time, in a development that was to be critically important for the future, a series of small but independent Christian pockets had emerged the whole way along the north coast, ranging across the foothills of the Pyrenees to the Mediterranean. Here stood Frankish Barcelona, initially pounded into being as an independent county by one Wilfred the Hairy, but now, just like León, recovering from the attentions of Almanzor. At Jaca, just under the Pyrenees, the kingdom of Aragón had put down its roots. The Basques too were becoming more organized and had set up the kingdom of Navarre, based on Pamplona, in broad sub-Pyrenean country. Cumulatively, this represented a considerable Christian growth. But more important still was the slow recovery for the Christian interest of the territory just south and west of the Basques, around the headwaters of the Río Ebro. This was highly strategic ground since Moorish raiding parties often came up the east coast and then straight along the Ebro valley to strike at the lesser kingdoms and finally Asturias–León. Little by little, León began to dominate this territory, building so many defensive strong points that both Moors and Christians came to call it the Land of Castles – Castilla, as it emerged in Spanish, and known, of course, in English, as Castile.

This was a rough, rude territory, fast acquiring its own momentum. First, it claimed independence as a county; next it laid claim to status as a kingdom, close cousin to León–Asturias but ultimately, of course, to dominate both its own elder cousin and the course of Spanish history, creating, for better or for worse, an apparently irresistible ethos. Castilian virtues were from now on to be held up as representative of all of Christian Spain. Castilian vices were to be identified, by Spaniards and foreigners alike, as equally representative of Spain. Even the language that we know as Spanish is still customarily called Castilian in Spain.

For the moment, the essential point is that the Christian royal houses of the north coast and Castile began to intermarry with the royal family of León, with one kingdom sometimes dominating others to create a larger unit, and this new unit quite soon splitting up again, generally with bitter fratricidal fighting, into its constituent parts. One way and another, kings of Castile often doubled up as monarchs of León.

The first to occupy this dual role was the extremely interesting but scantily documented Fernando I, originally of Castile alone. He married Sancha, daughter of Alfonso V of León, and the two of them set about all kinds of energetic ventures. Many of their activities depended on the fact that Castile was already becoming very rich.

This in turn reflected the most startling development of all in the eleventh century – the sudden and complete collapse of the Cordoban caliphate. What happened was in essence simple. Almanzor's son had taken over from his father as dictator, controlling the weak caliph to the extent that he himself was now proclaimed the heir to the caliphal throne. This broke the legitimate succession of the Umayyads; everybody who exercised power anywhere now wanted a share of the spoils; and a quarter-century of civil war began. The Slavs and Berbers brought in over recent decades to man the army were a formidable and unassimilated force and simply tore the place to pieces. By 1031 the caliphate was gone and in its place were almost thirty petty Islamic states – the *taifas*, or 'kingdoms by division', known in English as the 'party kingdoms'. Some, like Seville, became extremely accomplished in the arts and scholarship, outshining what had been achieved so far in Córdoba. Others again, like Granada, excelled in the creation of beautiful buildings. In early days, however, the *taifas* were extremely weak in political and military affairs.

The Christians quickly saw their opportunity. But, just like the fierce Almanzor, they did not seek to capture territory so much as to exact tribute from the Moors, a form of protection money known as the *paria*. If Almanzor had been the great master of the *razzia*, so now Fernando I of León–Castile emerged as the great master of the *paria*, successfully demanding payments from the *taifas*, from Zaragoza to Seville and on to Badajoz. Because of the existence of the Pilgrims' Way to Santiago right across the north and the presence of French clergy and merchants all along it – an immigration much encouraged by the Spanish Christians – Spain was no longer cut off from the northern European mainstream. Fernando I was a positive Francophile and began to divert huge annual sums of Moorish gold to the monastery at Cluny. Spain itself, in almost direct interchange, began to acquire Romanesque architecture, its noble, solid forms clomping across the land along the Pilgrims' Way.

Fernando and Sancha were apparently anxious to make their own contribution. From the workshops of the Leonese monastery of Carrizo, they commissioned two ivory crucifixes, both now famous. One is in Madrid, the other still in León, in the local museum in the cloister of San Marcos. More than any other Spanish work of art from the eleventh century it expresses a rural tenderness, a devout simplicity later lost as Castile rose to pre-eminence and Spanish Christianity moved on towards ecstasy, hysteria and sometimes savagery.

The Carrizo ivory in León is not very big at all. I make it, judging by eye, about ten inches or a foot in height. Christ's head is long, almost absurdly so, bent forward, solemn, sorrowing, with huge black pupils to enhance the sense of loss. There are some ornamental elements. The beard is curled schematically, the figure has long ropes of hair and the top of the head looks a little like a hand-coiled pot. Christ has a wide formal moustache like angels' wings. Chest, ribs and belly are shown in modest, carefully indicated relief, while the garment round his middle, belted and perhaps bejewelled and resembling a Malaysian sarong, falls in elegant folds to bended knee. The overall impression, however, is one of humble disproportion and innocence; the image of a simple man made in the image of simple people.

Now, too, the royal pantheon was reaching final form, at least in architectural terms. It consists of a pair of small low chambers whose vaulted roof is mounted on extremely solid pillars. The large, low capitals – as out of scale as the head of Christ in the Carrizo crucifix – are Visigothic still in looks, with apples and fir-cones and the curling tongues of leaf that we have met on Monte del Naranco outside Oviedo. The ground-plan certainly has an Asturian feeling but columns and vaulting say unequivocally that we are now in the presence of the Romanesque. Two of the capitals are also Romanesque, with small-scale sculpture on them that is often taken as one of the earliest and finest instances of the style in Spain. There is a particularly engaging Lazarus, in the very act of rising from the dead. He looks understandably serious, with just his head and shoulders showing clear of the tomb.

Here, in this Leonese crypt, 23 kings and queens, 12 royal children and an assortment of counts were laid to rest. For the church itself, Fernando had managed to obtain from Moorish Seville the bones of San Isidoro, sixth-century bishop, polymath and encyclopaedist. The church was now re-dedicated in his name, and church and pantheon together made a single, powerful statement, expressing dynastic worth and permanence beyond the death of the individual.

This, however, is only the beginning of it. For what strikes the visitor first and overwhelmingly, as unforgettably as the name of Wilfred the Hairy of Barcelona, is a later Romanesque addition, a set of dense packed paintings, astonishingly bold and vigorous, on every inch and curve and modulation of the low vaulted ceiling.

They hit you physically, first offering mass and line and colour – mostly black and white and ochre, yellows and reds and greys (the greys were perhaps blues which have now faded) and with just a little gold here and there for haloes. Then, little by little, you begin to take in detail, the richness and variety of subject-matter and, in the treatment, the very same simplicity and tenderness as in the Carrizo ivory. This, in a way, is another surprise, since the painting was probably done a whole century after the completion of the structure, round about 1180, when life along the Pilgrims' Way was becoming a good deal more elaborate. But the paintings, whether by French or Spanish artist, still offer a deeply moving guide to spiritual and human values in Old León.

All the scenes, as a matter of course, are from the Bible and the Apocrypha. Christ figures frequently: in the Last Supper (the Nativity is largely lost), the Passion, the Seven Churches of the Apocalypse and above all where he sits as Christ in Majesty surrounded by the Evangelists in figurative form. Mark is a lion, John an eagle and Luke has the head of an ox. Only Matthew wears a fully human form. Two royal figures also kneel at a lower level. Most scholars believe these are King Fernando I and Doña Sancha.

In essence, all this is straightforward enough. The delight and sense of revelation lie in the supporting details. The painter is almost as interested in architecture as was his predecessor in San Julián de los Prados in Oviedo. The churches of the Apocalypse come in all shapes and sizes, one apparently at least five storeys high, more of a Roman palace than a church. They have arcades and domes and towers. The tops of palaces float over indoor scenes like the Last Supper and these scenes are themselves contained within painted arches, interestingly misshapen to fit the curving surfaces of the real ceiling. As well as architecture, we learn about table-setting, clothes and hairstyles. But most of all we learn about the countryside.

Strip paintings on the underside of arches contain a rural calendar, with the activities of each month lovingly set out in round medallions. February is sitting at the fire, stiff as a board, his hands held out beseechingly towards the flames. March is pruning, September gathering the grapes. October is shaking down acorns for a pair of pigs, one red, one black, November is butchering the red one. All the activities shown, and all the tools in use, remained exactly as portrayed in León's villages until the 1920s. A few remain unchanged even today.

Even better loved by local people than the rural calendar is the treatment of animals and agriculture in the large panel of the Annunciation. The angel arriving with his message, in what one might call the bottom left-hand corner, comes upon a shepherd carrying a long crook and playing on a small reed-pipe. Another is sounding a horn under a tree. A third, seated quite comfortably on a schematic rock, turns and holds out one hand towards the angel – quite failing to notice that his mastiff, eye warily on its master, is gobbling down the bowl of milk forgotten in the other hand. In the remaining spaces, sheep, cattle, pigs and goats all go about their business – though some, it seems, are also listening to the angel. The bell on one sheep is so big it is a surprise that it can lift its head. Down in the lower right-hand corner, opposite the angel, their ferocity counterpointing his peacefulness, two bucks have risen on hind legs to battle. Horns locked, eyes angrily glaring, chins plumed with beard and testicles the size of udders, they box with their hoofs in front of a tree. From the Byzantine stillness and symmetry of Christ in Majesty to the surging energy of the bucks and the peaceful portrayal of the countryside, the pantheon in León is as full a statement as any ever made in paint of the main elements of Spanish Romanesque. It touches the human heart directly. Certainly it is a far cry from the grandeur of the caliphate; but as the caliphate disappeared and the *taifa* kingdoms themselves tottered, it was slowly becoming evident that another civilization was waiting in the wings.

Messages from the whole past of León are written everywhere in the town. The city walls, rebuilt after Almanzor, still stand in many places. With the eye of faith and a little expert help, you can make out the Roman pattern of bisecting streets. San Isidoro is built practically into the bastions. The cathedral, started 200 years later, stands at the Roman crossroads. The Pilgrims' Way, one of the great shaping forces on the physical construction of towns along its length, followed the outside of the city wall along a path known as La Rúa, a term as convenient in those days to incipient French speakers as to Spanish. Shops and inns and eating places grew along La Rúa and to the south of the city wall, making it necessary to construct an extra half circle of defences. Most of these still also stand and all the old activities are still pursued in exactly the same places – as witness the suppliers to sausage-makers. San Marcos, when it came, was built some distance off, across the fields and at a point protecting the main river crossing. The town reached a population of about 5,000 (compared to the 100,000 or more of earlier Córdoba) and so it stayed for centuries. Little happened now in terms of growth until the coming of the railway in the nineteenth century. Then, all of a sudden, a new bourgeois suburb grew up between the ancient city and the station on the far bank of the river. This district was called the *ensanche*, or extension, a name we will meet again in Barcelona. It is now, of course, a part of the city centre, and the late nineteenth-century buildings are fast being torn down to be replaced with altogether simpler-looking modern substitutes. On several sides of town, marking its contemporary limits, workers' apartment blocks fall from sky to earth in ugly cliffs, just as in Córdoba. You can see it all in an hour or two of hoofing. Sometimes, in just a second, you see how the whole grew up to fill the vacuum left by the Moors.

It's Saturday evening and Diego Alvarez, sixteen years of age, has been volunteered by his parents to show me an interesting phenomenon. Or perhaps he has volunteered himself, who knows. Young people in Spain are very forgiving of their elders. The phenomenon is the intense evening bar-life of the young, a kind of ambulant cocktail party known to older people as *La Movida*, or perhaps 'The Stir-Up'. This takes place in most of the Spanish cities, in its own little part of town, always referred to as the Barrio Humido, the Wet District. *La Movida* is at its most fashionable and gossip-column ridden in Madrid, with sociologists and newspaper editorialists debating whether it is merely pretentious or may in fact be setting new trends for society. In León it is a simple, seemingly good-hearted affair. Sixth-formers, university students, anyone up to about the age of twenty-five – all pack into the bars like locusts. The bars themselves fill up to bursting and the young people then spill out into the streets, stopping all traffic and rattling away to one another like songbirds on a summer morning.

There is nothing like it anywhere in northern Europe, not even on the night before a rugby international in Cardiff. It is cheerful, busy, oscillating, just what I would have wished, for myself and friends, in chillier student days in Britain. Diego leads me through the throng to greet a group of schoolmates. Most of them, I notice, are drinking grape juice. One wants to be a doctor, one an astronomer. Madonna is playing on the bar's sound system, not too loud at all. I look up to see a ceiling carpentered in Moorish style, with stalactites and wooden coffers. 'And have you noticed,' says Diego, following my eye, 'the bar is actually called La Frontera?' *Frontera*, frontier in English, existing as part of many place-names, generally means the frontier with the Moors.

2 Moors and Christians

Goodbye to Universalism

ARAGÓN AND CASTILE, twin pillars of the official version of Spanish history, are linked by the Pilgrims' Way to Santiago. The easternmost branch coming out of France runs from Jaca, first capital of Aragón, and all the way across Navarre to Burgos, chief city of old Castile, before it marches on to León and over the last stretch of mountain into Galicia. Jaca sits at middle altitude in the Pyrenees, point of arrival or departure for the Somport Pass above. The Moors had used the pass on their raids into France some centuries before. Now, in the eleventh century, the pilgrims are flooding in the opposite direction, confident their stay in purgatory will be reduced as a reward for the long trek to Santiago. And perhaps when they finally reach the shrine, the great St James himself will intercede with God on their behalf, doubling the effectiveness of the journey. They will experience hope and weariness, danger and exaltation. And then, of course, there is the long road back again. The twentieth-century journey I am now preparing begins in Jaca and will end in Burgos. The route crosses the territory of both Aragón and Castile, appropriate to this chapter in the story of power politics. I hope it will also offer at least some sense of the passage of the pilgrims, that vanished throng whose endlessly flowing streams were an accompaniment to all else that happened and in whose name and for whose convenience so many great buildings were erected and pious works of art created.

*

Jaca, today, is a cheerful little town, jumping-off point for Pyrenean ski resorts. There is a special freshness in the air, even when it is raining as it is for my arrival. Children paddle by in moon boots; grown-ups, in quilted trousers and jackets, bustle underneath umbrellas while cars go whisking by with skis in pairs on roof-racks. In a bar near the cathedral I try a dish of *migas* – fried bread crumbs tricked out with firm-fleshed, bright green grapes. A fellow-customer tells me you can have them done with eggs as well. One way or another, he avers, they are just the thing to satisfy cold-climate appetites. Cloud blots out the snow-peaks to the north, clearing every now and then to reveal a snowy, dog's-head lump of rock to the south. The glimpse of dog's head suits me well since stone and stony things are very much upon my mind today.

The glory of the Pilgrims' Way, as we perceive it now, lies in the array of Romanesque architecture that flowered all along its length: churches, resting places, hospitals and monasteries. Its hallmarks are the rounded arch and, in the churches, rounded apses, often with radiating chapels. Transepts grew larger so that the old three-aisled construction gave way to something closer to the shape of the cross. In monasteries, there would always be a cloister, serene and beautiful, beside the church. The inspiration was mainly French – indeed the Pilgrims' Way was known as the Camino Francés, or French Road – with here and there a highly individual single building or sometimes a whole series. One thinks of the cupolas, covered with fish-scale tiles, of the cathedral of Zamora and the collegiate church of Toro, far to the west of Jaca and a little south of the main pilgrims' route. Taken as a whole, this efflorescence of the Romanesque seems quite unique as a chain of buildings dedicated to a single purpose and covering so many hundreds of miles. But the most delightful aspect of Pilgrims' Way architecture is the astonishing range of sculpture that accompanied it, on portals and façades and capitals, on every crag, cranny and vantage point, all the way from Jaca to the final masterpiece of the Portico of Glory in the great cathedral of Santiago de Compostela.

Migas apart, my first intention in Jaca is to see a particular piece of sculpture – to be precise, the capital topping the column on the right-hand side of the door in the south porch of the cathedral. The capital to the left is also very fine, a rendering of the story of Balaam's Ass and its reproach to the master who is beating it. But the one to the right is even more special. The carving, of course, is necessarily small, and it tells the story of Abraham and Isaac. Unusually for the period, Isaac is shown naked. Just as he realizes that he is betrayed, the angel intervenes to save him. Abraham, interrupted in his macabre preparations, turns his blunt-featured face towards the interfering angel. It is a moment of arrested action, passions plain to see, unabashed naturalism brought to bear on a tale no doubt believed in its entirety. It is precisely this innocent acceptance of the marvellous that gives so special a quality to the sculpture and stone-carving along the Pilgrims' Way.

The cathedral is shadowy and solid, pungent with incense, heavily Romanesque despite some later changes, mainly the installation of Gothic vaulting overhead. It was erected very slowly as an act of state by one of the early kings of Aragón, anxious to re-establish in Jaca a bishopric whose territory was currently in Moorish hands. The aim was to dignify the capital and give it ecclesiastical as well as military and administrative status. 'Capital', though, is hardly the proper word for any of these early cities, whether Jaca, Oviedo or León. The royal families and their entourage were always on the move and wherever they happened to be at any moment was the administrative centre. But they certainly chose principal cities for themselves and accorded each the greatest architectural splendour that could be managed. The continual southwards movement of the Christians, from the ninth century till the fifteenth, meant that a great number of cities were used in this way over half a millennium, one of the deepest reasons for the abundance of early monuments in Spain. In the case of Aragón, the rolling Christian tide made Huesca 'capital' after Jaca and, not long afterwards, the great city of Zaragoza. Each received the proper embellishments.

As for the pilgrims, their route lay through what was in early centuries a comparatively narrow strip of Christian land running across the north of the peninsula. Leaving Jaca, they followed the River Aragón, fast flowing and yellow-grey as winter turns to spring.

Sometimes it runs comfortably along the valley floor, sometimes far below through deep-gouged cliffs of clay. The high peaks of the Pyrenees rise to the right; to the left, and tumbling down towards the Ebro plain, lie lesser but still substantial sierras, a sound defensive barrier. Occasional small towns are set on knolls but otherwise, right up to the present day, the prospect entirely rural, ravishingly beautiful. I have a little tape recorder with me as I drive and it has started to fill itself up with simple-minded cries of wonder and delight.

Things change a little in Sangüesa, a short distance into the old kingdom of Navarre. Here a noxious paper-mill releases an inverted pyramid of smoke above the countryside and wafts a sulphurous stench along the streets. Navarre, originally Basque but now considerably more mixed in population, played a much smaller part than either Aragón or Castile in early developments (it was not till the nineteenth century that it moved to centre-stage in Spanish history, with catastrophic consequences); but the pilgrims left their mark, obliging me to make a stop. Santa María la Real is the last building before the bridge across the Aragón, crossed here for the last time by the pilgrims. To the left of the church doorway three sculpted figures stand in almost Egyptian state, tall, thin and rectilinear. Across the road, surveying the sculpture, stand three young women, flesh and blood and considerably more rounded in figure. Hoping I will not appear too much the middle-aged adventurer, I cross the road to ask them what it's like to have this splendid edifice as their church? They answer, almost in unison, that Santa María la Real is something they all love. It stands at the centre of the way they see the town and they are studying it at this very moment for their sixth-form art class. The shortest and roundest is appointed spokesperson and proceeds to fill me in on the details of one of the most elaborate façades I have so far encountered. The three tall female figures are the Three Marys, she says – I know all about them, naturally? – and one – have I already noticed? – is signed by the sculptor, Leodegarius, who did the carvings in the twelfth century. Judas is over on the other extreme, and badly weathered; serves him right. Then up, look, up there – there is

Christ in Majesty among the Evangelists. Among a number of mythic beasts, I make out a lion chewing on the body of a headless man. There are various distinctly Nordic figures.

'Yes,' said the spokesperson, 'a lot of pilgrims were from the northern countries and these carvings were to welcome them and make them feel at home.'

I inquire about a blacksmith hammering a sword and, just above, what seems to be that very sword in action, its owner slaughtering a dragon.

'Ah,' says the spokesperson very sweetly, 'that's another Nordic story but I'm afraid we have all forgotten it. But do you see the oxen just above the door? They were to show the pilgrims, who were perhaps not very well-mannered, that they were entering a sacred place.'

The logic of the symbolism eludes me, unless it is a reference to Ezekiel and the ox as emblem of the priesthood. But the conversation seems to prove that the Pilgrims' Way belongs to local Spaniards as much or more than to visiting city-dwellers or foreign busybodies like myself. This has to be counted a good thing in any philosophy. I also wonder whether our own sixth-formers would have the same aplomb – or interest and courtesy.

The route runs on, through what I frequently tell my tape recorder is beyond doubt the loveliest countryside on earth, with widening views of hill, mountain and valley, and eventually, in the distance, the chimneys and apartment blocks of Pamplona. Soon the road reaches Puente la Reina, where the River Arga is bridged. This is a place of some significance, for here another large contingent of pilgrims, having crossed the Pyrenees at Roncesvalles above Pamplona, joined with the throng already pressing westwards from Jaca. I dump my car and walk down a long defile of freezing street, huge iron studs in wooden doorways, to cross a humpbacked bridge now closed to traffic. After the pleasures of Sangüesa, this seems a chill, unfriendly place, with more than its share of painted slogans accusing the Madrid government of terrorism against the Basques. Just at this time, as it happens, a group of political guerrillas – not Basques but members of the tiny group called Grapo – are on hunger strike in gaols all round the country and I have been stopped several times already by Civil Guard roadblocks. Pleasure in landscape starts to yield to a sense of political intractability.

In Estella, a tight little town along a river valley with straggling industry long in decline, the famous pilgrim church of San Miguel is *en obras*, under repair, invisible behind dust sheets. The steepest imaginable little humpbacked footbridge, deep in sheep's dung, springs up to cross the river and here, for no reason that I can fathom, an old man in farm-worker's overalls tells me indignantly that 'they don't even teach Basque at Pamplona university'. He lays his finger alongside his nose. 'Politics, politics,' he says.

In Logroño, sleepy old capital of La Rioja, home of Spain's best-known wines, there is an immense Civil Guard barracks. There would need to be, to support the amount of Civil Guard activity I have seen. In a tatty square in the old town, a group of young men, all seemingly unemployed, stand aimlessly, with a slightly threatening air. I take my lunch in the ageing Café Moderno, served by an elderly waiter among sepia photographs of the pre-Civil War city. I am joined by a youth with entirely rotted teeth who says 'Eh?' very loudly, when addressed by either the waiter or myself. Otherwise he draws silence round himself like a blanket in a manner most unusual among Spaniards. There is nothing for it but to watch the television, frequent restaurant companion of the single traveller in Spain. The news, of course, is bad.

My only serious duty in Logroño still lies ahead: to inspect the local church of Santiago, given special notice by the writer Edwin Mullins for the size of the genitalia of the horse that bears the sculpted saint on his reckless stone career across the outer wall. The writer of the *Rough Guide to Spain* has also made this pilgrimage, in honour of both Mullins and the saint, so I feel I am near the start of what may become a respectable tradition. Abandoning the Café Moderno, in only moderate spirits, I doff my cap, though rather briefly, to Mullins, Santiago and his splendid steed and leave the town, in the wrong direction, by a steel bridge across the river. Here the Ministry of Public Works has erected a sign saying that a recent coat of paint cost 27,172,681 pesetas.

Half-way between Logroño and Burgos there runs another river, the Río Oja, from which the Rioja district takes its name. A holy man by the name of Domingo – there are three saints of the same name from hereabouts, including the founder of the Dominican order – made it his life's work to build a *calzada*, or causeway, across the Oja for the benefit of pilgrims. It was a long job and he lived to be extremely ancient. The town that gathered round the causeway is called, quite properly, Santo Domingo de la Calzada. It has a cathedral and a monastery and a long approach past dismal garages and agricultural suppliers. From far away you see the cathedral's much-admired baroque bell tower, free-standing and rising like a phallus over the roofscape of the town. The cathedral itself, which is short from east to west but surprisingly lofty inside, has one extraordinary feature – a live cock and hen scratching away at first-floor level in a carved and gilded gallery like the back of a gypsy caravan.

The presence of the poultry commemorates a miracle. According to the tale, a youth unjustly hanged for theft miraculously survived upon the gibbet. The judge who had sentenced him, interrupted during the course of a chicken dinner, said he would only believe the news if the bird on his plate got up and crowed. It did, of course, and the judge rose up and cut the youth down from the gibbet and all were happy ever after. And since that day a white cock and his consort, replaced as necessary, have lived in the cathedral. The story may sound a little silly in the telling but seems, on the spot, as innocent and touching as any of the statuary along the way.

The bier of the saint himself is revealing of more modern attitudes. Santo Domingo's long-bearded effigy lies behind iron railings to which appreciative silver plaques have been attached. One comes from the Spanish Society of Gerontology, another from MOPU, the Ministry of Public Works. All declare him patron saint of their endeavours, some even claiming him as grandfather. The sense of Spain's familial allegiance is strong; and perhaps it was the saint, as a good grandfather, who dug into his pocket for that last peseta to finish off the paintwork on the bridge back in Logroño.

Now Burgos is not far off, and beyond Burgos the road goes reaching out over the wide cereal country to León, by way of the splendid sculpted churches of Carrión de los Condes and the ruined Benedictine monastery of Sahagún. Beyond León, there lies the wilderness of the Bierzo Mountains, where the Romans literally washed away whole hills in search of gold, and finally comes Santiago, goal of the pilgrims. One cannot contemplate the pilgrims' route without an overwhelming sense of the distances they travelled, how far and steep the mountains must have looked, how intimidating the cliffs that seemed to block their way along the upper Ebro, how achingly, how desperately wide the plains.

You could quarry away for an age along their route in quest of ancient and modern. For myself, I could not consider even the journey to Burgos finished without a diversion to the monastery of Santo Domingo de Silos, tucked away beneath the imposing Sierra de la Demanda. This particular Santo Domingo was an eleventh-century figure responsible for rebuilding an earlier monastery sacked by Almanzor during one of his summer campaigns. The oldest part now surviving is a double-storeyed cloister dating from 1042 and perfectly Romanesque in form. Neat little arches rest on double columns, holding up stone walls the colour of a lion's pelt. A single cypress rises within the cloister, a fraction mangy but a traditional subject for lyric poetry. Pigeons coo – it is now definitely spring, though very cold indeed – and sparrows blast away as if electronically amplified. There are many interesting minor features: a horseshoe arch at the top of a flight of stairs, an effigy of Santo Domingo on a bier that rests on the backs of three fine lions. Underneath is a tomb described by the monks as Visigothic, a body-shaped hollow carved from living rock. On the wall behind, in high relief above an altar, a thirteenth-century scene shows monk or abbot – perhaps Santo Domingo de Silos himself – securing the release of prisoners from a mysterious figure who may be a king, may be their captor. The prisoners themselves, crouching in dejection or raising their hands beseechingly, may possibly be Christians, may possibly be Moors. Scholars do a good job of complicating the issue. But you cannot be in the cloister for more than a minute or two without a clear awareness that these are only sideshows.

What matters at Santo Domingo de Silos, hitting the tender spots of the emotions, is the stone-carving all around you, integral to the architecture itself, covering the doubled-up capitals of the paired columns and the inner sides of the square columns at each corner of the cloister; sixty-four capitals in total in the lower storey and eight tall slabs of stone carved in relief.

The capitals are intricate to the point of astonishment. Some show lions in thickets of foliage. Some are composed entirely of foliage and arabesque. Flamingos are a favourite theme, repeated several times. The tall birds are topped by griffin-like wings and bend their long heads down to lay them on their feet. Their feathers, shaped as perfectly as any haircomb, are made of the tiniest stone filaments growing out from a central dividing line. There is a good supply of harpies, too; they have birds' bodies and women's heads, with fork-tongued serpents protruding from their mouths. There is also a cavalry battle, less well-preserved than some of the other scenes. You could easily spend a hour or two here, explanatory leaflet in hand, working your way quietly round the capitals, enjoying the diversity and strangeness and wondering whether they were really carved by Moorish craftsmen – prisoners, perhaps, as some scholars have claimed. But you will eventually find yourself distracted from the capitals by the rectangular reliefs standing in couples at the cloister corners.

Of the eight, one pair in high relief hold less interest than the rest. All of the remaining six, all more shallowly carved, may reasonably be claimed as masterpieces. There is an Ascension and a Pentecost, both featuring a layer of schematic cloud like heavy ruffles in a curtain. In the Ascension, Christ's head shows above the cloud; in the Pentecost a pointing hand reaches down out of it. There is a portrayal of Christ's burial, combined, in the same panel, with his Resurrection and a posse of soldiers sleeping like upright chessmen. There is a Deposition from the Cross, a mournfully flowing piece in which the helpless sagging of Christ's body is mirrored just a little lower down by the supporting curve of Joseph of Arimathea's waist and knee. The panel of Doubting Thomas, like several of the others, shows all the apostles ranged on the flat surface as in a Byzantine icon. Only Thomas, head tucked inquisitively into Christ's armpit to inspect the wounded ribs, stands apart fractionally out of sequence. It is a truly moving composition.

But still more beautiful, for me at least, is the relief of Christ and his two companions on the road to Emmaus. The left-hand figure, first of the companions, stands erect and meditative. The second companion occupies the centre. With swaying movement, raiment tightly pressed against his body, he raises one foot to take a step and one arm in a supplicatory gesture. Christ, on the right, looks back over his shoulder, halo behind his head, his head-dress almost like a helmet. The long, triangular nose, the shape of a bar of Toblerone, is that of a Christian warrior, no sacrificial lamb.

Others who have followed the Pilgrims' Way hold out the Santiago Portico of Glory as the supreme moment, with Christ surrounded by the twenty-four figures of the Apocalypse, Santiago himself half-way down in intercessionary station and at the bottom Master Mateo the sculptor, ideal for pilgrims and contemporary tourists to bump heads with, hoping to gain a little of his wisdom. All this is quite magnificent, hard to make excessive claims for. But it is in Santo Domingo de Silos, somewhere between the flamingos and the Road to Emmaus, that I find my own point of stillness along the Pilgrims' Way.

Alfonso VI is king in Burgos, not far to the north. Son of Fernando I, already familiar as creator of the León pantheon, Alfonso originally received only the kingdom of León as his patrimony. Another brother was awarded Galicia, but it was to the eldest that Castile was given. This implied the political judgement that Castile was now – and, as it happened, for all future time – top dog among the Christian kingdoms. In the seven years of civil war that followed this division – as automatically, it seems, as night follows day – Alfonso initially came off worst. Captured by the Castile brother and subjected to a long forced march in chains, he was exiled to the Muslim *taifa* of Toledo, the other side of the frontier zone south of Castile. Toledo was one of the most important pieces on the Hispanic chessboard and here, in a neat example of the interpenetration of the cultures, Alfonso formed an effective working relationship with the ruler. It was only after the murder of his Castilian brother – a murder for which he and his sister Urraca have often been blamed – that Alfonso finally made himself king of the whole of his father's old domains. The Galician brother, happy perhaps to have avoided assassination, spent the rest of his life in captivity. Alfonso, for his part, now set about one of the longest and most dramatic of medieval Spanish reigns, effectively from 1072 to 1109. Along the way he had six wives and two well-established mistresses – one of them, a high-born Muslim woman named Zaida, providing the long-awaited heir to the Christian throne. Alas, though, for the future of the kingdom, the young man died in battle before he could succeed. Alfonso's enemies accused him persistently of incest with his sister, Urraca. He was also, it should be mentioned early on, the monarch who had to deal with the frequently insubordinate behaviour of one Rodrigo Díaz de Vivar, better known to myth, and history, as El Cid Campeador. These were, as all who contemplate them must agree, extremely exciting times.

Coming up to Burgos on the Madrid road, as you would necessarily do after a visit to Santo Domingo de Silos, you see at once the military attractions of Castile's first capital or quasi-capital. Up in this high, windswept landscape, spare, often eroded, whitish-grey – though formerly, perhaps, it was a good deal better timbered – Burgos is sited at the end of a spur of hill that reaches down at right angles to the slim and pleasing Río Arlanzón. The crest of hill closest to the river makes a strong defensible point and here, inevitably, the castle was located.

Nowadays the castle is a ruin – burned in the eighteenth century and finally razed by the French in 1813. What you take in first is the cathedral, the city's most famous landmark and one of the most distinctive in all Spain. As well as its two instantly recognizable open stonework spires, suggesting a matching pair of bluebells or grape hyacinths, Burgos cathedral heaves up a gallimaufry of lanterns and pinnacles and lesser spires, a dottily inspiring festival of stonework on the side of the hill that the castle previously dominated. Immediately around the cathedral lies the old town, with narrow streets and the usual Castilian cold-season display of women in fur coats – sensitivity on the issue of fur, as on environmental questions generally, has scarcely yet arrived in Spain – and the year-round spectacle of pleasingly old-fashioned little shops. As in many of the Spanish cities, the discovery of an antique pharmacy with deep-stained hardwood counter and scores of phials ranged on hardwood shelves finally becomes a pleasing commonplace. One realizes, as well, that most of them have snappy fridges in the back room, containing the latest in antibiotics.

The Río Arlanzón abuts the old town, shallow and swaying with weed. It is set between stone walls and here, in summer, frogs bellow at dawn and small boys come later in the day to fish and dabble. The cathedral side of the river is stone-paved and shaded by an *alameda*, that most Spanish of arboreal constructions. In a classic *alameda*, the branches of adjacent trees are grafted together so that a whole avenue, or a carefully disposed group of individual trunks in the middle of a square, leads the eye upwards towards one single, intertwined canopy above, branch flowing into branch. Whether or not it may be said that the trees now form a single plant, it is clear the canopy at least consists of one integrated, organic whole of rustling leaf. *Alamedas* are a delicious, cooling fantasy, one of the most perfectly executed features of a country where edges are often tatty and lack of urban finish is a byword. You find *alamedas* all over the place, from the big cities on the coasts to little villages and townships strung along the Pilgrims' Way. One of the prettiest of all is at Zamora, where Alfonso VI's brother was murdered as he lay in siege.

The Burgos *alameda* is called the Espolón and it is the city's favourite strolling place. At the end furthest from the cathedral, municipal offices occupy most of an old theatre. Here, throughout the chilly day of my arrival, a long and muttering queue has been protesting about lack of public housing. Both in Castile and across in Aragón, where farmers are unhappy over European Community exactions, I am discovering that Spanish demonstrators will put their case at length to foreigners, especially to foreigners prepared to represent themselves as journalists. There is no doubt at all that the queueing group in Burgos are poorly dressed – poor people, that is probably to say – and believe themselves to have come off badly through the machinations of local administration. Another certainty is that for two centuries at least, and probably much longer, Burgos has been one of the most right-wing cities in Spain, often strongly militaristic and reaching a military climax when it served as Franco's own headquarters during the Civil War. The city's leaders have shown little interest, so the left-wing argument asserts, in the daily welfare of the common people.

As it happens, I have a date with a left-wing intellectual, just about the only one in Burgos, in the Pinedos café, also in the former theatre on the Espolón, looking out along the *alameda* and up to the open stonework of the cathedral spires. Pale, lilac light shines through them.

Left-wing or right, Daniel de la Iglesia, formerly a socialist deputy in the Castilian 'autonomous' assembly and now in dispute even with his own party, is a man after my own heart; Señor Capdevila of Córdoba would also approve. He grounds his analysis in history and expounds it with the marvellous fluency one often meets in Spain. What starts him off is the remark made by a friendly publicist in the local tourist office, which I have rashly repeated, that Burgos is a 'seigneurial city'.

'Seigneurial indeed,' scoffs Daniel. 'The whole point is that it was bourgeois, just a trading city to begin with,' and off he takes me on a romp through the period after the Christian Reconquista, when most of the *meseta* had become a vast ranch for sheep and cattle, with the wool flowing down through Burgos to the ports of Cantabria and so to Flanders, wealthiest and most industrialized corner of fifteenth-century Europe. Burgos, says Daniel, was a dealer's town, living off the backs of sheep, till Spain's Low Country Wars of the sixteenth century brought ruin to the garment manufacturers of Flanders and a long decadence to Burgos. The people who now lay claim to aristocracy are trading families who bought their land at the dissolution of the monasteries in 1836 – and these very people currently proclaim themselves good Christians and good friends of the Church! Best of all, he snorts sarcastically, they see themselves as Castilian heroes, like the mythical version of El Cid. 'But even if it's not a seigneurial city, it's certainly right-wing,' says Daniel. 'The right runs public administration, local industry, even the savings banks. Nothing ever happens, nothing ever changes. Getting on means going right.'

With or without the dissolution of the monasteries, says Daniel, continuing his disquisition, Burgos has always been an important centre for Spanish Catholicism, with its own archbishopric to match the splendour of the cathedral. In the latter part of the nineteenth century it became a bureaucratic centre too, home-base for an army captaincy-general and therefore seat of the military courts. These courts deal with the Basque Country – symbol, one might say, of Castilian dominance over the Basques. And in Burgos more than almost anywhere in Spain, Church and army go hand in hand. Up till just a few years ago, the place was full of men in uniform. No function of the Church's was complete without the captain-general, no army event carried much status without the attendance of the archbishop or at least a good scattering of senior priests. No rich businessman married his daughter to anyone except an army officer.

I find myself nodding away vigorously, for quite apart from the housing demonstration two things have happened to me during the day that tend, in an impressionistic way, to confirm the view of Burgos as a military city and one in which the economic underclass might not receive much sympathy.

The first occurred outside the handsome army headquarters in the city centre, right beside the tourist office. Standing there in the rain, trying to transcribe a pair of triumphal Civil War inscriptions about Generals Franco and Mola, I had been warned off sharply by a sentry with an automatic weapon. Were these inscriptions not written to be read, I ventured to inquire, getting a very dusty answer for my impertinence; quite rightly, some would say, in a country with problems from terrorism. But certainly the tone of military authority rang out brisk and unselfconscious as it used to in the days of Franco. Then there was a lunch-time encounter that seemed a good deal more significant.

Again, I had been alone in a restaurant, on the far side of the river, in the seediest part of Burgos. There was just one other customer, an old man with a white moustache and, so far as I could tell, no teeth at all. I watched the television, taking in even more dismal news, of storms and parliamentary confusions in Madrid and nitrates making the water undrinkable in the rich strawberry land round Lepe, down on the Atlantic border with Portugal. The old man was now smoking a huge cigar and sneezing, taking out the cigar during convulsions, then promptly popping it back again, rolling it round and round between his gums until the following seizure. The advent of each sneeze gave him just enough time to snatch the cigar from his mouth. He was also, unusually for Spain, becoming visibly drunk.

After a while he heaved himself to his feet and marched across to my table, where he bent to place his face close up to mine. Exhaling almost into my mouth he told me, fiercely but not aggressively, that he had been a shepherd all his life and had a little land but not enough to live on. 'You,' he said, jabbing with his cigar, 'you have more land than I, more land than I, more land than I,' – over and over and over again. I felt like a rich simpleton caught slumming, disgusted at myself, bruised and confused and convinced that whatever support was available to the old man, whether through family or state, was not enough. It turned out in the end that he could not pay his bill, something I had never seen before in a Spanish restaurant.

As for the Castile of Alfonso VI, for whose sake I have come to Burgos, remarkably little is on view in a physical sense. This is mainly because the city was a success story right up into the Gothic period and beyond, remaking itself continually and losing in the process the Romanesque buildings of Alfonso's day. But many historically important events occurred here under Alfonso: debates on the vexed question of whether the Spanish Church should follow the old Mozarabic rites or the forms of service in use throughout the rest of the Roman Catholic world (the matter was actually put to trial at one point by combat between two knights representing the rival rites), a formal visit from the great Benedictine abbot, St Hugh of Cluny, and the signing of a great many charters, legal documents and so forth. For the rest, the king was continually on the move, governing literally by itineration.

Given the tiny population of the towns and villages, the travelling court was a surprisingly large affair. There were the king and his courtly officials and always his sister Urraca, a swarm of squires and falconers and masters of hounds, the local aristocracy in any area they were traversing, a bishop or two perhaps, a military escort suitable to the dignity of the procession, pack animals, even cattle and sheep for provender. Outside the cities, the court was mostly obliged to camp, its members living a rough and ready life and hunting continually as they went. There is no evidence that Alfonso could read or write but every evidence that he ruled most shrewdly as he travelled.

Alfonso was perfectly happy to go to war with his Christian neighbours over small pieces of desirable real estate such as La Rioja, today the smallest of Spain's regional autonomies. He quarrelled viciously with the Aragonese when they showed signs of moving down into the Ebro Valley, threatening Castile's traditional rights to tribute money from the *taifa* of Zaragoza. These, though, were matters of adjustment, rather than of territorial conquest on a large scale.

By and large, in the early part of the reign, he also felt it wise to plunder the *taifa* kingdoms without taking over too much of their territory. This emerges with the greatest clarity from the autobiography of Abd Allah, ruler of contemporary Granada. Finding himself hard-pressed for cash by the Christian king, he tried to reason out Alfonso's approach. It must have gone, Abd Allah thought, like this:

I am a foreigner to them and they all hate me. Why should I decide to take Granada? That it should surrender without a fight is impossible! Thus I would have to wage war, risk the lives of my soldiers and spend money – and I would then lose more than I could hope to gain if it fell (without a fight) into my hands! Even in the latter case itself, I would not be able to hold it unless I could be sure – and this would be impossible – of the loyalty of the population. I couldn't even massacre the latter and populate the town with men from my own country! No, in reality what must be done is to set the Muslim princes against each other and continually take money from them in order to weaken their resources and exhaust them. Once they have reached that stage, they won't be able to do anything except give in and come to surrender to me spontaneously. That is what has happened at Toledo, which I will obtain without trouble, thanks to the impoverishment and dispersal of the population as well as to the flight of its ruler.

(Taken from Les 'Mémoires' d'Abd Allah, as quoted by Angus McKay in Spain in the Middle Ages)

Abd Allah's analysis seems entirely convincing. But what he was witnessing at Toledo in fact implied a slow but fundamental shift in Alfonso's policy. Here, in his former place of exile, his somewhat equivocal ally al-Mutamid had for a while done well, successfully taking Córdoba from the Abbadids of Seville. Within five months, though, al-Mutamid was dead by poisoning. Córdoba was again under Sevillian power and Toledo itself was in far weaker hands, its new ruler actually kept in place by the efforts of Alfonso (for which, of course, a hefty charge was made). Toledo's new instability threatened chaos through the frontier districts of the Duero, which Castile was actively attempting to repopulate. Most probably seeking order above all, Alfonso little by little crept up on Toledo, taking fortresses to the north and south of it. With some 30,000 people, Arab and Berber, Jewish and Mozarab, Toledo was undoubtedly the hub of central Spain, larger than all the cities of Castile–León combined. Alfonso now simply waited until it fell, weakly and passively, into his open hands.

When the Castilian king finally clattered across the Tagus in May 1085, through the old Visagra gate – it still stands very much as it was in those days, with horseshoe arch and flanking towers – and up the steep streets of the town, he was ushering in a new phase in Spanish history. Instead of simply exploiting the kingdoms to the south, Alfonso had actually taken one over for himself. From now on he would be responsible for its large and racially mixed population; he would have to find men of his own to hold and administer the territory; he would have to spend where once he had merely exacted, just as Abd Allah had foreseen. All the future problems of the Reconquista were implicit in that moment. Nor could he have realized immediately that in winning back the ancient capital of the Visigoths and former centre of Hispanic Christendom he had stirred an Islamic hornets' nest that was now taking shape in Africa. Toledo, for the moment, must have seemed the juiciest of plums.

Alas, poor *taifas*. Had they paid less attention to leadership disputes and mutual rivalries, all might have been otherwise. For they were in general extremely rich. Across the whole of the south of the peninsula, from modern Portugal to Valencia in the lush Levant, and up to sterner Zaragoza in the north-east, the *taifa* kingdoms flourished so long as they paid their tribute to the Christians. Their agriculture was accomplished, their decorative arts profuse. Unlike their increasingly martial Christian neighbours, they were the immediate heirs to a great literary culture. The scholarly and lyric spirit of the Cordoban caliphate lived on among them and was deliberately cultivated in their courts. Some of the finest scholars, such as the poet and theologian Ibn Hazm, were born and educated in Córdoba itself, then spent most of their careers elsewhere, distributing the benefits of Córdoba's tradition.

Poetry was the most admired of all the arts and here, undoubtedly, it was Seville which glittered most, not least because two of its foremost rulers, al-Mutadid and another al-Mutamid, father and son of the Abbadid dynasty, were among the leading poets of the age. It is true that poetic forms were largely traditional and subject-matter tended to the escapist, concerned with love and nightingales and pools of water in the desert, but the effects achieved were often beautiful, if rather fragile, and may even have been the starting-point for the troubadour poetry that would soon sweep across Christian Europe. Rising poets addressed long panegyrics to their princes and might well be rewarded with court appointments – though these, like any other political involvement in the *taifas*, carried considerable perils. Ibn-Ammar, much favoured court poet of Seville, attempted to carve out his own dominions and ended up being killed by the hand of al-Mutamid personally. Yet al-Mutamid himself fared little better, dying in exile in Africa among a heap of piteous laments, a victim of the political convulsions in the Arab world brought on eventually by the fall of Toledo.

With the possible exception of Seville, the most interesting of the *taifa* kingdoms was Zaragoza. Here, though the local rulers had centuries of their own effective independence to look back on, the present incumbent was a near-perfect representative of the Cordoban tradition. Al-Muqtadir, chief of the fairly recent Banu-Hud dynasty, was himself philosopher, mathematician and astrologer – astrology was then regarded as a science and would retain its high prestige well into humanist, Renaissance Spain. Al-Muqtadir attracted other scholars, Muslim and Jewish, to his capital. His vizier, incidentally, was Jewish, as had been the case in several other *taifas*.

In architecture, the *taifas* had done rather less to emulate the caliphate than they had in poetry and scholarship. A few large projects had been carried out, most notably the walling of a string of cities, but now, in Zaragoza, al-Muqtadir built a palace foreshadowing the future triumphs of the Moorish style in both Granada and Seville. There were in fact two, of which only one survives; but for me its continuing existence now prescribed a visit to the 'Immortal City' on the Ebro.

This lengthy river starts its travels north of Burgos in a wide and dreary landscape, a Thomas Hardy heath set at a high altitude. But the visitor's sense of being on a plateau is partially dispelled by the swivelling incisions of a deep gorge. Peering into it from above, or travelling down and up again as you do on the road from Burgos to Santander, you see a mountain torrent dashing along full tilt. By the time the Ebro reaches Zaragoza, more than 300 kilometres closer to the Mediterranean, it is broad and powerful and running through a wide, dull valley whose agricultural possibilities have been of interest since Roman times. The city's name is a corruption of Caesar Augustus and there is no end to the digging up of Roman remnants. The plaza in front of the cathedral has recently been dug up revealing the old forum. Just a few blocks away a ruined amphitheatre lies half disclosed, the dig in a state of perpetually suspended animation.

Nowadays the city is famous for its General Motors factory and for one of the most sacred cult objects of Hispanic Christendom, the little statue of the Virgin on the Pillar commemorating Our Lady's appearance to St James during his supposed ministry in Spain. This is housed in a giant brick basilica beside the river, gaudy with domes and with a pinnacle at each of its four corners. The basilica looks, to be a trifle blunt about it, like a giant sow flat on her back, her legs aloft, the multitudinous ceramic domes resembling multi-coloured teats, the biggest, in the centre, like a hugely swollen navel. Behind the basilica and up from the severely elegant *lonja*, or exchange, the narrow streets of the old town go running away at right angles to the river till they reach the huge, inevitable zone of modern apartment blocks. The streets of the old town, bustling for the evening *paseo*, or promenade, are full of brightly lit little sweetshops selling *tartas de azahar*, orange blossom cakes, boiled sweets pleasingly named *frutas de Aragón* and *adoquines*, cobblestones. This is a city with a reputation, among its own people, for openness and generosity and, among outsiders, for a confrontational approach. But never believe the Aragonese are angry, I am told by a Zaragoza friend, it is just their hearty, straightforward way of speech.

For the Moors, the city was a major frontier settlement. Later of course, when the Christians took it, it became the capital of Aragón, in succession to Jaca and then Huesca. Aragón being Aragón, that is to say extremely important within evolving Spain, Zaragoza was used first as a base by its own powerful royalty and later as a fairly frequent stopping-place for the kings and queens of a unified country. It comes as no surprise, therefore, to find that successive monarchs have made a great many changes to al-Muqtadir's Moorish palace, the Aljafería. Isabel and Fernando added an upper storey and a long chamber with an exceptionally fine coffered ceiling, painted and gilded and hung with pineapple-stalactites in the Moorish style known as *artesonado*. Felipe II dug a moat and added a wall in castle style. Later kings and queens stripped out great quantities of Moorish decoration. The Franco regime used it first as a barracks and as stabling for military mounts, buildings being valued at that time only for their utility, and modern custodians, while attempting restoration, have added a deal of what is fast becoming a standard solution – large sheets of blank and featureless plate glass.

Perhaps it takes an addict to enjoy the Aljafería to the full, but the mosque, which survives almost intact within, is certainly a thing of considerable beauty, octagonal and tiny, and in this respect at the far end of the scale from the great public statements of Córdoba. Like the Mezquita, though, it has a shell-shaped marble block roofing its little *mihrab*. Plaster patterning, cursive and intricate but in only moderate condition, ascends towards a gallery with multifoliate arches and windows in lattice-work. It is, to me, a pleasing and domestic-seeming place, enormously enriched by the intricate and never-ending geometrical patterning. From the outside, a fine multi-lobed arch guards the gorgeously patterned doorway, standing between mosque and a reflective indoor pool. Other exquisite arches are ranged round the pool, with blind arches up against the walls, framed by their rectangles of abstract patterning. In the central patio, just by the main entrance, an especially worn column on the corner takes the eye.

One man who may have slapped it with his gloves in passing was Rodrigo Díaz, El Cid. Being short of occupation for a moment in 1081, he had sent a message to al-Muqtadir offering his services. The result was five years of military campaigning as a servant of Moorish Zaragoza.

The Cid, of course, comes to us initially as a figure of romance, hero of one of Europe's great medieval epics. In this, he is presented as a frontier fighter whose vast inner nobility contrasts with the corruption of the hereditary aristocracy. Perpetually betrayed by a jealous king, he remains forever loyal, faultless in his duty as a feudal vassal. He is a constant husband and a loving father, a byword, irreproachable, in the doughty struggle of Christendom against the Moors. His honorific title is taken from the Arabic *sidi* and means lord or señor. Thus, the Christian usage *el mío Cid* is itself a mixture of Spanish and Arabic. He is also known as El Cid

Campeador, the last word a version of *Campi Doctor* or Doctor of the Military Field – professor, as it were, of fighting. There are many references to him as 'he who was born in good hour', suggesting, in a poem written from the Castilian point of view, that he was a long-term benefactor to that kingdom.

El Cid, in short, and forgetting for a moment the half-Arabic honorific, is a key figure in the version of Spanish history that begins at Covadonga and rolls on as an unstoppable national crusade, Christians against Moors. To the simple early story, there has now been added the extra ingredient of Castile, seen as the fount of martial values and noble attitudes. This version has proved an extremely heady one, endorsed to the hilt earlier in this century, in the most scholarly fashion, by Ramón Menéndez Pidal, universally regarded as the greatest of Spanish historians. Moreover, as pointed out by Richard Fletcher, the best modern historian on the theme, Menéndez Pidal also believed that 'Castile's historic destiny was to unify Spain.'

It is worth taking this a little further than Fletcher does in his extremely readable account. The key, it seems to me, is the question of unity. Beyond a doubt, Menéndez Pidal and his generation believed most fervently in the merits of Spanish unity. So, before and after him (he died in 1968 at the age of ninety-nine), has almost every other mainstream historian and, with the possible exception of the Habsburgs, each and every ruler of the Spanish state. The notion of unity was essentially Castilian, backed by Castilian propaganda. Isabel and Fernando gave it a powerful boost, at least ideologically. It waned somewhat during the sixteenth and seventeenth centuries but from that point onwards, the drive for unity, translated into centralism, has been the great theme of Spanish statecraft. It is, however, precisely this concept of centralism, identified with Castile and Castilian military values, that has permitted the modern persecution of the Basques and Catalans, the long suppression and poverty of the people of Andalucía, the marginalization of Galicia, the abandonment of the Canary Islands. Since 1975 and the death of Franco, sternest of all the centralists, it has become a great deal easier to see the underlying many-ness of Spain and indeed it is this alternative history that has recently been endorsed, feebly or not, according to one's analysis, by such developments as the setting up of the regional 'autonomies'. What has happened both with Covadonga and El Cid is that the legends that grew up around them after the event, bearing the political messages of their successors, have been accepted as historically truthful and used to underpin a subsequent historical process. It is only since the death of Franco, and with the arrival of democracy, that it has become acceptable to look for other versions of history.

The real Cid lived at a time when the concept of Spanish unity, or even Spain, lay several centuries ahead. The notion of Castile, however, was already powerful and closely tied up with concepts of frontier fighting and nobility of conduct. In this sense, the legend is realistic enough. There is also an element of realism, however it may have applied in the case of El Cid individually, in the theme of conflict between hereditary aristocracy and those whose personal nobility brought them elevation. The powerful aristocracy which had been formed in the early days of Asturias--León had now become a feature of Castile as well. It worked on the principle that profit lay in military might, in lordship over men, cattle and sheep and scarcely at all in working the land. These fairly primitive pastoral and élitist notions, quite possibly Visigothic in origin, were to underlie Spanish history for centuries and may still be seen at work in remoter areas such as Extremadura and inland Andalucía.

During the Middle Ages, however, there were not enough aristocrats to undertake control of all the frontier areas. Settlement was encouraged, particularly by Alfonso VI, through the planting of monasteries and the granting of especially favourable charters to those prepared to act as pioneers. This produced what the historian Sánchez-Albornoz has described, with only a little exaggeration, as a 'whirlwind of liberty', inevitably muted as law and bureaucracy at length caught up with the pioneers. Out of this initial whirlwind, a new aristocracy was continually emerging, its members ready to take their place alongside the existing *ricos hombres* – literally rich men, in fact the ancient master class. Sometimes, though, as the Cid epic makes clear, there were serious clashes.

Unfortunately for the poetic version of El Cid, which has him as a rising man confronting corrupt nobles, he was himself a member of the minor aristocracy. Tradition sees him born at Vivar (now Vivar del Cid) a few kilometres north of Burgos. This is a fairly dreary little place, with enormous tractors, a commemorative restaurant in a mill and otherwise not much except a fresh little river, the Ubierna, a tributary of the Arlanzón and likewise dragging prettily with weed. Here the young Rodrigo Díaz may well have dipped his toes. As a Castilian, Rodrigo first served Sancho, Alfonso VI's elder brother, who had inherited Castile. But following Sancho's murder in the ditches of Zamora, he transferred his loyalty to the new king. Tradition intervenes again here, offering us a scene in Burgos, in the church of Santa Gadea, one of the few contemporary buildings that still survive, though not, it must be said, an especially remarkable one. Here, according to a doubtful tale, the Cid obliged Alfonso to swear in a great oath that he and his sister Urraca were innocent of Sancho's murder.

The Cid flourished under Alfonso, though not perhaps as much as under Sancho. Unlike his new sovereign, Rodrigo Díaz was literate and very probably had a good knowledge of law. His signature crops up quite frequently as a witness to charters and he was involved in adjudicating legal cases. He married a woman named Jimena, possibly an Asturian aristocrat. An early copy of the marriage settlement, exhibited in facsimile in the museum in the cloister of Burgos cathedral, shows him as owning clusters of properties in the area. The document has been folded over and over again, to the size of a pocket book, giving it a marvellously familiar, well-used look.

Above all, though, Rodrigo Díaz was a military man, a fighter and commander. It was here that he fell out with Alfonso, conducting murky brawls involving cross-alliances with Moorish factions and even the capture and ransoming of other Castilian aristocrats. In 1081 he led an independent raid into the area around Toledo, upsetting Alfonso's slowly emerging system of control. Banishment being then a common weapon – Alfonso himself, of course, had spent his months of exile in Toledo – Rodrigo Díaz was now dismissed from Alfonso's realms. He departed with his followers leaving his wife and daughters, for a time, in the care of San Pedro de Cardeña, a monastery near Burgos, well worth a visit for modern followers of the Cid.

It is hard to say whether the Cid's military activities were those of a mercenary in the modern sense or whether he was merely maintaining himself by warfare in the aristocratic style. He was now without a ready source of income and it was this that led him and his men to Zaragoza.

However embarrassing for the Christian, Castilian legend, El Cid did well in Moorish service at Zaragoza. Al-Muqtadir had died, leaving his realms divided between two sons. Rodrigo Díaz remained in the service of the son with the more westerly domains, fighting vigorously in his various campaigns and defensive actions. On one occasion he captured and ransomed the Count of Barcelona, an action he was to repeat a little later, to the considerable chagrin of the Count. As with many other successful generals, he seemed to have luck continually on his side and it is from this Moorish period that much of his military reputation derives.

In exile and in disgrace with King Alfonso, and thoroughly occupied with Zaragozan affairs, El Cid was an absentee on the day Toledo finally fell to Alfonso. Events, however, were soon to bring the two together.

Toledo's undignified collapse, and signs soon afterwards of a more aggressive Christian attitude, had already provoked the *taifa* kingdoms to appeal for help to the new Muslim rulers of Morocco. The Almoravids were recent arrivals on the North African scene but enough was known about them to suggest that the *taifa* kingdoms might have been wiser to stick with the Christians. The Almoravids were extremely militaristic, pursuing a Saharan code of asceticism and a fundamentalist interpretation of Islam. They now came over to Spain under their leader Yusuf and in 1086, the year following the fall of Toledo, soundly defeated Alfonso, who remained for the rest of his long reign almost entirely on the defensive.

Yusuf, slightly to everyone's surprise, went home to Africa again, retaining some control but also declaring that the *taifas* knew better than anybody how to manage their own affairs. Very soon, though, he was back and it was in the face of this growing pressure from Africa that El Cid and Alfonso VI were eventually reconciled. But their friendship and cooperation lasted only briefly. Accusing the Cid of treachery, Alfonso banished his awkward subject once again.

Retiring to the east, El Cid now set about carving out an independent state. There were several seasons of scavenging and extortion, a raid into the Rioja whose savagery shocked even a contemporary Christian biographer and finally a successful siege of the great Moorish city of Valencia, controlling the richest agricultural region in all Spain.

I reach Valencia in spring, in company with my wife, after one of those endless drives that leave you mutton-headed and despairing. Dark has caught us on the road and we have been lost in the famous *huerta*, or 'garden', of the coastal region, making our way through the nether end of scores of small industrial settlements, with little energy for the dusky fields of artichokes between the towns or even orange trees in blossom. We pass the night in a modest *hostal* to the south of the city. *Hostales*, particularly those most used by lorry drivers, are cheap and often excellent, but this, it must be confessed, is a very strange place indeed. There are sounds of fighting and a rough bumping and clashing, never explained, as if of mechanical monsters copulating. We wake to find, to our surprise, that it is a local bank holiday. All around lie orange groves and factories and litter. Across the fields we spot an unexceptional stretch of water backed by tall buildings creeping in from north and south. This has to be the famous Albufera, the fresh water lake just south of the city, source throughout history of duck and eels, and divided from the Mediterranean by only a narrow strip of sand – encroached on now by out-of-scale construction. I have always associated the Albufera with the duck-shooting scene in Lawrence Durrell's *Alexandria Quartet*, with mist and reeds, with dogs and shallow punts. I regale my spouse, and at some length, with a passionate account of my disappointment.

As it happens, I have visited Valencia two or three times before but hurriedly and always willing to respond to the guidebook charge that its nineteenth- and twentieth-century attempts at self-improvement have made a dreadful mess of a long inheritance. I hold out relatively little hope on this occasion.

We begin with what we realize is becoming a routine: terrible warnings from friends waiting to greet us that our car, being not only out-of-town but foreign, will be ransacked if we leave it on the street. Not wishing to respond to what may be alarmism, we park instead, in the middle of the morning, outside a smart hotel bedecked with flags. The hall porter, seemingly inspired by kindness rather than territorialism, comes dashing out to tell us that his own car, bearing Majorcan number plates, has been broken into twice in the past six weeks. We find a space under a department store and pay the kind of ransom El Cid demanded from the Count of Barcelona. Such is the state of fear affecting the car-owning classes.

The bank holiday proves a bonus. For a start, there is relief from traffic. Spaniards live in apartments, which means their cities are far smaller physically than, say, British cities with their individual homes and gardens. A recent, colossal growth in Spanish car owner-ship has combined with growth in the size and number of lorries to ensure there is hardly an inch left in the streets and an almost perpetual stalemate among those attempting to use any kind of vehicle. Madrid is choked to the point of despair. Seville is dreadful. Valencia is as bad. The country roads of Spain, even in remote places, are faster than they ever were and often wonderfully empty; driving, that most mundane activity, can often be a delight; but somehow, as a traveller, you have to come to terms with the traffic in the cities or you will wish that you had never set out in the first place.

Perambulating through the almost empty streets of Valencia, we find ourselves pleased, if not quite thunderstruck, at many inci-dentals. The 'northern' railway station, confusingly to the south of the city centre, is a stark up-and-down twentieth-century building relieved by towers and turrets, decorative stars and shields, oranges and orange blossom. There are ceramic plaques showing naked children, gypsy-looking ladies in gorgeous dresses, a profusion of flowers and, once again, oranges. The cafeteria, which has a highly fancied ceramic ceiling, is closed for *obras* – fate of many a public place in Spain – but the ticket hall itself is worth inspection as an example of the Modernista style that flourished in the late nineteenth and early twentieth centuries in Valencia as well as Barcelona. The Bank of Valencia, in a street named for the nineteenth-century painter Sorolla, master of sunny beaches with parasols and ladies in long dresses, rises through several layers of sculptural adornment to an upper storey positively pirouetting in green and yellow ceramic tiles. And so it goes, with plenty of average contemporary buildings but also streets of Neapolitan narrowness and peeling plaster, a dignified cathedral – possessed of what it claims to be the Holy Grail – a pair of surviving city gates, a dried out river bed with handsome bridges and, on the far side of it, a park with palms and careful gardeners, the university and then the usual extension of large apartment blocks. To the east, a mile or two into the urban haze, there lies the city's busy harbour and to the south the Albufera and its outsize buildings.

We notice posters for photographic shows and avant-garde music, for cinema and theatre. Valencia, Spain's third city, is culturally alert. Outside the Gothic *lonja*, the most beautiful single building in the city, we run by purest chance into the Valencia art historian Santiago Sebastián. This is a particular pleasure since I have just been reading a work of his on Renaissance Salamanca. We find the professor effervescing over a pet theory, an alleged Renaissance parallel for Picasso's *Guernica*. He claims the resemblances are so close that the Picasso work, whatever its title, should not be linked directly to anything so specific as the Spanish Civil War. The professor is getting a lot of mileage out of his theory, with lectures to give all over Europe. But now he takes time off to explain the sculptures on the *lonja* door. The building's church-like look, he says, springs from the fact that it was genuinely seen as a temple of commerce. On the lower courses of the outer door, he shows us Leviathan swallowing up sinners, presumably dishonest tradesmen. But some, high up on the left, appear to be in trouble for their sexual proclivities. A small stone couple, naked and relaxed, are making love with some enthusiasm. Chuckling with pleasure, Prof. Sebastián shows us another figure, on the adjoining building, with naked backside and erect member – definitely a dirty piece of carving, this – then leads us back again to the *lonja* doorway for simple scenes of duck-hunting, immediately suggesting the Albufera in better days.

Apart from the lack of traffic, there is a second blessing in the bank holiday. The day turns out to be the feast of St Vincent Ferrer, Valencia's patron, and is being celebrated all over the city in scores of open-air plays performed by children. Each shows one of the saint's miracles. The temporary scenery is huge, with ecclesiastical backdrops reaching high above elaborate wooden stages. The young players have microphones; you can hear the roughened contralto of the boys and the thin soprano of the girls echoing from walls of houses long before you come upon the players. Each play is like a school performance much enlarged, with long parts for the children to commit to memory. Adults sway with laughter at innuendoes in the text. Fathers stand up to shoot videos. Priests prompt and little brothers, reading comics, mouth the words they already have by heart. It seems to go on and on. We set out for an evening meal during the first performance and return hours later, close to midnight, to find the final scenes of the second showing still in progress.

Valencia's role and character spring from its position on the sea, with flat and fertile *huerta* all around, with easy access north to Barcelona and westwards over the mountains to Madrid. Valencia acts as an intermediary, accepter and transmitter of influences, a diplomatic city with a tradition of tolerance and liberalism and also some lack of confidence about its own identity. In Spanish terms it is neither of north or south, but being in between, is blessed with a measure of northern, Catalan practicality and with a sun-filled meridional generosity. Nor must one think that people have things easy. The area is quite disaster-prone, with devastating floods and rivers that suddenly change their courses. The *huerta* itself is only fertile because humans have cared for it for millennia, irrigating it, as they still do, and working every corner. Valencians, above all, are a hard-working people.

This generally agreeable picture emerged from lengthy negotiations with our Valencian 'minders', Antonia Sánchez and Carmen Aranegui. Toñi, short for Antonia, is a linguist and Carmen an archaeologist. Both are naturally sensitive to the implications of language and pleased, they say, with another aspect of Valencian life, the general use of the local Catalan dialect (some believe it indigenous and call it Valenciano) in place of Castilian Spanish. By the same token, they are indignant with me for planning to write about El Cid, no doubt assuming what I write will be one more piece of pro-Castilian hero-worship. Carmen is running a big dig at Sagunto, the nearby town that provoked the Second Punic War between the Romans and the Carthaginians and which El Cid much later captured after a particularly interesting siege. But she is unrelenting and presses me with alternatives. Why don't I write about the Borjas, she asks, better known to me perhaps, in Italian, as the Borgias? They came from just down the road at Játiva, in the province of Valencia, and if you leave out Cesare, then they were very representative of the area – wonderfully outgoing people, brilliant diplomats. And what about Alfonso the Magnanimous? And what about our fine Renaissance painting? 'Honestly,' says Toñi, pleading in her eyes, 'the Cid was just five minutes in the history of Valencia.'

Toñi is right, of course. El Cid took the city in 1094, conducted his wife and daughters to the top of the fortress tower to show them their new home, and proceeded to rule with shrewd rapaciousness and considerable violence. He subdued the area round about Valencia, defeated an Almoravid army – the first time this had been achieved – and died in his bed in 1099, much mourned by Jimena.

During our time in Valencia, my wife and I do our best as Cidian tourists, following step-by-step an engaging description in Richard Fletcher's book. As a substitute for the vanished fortress tower, we climb the Miguelete, the cathedral belfry, and find, to our surprise, a team of French workmen changing the clapper on the bell. We look out for the Albufera but cannot see it, thanks to industrial haze and apartment blocks. We survey the long-drained river bed to the north. But really, the case is as it was in Burgos. There is practically nothing of the period to be seen and it is the more modern city that carries the weight of imagining.

The one exception is in ceramics, a Moorish speciality flourishing here as a popular art form before, during and after the time of Rodrigo Díaz. Behind one of the most extraordinary doorways in all Spain, the baroque extravaganza, all gush and alabaster, of the former palace of the Marquis of Dos Aguas, there is a huge collection of ceramics – two collections, to be precise, one originally private and one assembled by the city council. It is a confusing place with impossible problems of display. The only answer is a comfortable, unhurried wander allowing the visitor eventually to make out a progression from the geometrical patterns of early times, generally in tender blue or green on a white background, and often enhanced with Arabic inscriptions, then on through an increasingly large palette, to culminate, in the Renaissance and after, in the happy polychrome of Talavera near Madrid and the continuing delights of Manises and Paterna, both now suburbs of Valencia. In this single cluttered museum, one may inspect Valencian lustreware – the so-called *reflejo metálico*, glinting with coppery tones, whose export first made the city famous internationally – and gain some first perception of the art of the Hispanic tile-makers. The tiles themselves point on towards Seville and Granada, on again through the necessary shifts in style to seventeenth-century Dutch interiors and finally come home again to the Arabic-inspired designs to be seen in porches and patios the length and breadth of southern Spain today.

Afterwards, or perhaps before, the enthusiast will make a visit to Manises where a new municipal museum shows how it was all done and offers a smaller, simpler and equally rewarding display. There is little truth in the rumour, beloved of guidebooks, that some of the kilns here have been in use since Moorish times. But if a kindly person will direct you to one of the traditional potteries, and away from the otherwise prevailing tat, you will witness the continuation of the most remarkable, and most delightful, of all Spain's popular arts.

The Almoravids grew stronger and stronger. Even with Alfonso's help, the widowed Jimena was unable to hold Valencia. Abandoning the city in 1101, she fired it, an act that has not been forgotten. Valencia and the rich *huerta* of the Levant passed back into Moorish hands where they remained for the next 130 years. Meanwhile the Almoravids, as had always seemed inevitable, decided the *taifas* were a hopeless case and took them over one by one, removing such figures as Abd Allah of Granada and al-Mutamid of Seville to exile in Africa. But powerful as the Almoravids were, they never retook Toledo, whose loss had provoked their own invasion of Spain. Nor did their power last long, for in 1118, in another key episode of the gathering Reconquista, the Aragonese took Zaragoza.

With this defeat, the Almoravids began to crumble. But already, by the early twelfth century, a new and even more urgent Islamic sect, composed mainly of Berbers, was emerging in northern Africa. These newcomers, named the Almohads, drove eastwards towards Egypt and north into the Spanish peninsula, resisted at first, though, briefly, by Seville. Like their predecessors they professed a desert fundamentalism, austere and inflexible. More so than their predecessors, they were seen throughout their period in Spain as foreigners and tyrants.

Making Seville their capital, the Almohads erected a number of handsome monumental buildings, including a pair of octagonal towers, one on each side of the Guadalquivir, just where it met the city, and with chains to sling between them, blocking passage to the unwelcome. One survives today. It is called the Torre del Oro, or Golden Tower, and is one of the picture postcard trademarks of the city. The Almohads built a public mosque with a large patio for ablutions – this had a particularly fine bronze doorway in severe but harmonious patterning – and a tall brick tower which became a landmark in the lush, fruit-bearing valley. Today it is known as the Giralda, making an excellent pair with the tower of Kutubiyya in Marrakesh. Two hundred metres to the east was the *alcázar*, or fortress, and this the Almohads refurbished in their own dignified taste.

It is conventional to say two contradictory things about the Almoravids and their successors, the Almohads. The first is that like all settlers in the south of Spain, they were seduced by its beauty and luxury, becoming more Andalusian than Arabic or Berber. The second is to present these New Andalusians as cultural vandals and religious oppressors, undoing the achievements of caliphate and *taifas*.

First, then, their cultural achievements, or lack of them. Under the Almoravids courtly poetry went out of fashion. Ceramics flourished, however, as did other decorative arts. Under the Almohads, despite their dogmatism, philosophy reached heights not matched before or after in the peninsula.

The Jewish scholar Maimonides, born and raised in Córdoba during the Almoravid period, was a precursor. Finding the climate by now unkindly towards Jews, Maimonides travelled widely and most of his writing was actually done in Fez and Cairo. His contributions to medicine were considerable but his enduring reputation lies in the codification of Jewish law. His, in the deepest sense, was a Jewish career, although it was conducted entirely within the Muslim world, and it seems appropriate, Almoravids notwithstanding, that his turbanned statue should sit so tranquilly in a floral corner of the old Jewry of Córdoba.

Maimonides was still alive in Cairo when Ibn-Tufayl, known to the medieval west as Abubacer, was court physician to the Almohads in Seville. Abubacer was himself a philosopher, author of a fine allegory on the conflict between the inquiring nature of thought and the more rigid tenets of religion. His successor as court physician, for a brief period, was Ibn-Rushd, better known as Averroes and still the most intensely admired of Hispanic philosophers. It was Averroes who reinterpreted Aristotle for the later Middle Ages, for Europe as well as the Arab world, clearing away the accretions of Neoplatonism and revealing once again the obscured intentions of Plato himself. And bizarrely enough, given the fundamentalist views of the Almohads, it was the Almohad ruler who encouraged Averroes to the undertaking.

All this being acknowledged, it is also true that the twelfth century saw a general hardening of Muslim attitudes, a more thorough Islamicization of al-Andalus than had occurred before. Mozarabic

Christians found they were no longer acceptable and moved out of Moorish areas. Many Jews were actively persecuted and also moved to Christian territory, bringing their skills in scholarship and finance. It was a reversal of the early days of the Moors in Spain, when the Jews had taken refuge among the Muslims to escape Visigothic harassment.

It is hard to be too positive on the point, but over and over in the early Middle Ages one gets the impression that early Hispanic Christianity was a tolerant, almost benign affair in its dealings with the other great religions. Certainly, there was no great intellectual interest in Islam, no suggestion but that the Christians, possessing the ultimate in revelation, were anything other than superior in their own estimation. Yet Moorish skills of civilization were deeply admired; scholarship, styles and luxury products crossed the frontier line; Christian lords and princes embraced Moorish wives and mistresses – all kinds of currents ran back and forth between the two communities and cultures.

It would be 200 years before those currents finally evaporated. But from about this time, Christian attitudes also began to harden. It is pleasant, even if a little xenophobic-by-adoption, to blame the French and the papacy. But there is some case for doing so, since what was finally arriving, as counterpoise to the new Islamic Holy War, was the full-out Christian crusade. Promising forgiveness of sins in much the same terms as Islam, the papacy spurred on its Christian fighters, men who were as interested in a good share of the spoils as they were in the fortunes of their religion. The French Cluniac clergy, now so powerful in Spain, played a large part; many Christian knights came down from France, seeking their own castles in Spain. At the same time, as a largely indigenous product, the concept of the noble Castilian conquistador was in the making; the *Poema del mío Cid*, embodying these ideas in terms hard to resist, even today, was probably composed around the start of the thirteenth century. St James of Compostela now became St James the Moorslayer, soon to be seen astride his horse on a thousand church fronts, pinning down human adversaries with his spear just as St George dispatches dragons.

It was Alfonso VIII of Castile and León who decisively turned the tide against the Almohads at the battle of Navas de Tolosa in 1212. Though this had been planned as an international crusading operation, the alliance finally fell to pieces. On the other hand, Alfonso had the support of all the Hispanic Christian kingdoms: Aragón, by now including the Catalan counties; the Basques of Navarre; the kingdom of Portugal, which had emerged during the previous century under the house of Burgundy; and finally his own home-base – Castile, including now Toledo, and the appendages of León, Asturias and Galicia. Not too surprisingly, given the spirit of the times, Alfonso was guided to victory by a shepherd whose face remained invisible to all but himself; not just St James, perhaps, but conceivably, given the importance of the occasion, the Divinity in Person.

Now the Reconquista proceeded irreversibly. By 1238, Valencia and the Balearic islands, rich and important, had fallen definitively to Aragón–Catalonia. Down in the deeper south, Fernando III of Castile, who later became a saint, was mopping up huge areas. Córdoba, shorn of its former greatness, fell to him in 1221; Murcia, then as today an agricultural centre not far short of the Levant, came into the Christian fold in 1243. In 1246 it was Jaén and finally in 1248, diamond in the diadem, Seville. This left only Granada where a new ruler, of Arab origin, had lately established himself. He had become a vassal of Fernando's, actively helping in the conquest of his co-religionaries; when finally Fernando died in 1254, a troop of Muslim knights from Granada attended his funeral. His tomb bore the inscription 'King of the Three Religions', eloquently making the point that though his victories had been won in the name of the new and tougher Christendom, Spain was still a richly heterogeneous society.

For us today, the greatest witnesses are architectural, reflecting the interwoven population patterns. In much of Aragón, Valencia and around Toledo, many Moors – now known as the Mudéjars – stayed on to work the land for Christian masters. Under their hands, agriculture remained rich and profitable, especially where it was based on irrigation. *'Quien tiene Moro tiene oro,'* went the

Christian refrain – 'Whoever has a Moor has solid gold.' Among the Mudéjar population there were many skilled craftsmen and it was they who possessed the skill and taste that lay beneath the popular architecture that now emerged, expressed above all in churches built in brick, their towers elaborately patterned with brick bands and elaborately varied zigzags protruding just a little from the surface. Under the sun, these cast tiny, geometrical shadows. The finest of all, perhaps, are the strange towers, fantastically patterned and with ceramic inlays, in the high Aragonese city of Teruel. The Mudéjars also fashioned magnificent wooden ceilings in the *artesonado* style, still to be seen throughout the whole of Spain.

Meanwhile, at the far end of the scale from the Mudéjar churches, the grandest of Christian buildings were going up in stone. These were the great Gothic cathedrals, which now appeared in the city centres, built entirely under European influence. León cathedral, totally French in style, was constructed over a long period from 1221. In the same year, Fernando el Santo personally laid the foundation stone of the great cathedral of Burgos, designed mainly by German craftsmen. Six years later, he laid the foundation stone of a new cathedral in Toledo.

To understand the force and complexity of Catholicism in Spain there is no place like Toledo, now – as in Visigothic days – the seat of the primate. It is a truism that most of us know how the city looks, humped under summer lightning, ringed by the Tagus, flaring mauve and grey from the brush of El Greco. So it was in the sixteenth century, give or take some painterly exaggeration; so it is in the twentieth, with a view of climbing roofs and steep declivities, the *alcázar* towering above one half of it, as reconstructed in the Franco era after the bitter siege of the Civil War. The cathedral itself is somewhat buried in the side of the hill, though there is a good view of the whole from the parador across the river. Most of the new apartment buildings are hidden away on what is virtually a separate site, preserving the old city in its tight-packed visual poetics.

Enter the city, however, even in midwinter, and your impression will change. A friend from Madrid, though a true Castilian, has refused to accompany us, saying he cannot bear the way the cars pursue pedestrians along the narrow streets, forcing them to clamber into doorways or stand spread-eagled with their backs against the walls. There are more tourist shops than one can easily imagine, loaded with damascene paper-knives and cheapjack swords, with gaudy pottery and blatantly coloured reproductions of El Greco. We stay a few days amid the bedlam and are amazed to find the Toledans going about their ordinary business, chatting and shopping on the calmer fringes or cutting their way straight through the crowds, as though the tourist floods were immaterial. We try to emulate their calm.

As all good tourists know, or should, the physical city reflects Toledo's jumbled past, with a mosque and synagogues, Mudéjar churches, ancient walls and gates. El Greco lived and painted here and two of his greatest masterpieces are still in the city, together with an ancient building, a very pretty one, dolled up to represent his home and studio. Toledo's tourist spots attract their thousands because of their genuine interest and beauty; all of them are on our list. Our real intention, though, is to pass what time we can round the cathedral and all that it represents.

When Alfonso VI took the city in 1085, he may quite possibly have held conciliatory views about the principal mosque and the site it occupied. This was certainly the case with his first governor, a distinguished Mozarab named Sisnando Davídiz. Davídiz, anxious to restore public confidence, was willing to let the mosque simply carry on. But Alfonso's current queen, a Frenchwoman and niece of St Hugh of Cluny, adopted harsher measures in the king's absence. A faction representing the queen and her ally Bernard of Sahagún – a Cluniac monk who soon became archbishop of Toledo – appears to have entered the mosque forcibly, erected altars and turned the minaret into a belfry. Alfonso finally fell in with the forced conversion and a Romanesque cathedral was erected on the spot. This was the bruising side of the Catholicism then emerging. Oddly enough, one major memorial of the older, gentler Catholicism has survived right through from Romanesque to Gothic and may still be found at work within. This is the ancient Mozarabic rite.

The building that we see today is later than Alfonso's. Spare and pure in Gothic style, it is complicated with many trappings, some grandiloquent to a degree. You enter either down an alley flanked forbiddingly by cliffs of stone or, less challengingly, from the grand, wide cloister. Step down here through a gleaming Renaissance doorway, under a sculptural medallion, and at once you are in older territory, with massive, fluted columns soaring to pointed arches and above, depending on the light, a richness of medieval glass. Chapels cluster all around; the hats of departed cardinals hang on strings like fishing floats suspended in the murky air. There is a great carved choir, its walnut seats incised with scenes from the capture of the kingdom of Granada at the close of the fifteenth century; siege upon siege, sally upon sally, turbanned heads and knights on chargers, even, on one of the seats, a cannon firing. Opposite the choir, above the altar-table, rears one of those vast Spanish altar backdrops known as *retablos*, a cross between sculpture and architecture. They rise in storeys like apartment blocks, each storey full of sculpted figures, usually in wood and painted and known by the general term of polychrome statuary. As in Toledo, the major subject is usually the life of Christ, often with a Calvary to top out the construction. Just round behind this *retablo* there waits Toledo's challenge to Valencia's portal of the Marquis of Dos Aguas – an enormous sculptural extravagance known as *The Transparency*. White legs of angels kick out into space as their owners descend head first into a baroque froth of white and gold.

Processing right round this sonorous cathedral we come at last to the sizeable chapel close to our point of entry where the Mozarabic service is celebrated. Though Alfonso VI had delivered Spain to the papacy, ritually speaking, by agreeing to follow the Roman rite, the old order of service had remained in at least occasional use in Toledo. Four centuries later, Cardinal Cisneros, servant of Isabel and Fernando, took the conscious decision to preserve it, licensing its use in the cathedral, in two Toledan parish churches and a single private chapel.

1 Santa María del Naranco. The immaculate mid-ninth-century palace now does occasional duty as a church.

2 San Salvador de Valdedios, south of Villaviciosa, built in the late ninth century and showing Mozarabic influence.

3 Mud and muck – Asturias in winter. Behind the house is an *hórreo*, a granary on granite stilts.

4 The Virgin of Covadonga, tiny but resplendent in her cave-shrine, marks the start of Spain's portrayal of herself as heroine of the Reconquista and sword-arm of Christendom. The image is an eighteenth-century replacement of the original, destroyed by fire.

5 A modern chapel in the cave mouth at Covadonga. Altar and Virgin are hidden away behind, while to the right, behind the railings, pews provide a resting place for pilgrims at prayer. The cave, once almost inaccessible, is easily reached today by stairs or tunnel.

Large, ceremonial arches on the eastern side of the palace site at Madinat al-Zahra. The accretion of buildings on the plain, glimpsed through the central arch, points the way to modern Córdoba.

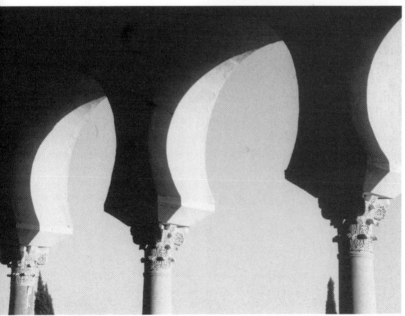

7 Restored, certainly, but once again creating an irresistible pattern of light and shade on stone. These horseshoe arches at the palace of Madinat al-Zahra, Córdoba, give access from the caliph's chambers on to the central terrace.

Above: 8 The Aljafería, Zaragoza. The Moorish fortress-palace of the Banu-Huds later became a home to the kings and queens of Aragón. Restored and refortified time after time, it was embellished by Isabel and Fernando. Now open to the public, it has also served as hospital, prison and military stable.

Left: 9 The interior courtyard at the Aljafería with characteristic paired windows, cursive stonework and interlocking arches. Much is the fruit of restoration but the original mosque and *mihrab* still survive, tiny, dark and evocative. In the way of these things in Spain, the mosque was later used as an office by the Inquisition.

Opposite: 10 Tiles and turrets observed during the ascent of the Miguelete, the belfry of Valencia cathedral.

11 An ox's head surmounts the doorway of Santa María la Real, at Sangüesa, on the Pilgrims' Way.

12 The bridge at Puente la Reina, nearby in Navarre. Two streams of pilgrims met here after crossing the Pyrenees by different routes.

13 Graffito in Puente la Reina echoes the accusation that the police have used government money to fund a secret death squad. The camels are drug dealers, condemned by ETA.

14 Charles V landed, by mistake, at Tazones in Asturias, at the mouth of the river seen here in the foreground.

15 and 16 Details from the cloister of Las Dueñas, Salamanca. Others, far more horrifying, await the visitor.

17 Upper storey, cloister of Las Dueñas.

We join a congregation of two. '*Adesto, adesto Jesu bone pontifex,*' intones the priest, while his assistant equips us with vast tomes from which to follow the service. The priest goes pounding away in Latin, racing through the names of Visigothic saints and martyrs – among them Isidoro and Leander – like a small boy counting to one hundred as quickly as he can. Whenever we lag in our responses, and there are many that we should be making, the assistant priest looks at us with troubled eyes and small encouraging gestures. The centre-piece is the creed of the Nicenes, put forward in 381 AD at the Council of Constantinople to counteract the Arian heresy. It is antiquarian sentimentality, perhaps, but a treat all the same to hear the key words still spoken with serious intent, spelled out both in Greek and Latin so clearly that no one theologically attuned – as many people were in the early Middle Ages – could fail to miss the critical point about Christ's nature. He is '*homousion to patri,*' of one substance with the Father.

Our fellow-worshippers are two Californians, both with large moustaches and neat jackets. I have run into them previously in the sacristy among the extraordinary collection of canvases by Greco and Goya, Velázquez, Zurbarán and the Italian masters. Now it is revealed that one of the two friends is a professor of theology and former cantor of the Russian Orthodox cathedral in San Francisco. All of us linger after the service, chatting to the assistant priest. Making a musical point, the former cantor raises head and voice and the Russian chant rings out, perhaps for the first time, in this side chapel of the great cathedral.

Next day is the feast of St Ildefonso, patron of Toledo, and occasion for more music. Ildefonso was a Visigothic bishop of the city long before the first arrival of the Moors and wrote a treatise asserting the completeness and totality of the Virginity of Mary. Recognizing good theology when she read it, Mary came down from heaven and, right there in the earliest cathedral, antedating the mosque by centuries, she presented him with a special chasuble as a reward. What happened to the chasuble is not recorded, but the stone on which she set her foot is still in place – a plaque on the wall nearby assures the faithful of its authenticity. If you reach through a set of railings and press your fingers through a grille you can actually touch a small section of it, though it is, as you discover, a little damp and oily. Next, following the injunction of the plaque, you kiss your fingers.

As so often on the Castilian *meseta*, it is bitterly cold on St Ildefonso's feast day. Women wrapped in overcoats and furs, with scarves across their mouths, come up to the railings and perform the ritual, pulling down the scarves only enough to kiss their finger-tips. One, a housewife from Salamanca, who assures me she visits this spot every day, borrows my pen and a page out of my notebook and in a large, loose hand composes a poem to the virginity of the Virgin Mary. Alas, she carries it away with her.

We are all awaiting celebration of a 'pontifical' mass, and soon the congregation is packed into the space between the choir and the *retablo*. A procession forms in the side aisle, choir and priests in gleaming soutanes, auxiliary bishop, as it proves to be, ushered along in the centre of the throng, in gold, with swelling stomach and large lips, a mitre on his head, a huge golden crook in his left hand. The choir file into the screened *coro*, press up against its bars like creatures in a zoo or slowly seat themselves among the stalls carved to celebrate the capture of Granada. In front of us, we see the whole huge *retablo*, its upper portions deep in dust, the Calvary on the top invisible at this angle. Above and to our left is the statue of the miraculous shepherd from the battle of Navas de Tolosa, supposedly carved by Alfonso VIII himself, since only he, of course, had seen the shepherd's face. The choir has begun to sing, loftily, majestically.

Now, in a pause in the exultant music, the auxiliary bishop begins his sermon. A press photographer bangs away with a flash. A woman journalist takes down a shorthand note for publication in the morning. Naturally enough, the auxiliary strikes the theme of San Ildefonso, praises the saint's lesser works, including his advocacy of daily communion, and arrives at last, quite firmly and openly, at the main issue. What Ildefonso praised and what we should admire and venerate and hold before our eyes continually, he says, is none other than the perfect and total virginity of Mary. He shows no consciousness at all of the contrary view, that the concept of virginity has been used by the Catholic Church across the centuries as a means of subjugating untold millions of women. Nor does he evince uneasiness that he, a celibate male, should be pronouncing on the subject.

'And now,' he concludes, 'since tomorrow, as you know, I take my vows as a full bishop, pray for me, pray, using my own name, to the White Virgin of Toledo.' We feel, and perhaps it is truly so, that we have arrived at the epicentre of the other, darker Catholicism and that it still has a stranglehold on half of Spain at least.

We find ourselves in Seville in dappled sunlight, tempted to go jangling in a tourist horse and carriage along the banks of the Guadalquivir, clip-clopping past the cathedral and among the tall Latin American trees that give such grace and height to the María Luisa park. And then again, we think we shouldn't, we had better wait till we have the children with us so that we can blame the frivolity on them. Seville is champagne bubbles and polka dots, orange blossom, Carmen, southern warmth, every cliché you can think of, though we can't think why. It has an atrocious rate of unemployment, of crime and misery and family collapse. It has a long record of discrimination against gypsies and a monstrous gap between the rich and poor. We meet a social worker who reveals the worst in sober facts and figures. But by next morning, I am ashamed to say, we feel once more that we are dancing. This has to be what people mean when they say Seville turned even the fiercest Moors into Andalusians.

Instead of the carriage ride, we take the more arduous path to the highest point in the city centre, the old Almohad tower of the Giralda with its Christian belfry and diminishing stages perched on top. Some say the belfry is ridiculous, a Renaissance outgrowth spoiling the purity of a serious piece of architecture. I am more relaxed on this, valuing the Giralda more in its role of landmark – in which case, obviously, the taller the better. You see it from a long way off as you beat southwards from Mérida and Salamanca. It dominates the skyline as you come in from Huelva in the west and take the steep hill down into the Guadalquivir valley. Unfailingly it reminds me of another traveller on his way to Seville, Antonio Torres Heredia, gypsy hero of Lorca's shivery poem, idling along with a willow switch in hand to see the bullfight in Seville. Instead of finishing his journey, he is enveloped in a brawl and as his blood runs out into the sand, he lies, in all his lost nobility of soul, dying 'in profile'. I imagine Antonio Torres Heredia and a thousand other travellers drawing towards the old Andalusian capital and looking out with affectionate recognition for the distant Arab tower, topped with its stack of belfry.

On a hot day, it is a long pull up the ramp of the Giralda. The rewards, however, are sufficient, mainly because the Sevillians have been wise enough to leave the old part of their city low. The apartment buildings, ranged round one side of town, are a long way off and in any case lower than the Giralda itself. The only buildings that have crept too high have themselves become environmental *causes célèbres*. The watcher from the tower looks down over a city of palaces and courtyards, the patios of smaller dwelling places, ancient roofs with Roman tiles, satellite television dishes, washing, rooftop gardens, even, not far off, a rooftop swimming-pool. Beyond the river lies the district of Triana, its name a corruption of 'Trajan' and famous to tourists as a place to hear flamenco and eat *tapas*, the inventive bar snacks that add so much to the pleasure of a glass of wine or sherry. Just as Seville itself has produced the jolly flamenco rhythms of the *sevillana*, so Triana has given its name to another of the traditional flamenco forms. Rodrigo de Triana, sailing with Columbus, was the first man to spot land on the far side of the Atlantic, earning his adoptive city – it is probable he came from Huelva – a place in the consciousness of every Spanish child.

Seville, with its good harbour on the river, was given the monopoly of the Atlantic trade almost as soon as America was discovered. Conquest and colonization brought a huge growth in maritime movement; the treasure fleet brought gold, and especially silver, beyond imagining. This meant that right through the sixteenth century Seville was the dominant city in all Spain. One of the most significant rooftops on view from the Giralda is that of the Casa de

Contratación close to the foot of the tower. This severe but palatial building housed the bureaucracy that controlled the American trade. Oddly, the rectangular roof around its courtyard is covered in little bumps and humps like the roof of a Turkish bath. The roof of the cathedral right at your feet – the largest Gothic cathedral in Spain, erected in a spirit of pure triumphalism – is an essay in the moss-covered shapes of Gothic vaulting, here seen in mirror image.

By the seventeenth century the river was silting up and the American monopoly was moved to Cádiz. Seville began the long decline whose aches and pains are still so evident. Today, though, ships are back again. You can see them from the Giralda, incongruous so many leagues inland. And there on the opposite side of town is another visible expression of hope, the dashingly modern bridge that goes arcing across to the site of the 1992 Seville World Fair. The earlier fair of 1929, for which a cluster of extravagant buildings was erected, had the misfortune of coinciding with the Wall Street crash.

There is hope, too, or at least evidence of energy, in the city's Holy Week, with its great hooded processions, laments and bare-footed flagellants. Then, hard on its heels and even more energetic, comes the Seville *feria*. Down past Triana, on an expanse of open ground visible from the Giralda, thousands of gaudy pavilions are erected. These are private affairs, belonging to grand families or businesses in search of self-promotion. Those invited circulate night and day in the proper whirl of wine, guitars, flamenco and flounced dresses. Horsemen in tight waistcoats and flat hats mince through the streets in a celebration of dressage, their polka-dot ladies up behind them, carnations in raven hair, just as in the tourist posters. And no matter how private the pavilions, the whole of Seville gives itself to the party in the unstinting spirit of southern Spain.

This is something one may not see from the Giralda; but standing high on the great Moorish tower, overlooking the river and the Torre del Oro, the visitor will feel the intimations of the Moorish presence more strongly than in any other Spanish city.

Partly, it is a question of lifestyle. Women, to take the most obvious issue first, and even though the number taking jobs is growing, still remain hidden in the home in Seville as in southern Spain in general – to an extraordinary degree compared to northern Europe. This spirit of seclusion is a clear survival from Moorish days. It was expressed in Moorish times in the infinitely graceful little lattice windows made of plaster, stone or alabaster – in Spanish, *celosías*, or 'jealousies' – which allowed female members of a household to look down into public rooms without revealing themselves. Houses themselves were constructed so as to hide their women, with completely unrevealing exteriors. Within lay the private kernel, the flower-filled, water-plashing patio for the exclusive pleasure of the family. The tight packed little quarter of Santa Cruz, just under the cathedral and beside the Seville *alcázar*, touristy but lovely, is full of houses built in just this style. The inexpressive, curious, white little streets, the glimpses of patio, with geraniums and tiles in Arab patterns, doorways so ancient they are a foot or two below street level – all this, though it has done later service as a Jewish quarter, seems to speak of the Islamic inheritance.

Another side of that inheritance is represented by a building whose most obvious references are Latin American. This is the Tobacco Factory, a huge and astonishingly monumental building – anybody who doubts me should inspect the sculptural grandiosities of its main entrance – which provided a considerable proportion of state revenues from the time of its construction in the eighteenth century. It is also, of course, the starting-point for the plot of *Carmen* and the setting of parts of the opera. Nowadays, it is occupied by Seville university. The ancestor of this institution, and here is the Moorish connection, was an academy set up by Fernando el Santo, shortly after he captured the city in 1248, its object being to study Latin and Arabic.

The Spaniards may have adopted some of the social behaviour of the Moors. They and many other Europeans were also determined to acquire what they could of Arab learning, readily acknowledged as superior. The key here was the translation of texts, Arabic works on astronomy, geometry and so forth but also, more particularly, the philosophy, medicine and mathematics of the ancient classical world that Islam had patiently protected since its conquest of so much of the Byzantine Middle East in the very early days. The work of translation began in the great monastery of Ripoll in Catalonia and continued in the Ebro valley, newly under Christian control, in the twelfth century. The torch passed finally to Toledo where Jewish translators quarried the essence from Greek and Arabic, while Spanish and European scholars readied the final Castilian or Latin version. The process reached its climax in the late thirteenth century under Alfonso X, el Sabio, the Wise or Learned, who established a 'translators' school' quite consciously intended to transmit the culture. Fernando el Santo was Alfonso X's father and played an intermediary part by setting up his academy of Arabic here in Seville.

The next great act of homage, though it may have been intended to surpass the civilization it imitated, was paid in the fourteenth century by Pedro I, another king of Castile, in his contribution to the *alcázar*.

You enter this entirely wonderful building through Almohad walls. The site had been in continuous use since Roman times at least, always the centre of power in the city and often, accordingly, of the whole of al-Andalus. It was a palace that people enjoyed, not just the Romans and the Arabs but almost all the Christian kings and queens who followed. They came to visit and as like as not remained for months at a time. Franco used the *alcázar* frequently. So too, at the start of his reign, did the present king, Juan Carlos. (Nowadays he tends to stay instead with the Duchess of Alba from whose palace there is a better view of the Easter processions.) Often parliaments have sat here and here too, in an assertion of continuity, the first assembly of the Andalusian autonomy was held.

Naturally almost all the longer-term occupants of Christian times have left their mark. Isabel and Fernando were responsible for a large formal chamber, one which might appear grave and handsome elsewhere but which here appears little more than clumsy. Isabel, incidentally, gave birth to her only son here in the palace. Charles V created a large and opulent suite with boldly extravagant tiling, representational, gaudy in polychrome. Outside, in the delightful garden, are tall trees from Latin America, a pretty Mudéjar pavilion, a fishpool and an eighteenth-century wall rising above, astonishing in the grotesquerie of its huge and roughly rusticated stonework. All of these elements, however, except for the garden and its summer house, seem merely afterthoughts compared to the contribution of Pedro I.

Pedro's starting-point was a palace which already contained work of the Umayyad, *taifa* and Almohad periods. He took the early palace and enlarged it, subsuming its elements and decorations, changing it, adding his own, working entirely in the Moorish style, until it is impossible to say which are his own contributions and which are genuinely Moorish.

The mere attempt to discern which is which brings out the acerbic in Rafael Valencia, an Arabist at the university who has joined me here on a spring morning. 'It is like taking a blood sample from a living person and saying, this bit is Jewish, this is Arabic, this bit, I think, is Spanish.'

His point, of course, is that it hardly matters, for this is one of Spain's great buildings, founded in the culture and aesthetic that was the most admired right across Spain at the time when it was built.

I stand with Rafael Valencia in the courtyard facing the main façade of the *alcázar*. Pedro's craftsmen were Mudéjars from Christian Toledo and Moors from Nasrid Granada – so called after its new ruling house. Already, by 1336, it had endured for a century as Spain's only Moorish kingdom. Presumably it was the Granadans, acting on Pedro's orders, who inscribed here eight times over in Arabic script, on the Christian king's façade, the famous 'Nasrid Ghaliba' – *'la galib illa allah'* – 'God alone is conqueror'.

This was familiar to me. What Rafael had to say about the colours of the façade and interior came as entirely new. Did I know, he asked, gesturing at the brilliant ceramic-tiled walls, that blue kept away demons, while green – omnipresent in the *alcázar* – was the colour of the Prophet himself? White was the Umayyad colour, its use stretching back to the caliphate, so that the green and white flag of the modern autonomy of Andalucía, which made its first appearance in Almería in the eleventh century, celebrates both prophet and caliphate. The dreaded Abbasids adopted black; you will not see very much of that in the *alcázar*. As for the kings of Granada, their colour was deep red, just the same as the red used by the kings of Castile – one more example of cultural parallelism or crossover. We move on into the vestibule of the *alcázar* and Rafael strikes a plain green tile with the heel of his hand, saying that this very shade of green has been in continuous production in Seville for well over 1,000 years.

Next comes the Courtyard of the Maidens, tranquil with paired marble columns installed during the sixteenth century, alive with plaster filigree and geometric tiles in Arab style. There are pilgrim shells here too, but Rafael assures me these are also Arab in origin, the Christians having had no monopoly of the seas. We make our way to the Hall of the Ambassadors where every force conspires to lift the eye upwards through an elegant profusion of plaster-work to a 'half-orange' dome, its stalactites suspended like a thousand swallows' nests. Here, in this entirely Moorish setting, the emperor Charles V was later to wed his beloved Isabel of Portugal; it comes as no surprise to find a few Habsburg crests let into the plaster decorations. Elsewhere there is a frieze of falcons, symbol of eternity in pre-Islamic myth. Certainly we both admire, though rather doubtfully, the highly ornamental little rooms, like gilded birdcages, which were devoted mainly to the use of women. On and on we go, through what seems in small compass an infinity of decoration laid out over strongly defined architectural forms.

I do not know about Rafael but two things amaze me, now as previously. One is the beauty of the tiles, their gleaming colours, their strange and lovely patterning with here and there the coppery glint of *reflejo metálico*. The other is that this great Christian palace was built early enough to be reflected back in the last of the Moorish masterpieces, the world-famous Court of the Lions, in the Alhambra, in Granada.

3 Isabel and Fernando

Catholic Kings, Catholic Conquests

I N A LAND OF BEAUTIFUL and striking names, few sound so sweetly on the ear as Madrigal de las Altas Torres, Madrigal of the Tall Towers. The reality of the original was considerably more martial than the name suggests, for this was a strong point out on the Castilian plain, its high towers joined in virtually a perfect circle by chunky walls protecting a surprisingly large acreage of settlement. Here, when their itinerations brought them in this direction, Juan II of Castile and María of Aragón inhabited a part-Mudéjar palace. After María's death, Juan II came sometimes with his new queen, Isabel of Portugal; and it was here, in Madrigal, on or about 22 April 1451, that Isabel of Portugal gave birth to a baby known variously to history as Isabel of Castile or Isabel the Catholic.

It was, let us be frank about it, a birth that seemed at the time of no particular significance. The king had an heir already and nobody outside the family was particularly concerned about the new arrival. Even the date of her birth went unrecorded; it has been deduced for posterity from documents dealing with other matters. But for those who were alive during Isabel's maturity, and for all since then who have been of Spanish blood or taken an interest in Spain, it has been crystal clear that Isabel was, at the least, a mighty phenomenon. With hindsight, we can see that actions she took, in common with her husband, Fernando of Aragón, still give a particular shape to modern Spain, a shape which provides it with much of its 'national' character and by the same token underlies some of the most harrowing problems the country has to face in the twentieth century. Indeed, it is not too much to say, though it is extremely unfashionable to say so, that the legacy of Isabel and Fernando, undoubtedly the cornerstone for Spain's two centuries of subsequent grandeur, now works away as a poison inside the Spanish body politic.

For the moment, all this lies in the future. Sor Angeles, a nun of the Augustinian order – which has occupied the palace at Madrigal for close on 500 years – leads us reverentially into a whitewashed alcove on the first floor, a cube of deadened air tucked in like a cupboard behind a larger chamber. It is little bigger than the four-poster bed she says it once contained. 'To think,' says Sor Angeles, clasping her hands, then making a little washing motion, 'to think so great a woman could have been born in so tiny a room.'

As it happens, we have come to Madrigal from Medina del Campo, site of the great medieval trade fairs, where Isabel died in 1504 in a handsome house on the corner of the Plaza Mayor. Medina stands just sixteen miles from Madrigal. Despite the fact that she travelled continuously, and extended Europe's vision of the world by sending Columbus out across the Atlantic, the physical proximity of the places of her birth and death have made a great impression on us, as if all Castile had been reduced to the size of a handkerchief with Isabel's short journey a kind of pilgrimage across it. The sense of tragic concentration is now augmented, almost beyond reasonable measure, by the small space to which Sor Angeles, in line with long tradition, ascribes the birth of this most forceful, perspicacious and ultimately questionable of great Castilian women.

Coming south out of Medina in evening light, the landscape is grassy to begin with, large pine trees making blunt, round silhouettes against the sky. Pines soon give way to cereal lands, with a little lift and contour in them, but nevertheless flat in appearance and effort-lessly bleak. In Isabel's day this was rough pasture land, grazed over by the ubiquitous sheep whose wool was traded first in Medina, collected in the great entrepôt of Burgos, then sent on down to the Cantabrian coast by mule to be shipped eventually in merchant fleets that left Bilbao for Antwerp. Isabel, born in Madrigal, and raised nearby in Arévalo, would have grown to maturity within sight and smell of sheep, in an atmosphere where stock-rearing went along with aristocratic militarism and an odour, increasingly harsh, of Christian piety.

Nowadays at Madrigal, as everywhere on the Castilian plain, it is grain silos that dominate the approach. One is large and round and made of steel, the other made of concrete and looking very much like a cement works. The town is meagre but well-swept, with much of its girdle of wall surviving, along with a clutch of gates, now ruthlessly restored. Outside the walls lies the collapsing monastery where Fray Luis de León, mystic and teacher, was to die in 1591. The setting is undoubtedly a depressing one – depressing, that is, until one reaches the convent of Santa María de Gracia, the one-time palace.

Proceeding round with a beaming Sor Angeles, in gathering darkness and at the very limits of visiting hours, we find a calm and sober cloister on two storeys, a church with the capacious wooden chairs used by Isabel's own parents, a letter written by Isabel and signed in her own appalling handwriting 'Yo la reina' – 'I the queen' – the deeply patterned woodwork of Mudéjar ceilings, doors of ancient, faded wood, with time-worn panels or breezily energetic inlays and, finally, the nuns' garden enclosed behind high walls like a fertile prison yard; their number has dwindled from sixty to sixteen and the land is worked now by a local market gardener. Sor Angeles gestures with enthusiasm to the portraits of prioresses. 'All great ladies from great families,' she says, 'but their portraits are not here because of that. They are here because of the particular virtues of each of the prioresses.' Sor Angeles's sentiments, which seem to imply considerable confidence in the nobility, combine with the alcove in the royal apartments to give one a strong sense both of the faded glories of Castile and of the presence of the infant Isabel. We are to travel far in pursuit of this princess and future queen, and of her formidable husband Fernando of Aragón, but nowhere is Isabel herself so clearly perceptible as at her point of setting out at Madrigal de las Altas Torres.

*

To understand the circumstances both of Castile and of the young princess it is necessary at this point to look back one hundred years to the time of Pedro I, the Castilian king who built, or at least remodelled, the great Islamic-style *alcázar* of Seville. Pedro, as it transpired, was to be the last of his immediate dynasty. Coming to the throne in his teens, at a time of bitter dispute over the succession – and ill-advised by his foremost counsellor, the first of Spain's *validos*, or ruling royal favourites – he made the irreparable error of executing Leonor de Guzmán, his late father's beautiful and beloved mistress. The rival claimant to the throne, Pedro's half-brother Enrique de Trastámara, was the illegitimate son of Leonor and the dead king; and following his mother's death Enrique Trastámara pursued Pedro through almost twenty years of civil war until the moment when he could kill him with his own hand. Trastámara propaganda has fastened the epithet 'Cruel' on the name of Pedro, apparently in perpetuity, and certainly he has much blood to answer for. But Enrique was at least as cruel; his slaughter of the royalist leaders deserves to be remembered as much as any deed of Pedro's. Enrique Trastámara also added a new and sinister ingredient to peninsular history. Rallying his forces behind a narrow Castilian chauvinism, he whipped up hatred against Pedro because of his tolerance of Jews and Muslims. Pedro's allegiance to Muslim values is expressed in the Seville *alcázar*. The Jews had also achieved great importance, both as tax-gatherers and as the nation's only money-lenders. But now the Trastámaras, in the person of Enrique II – as he became in 1369 – began to define Castilian identity in terms of exclusion, rather than the once traditional inclusiveness. Wider social forces were also at work, meaning it would be wrong to thrust the entire responsibility on the new dynasty, but before the end of the fourteenth century, pogroms were in full swing – evidence of a 'Jewish problem' to which Isabel and Fernando were later to apply a drastic solution.

Enrique also brought in the French, to deal with what he no doubt considered the English menace. Pedro I had married one daughter to England's John of Gaunt, another to Edmund Duke of York. Edward the Black Prince achieved great victories for Pedro during the early portion of the Castilian civil war. Increasingly, however, the struggle became entwined with the wider European conflict of the Hundred Years War. As France and England fought one another across the peninsula, the prospects of the rival Castilian clans rose and fell along with the performance of their northern allies. Enrique's final victory depended greatly on the French, helping to cement once more a relationship that had already had great consequences for art and the practice of religion.

Then there was the question of the aristocracy. Wishing for strong support from powerful allies but finding the Castilian nobility devastated by the civil wars, Enrique II simply created a new one. For the many families whom he ennobled, there now ensued an age of wealth and arbitrary power; an age of outrage for the tenant population over whom they exercised both feudal and judicial rights, in effect hanging or severely punishing anyone within their domains who bothered them. This was just as true in the vast lands of the Church and in the huge fiefs belonging to the crusading orders – the knights of Calatrava, Santiago and Alcántara. These orders had sprung up over recent centuries as part of the Reconquista, creating a world within a world, and owning fully a twentieth of Spain's land surface, mainly in what had once been frontier areas.

The new Trastámara-sponsored aristocracy, civil and ecclesiastic, was responsible for a great wave of castle building in Castile, their fortifications often taking over from those that centuries before had given the kingdom its name. The new constructions, of the fourteenth and fifteenth centuries, are by and large the castles that still survive today in northern and central areas (those in the south are mainly Moorish), helping Castile in particular retain its image as a place of intense, almost savage fortification. The most spectacular of them, as it happens, is one of the mildest, built more for show than serious military striving. This is the pink-brick effusion of Coca, rising above pinewoods and river valley not far from Medina del Campo and Madrigal. Elaborate and loftily, Gothically sculptural, with bartizan turrets and a huge dry moat, and instance after instance of Islamic reference, it was built early in the fifteenth century by one of the archbishops of the Fonseca family; the local forestry college has premises here today. Another great castle of the period, built in the 1440s, is La Mota, at Medina del Campo itself, with dramatic fortifications, also pink, and an interesting history. Passing eventually into the possession of Isabel and Fernando, it was used as a prison between 1506 and 1508 for one Cesare Borgia, famous sprig of a well-known Valencian family. But Coca and La Mota are only two of many. Any traveller setting out into the cereal plains of Castile and the gentle depression of the Duero valley will soon encounter, willy-nilly, bristling ramparts in villages now sunk into insignificance or make out a mighty ridge of wall outlining a distant horizon, impossibly vast, impossibly forbidding. This, by Isabel's time, was a land where tiny towns were sprouting great cathedrals, and every town and almost every crag was rendered grey and terrible by the presence of its castle.

Isabel, like Enrique de Trastámara, clawed her way to the crown through civil war. Following the death of her father, Juan II, when she was a small child, her elder half-brother, Enrique IV, son of Juan II and María of Aragón, came to the throne and held it for twenty shuffling, shambling years. For the last ten of these, the aristocracy was in open revolt, with many of the largest families engaged in full-scale warfare among themselves. Embedded in the contest was the question of the succession. Isabel's elder full brother, Don Alfonso, played a leading part in the rebellions but his death in 1468 made Isabel herself an immediate contender. Her rival was a young woman known to history, again with a somewhat unfair epithet, as Juana la Beltraneja. This carried the undisguised allegation that she was the daughter of a courtier named Beltrán de la Cueva, and not of Enrique IV, believed to be impotent by many contemporaries. The reverse may perfectly well have been true and Juana the genuine heiress. (A present-day Beltrán descendant, one of the Dukes of Albuquerque, has competed several times, and at a ripe old age, in the British Grand National.) Isabel herself had no doubts on the score of La Beltraneja's illegitimacy and was totally, almost messianically committed to her claim. As for Enrique, he acknowledged now one candidate and now the other, according to political necessity, so that both sides realized they would have to fight when he died. For Isabel and her coterie, the question of whom she married therefore assumed the greatest significance.

Compared to French and Portuguese candidates, Fernando of Aragón had the merit of youth and was reportedly a well set up young man, seventeen years old to her eighteen and already father, though she may not at this stage have known it, to one illegitimate child at least. Isabel seems to have loved him from the moment that she saw him. Unfortunately, Fernando, like Isabel, was a Trastámara – the family had been on the throne of Aragón from 1412. They shared a common great-grandfather, a fact that placed them, in theory, within forbidden limits of consanguinity. On the other hand, Fernando brought with him not only Sicily, an Aragonese possession of which he was already king, but the expectation of almost all the east of the peninsula.

The countryside around Fernando's birthplace at Sos del Rey Católico is high and fresh, with glimpses of distant Pyrenean peaks. The contrast with the plains encircling Madrigal could scarcely be more forceful nor more favourable to Sos. I reach it on my own in shining winter weather, cutting down from the Pyrenees across the Pilgrims' Way and the valley of the Río Aragón, then on a little southwards through a final barricade of lesser hills. Here Fernando's mother, hastening into Aragón in the final stages of pregnancy, gave birth to her baby in 1452.

The birthplace itself is a disappointment, a shabby old *palacio*, much remodelled, now barred and bolted and with a bureaucratically phrased notice announcing plans for *Rehabilitación*. There have been, one feels, too many *rehabilitaciónes* already. But the stout little town is a delight, so steep that instead of pavement it has steps running up the sides of its narrow, cobbled streets. Above the arched doors of the older houses, small but stately, immense spokes of stone, known to students of the art as voussoirs, wheel in that most noble of Spanish architectural forms. Newer houses, nineteenth-century perhaps, have straight stone lintels over wooden, stable-style doorways, with the upper half or quarter opening separately from the rest into cold and shadowy basements full of firewood, with dark internal steps to first-floor living quarters. I lean over a parapet towards the top of town, looking right out into the countryside, and watch two hawks quartering the valley. Into their territory now a mixed flock of sheep and goats threads its way with patient shepherd and plaintive clangour of bells. Shadow deepens in the valley. Sun fades off the snows of far sierra. The hawks retire and for a moment before nightfall the valley tweets and twitters with an innocence of birdsong. Next morning, I head downhill towards the acrid smoke of the Sangüesa paper-mill that suddenly intrudes itself into the idyll and once more meet an earnest Civil Guard road-block, young men wide awake, their automatic weapons at the ready and obstacles like tiny tank traps strewn across the road. The whole of northern Spain is tense, waiting for the next public outrage or killing of policemen.

The same kind of emotional switchback, deep peace followed instantly by intimations of strife, perhaps also afflicted the young Fernando, for he, as much as Isabel, was born to a complex, troublesome inheritance.

Two centuries before, the Aragonese had taken Zaragoza and the fertile middle reaches of the Ebro. Now their domain stretched down in a descending triangle through the high country round Teruel, which still retained, as its Mudéjar towers attest, a large Moorish population – extremely useful to the Christians given the paucity of their numbers. But this was only the start, for during the twelfth century, through a marriage that has been described as the diplomatic master-stroke of the Spanish Middle Ages, the kingdom of Aragón had taken effective and permanent possession of the County of Barcelona, chief city of the emergent region of Catalonia. And Barcelona, thanks to its Catalan energy and aggression, almost immediately embarked on an extraordinary period of commercial, territorial and artistic growth.

Early Catalan forays into France were eventually rebuffed; one of Fernando's greatest sores was the loss in his own time of two of his richest counties to the French. These are the present-day French–Catalan areas of Cerdaña and Rosellón (Cerdagne and Roussillon).

One of Fernando's most valued achievements was to win them back, temporarily, by diplomacy. Far more spectacular, however, was the Catalan–Aragonese incursion into the Mediterranean during the thirteenth and fourteenth centuries. Territorial expansion followed trade and brought them at one time or another Naples, Sicily and Sardinia. From 1309 to 1398, a freelance Catalan contingent, the Almogàvers, held the Duchy of Athens, including a large chunk of mainland Greece. Apart from its romantic extravagance, the Greek adventure was of no lasting importance to Catalonia; but the Italian connection had enduring consequences, explaining, in part at least, how the Renaissance arts of Italy were able in due course to penetrate the Spanish mainland as thoroughly as they did and also foreshadowing Spain's involvement, during the sixteenth and seventeenth centuries, in Italian wars and politics.

Valencia and its *huerta* were also part of Fernando's portion. Retaken by the Moors after the death of El Cid, Valencia had eventually re-emerged as an independent Christian kingdom, then finally become part of the Aragonese domain. In fact, the three territories of Aragón, Barcelona and Valencia were separate and separately ruled. All were considerably more liberal in their arrangements than autocratic Castile; successive Aragonese kings swore to uphold their rights and customs. This was all very well and might have pointed to a better future had matters turned out other than they did. The trouble for the moment was that the Trastámara kings of Aragón, though they enjoyed the support of an unhappy peasantry, were seen as an alien dynasty by the Catalan nobles. At the time when Isabel of Castile required a husband, Fernando's father, Juan II of Aragón, was on the verge of defeat in a long-running civil war. Providing her interest prevailed in Castile, Juan needed Isabel's support as badly as she, in her turn, needed the support of Aragón – provided only that the Trastámara cause won out.

The marriage of Isabel and Fernando was, one might say, an arrangement made on earth and not in heaven, celebrated in a private house in Valladolid on 19 October 1469, with Isabel on the run from her brother Enrique IV and on the basis of a forged papal permission to marry within the prohibited degrees. This mildly illicit start, eventually put right by the Pope, was to cause embarrassment much later on when supporters of General Franco made efforts to secure sainthood for Isabel, their chosen patroness, a campaign recently resuscitated. In immediate terms, however, the political aim was achieved; Isabel and Fernando had established the alliance that carried them to victory in Castile after Enrique's death in 1474. This took five years of civil war, though the turning point was the defeat of the Beltraneja's Portuguese allies at Toro on the Río Duero in 1476. The civil war in Aragón was also brought to a successful end.

Juana herself was to outlive her opponents, retiring to a Portuguese nunnery but continuing to style herself, in letters and other documents, as the Queen of Castile. Isabel and Fernando saw her, perpetually, as a threat. But they were duly grateful for the victory of Toro and celebrated it in one of the greatest artistic achievements of their reign. Isabel also celebrated, in even finer monuments, the parents who had brought her into this world and the brother whose death had opened her way to the throne. But before we turn to the magnificent sculpture and architecture of the Isabelline epoch, it is appropriate to make another journey into a very different culture. For over a period of what was now almost two centuries, the Moors of Granada had been developing a civilization whose mere existence was to be a critical factor in the story of Isabel and Fernando.

Imagine a nation about the size of the Basque Country or Catalonia but tucked down on the southernmost shores of the peninsula. For all its Mediterranean warmth, this coast itself is rugged, somewhat forbidding. Here and there, however, there lies a fertile plain where rivers meet the sea, or a valley mouth well suited to intensive agriculture. Gibraltar for a time belongs to this kingdom. So, almost from first to last, do the heavily fortified towns of Málaga and Almería, likewise notable ports. But overwhelmingly the essence of Granada (the name means pomegranate in Spanish) is the splendidly, wildly mountainous nature of its interior. Up through the Alpujarras the land goes soaring, to reach a lofty climax in Mulhacén and the

Pico Veleta, high points of the Sierra Nevada – literally the Snowy Range – and the highest peaks of mainland Spain. This is a rigorous, untamed, perhaps untameable countryside, broken by small valleys where ploughland still gleams dark and rich and pine and poplar stir restlessly in the breeze. The city that gave its name to the kingdom lies just to the north of this sierra and was selected, as a defensive stronghold, by the thirteenth-century Arab chieftain, Muhammad Ibn-Yusuf Ibn-Nasr, retreating southwards from Jaén. The actual position that he and his men chose for their fortress is high over the agricultural plain of the Río Genil, and high over the modern city too, commanding wide views and offering good prospects for holding off attackers. For most of the year, the Sierra Nevada gleams behind like a great white whale. The name of the strong point, which grew and grew till it contained the patios and jewelled chambers of a palace complex, is, of course, the Alhambra.

From the start, Granada had been a tributary state, owing allegiance to one or other of the Christian kingdoms. At times, as during the reign of Fernando III, the relationship was genuinely warm. But over the years Islamic philosophies had grown sterner, meeting at the same time a hardening response from the Christians. The two camps became progressively more hostile.

People who come new to Spanish history often express surprise, indeed amazement, that the little Muslim kingdom of Granada, ruled by the Nasrid dynasty, just 200 miles from east to west and only seventy or so from north to south, somehow survived for over 200 years, all on its own, despite Christian hostility. This, however, is to ignore a whole series of factors. The first, as we have seen from earlier encounters, is that it was scarcely economic for the Christians, already badly overstretched in terms of manpower, to add a whole new chunk of land, and very difficult land at that, to their thinly populated dominions. In addition, the Christian kingdoms were often divided among themselves and paralysed internally by civil wars. The final factor, perhaps the one most frequently neglected, is that the inhabitants of Nasrid Granada, more so than those of the earlier *taifas*, were a warlike people, almost as rugged as their own sierras. And who could say, if they came under direct

attack, what North African or Eastern allies they might not introduce to the peninsula?

One way and another, then, though the Granadans themselves
were pessimistic about their long-term prospects, they were considerably more secure than might be at first supposed. This allowed
them to raise their accomplishments to a high level. The few but
magnificent Granadan silks in the Lázaro Galdiano Museum in
Madrid, for example, and those others scattered through the cathedral sacristies and treasuries of Spain make the point eloquently. It
is no wonder that grandees from the Christian kingdoms abandoned
ideology to purchase whole wardrobes from Granada for marriages
or great occasions of state. These were made to order and often
revealed an interesting mixture of Christian and Islamic styles. But
straightforward Moorish dress was also highly fashionable and was
often worn by Christian kings and queens.

Granada also produced notable ceramics – the example often
quoted is the magnificently elaborate vase in the Museum of
Hispano–Muslim art in the Alhambra, shortly due to move to new
quarters. It is a shame, though, to think of the phenomenon as
limited to works produced in Granada itself, for the Islamic tradition
of ceramics, influenced like textiles by the demands of Christian
purchasers, continued to prevail not only in Granada, but even
more so in Valencia, flourishing right across southern Spain and up
into Aragón as well. All these styles are represented in the National
Ceramics Museum in Valencia, making this the best of all moments
to stage a small diversion in that direction.

During what one might call the Granadan period – that is to say,
from the thirteenth to the fifteenth century – both Manises and
Paterna, behind Valencia, were producing some of their loveliest
work, mostly in light greens achieved by copper oxide glazes, but
also in a cobalt blue very often used for decoration in Arabic
scripts. Both colours are well represented in the Valencia collection.
The patterns as much as the script-decorations have a distinctly
Middle Eastern look, often abstract but with a fair sprinkling, too,
of birds and fishes, often strangely jagged. There are human figures:
fishermen and warriors and sometimes couples, male and female,

happily together. Rabbits may have long, loopy ears, anticipating the work that was to flourish much later, in Italian Renaissance style, at Talavera de la Reina and Puente del Arzobispo south-west of Madrid. Teruel, of Aragonese Mudéjar fame, also produced a very handsome range of green ceramics, often carrying heraldic devices as well as basically Arabic patterns. These too may be seen in the Valencia museum.

But what is perhaps even more intriguing for the traveller in Spain is that many of these designs have either survived continuously up to the present day or have been revived in recent times and may be encountered almost anywhere. I cannot forbear to mention the ceramics shop opposite the cathedral in Teruel, full of Islamic splendours reinvoked by a successful modern pottery, or the professionally marketed Paterna greens, a vivid tribute to the Moorish years, which turn up in the crockery departments of the biggest chain stores all over contemporary Spain. Many localized pottery styles survive within the former borders of the kingdom of Granada, compulsively beautiful though often rather strange to the unaccustomed eye. Examples range from the shimmery, streaky ware of Coín near Málaga to the delicate but smudgy green, brown and blue of Albox in the modern province of Almería. Meanwhile, the best known pottery anywhere in Spain is probably that produced in and immediately round the one-time capital itself. Granada ware, though rather predictably centred on the perennial pomegranate, is a teasing swirl of Islamic-looking greens and blues.

It seems appropriate to mention all of this – the military strength, the textiles and ceramics – before setting out on a visit to the Alhambra, a place very often conceived of, and certainly presented to tourists, in a romantic vacuum. Romantic the Alhambra certainly is, but it acquired its extraordinary qualities against a background of wider achievement.

On the unofficial tour of the Alhambra, the place to begin is either on the main road snaking down into Granada from the east or in the Albaicín, the old Arabic settlement now inhabited by a rich mixture of Granadan townsfolk and local gypsies. It occupies a steep hill just opposite the palace, with the unimpressive Río Darro running down the valley in between. From either of these vantage points – best of all perhaps from the terrace of the church of San Nicolás in the Albaicín – you see at once, when you have recovered from first impressions of the physical beauty of the site, that the outer shell of the Alhambra is stern and thoroughly unwelcoming. This is first and foremost an exceptionally strong fortress, long and reddish-coloured on its sloping shelf of land beneath the mountain. (The name Alhambra comes from Arabic Al Hamra, the Red One.) But since we know in advance that within those awesome walls there lies concealed an unrivalled display of finery and ornamental art, we also realize from the start that the Alhambra will function on the analogy of any ordinary Moorish house, whether in Granada, Zaragoza or elsewhere – stern and protective without, tenderly delicate within.

The construction of the Alhambra is so jumbled that it is not possible to take its various parts in chronological order. But by making a start in the Alcazaba, the fortress on the furthest tip of the promontory as it extends, so to speak, from the mainland of mountain, one does get a firm impression of military origins. Later building, mainly by Fernando and Isabel, has added somewhat to the sense of scale and height, but the original Moorish keeps and towers still survive and from their eyrie-like position they offer thrilling views out over the plain as well as over the steep-pitched whitewash of the Albaicín. These views are seen through filigree lattice-work and horseshoe-shaped, paired windows, divided by a single, slender column. Called *ajimez* in the singular, *ajimeces* in the plural, these paired windows, most graceful of Moorish features, are entirely characteristic of the palace, or group of palaces, the visitor will soon traverse, tucked in behind the Alcazaba but following the ridge of high ground back towards the mountain. The original Arab city, now long gone, clung to the perilous slope beneath the fortress.

After the Alcazaba, visitors enter the palace complex through a small, rather sunken doorway and find themselves almost immediately in a not very large rectangular chamber with gallery and ornamental tiles and plaster-work. This is the Mexuar, or Hall of

Audience. Considering what is to come, it is not exactly an earth-shattering room but it has the effect of stopping first-time arrivals dead in their tracks – and still does the same to me, no matter how often I enter it. Since it contains many of the elements one will encounter later, even though later they are often in more elaborate form, it will perhaps be worth enumerating them so as to provide at least an initial skeleton.

First, then, the *azulejos*, or tile-work. This forms a high dado, coming up to about rib level, the characteristic way in which tiles are employed throughout the Alhambra. The pattern in the Mexuar is relatively simple, made up of six-pointed stars, obliquely orientated and creating a jazzy effect. Elsewhere in the Alhambra one will come on larger patterns made of many tiles, seemingly intermediate between the wheel and star, on little upright forms that look like endlessly repeating Christmas trees, on simple squares of tile set cornerwise like diamonds, on complex squares made up of half a dozen different little insignia – one will come, in short, on more different shapes and patterns than one can carry in the visual memory, even from one room to the next. The keynotes are elaboration and unending variety. Even with the diamonds, where the pattern at first seems simplest, a moment's close attention will reveal that the elaboration comes not from the form but from the use of colour, the whole comprising a playful, almost musical exercise in variation. The tiles in the Seville *alcázar* are quite ravishing but it would take a stern critic to deny that those in the Alhambra are even more beautiful, often bewilderingly so. Many of the simpler Alhambra patterns are still in use, in proper homage, right across Mediterranean Spain.

Above the tiles comes plaster decoration. In the Mexuar this takes the form of distinct bands, here both topping the tile dado and forming a cornice underneath the ceiling, with quite large areas of plain wall by way of contrast. Elsewhere in the Alhambra the whole wall-space above the tiles may well be covered in raised plaster decoration creating an effect of totally unrestrained elaboration. It rises in shallow relief from a base once painted blue or red and still, in patches, retaining tantalizing glimpses of these colours,

faded and delightful. Arabic scripts, with all their cursive elegance
and curlicues, form quite a large element in the decorative scheme.
But in the plaster-work even more than in the tiles, the watchword
is quite unrivalled inventiveness in abstract patterning. If it is really
true that lines that have no end express the infinite in Arab art, then
certainly the concept of the Infinite is appealed to over and over
again in the Alhambra. And one of the loveliest elements of the
whole, though it does not figure in the Mexuar, is the way the
plaster decoration climbs the walls to meet and join the descending
plaster-work of ceilings. The grander ceilings are even more astonishing in their elaboration than the walls, full of pendant shapes clus-
tered like swallows' nests, of tiny hanging alcoves, of stalactites
descending like a thousand stiff little sticks of sugar. These tiny
basic shapes form larger shapes again, repeating and varying the
whole of the smaller pattern, until a ceiling looks as if it is composed
of an endless comb of wasps' nests, mounting higher and higher.
These wonderful constructions reveal themselves one after the other,
to cries of admiration, as one takes the tourist trail round the Alhambra.

Perhaps we should return to the Mexuar, though, just for a final
moment, to note the Habsburg heraldry that has been introduced at
a later date – and very effectively, in my opinion, if it does not seem
profane to say so. This may serve as a reminder that the Mexuar
itself is something of a hotch-potch decoratively, with elements
brought in from elsewhere in the Alhambra as well as those which
have accrued over the course of time. It is as well to make a mental
note of this early on, for the whole of the complex has been repaired,
restored and even revamped, reflecting the great delight that the
successors of the Nasrids have taken in the building. One may as
well be grateful, rather than critical, for without this interest the
buildings would probably not have lasted in any shape or form.

Where the Mexuar comes to the edge of the precipitous ridge it
stands on, there is a little oratory, set at an odd angle and offering
views of the Albaicín. With *ajimeces* below and lattice windows
above, and a delightful complication of plaster tracery, it is one of
the true treasures of the Alhambra and may do duty in this brief

overview both in its own right and as an example of many little balconies and vantage points, both here and in the summer palace of the Generalife a little further up the mountain slope. Apart from the larger, more palatial rooms, typically those with the most elaborate of the ceilings, the other main elements in the Alhambra complex are courtyards, fountains, pools of cooling water and delicate pavilions set on slender columns.

The two most famous courtyards, the Court of the Myrtles and the Court of the Lions, seem to me to make a point that runs rather contrary to accepted wisdom about the Alhambra. In the conventional view, which I accept entirely as a starting-point, the buildings are seen as supremely decorative. But then a further leap is made that is not so convincing. This is the assertion that the underlying architectural form has been neglected, because of the commitment to superficial ornament.

The Court of the Myrtles dates from the mid fourteenth century when Yusuf I was ruler of Granada. It is a long and striking rectangle, looking up to the solid bulk of a tower of the same period, built to house Yusuf's throne room. This chamber, reaching through a full two storeys, is one of the most elaborately lovely of all the main rooms of the Alhambra. A porch with seven arches, topped by lattice-work, stands between the long water pool and the sturdy tower, so that both are quietly reflected on the surface. A view is offered right through the porch from the courtyard, right through the throne room and out on to the landscape, seen as a patch of purest light framed by the double embrasure of an *ajimez*. At the other end of the courtyard, though much has been destroyed by a large, later building – the palace of the emperor Charles V – extremely elegant wooden balconies survive. The whole of this courtyard and its surroundings, known broadly as the Comares palace, seem to my expectant and possibly over-willing eye an example of the clearest and most obvious architectural shaping, strong and vigorous and illuminated by the contrast of its moments of tenderness.

The Court of the Lions is just the other way around, for here the accent is entirely on tenderness, with the sweetest little pavilions protruding out into the gravelled courtyard, their roofs held aloft on fragile columns grouped in ones and twos and threes like Botticelli virgins dancing in a glade. The effect, if one may still say such a thing, appears entirely feminine, though no less architectural for being so, and with only the bluff fountain and its snub-nosed lions to introduce a hint of masculine ponderousness.

The Alhambra is a tricky subject since it obviously deserves rescue in our minds from its rather simple tourist status as one of the best known groups of buildings in the world. Somehow, in order to achieve this, we have to steer a way between the standard picture-postcard image, whatever we can assemble by way of legitimate background and the peculiarities of our personal responses. My own feeling is that the Alhambra varies enormously in mood from part to part, presumably in original intention as well as in its ultimate effect; that it is a deeply architectural as well as a decorative achievement; and that to call it decadent, as some have done, is to reveal an unbecoming censoriousness. It was, on the contrary, a triumph, in a real sense the climax of Moorish civilization in the Hispanic peninsula. And it was into this high civilization, a hundred years after the last parts of the Alhambra took shape, that Isabel and Fernando were to come, thrusting and destructive, in a well-organized display of muscular Christianity.

One of the most agreeable aspects of Spanish history is that from about this point in time – and in sharp contrast to Spain's early medieval period – most people know, roughly at least, what happened next.

Isabel and Fernando captured the Moorish kingdom of Granada in 1492. Through the alliance of Castile and Aragón, they laid down the foundations, or at least cleared the ground for the modern Spanish state. They witnessed the emergence of Castilian dominance in both language and culture, established the Spanish Inquisition, expelled the Jews, and, by despatching Columbus on his great adventure, almost by accident provided the springboard for Spain's Latin American empire. After their deaths, the Spanish monarchy fell into the hands of the Habsburgs. At this stage, in the person of Carlos I of Spain, who was simultaneously the Holy Roman Emperor Charles or Carlos V, the Habsburgs ruled not only Spain and most of the Americas but also many of the richest and most important parts of Europe. It was Carlos V's son Felipe II (Philip II of Spain in English history), struggling to hang on to the old certainties and battling hard in the counter-Reformation cause, who sent out the Great Armada against England. Soon after that, so the story goes, Spain fell into irreversible decline. Miraculously, however, and for reasons that naturally remain unexplained, except by such hollow theories as a 'culture lag', she was at the same time turning out quite extraordinary works of art and literature.

Little was heard of Spain during the eighteenth century though it is generally accepted that she was now ruled by the Bourbons and there were rumours, even at the time, that she had experienced some faint apology for a French-style Enlightenment. Then came invasion by Napoleon, the Spanish War of Independence against the French – popular with radicals as the first modern war of liberation and with the British in particular because of Wellington's involvement – and an extremely bleak nineteenth century of frivolous plots and counterplots, of civil wars, a First Republic, a restoration monarchy and so on. This brings us to the present century, ready for the twilight of the monarchy under Alfonso XIII, the dictatorship of Primo de Rivera and then the Second Republic of 1931–6, or 1931–9 depending on your viewpoint – an episode that stirs the imagination in all kinds of ways. The Spanish Civil War of 1936–9 was one of the climactic conflicts of modern times and often viewed as a practice bout for World War II. This was followed by the thirty-six-year-long dictatorship of General Franco and finally, under a Bourbon monarchy now re-installed, the emergence of a fragile democracy made stronger by entry to the Common Market and the Western military alliance. Countries such as Britain might not care to admit it, but in the 1990s Spain is poised to surpass them in wealth and style and possibly a new round of artistic achievement. Throughout all this, nobody in the world was quite so noble as a Spanish aristocrat, nor indeed so aristocratic as a Spanish peasant.

This version, give or take a bit, is not far off the commonly accepted one. It may not be precise in all its details; some of it, indeed, is positively misleading. But by and large the acknowledgement that such a stereotype exists will save a deal of explanation and serve, from time to time, as starting-point for more detailed discussion.

In the case of Isabel and Fernando, there is no doubting that the commonly accepted version is true. Though themselves medieval rather than 'modern' in their political solutions, they do indeed stand as cornerstone to a huge part of the Spanish future, in particular to the subsequent nation-state based on Castilian values. What one may question now, however, along with a few other customary value judgements, is whether that nation-state, especially so constituted, was such a good idea.

In 1474 Isabel was proclaimed queen in Segovia, most Castilian of cities. With its sandy walls, its sandy-pink cathedral and sandy-coloured *alcázar*, invariably but tellingly compared to the bows of some great ship, this is a fine place for a day out from Madrid. It has a little of the freshness of the nearby mountains and a water-supply that likewise comes from the mountains, brought from early days by a Roman aqueduct. The aqueduct, as is well known, rises to great heights, arch riding upon arch, as it crosses the last valley before town – this valley, of course, is now very much a part of town, a place of dreary tarmac and with traffic scuttling through the lower arches of the aqueduct itself. But except for this great architectural phenomenon, besieged but still magnificent, almost all of the visual assembly of Segovia post-dates Isabel, making it hard to imagine what the town was like.

We get a clearer glimpse of the woman herself, still in Segovia, just two years later. Now she has given birth to a male child – the arrival of an heir, assuring the succession, was almost as important in swaying the opposition to her side as the victory over the Portuguese at Toro – and she and her husband are presenting him to their loyal supporters. Fernando rides on a white hackney, the queen on a white palfry with gold and silver harness. Though Isabel was known for the sobriety of her clothing, on this occasion her dress is encrusted 'with pearls of many different kinds'.

Isabel and Fernando have also been caught at about this stage of their lives in a double portrait, which hangs in the convent at Madrigal de las Altas Torres. The royal couple bear a distinct family resemblance to one another, with fleshy, rounded faces, and small, dark, oval eyes. Fernando's mouth is also very fleshy, with a deep and slightly protruding lower lip. Isabel's mouth seems by contrast a little more buttoned-up, and definitely more determined. But truly, their features are unremarkable.

Nobody could say the same of their characters or abilities. The impression created by Fernando's career is that of a cool and calculating man, skilful as diplomat and military leader, well able to lie to gain his political ends. He seems at this distance more a fox than a lion and it was his contemporary, Machiavelli, who saluted him as 'a new prince', one transformed from the status of 'a weak king' to being 'for fame and glory, the first king of Christendom'.

Isabel's exceptional abilities were recognized by all who met her. We know of her also that she was fervently pious and deeply dedicated to the furtherance of Catholicism, zealously faithful to her husband and jealously irritated by his amours. The two of them maintained a court where learning was much respected, even if not much practised personally by the sovereigns. Fernando as a young man acknowledged that he had 'read little but seen much'. Isabel's reading matter was largely devotional and, for the rest, decidedly middle-brow. But she patronized scholars, made some effort to learn Latin and caused a Latin grammar to be written, because, she supposedly said, up to that time women had been obliged to learn from men. Another scholar at her court, Antonio de Nebrija, Jewish and formerly at Oxford, produced the first ever Castilian grammar, explaining in his dedication to Isabel that Castilian was the appropriate language of empire.

It is scarcely surprising that a royal couple who gave house room to scholars should also have sought to embellish their realm with works of art. In painting, their taste was for the small-scale, surface exactitude of the Northern Realists and Isabel's collection contained many Flemish and German works. The connection with Flanders had been established long before by the comings and goings of the wool trade. In 1428 Van Eyck had made a celebrated visit to Spain and it still seemed almost a matter of course that the portrait painters of the court of Aragón and Castile should be northerners. Of native-born Spaniards, Pedro Berruguete is the most exciting – taut and precise and commenting on often very painful subjects. Take, for example, his series on the death of St Peter the Martyr in the Prado, where the saint is seen first praying, then preaching. Next he is on his feet, holding up a prayer-book open at the creed, despite a great machete lodged in his cleft skull. After this, we see him on his knees, machete still in place and gouts of blood on his slightly pained face while a soldier stabs him fiercely in the back. Behind this scene there are attendant figures, religious and military, in contrasted states of shock and aggression, and behind again a lake or inlet with boats crossing it to reach a multi-turreted fantasy castle. Leaves are shown with miniature precision; a horse is drinking in the lake. What matters is the accumulation of detail, ordered with a quaint formality, in and round and endlessly receding from the central tableau. Scenes like this remind one inescapably of Auden's visit to the Beaux Arts in Brussels where, even though Bruegel's Icarus is falling to the earth and who knows what acts of horror and destruction are afoot, the torturer's horse still has an innocent behind and calmly scratches it against a tree.

In sculpture and architecture Isabel and Fernando were particularly fortunate, nowhere more so than in Burgos. The style here was of course Gothic, as represented by the cathedral and also the great monastery of Las Huelgas. Today, Las Huelgas is well within the city limits and it is hard to get a good view of it from any distance in which the local aluminium factory does not also figure. In the original conception, however, it stood on its own among the meadows a little way along the Río Arlanzón, serving both as convent and occasional resting place for the Castilian royal family. (The name Las Huelgas comes from *huelga*, meaning leisure or repose; whence also *huelga* in the sense of strike or industrial stoppage. Pronounced in the Andalusian style, it came back to Castilian as *juerga*, a party or carousal.)

The combination of palace and monastic retreat, sometimes

including a pantheon or burial place for members of the royal family, was a very common pattern in Spain's medieval Christian kingdoms and was to have an abiding fascination for the Habsburgs, too. It is going too far to claim the formula as evidence of a theocratic state, but certainly the monarchs used these establishments both to assert their own Catholic allegiance and to ensure that masses were said continually for them after death. Perhaps it reveals, as much as anything, the medieval terror of hell and the desperate attempts of the powerful to insure their futures for perpetuity.

Las Huelgas had been founded by Alfonso VIII, victor over the Moors at Navas de Tolosa in 1212, at the request of his wife, Eleanor of England. It was inhabited only by ladies of the highest lineage and it was said that if the Pope should ever marry, his bride would surely have to come from here. By Isabel's time it contained, along with the tombs of many of her forebears, a splendidly spare Gothic church and Gothic cloister (the latter now somewhat spoiled by a more recent upper storey), an archaically handsome Romanesque cloister and quite remarkable quantities of fine Mudéjar work. The most interesting example is the little freestanding Chapel of Santiago, with horseshoe arch, elaborate decorative plaster-work and a polychrome *artesonado* ceiling, all completely Moorish in style. Here young aspirants kept vigil on the eve of receiving their knighthoods, wearing white gowns and with no earthly possession other than a candle or two to shed a little light. It is a ritual that has given several lively phrases to the Spanish language, according to my guide, among them *estar a dos velas*, literally 'to be with two candles', or, by extension, to be completely penniless. Here, amid the riches of Islamic art and in common with almost half a dozen Castilian kings, the future Edward I of England kept vigil and was duly knighted. The interpenetration of the cultures reached out even to northern Europe.

Fernando III, El Santo, was also knighted here – supposedly dubbed by the articulated arm of a statue of Santiago, still to be seen in the chapel today. To make it work, you pull on a length of cord and down comes Santiago's sword arm, a rather simple-seeming arrangement. The reason given, both by respectable history books and by the enthusiastic young ladies who show visitors around, is that Fernando felt there was no human being sufficient in status to knight him.

Isabel stayed at Las Huelgas when she was attending to the funerary monument for her parents, Juan II and Isabel of Portugal. This was to be in yet another Burgos monastery, the Charterhouse of Miraflores, about two miles to the east of town. Juan had commissioned the construction of the monastery and now, a decade and more after his death, he had the posthumous good fortune that one of the greatest of all Gothic sculptors was on hand to make his monument.

The artist in the case was Gil de Siloé, possibly a native of Orléans, though now, by habitat and volume of local work, surely to be regarded as a Castilian. The tomb he built for Juan II and Isabel of Portugal stands close to the altar of the monastery church and is reached by passing through the normal Carthusian arrangement of separate divisions for public, lay brothers and monks. The monks, of course, had far more splendid seating arrangements than anybody else, high carved stalls clinging to either side of the fabric of the church and looking across to the tomb before the altar.

In the royal tomb, as much as in the Alhambra, the essence lies in elaboration. The large plinth on which the royal couple lie is octagonal, of precisely the same shape as one of the more common Islamic tile designs. You would make the shape by placing a square sheet of paper on top of another the same size, then rotating one of them through forty-five degrees, at which point the form under your hands would be revealed as an elegant, shallowly indented, eight-pointed star. The king and queen lie on the marble star amid a host of smaller figures, of varying size and the greatest naturalism. The robes, brocades and pillows of the royal couple are ornate to a degree, contrasting with the full and sleepy sweetness of their faces. The queen appears to have fallen asleep while reading a book, presumably a sacred text. The upper surface of the tomb ends in a fringe of cursive vegetal forms alive with putti and little animals. On the sides, amid a riot of pinnacles, there are niches with small-scale sculptures, among them lions with lean torsos, huge heads and long tongues delicately curling.

Despite some broken pieces – the king's sceptre is gone and the tiny trellis dividing king and queen is damaged – the whole is most evidently a masterpiece. Nor is it alone. On the left-hand wall facing the altar, there rises the monument to Isabel's brother Alfonso, also carved by Gil de Siloé. Here the effigy is in a kneeling posture, creating an entirely different rhythm, though the work is almost equally elaborate in its details and contains, so it is said, a portrait of the sculptor; he is in spectacles, low down on the left.

Behind the altar, rising high over these two great works, stands a *retablo*, also by Gil de Siloé, easier to make out than most. At its centre is a flowing circle of angelic figures. Christ hangs crucified and above his head the pious pelican savages her own breast so that her blood will feed her young.

The architecture of the Miraflores church has disappointed some critics. Not so the Condestable chapel in the cathedral, built on to the eastern end of the structure during Isabel's reign. Cousin and contemporary of English perpendicular, it is in the grandly elevated style now known as Isabelline Gothic, sweeping upwards towards a glass-filled star, also eight-pointed but with each point considerably more elongated than in the Miraflores tomb. From far below it looks just like a kite. The chapel contains sculpture by Gil de Siloé and, by another hand, an extremely pleasing sepulchre to its founders. It also possesses, quite startling at a first view, huge armorial devices set at an angle on the lower walls.

These are bold, handsome, regal. They express with absolute clarity the spirit of the age; from now on in Spain, escutcheons and emblems become an architectural commonplace, almost a sign of Spanish-ness, certainly a signal of aristocracy and aristocratic aspiration. Today, I must confess, I find their hierarchical implications disturbing; but time was when I loved them with a passion and I still admit, regretfully, to finding them beautiful.

San Juan de los Reyes in Toledo was founded by Isabel and Fernando as thanksgiving for their victory at Toro (it has, incidentally, one of the most beautiful of all cloisters in Spain). Before the fall of Granada offered them a still more striking venue, the royal couple intended it as their burial place. Armorial escutcheons very similar to those in the Condestable chapel are a leading feature in the church, another powerful example of Isabelline Gothic. The escutcheons here are attended by rampant lions and vast eagle heads and over and over again by bundles of arrows, tied round the middle and fanning out at top and bottom, the fasces that Isabel and Fernando made their special symbol. They were also, in due course, to become the symbol of Franco's Falange.

Along with Isabelline Gothic, one should perhaps mention another architectural style that originated during the reign, though reaching its greatest glories later on in Salamanca. This is the so-called plateresque, where huge quantities of ornament in low relief adorn façades divided into compartments rather in the manner of *retablos*. The word 'plateresque' is a reference to the decorative work of silversmiths but it has also been argued that the real origin of this shallow ornament may lie in woodcarving. Its great elaboration also shows a clear Mudéjar influence. Increasingly, though, as the Italian Renaissance made itself felt in Spain, this type of decoration was applied to buildings of generally classical proportion.

San Juan de los Reyes was designed by the architect Hans Wass, hispanicized to the more familiar Juan Guas. (The church's north-west façade is rather later.) In Guadalajara, a dull provincial capital to the east of Madrid, Guas built a magnificent palace for the first duke of Infantado, one of the powerful Mendoza clan. Here the basic structure is solidly Italianate but the large columns to either side of the doorway are decorated with a kind of stone-carved noughts and crosses, like diagonal plaits of basketwork with little cannonballs inside. Above the door two hairy satyrs hold up a shield at forty-five degrees, complete with kettle drum and swan, or perhaps it is another eagle. The whole surface of the façade is decorated with diamond bosses like the business end of a mace. There is nothing else of the period quite so extraordinary, unless it is the façade of the College of San Gregorio in Valladolid – architectural design by Guas, carving attributed to Gil de Siloé.

The Infantado palace is classed as plateresque. The San Gregorio façade stands at an intermediate point between Gothic and plateresque, the work of two great artists here seeming to summarize the best of Isabel and Fernando, architecturally and sculpturally speaking. Essentially, it is an elaborate gateway, whose arch and archivolts, panels, canopies and niches provide enormous scope for sculptural invention. Nor has Gil de Siloé been found wanting. Here, as at the Infantado palace, but in enormously greater profusion, hirsute satyrs, heraldry and mythic beasts compete for the attention of the observer. Right in the centre, under shield and outsize lions, babies dangle from the branches of a tree with all the playfulness of kittens.

Valladolid was for many years the main administrative centre used by Isabel and Fernando; from here, though also travelling extensively in the manner of previous monarchs, they governed a realm growing swiftly in prosperity. The north coast ports were thriving. Bilbao was already making steel. Trade in Castile was increasing quickly with wool, as ever, at its centre. Centuries earlier Alfonso X, the Learned, had set up a body to govern and protect the transhumant ranchers who moved their flocks each year, according to the season, from north to south of Spain and back again. This body acquired the title of the Mesta and it enjoyed enormous privileges. Traditionally, Isabel and Fernando have been accused of favouring the Mesta disproportionately, so that sheep took an easy precedence over much-needed corn. Recent scholarship has chipped away at this a little, but the blunt fact remains that both Castile and Aragón (which had a body of its own closely resembling the Mesta) were dedicated to stock-rearing rather than to the more laborious and productive kinds of agriculture. This fundamentally aristocratic notion, downgrading labour in favour of dominion over men and beasts, still lay deep in the Castilian concept of self. It had recently received reinforcement from the concept of chivalry, developing fast in France and Flanders and tending to confirm the view that honour lay in war and nowhere else. Perhaps no group in Europe was at this stage so warlike as the Spanish aristocracy.

Fernando and Isabel nevertheless made it their business to control the nobles. They did nothing to reduce their overwhelmingly high status, either socially or as the owners of rural *latifundia*, the huge estates whose mere existence conditioned much else in Spain. But they used the nobles remarkably little for any tasks of state, preferring instead what chroniclers described as 'men of prudence ... of the middling sort', 'well-informed, discreet and subtle'. The monarchs firmly discouraged aristocratic wrangling, forbade the building of new castles and even, on occasion, seized back whole cities for the commonweal – among them Cádiz, which up till then had been entirely the personal possession of the local duke. They moved in on the towns as well, adding royal officials called *corregidores* to what had, in many cases, been virtually independent local rule.

Few would question the good sense of this approach. Their method of achieving order in the countryside, however, was much more dubious. At a famous meeting of the *cortes*, or parliament, in Madrigal de las Altas Torres in 1476 – held in the handsome room where the nuns now have their refectory, tables crammed against the wall along a narrow dais – Isabel and Fernando set up a rural police force called the Santa Hermandad, or Holy Brotherhood, financed by local taxes. This proceeded to 'pacify' the countryside, apprehending those who fell foul of it and itself passing sentence on them. 'There was,' wrote the royal physician approvingly, 'much butchery, with the cutting off of feet, hands and heads.' So effective was the butchery, and so much was the expense resented locally, that this first version of the Hermandad was abolished in 1495. But it had established a notable precedent; and the whole of Spanish history, even the so-called liberal era of the nineteenth century – which incidentally saw the foundation of the present Civil Guard – has been marked by extraordinarily vicious episodes of repression in town and countryside.

The particular repression for which Isabel and Fernando are best known, however, was that of the Inquisition. The background to its establishment was the presence of a considerable Jewish population, the pogroms of the late fourteenth century and the consequent conversion of many Jews to Christianity. This allowed the (Jewish) New Christians, known as *conversos*, to marry into the community of the Old Christians (native Spaniards) and they made very rapid progress up the social scale. Many grand Spanish families soon had Jewish blood. Fernando himself was partly Jewish, as was St Teresa a century later. *Conversos* were also deeply entrenched at court and seemed quite indispensable as administrators of the royal finances.

But now, partly out of jealousy at their success, there arose the sinister question of whether they were true Christian converts or merely hypocritical 'Judaizers'. Accusations were as plentiful as they were fervid and during a journey to Seville, Isabel was much impressed by evidence she heard about this kind of heresy in the southern part of her realms. Soon we find king and queen petitioning the Pope for permission to set up a special Castilian inquisition, under their control and not the Pope's. Permission granted, orders went out from Medina del Campo in 1480 and one of the most repellent tribunals in history was under way. Its purpose was to eliminate semitic elements from Spanish Catholicism.

Seven hundred *conversos* were burned in Seville during the first eight years, thousands throughout Castile, with many more suffering lesser penalties. These included the seizure of property, often in a manner that served the personal interest of the inquisitioners. In 1484, under Tomás de Torquemada, himself of Jewish blood and one of those who had originally given evidence on the issue to Isabel, the Inquisition was extended into Aragón, and in 1487 into Catalonia. When people there protested, Fernando replied, 'No cause or interest, however great, will make us suspend the Inquisition.' In 1491, in the incident of the Niño de La Guardia, Jews and *conversos* were accused of the ritual crucifixion of a Christian child. By now voices were being raised to claim that Spain could not be pure so long as unconverted Jews remained within the kingdoms.

Historians have pointed out, in a spirit of apology or at least of explanation, that the number of women burned in Germany on charges of witchcraft in the seventeenth century exceeded the number executed by the Spanish Inquisition over three centuries. This may very well be true, along with many other possible parallels. What is so horrifying about the Inquisition is that it was formally and knowingly adopted as an instrument of state. The identity of witnesses was concealed, opening the tribunal to every kind of private vendetta and creating, well ahead of the secret police forces of our own century, an atmosphere of terror and denunciation. Moreover, and this is the most serious aspect for the future, it was part of a deliberate attempt to create a unified, ultra-Catholic ideology across the whole of the realms of Isabel and Fernando. That this was done by force, and from the centre, was to establish a precedent far more grievous than that of the Santa Hermandad.

In constitutional terms, however, Isabel and Fernando were careful to keep their differing possessions separate. Having inherited medieval institutions they sought to make them better rather than replace them. Fernando carefully respected the historic 'contract' by which he governed Aragón, Catalonia and Valencia. In 1476 he swore under the sacred oak at Guernica to uphold the freedoms of the Basques. Thus there remained at least a possibility that a pluralist or federal state might yet emerge. The common but mistaken belief that Isabel and Fernando were consciously trying to create a unitary state seems to have arisen because they ruled together, establishing an effective common will that became the great engine of state. Their motto *tanto monta, monta tanto/Isabel como Fernando*, origin of the English 'tantamount', has posed continual problems for translators interested in achieving a comparable neatness. The implication, however, is plain: whatever achievement redounded to the fame of one of the monarchs, that achievement was to be credited equally to the other. It was a remarkable arrangement, the more so given that Fernando was not king of Castile, nor Isabel queen of Aragón.

There lay hidden within it one enormous disadvantage, whose consequences are still a plague to Spain. Given that the monarchs had one indivisible will, it was only natural that they should exercise it most in those parts of their territory that mattered most. Castile's population was five times that of Aragón and the Levant; the Castilian economy at the time was exceptionally buoyant; here above all military might was concentrated. Fernando lingered in Castile, spending only four years out of thirty-seven in his Aragonese realms. At the crucial moment when trade with America opened up, Seville received the monopoly and Catalans were held at arm's length.

They subsequently worked their way back into the trade but the initial Seville monopoly justly forms part of their great complaint that Catalonia has been held back for centuries by the central government in Madrid.

Defying a somewhat theoretical truce, Abu 'L-Hasan of Granada, known more familiarly to Christian writers as Mulay (or prince) Hassan, staged a surprise attack on Zahara in December 1481. Zahara lay on the frontier, due north of Gibraltar and a short way west of Ronda, that little white Arab town rent by the most spectacular of gorges. The attack was just what the Christian aristocracy required. The following February they made a reprisal raid deep into Nasrid territory, taking the town and castle of Alhama. This was the start of the war that ended with the fall of Granada.

There is a story, as charming as it must be apocryphal, of Mulay Hassan summoning his wise men to him in the Alhambra and laying a gold dish in the centre of a large carpet. The dish belongs, says Mulay Hassan, to whoever can take it without stepping on the carpet. The wise men think a while, then shake their heads regretfully. It is left to Mulay Hassan to roll up the carpet from the edges and retrieve the platter. 'So,' he says, 'will Fernando possess himself of Granada.'

As a summary of events one could scarcely do better, for Fernando, now that the Spanish kingdoms were at last free of civil war, was able to play upon divisions in the Nasrid camp – particularly the conflict between Mulay Hassan, his brother al-Zagal (The Valiant) and Hassan's young son Boabdil – and so take Moorish territory piecemeal. The motives behind the campaign were partly religious; 'our zeal for the Holy Catholic faith' was the phrase used by Isabel and Fernando in reporting to the Pope. The war was officially declared a crusade. Isabel and Fernando also wished to control Granadan silk production and the traditional gold route out of Africa. In addition, there was already a belief, at least among their subjects, that the joint sovereigns were destined to conquer a large empire, starting with Granada. Yet even with so many layers of motivation, the war took ten years, involving many bitter sieges and innumerable episodes that have entered Spanish martial legend. Fernando managed the campaigning personally and Isabel herself appeared in the Christian camp whenever serious difficulties were encountered.

There are two ways to follow the course of the war. One is through the choir-stalls of Toledo cathedral; the other is to visit at least a few of the key sites, revelling in the tremendous mountain scenery, the crumbling castles and the townships, decaying or prospering depending on local circumstance. After a little of both kinds of tourism we find ourselves in Granada once again, in the Generalife gardens above the Alhambra.

The Alhambra is often thought of as a place made beautiful by running water. This reputation is borrowed from the reality of the Generalife, where fountains splash as busily as market-day and little water channels gurgle alongside steep stairways, past cypresses and zinnias, marigolds and custard-apple trees. The pavilions looking out over the Albaicín are as lovely in their more modest style as anything in the Alhambra proper. As for my wife and I, we have come for a moment's mourning on behalf of Spanish Islam.

All, however, is not quite as it should be. In the cheap *hostal* where we are staying, a few miles from the city and without so much as a window in its bedrooms, we have been receiving warnings against gypsies. Setting out on a walk through the village, we are hauled back in again by a waiter who tells us excitedly of a dangerous local gang. The proprietor joins in, assuring us that we will be safe with him if we will only stay indoors, but we are bound to be mugged in the Generalife and on the paths roundabout. Gangs lie in wait with guns and knives, he says, adding that there was nothing like this under Franco. He says that most people can only recognize gypsies because they are dark and dirty and have long hair, but he can tell them, infallibly, by the lobes of their ears. Throughout this diatribe, Lola Flores, Spain's most famous gypsy singer, is performing lustily on the *hostal* television. My wife remarks on this in quite respectful terms. 'Listen,' says the proprietor, 'anyone can sing.'

This was a conversation to linger in the mind, matching others we had had elsewhere, particularly in Seville. It made us think of

Lorca, shot in Granada during the Civil War, allegedly 'with two up the arse because he was a queer.' Lorca had written that Granada, more than anywhere on earth, had made him understand the experience of the outcast, the Muslim and the gypsy. His view was certainly an invitation to us to avoid the racist views we had encountered. Yet we were also, despite ourselves, a little impressed by the warnings of our *hostal* proprietor, the more so since I had come adrift from my wallet just a few months earlier in the Albaicín. Now, in the Generalife, we found the area patrolled by tough-looking security men with guns and coshes, as if there were objective dangers to be dealt with or at least a need to provide visible reassurance. What in all this mishmash of warning and alarm was true and what was false?

Next day we learnt a little more in Santa Fe, a small, rectangular, walled town laid out by Isabel and Fernando for final operations against Granada. It looks up over the flat lands of the Genil to the Alhambra and the Sierra Nevada. Here there was a little festival in progress, with a performance due to start at any moment. A restless crowd had gathered in the square, dark men in leather jackets and striped trousers, with old-fashioned spiv haircuts. Many of the older women were wearing slippers and aprons, hair pulled tight into a bun like Lola Flores. The girls wore jeans and pressed up close against the men. It was an entirely gypsy audience in a town that turned out to be almost half gypsy; and when we tried, with the crudity of journalists, to strike up friendly conversation, the replies were minimal, only just within the bounds of courtesy.

Wandering into the church we found evening mass in progress. Here the congregation was entirely 'white Spanish', except for one gypsy woman at the back and another who came in with a shopping bag. Afterwards, we repaired to the Rey Fernando, the King Fernando café, another 'whites-only' establishment. The waiter was friendly and let me blunder on with my questions.

How do people get on together in the town? I ask.

'Fine,' he says, 'no problems.'

How do the gypsies live?

'In houses, just like us.'

Work?

'Almost all of them are travelling salesmen, you know, *venta ambulante*, door-to-door sales. They are much better off than the people in Granada. No problems at all.'

Marriage? I ask, and then add, Intermarriage?

'Well,' he replies, consideringly, anxious perhaps to give a good account of Santa Fe, 'that's frowned upon – *mal visto*. Until people get used to it, of course. You see, we all go to the same school, no problems there at all. Except that the gypsy children don't come very often, they have to work with their fathers.'

It must, we suppose, be quite hard work. He agrees with us, shaking his head sadly. All over Spanish cities, in Catalan, Castilian and Basque, and quite as plentiful as notices in Britain banning ball games, there are stern signs forbidding *venta ambulante*.

The Spaniards brought the siege of Granada to a successful conclusion in January, 1492. Boabdil handed over the keys of the city to Isabel and Fernando with all the chivalry expected of him. According to the *Oxford History of the Spanish Kingdoms*, the royal couple were in Moorish dress. This is contradicted by a nineteenth-century painting in the Royal Chapel of the cathedral. Somebody, not I, may know the truth. Romance has Boabdil weeping as he departs for the estate in the Alpujarras that has been reserved for him (he died, not too long afterwards, in Africa). 'Weep like a woman,' chides his mother, 'for what you could not keep as a man.' Soon the Pope was to honour Isabel and Fernando with the title by which they are still known today – los Reyes Católicos, the Catholic Kings.

Granada had fallen on 2 January, ending the last vestiges of Islamic authority on the Iberian peninsula. On 31 March, after delays caused by the pleas of the community, a royal edict was published expelling all Jews from the Crowns of Aragón and Castile. At Santa Fe, on 17 April, Isabel and Fernando commissioned Columbus to sail west on their behalf to Asia to open a new route to the Orient and convert the infidel.

Columbus had been present to see the royal standard fly over the

Alhambra and witness Boabdil kissing the hands of Fernando, Isabel and their son, the inadequate Infante Juan. The opening paragraph of his ship's log, addressed to his royal sponsors, makes it clear that he saw a common thread in the three events: the reduction of Granada, the expulsion of the Jews and his own, potentially moment-ous journey. So did others; and it would be blindness not to make the connection. All were part of Spain's 'self-purification' and im-perial zeal for Catholicism.

Columbus had by now been peddling his visionary scheme for years. Henry VII of England laughed his emissary out of court. The Portuguese, extremely advanced in navigation, knew there was some-thing wrong with his *idée fixe* that Japan, Marco Polo's Chipangu, was less than 3,000 miles away. They, too, gave him short shrift. But now, after seven years of pleading, poverty and ridicule on the fringes of the Spanish court, the moment for action had arrived. With letters of royal command to help him find suitable ships and crew, he departed for the little port of Palos in what is now the province of Huelva. From here he set sail at eight in the morning on Friday, 3 August, for the Canary Islands, the final staging post before the unprecedented assault on the Atlantic.

Readers of the log, even in the slightly mangled form in which it has come down to us, can experience some of the drama of the voyage, the fears, the long duration, the disappointments of the many-times delayed arrival when what appeared at first to be dry land turned out to be cloud or mist or simple illusion, and finally the greatest illusion of all – the determined belief that they had made their actual landfall in Asia. There is a little, but only a little, of the same sense of excitement to be had in Palos, where the big old church in which Columbus and his crew prayed before departure stands up on a bluff above a creek. This has long been dry and looks thoroughly dingy, awaiting radical refurbishment. But formerly it opened on the wide river, serving as an adequate harbour for the tiny caravels in which the expedition sailed. Today, the view on the far side is of the drearily industrial city of Huelva.

Another mandatory visit, and one less likely to disappoint, is to the nearby monastery of La Rábida. Its abbot had previously been confessor to Isabel; he had helped Columbus in various important ways. Now, during the first voyage and for several years after, the monastery gave shelter to Columbus's son Diego. Parts of La Rábida fell in during the earthquake that destroyed Lisbon in 1755, but enough survives to give a sense of contemporaneity with remarkable events. Best is the heavily beamed upper chamber where planning meetings were held to settle vital details for the trip.

For me, though, there is more for the imagination in the island of La Gomera in the Canaries. For several decades, the Spaniards had been trying to wrest these islands from their original inhabitants, the ill-provisioned but attractive stone-age people named the Guanches. The Guanches fought back with the greatest tenacity and Tenerife had still not been subdued at the time of the 1492 expedition. As Columbus and his men sailed past the island, the 12,000-foot cone of Mount Teide erupted, terrifying the crew. Columbus, usually most inept in his personal dealings, successfully soothed the men and sailed on to La Gomera, a lofty lump of granite the shape of a bowler hat. Mists swirl about its highland forests; ravines slash its rocky walls.

No credence need be given to the story that Columbus conducted an affair here on his later journeys with the governess, Beatriz de Bobadilla, a tough operator whose portraits show her to have been extremely fetching in appearance. This rules out Beatriz's stout round fort as a Columbus monument but leaves as a strong candidate a little low well in the old customs house where the ships are meant to have taken water before their final setting out. But really, what counts is the physical shape of the island and the fact that it served as a stepping stone for this extraordinary adventure. Wandering one evening in the highest part of La Gomera, near a great rock supposedly used for Guanche religious ceremonies, I found myself just at sunset on a viewing platform looking due west across the ocean far below. As the great red balloon sank down to be engulfed I had a momentary vision of the three tiny vessels bobbing off across that immensity of water, destination Japan. Never, ever, could one feel anything but awe at the bravery and the crazily mistaken certainties of Christopher Columbus.

Which is not to say that his journeys brought admirable results. He was himself destroyed by them. Though notionally an hereditary admiral, viceroy and governor of all that he discovered, he fell into mortal conflict on his third journey with the settlers who had followed him and was returned to Spain in chains by a royal official sent to sort out the dispute. He never recovered from this dreadful event which left him, as his subsequent letters to the Catholic Kings reveal, a mass of self-pity and painful recrimination. Even after death, his shadow was pursued by years of litigation, his family fighting unsuccessfully for the inheritance they believed was rightly theirs.

It is said that his own age acknowledged Columbus as a man of destiny; the ending of his personal story was pathetic. Nor can one make great claims for the conquest and settlement that followed. It was the misfortune of America to be 'discovered' by a medieval warrior society and to suffer the importation of the brutal ideals and limited institutions of the later Reconquista. Considering not only the Americas but the fate of Jews and Moors, no Spanish anniversary is more double-edged than that of 1492.

Isabel, mother of the Inquisition, died in 1504. Her final testament asked those whom she left behind to 'devote themselves unremittingly to the conquest of Africa and to the war for the faith against the Moors.' This burden was shouldered by Cardinal Cisneros, who had in the meantime been involved in the forcible conversion of the remaining Moors of Granada. When they revolted, all adult males were expelled. Now Spain launched successive invasions of North Africa. Cisneros himself led an attack on Oran in 1509. The campaign is celebrated in a series of painted scenes in Toledo cathedral in the very chapel where the Mozarabic rite survives – thanks, of course, to the good offices of Cardinal Cisneros. We see the embarkation in Cartagena, the landing in North Africa and finally the contest for the town itself. Men with cuirasses, dressed in what look like red pyjama bottoms, struggle against the Moors while the cardinal, grand in his red hat, looks on in person. The hat itself, which has now lost a good deal of its colour, hangs just above the spot where the auxiliary priest intones his Mozarabic responses.

Isabel's death brought difficulties, even humiliation, to Fernando. Not being king of Castile in his own right, he promptly lost power there and had to look on as the power structure started to unravel. Throughout his career, he had been anxious to break Castile's traditional close contact with France, the country which had mis-appropriated his own Catalan counties of Rosellón and Cerdaña. This led him to marry his young daughters to anti-French interests (the two elder daughters had been married into Portugal in hopes of bringing the whole peninsula together in a single federation of kingdoms). A series of ill-timed deaths, first of the heir Prince Juan and then of all three elder daughters, meant that the succession to Castile devolved upon the youngest of the family, Juana, married to Philip the Handsome. Philip was a Habsburg prince from northern Europe, son of the Emperor Maximilian I. Juana was mentally unstable; Philip the Handsome had no knowledge of Spain and precious little interest in it. After Isabel's death, the couple dallied for an age but finally reached Spain. Now, however, Philip died of fever and Juana, grief-stricken, descended into total madness. It therefore seemed inevitable that the eventual successor to the throne of Castile – and to that of Aragón as well – would be Juana's eldest son, a young man named Charles or Carlos, brought up in Flanders as a Dutch-speaking Fleming. Fernando could hardly abide the prospect, nursing feelings of profound ill-will towards his grandson. Meanwhile, he had annexed the kingdom of Navarre for Spain; and campaigns in Italy under Gonzalo de Córdoba, known as the Great Captain from the Granada war and one of Spain's all-time military heroes, had established a tough professional army, laying the base for future military supremacy in Europe.

Such, broadly, was the state of play when Fernando went to his grave in 1516. He and Isabel were buried in Granada under the soaring vaulting of the Royal Chapel they had ordered, behind a magnificent wrought-iron screen adorned with fasces and apostles, eagles and lions. The bodies are in caskets underground – you file through the little crypt to enter the presence of the royal dead – and above, on a large plinth, more easily visible to God than visitors, the royal couple lie in an Italian marble version of 1517. The adjoining sacristy is hung with the small, detailed Flemish pictures that Isabel so loved, along with a quite beautiful Botticelli.

It is the kind of mixed memorial appropriate to Isabel and Fernando. But if a visitor to their times should wish to end on a calmer, more reflective note, nowhere is so suitable as the cathedral of Sigüenza, stony little medieval city tucked far away from all main roads in mountainous moorland east of Madrid. Here lies the most beautiful effigy in Spain, that of Martín Vázquez de Arce, known generally as El Doncel. He died in 1486 in the struggle for Granada, at the age of twenty-five; *doncel* is the masculine of *doncella*, a maiden, and must, in its primary sense, mean 'virgin', better rendered here perhaps as 'young person of delicate beauty'. Though wearing chain-mail underneath his shirt, he lies at ease on his right elbow, left leg gently inclining over right, reading a stubby little book with rapt attention. His face is the face of a young man perfectly at peace, the intellectual soldier, gentle master of his passions.

4 Imperial Might

Dark Deeds in a Brilliant Land

CARLOS, CHARLES OF GHENT, already Charles I of Spain and soon to be Charles V of the Holy Roman Empire, first glimpsed his Hispanic dominions in late September 1517. Aiming for Santander, his pilots had arrived in error – for which, says the entertaining Flemish chronicler Laurent Vital, they were heartily ashamed – off one of the wildest reaches of the Asturian coast. At six leagues out, the Picos de Europa loomed over them so large it seemed as if the distance were a single league. The sight amazed the flat-country, Flemish courtiers who accompanied the king. The expedition's forty ships were not far off Tazones, today a tiny fishing harbour and as pleasant a place as any for a Sunday lunch of freshest fish and cider – poured from an arm fully extended above the head into a thin, clear glass held in the other hand at the furthest possible downward extension. Visiting Tazones, I feasted on *pixín*, a fish unknown to my dictionary, after watching the lady of the house come out to gut my order on the wall outside, tossing the discarded portions to the waiting seagulls. Sizeable fishing boats rested on wooden sleepers on the concrete quay; others bobbed in the harbour with fishermen mending their nets on deck in the midday sun. In the village, cement-mixers chugged away, doing their best to spoil the look of things. Steep bracken-covered hills climbed up behind the village, their pure silhouettes broken by eucalyptus, while just a little further east, there rose a handsome headland. Now I watched the sunlight shift on cliff and headland

and on the white lighthouse which, had it existed in the sixteenth century, might have alerted Carlos's pilots a little earlier.

In the village, they believe devoutly that Carlos landed on the site of the present quay and that he was then helped on his way to the nearby town of Villaviciosa by a local fisherman who carried him on his shoulders. The fisherman received as his reward the title of Marquis of Royal Transport, el Marqués del Real Transporte. I check the story out in the Bar Breakwater (or *Rompeolas*) and am assured of its absolute veracity. Alas, Laurent Vital is positive that the royal landing party rowed all the way up the river to Villaviciosa, receiving a warm welcome from the locals who had come down to the coast armed to the teeth. They believed so large a fleet, the like of which had never been seen before, might well be French or even Turkish and was almost sure to have hostile intentions. When they saw the Castilian standard carried by the royal barge, they were first reassured and then, as they discovered the identity of their guest, delighted. Presumably they were the proverbially rough and ready folk of old Asturias; Vital refers to them throughout as 'mountaineers'. They provided lodgings for the king and his sister Leonora in a dignified house at no. 31 Calle del Agua – Water Street – and laid on a bullfight. '*Spectacle sauvage*,' said Carlos's Flemish chancellor, an early protest against this particularly Iberian avocation and the first recorded instance of the lofty tone adopted by Carlos's foreign advisers. The foreign intrusion was very soon resisted, to the point of outright rebellion, by resentful Spanish subjects.

The young monarch spent four nights in Villaviciosa, there receiving gifts of local provender – skins of wine, baskets of bread, sheep and half a dozen cows. He then went on a short tour of the Asturian coast, visiting Colunga, Ribadesella and Llanes, all haunts of my own and giving a special piquancy, for me at least, to this stage of the royal arrival. As for the Marquis of Royal Transport, the title does indeed exist. The last holder lived in Villaviciosa, his place of residence perhaps fuelling the rumour. He died, as it happened, in extreme old age, while I was in Asturias in quest of Carlos; obituary notices explained that the title was conferred only in 1760 and then on an ancestor who had helped the monarch of the day towards a happy landfall in Barcelona, a far cry from tiny Tazones.

Having seen a little of Asturias, Carlos and his royal party now headed inland for the *meseta*, following the remnants of the old Roman road up over the passes to Astorga and León. The route is a considerable distance west of the modern motorway, mostly track rather than road but apparently passable in a four-wheel drive vehicle. Friends of mine have done it, reporting that the Roman road runs high on the mountain slopes, dizzyingly high in places, presumably to avoid the possibility of ambush from above. This is the road the Moors came down when they invaded Asturias.

Carlos at seventeen had so pronounced a Habsburg jaw it was almost a deformity. His teeth did not meet exactly and he had difficulty eating, though his appetite was voracious right through his life, even later on when he had gout and knew the consequences would be painful. His mouth was generally half open, as may be seen in a remarkably frank terracotta bust in Bruges. Even when he had a full beard, he retained the same open-mouthed appearance, as witness an otherwise charming alabaster relief, also in Belgium, done at the time of his wedding. There was, however, no lack of alertness. Carlos had a piercing eye and gave his close attention to those he had business with. If he appeared weak in youth, by middle age he had grown into an impressive figure.

The aim of this first journey to the *meseta* was to visit his mother Juana – history's Juana la Loca, Joan the Mad – in the remarkable town of Tordesillas. Indeed, of all those little Castilian townships whose present-day decrepitude conceals a quite tremendous history, Tordesillas must surely be reckoned foremost.

The country roundabout glows a dull gold with ripening cereal crops in summer. In winter, the underlying soil shows white as a skeleton through hectic green. Shepherds wrapped in blankets, woolly dogs at heel, trudge along sandy tracks beneath the walls of ruined castles. The town itself is on a crossing-point of the Río Duero, which gave it a natural importance from the beginning, the river bank rising steeply on the northern side to offer views far south over the flatter country. There had been an *alcázar* up on this bluff from time immemorial. In the early fourteenth century, a palace was erected by Alfonso XI, with additions by his son and successor Pedro the Cruel. This seems to have been the first of all royal buildings in Mudéjar style, harbinger of much to follow. It is now a convent belonging to the Poor Clares with a purely Moorish courtyard of great beauty and, in the church, one of the finest of Spain's coffered ceilings. It is an excellent place to visit, especially when the storks are nesting.

The Treaty of Tordesillas, known otherwise as the Treaty of Demarcation, was signed here in 1494, an amazing thought today as you tread the sleepy streets. Effectively, the treaty gave Brazil to Portugal and the rest of Latin America to Spain, a line of political and linguistic division still, of course, of great significance. Juana la Loca arrived in Tordesillas a few years later bearing the body of her husband Philip the Handsome. She had travelled through Castile for several years in a macabre progress, remaining as attached to the corpse as she had been to the living man. Philip's remains were given some repose in the royal palace while Juana herself became so difficult to manage that she was confined in the now-vanished *alcázar*. A little park and modest apartment buildings mark the spot. Here she was to spend forty-six years, always as titular queen of Castile. With her, as a reminder of her husband, she had her daughter Catalina, born after Philip's death. Juana would not allow the child out of her sight. Severed from all contact with the world, young Catalina sat by a window from which she could see the local children play, sometimes throwing down small coins to attract them back again.

Carlos needed Juana's consent to his taking over the government following the death of her father and his own grandfather, Fernando of Aragón. He won it without difficulty but failed to rescue his sister Catalina. This came eight years later when she was married to the king of Portugal. Carlos himself now went on to Valladolid and then into Aragón, where, in months of wrangling, he got no joy at all from the independent-spirited Aragonese *cortes*. The constitutional ability of the eastern kingdoms to resist demands for men and money, of which Carlos now had a taste, was to have profound consequences for the whole of Spain, long-term as well as short, leading to bitter tussles as the kings attempted to increase their power. But soon events occurred that were considerably more exciting than arguing with the Aragonese.

The death of Carlos's Habsburg grandfather, Emperor Maximilian, suddenly opened the possibility that with adroit manoeuvring Carlos might himself be elected emperor. Gathering his courtiers about him, he promptly departed northwards from Galicia, in the first of what proved to be multiple absences from Spain. The longest lasted fourteen years.

The people of Castile were already seriously disaffected. Here was a monarch who at the time of his arrival spoke no Spanish (his first Castilian *cortes* petitioned him to learn the language). His Flemish advisers were pillaging Spain (two of their wives were permitted to leave with hundreds of mules and horses laden with valuables; the seventeen-year-old nephew of another was appointed archbishop of Toledo). Now Carlos was leaving Spain to further his non-Spanish interests. One by one, the towns of northern Castile rebelled, setting up communes to rule themselves. Toledo and Segovia led the rest.

For Spaniards, both of left and right, this is one of the key moments, a point at which their history might have taken quite another turn. This makes it important to understand what happened.

The commune movement was in fact intensely conservative in its beginnings, looking for nothing more than an end to foreign interference and a return to what was already seen as the golden age of Isabel and Fernando. The movement flourished strongly to begin with, not least because the loyalist armies acting for the king succeeded in burning down more than half of Medina del Campo, thus provoking the intense hostility of all the other towns. The *comuneros* now captured Tordesillas and did their best to pressure Juana into signing documents that would give legitimacy to their cause. Juana was sympathetic and confused but managed not to sign. From about this moment the movement, which had in any event been marked by factionalism within the towns, began to decline. As it did so it acquired a far more radical edge, with urgent demands for liberty for the peasants, freedom from unjust taxation and the insistence, by some theorists, that government must rest on the consent of the governed. In Madrigal, peasants refused to pay seigneurial dues. The aristocracy, who had tacitly supported the *comuneros*, now withdrew and soon the revolution was over. It had, in other words, proved weakest when most radical.

But just for a few brief months the monarchy of the emergent nation-state had undoubtedly faced a substantial challenge. The radicalism that the communes possessed in their later phase was written into the record, along with great acts of heroism and honour by the *comuneros*. Juan de Padilla was leader of the Toledo rebels, Juan Bravo of Segovia. Both were captured in the decisive battle of Villalar. When Bravo began to protest at the summary trial that followed, Padilla restrained him. 'My beloved Bravo,' he said, 'yesterday we should have died fighting like gentlemen. Today, let us die like true Christians.' And then, less honourable but more colourful, there was the bishop of Zamora, Antonio de Acuña. Last and fiercest of the warrior priests, he fought like a dervish for the *comuneros*. He was captured and imprisoned for five years at the castle of Simancas, close to Tordesillas – soon to become, as it still remains, home of the national archive. Killing his gaoler, Acuña finally escaped, only to be recaptured, tortured and garrotted.

Perhaps even more important than the *comuneros* in its implications was an almost simultaneous revolt in Valencia (and there was another in Galicia as well), that of the *germanías*, or military brotherhoods. Valencia had been struck by plague and its citizens, led by local craftsmen, concluded this was a punishment for sin. Homosexuals were first singled out for persecution and then the local Muslim population. Soon the movement turned on the aristocracy, becoming a genuine social revolution. By the time they were defeated, and ferociously repressed, the leaders were planning extensive land-reform and hoped to set up a republic on the model of Genoa. This, too, though it was a ragged business, has entered the record as another serious challenge, at least ideologically, to the great central power block of monarchy and aristocracy.

When I was young and living in Madrid, critics of the Franco regime used to maintain, with the darkest of mutterings, that the defeat of the *comuneros* and the Valencia *germanías* was where it all went wrong. I am inclined myself to place the turning-point somewhat earlier, with the defeat of Pedro the Cruel by the Trastámara line, and then with the ideological centralization on which Isabel and Fernando soon embarked, all of which, of course, had deeper roots in the evolution of Castile particularly. But it is undoubtedly true that some of the ideas put into circulation during the 1520s, no doubt particular to their own times, were so deeply informed with a libertarian longing for justice that they have ever since served as a touchstone for Spanish radicalism, helping to fuel one side in Spain's endless argument between the authoritarian centre and the country's other latent possibilities. This matters a great deal, for politically speaking there have been few countries more passionate than Spain, more ready to tear themselves to pieces for a principle, whether conservative or radical.

Carlos was absent while his regents met the challenge of revolt. He returned in 1522 as emperor. He was now the ruler of all the Hispanic kingdoms except Portugal, most of Latin America as it was progressively discovered, the Burgundian inheritance with the Low Countries as its key piece, important parts of Italy and great swathes of central and eastern Europe. In 1526, still pursuing the quest for Iberian unity initiated by Isabel and Fernando, he obtained papal consent to marry his first cousin, Isabel of Portugal. The wedding took place in the Hall of Ambassadors in the *alcázar* of Seville, with Habsburg crowns now let into the brilliant Mudéjar ceiling. Extra rooms were added to the palace, decorated with the Renaissance-style tile-work which contrasts so utterly in feeling with the earlier, Moorish-style ceramics. 'When the bride and groom are together,' reported the Portuguese ambassador, 'though everybody may be present, they have eyes only for each other.'

Carlos's biographer, Manuel Fernández Alvarez, is confident the couple had the good fortune, not so common among royal alliances, to experience romantic love. They went almost straight away to Granada where they enjoyed a months-long honeymoon, lodging in the Alhambra and building a new palace right in among the buildings of the old. Carlos himself was later to protest at the Christian cathedral inserted during his reign into the Mezquita of Córdoba. What he did himself in the Alhambra was not so different in the way it commandeered a key part of the site and introduced an alien style, perhaps intended as a challenge to the Moorish or at least as a showpiece of Christian architecture. There is just one small difference, though, between the cathedral-in-the-mosque at Córdoba and the palace-in-the-palace-complex at Granada. The former is a work of orotund pomposity; the latter is one of the finest buildings of its period, magnificent if one could only see it out of the context into which it has been so cruelly inserted.

Here though, before pursuing the point, it is necessary to pause for just a moment to look at the new influences entering Spain. The first effects of the Italian Renaissance were felt during Isabel and Fernando's time. The Mendoza palace at Guadalajara is a good example. Thirty years later, the ideas were pouring in, in an unstoppable spring tide, with troubled Valencia, open as ever to ideas, the main point of transmission. You can see what was happening by taking a stroll through that city's not over-large but outstandingly rich Museum of Fine Arts, the Bellas Artes.

There are fine paintings from many periods. Those that concern us at this moment were produced in Valencia, or by Valencian artists, in the early 1500s. Fernando Yáñez is famous for his scenes from the life of the Virgin on the altar shutters in the cathedral. The most striking work of his on show in the Bellas Artes is a Resurrection, full of clarity and quietude, its dramatic gestures contained by what seems almost a spiritual discipline of clarity. His Christ, rather rounded in figure, is as robust as any Leonardo character, with reddish hair and strong, serviceable limbs. Stylistically, Yáñez is regarded by art historians as having worked in parallel with, even in advance of, comparable Italian painters like Piero della Francesca or Fra Bartolomeo.

He seems to me a comradely though slightly formal painter, with considerable warmth under the formality. More dramatic, and by the same token rather more disturbing, is Vicente Juan Masip, active in Valencia just a little later. The influences adduced here are Raphael and his followers but for me Masip can again stand on his own. The Bellas Artes has a particularly fine Last Supper, tense and full of animation. One apostle is whispering in Christ's gently inclined ear, another is staring up as if he has seen a ghost. Some are standing, some sitting. Bare feet show under the table while behind Christ's head a window opens on to a dark little landscape, faintly Gothic. There is not a dull patch anywhere.

This picture is paired, interestingly, with another Last Supper hung just above it. The higher version is by Masip's son, Juan de Juanes, and though also a busy work it is a good deal blander, lacking in the emotional pressure that informs the father's painting. Juan de Juanes anticipates the sweetness of Murillo by more than a century, a fact which helps explain his great popularity in Spain – though it should be said that a very much more rugged Murillo hangs in the same room. The excellence of all these paintings, even allowing for a note of reservation on Juan de Juanes, is both a demonstration of the high levels of accomplishment in Valencia and of its role in propagating Renaissance styles.

In Castile, one of the leading painters of the day was Pedro Machuca; and it was he whom Carlos V commissioned to design the palace in Granada. This creation, unfinished because the emperor ran out of money – and only given its final touches at the command of General Franco – was a rectangular building of fairly straightforward Italian style, but with the notable flourish of a galleried circular courtyard at its centre. The outside is in two contrasting moods: a lower portion of enormous rough-hewn stone with vast iron rings set about ten feet up as if to tether the steeds of visiting giants; the upper portion more classically suave, though some have complained that the windows are contaminated by a hint of plateresque. It is the interior, though, that is the astonishment, with columns and balustrade of a strange composite rock, like cement pressed full of monster pebbles, giving the circular courtyard a craggy, weathered look of breath-taking severity. This is truly a place of stone, the spiritual opposite of the Alhambra. There was to be a good deal more of the same in the Habsburg repertoire in Spain.

Javier Coy is Professor of English at Salamanca university, not the earliest of Spain's learned institutions but historically the most famous, ranking with Bologna, the Sorbonne and Oxford. Javier, for his part, has the face of a suffering El Greco saint, cracking suddenly into an impish grin. I have known him, serious and laughing, almost thirty years. We knocked around together in Madrid in times of youth, our interest then in poetry, not history or politics. Now, as Salamanca becomes a focal point in my travels, we sit up late again with sheaves of poetry in front of us.

It would be easy to make out a case for Salamanca as the loveliest of Spain's old cities, climbing up gently from the Roman bridge across the Tormes on to a mound weighed down by its accumulation of venerable buildings. Though there are good views from beyond the Tormes, the city does not have quite the profile of Segovia or the gorge-enclosed intensity of Toledo seen from beyond the Tagus. What it does have is an incomparably rich interior and an incomparable colour, warm red suffused with gold. Two great cathedrals, one Romanesque, one Gothic, are held together by a common wall like Siamese twins joined right along the side. The small and effortlessly pure Romanesque church of Santo Tomás Cantuariensis was the first in Europe to be named for St Thomas à Becket. A famous fifteenth-century mansion is encrusted all over with pilgrims' shells. The sixteenth-century façade of San Esteban, with a seventeenth-century relief of the stoning of the saint, glows an earthy red in evening sunlight. In the eighteenth-century Plaza Mayor, beloved of Salamanca's citizens, cattlemen still do deals out in the open air. And then, of course, there is the university, with magnificent buildings of all ages, and a façade of quite exceptional elaboration. This was commissioned by Isabel and Fernando but designed and executed under Carlos V; it expresses, more surely and more beautifully than any other work, whether in architecture, sculpture or in painting, the spirit and the intended meanings of Spanish Renaissance culture.

'You get used to it all,' says Javier, 'and almost stop seeing it. Then one morning, perhaps you are more alive, perhaps you have had an extra cup of coffee, you suddenly notice something new in a building that you have passed every day for years. Salamanca is full of corners, sleepy little squares where nothing happens and you are in another epoch.'

We make a ruminative tour of the university, taking odd moments over several days and several visits. Teaching in fact began in the thirteenth century in the cloisters of the old cathedral. Today, the principal university cloister is that of the Escuelas Mayores, or Greater Colleges, begun in 1415. These colleges educated the élite within the élite of Salamanca university and here, surrounding the cloister, there are a series of historic halls and the university chapel. A picture in the chapel shows the graduating doctors of the university swearing, as they were obliged to, to uphold the Doctrine of the Immaculate Conception: not quite so simple as it sounds – the doctrine asserted that Mary herself was born without sin, rather than being sanctified during the course of her earthly existence. It was a serious theological issue, particularly in Seville, a city entirely dedicated to the veneration of Mary. A sermon advocating the opposed Doctrine of Sanctification could actually bring hostile crowds out on the street. Nor did the Pope get round to endorsing the Doctrine of the Immaculate Conception until the nineteenth century. You can quite see why it might be important in the leading university in the land of the great San Ildefonso of Toledo, specialist in matters of virginity.

Of the halls, the *paraninfo* or university main hall is grandest, with wide stone arches, wooden ceiling, a ceremonial dais and tapestries for decoration. The most intriguing is the lecture theatre used by Fray Luis de León, the mystic preacher and professor who later died at Madrigal. The lecturer spoke from a pulpit with a wooden cone above his head, like a shortened witch's bonnet or an inverted coffee filter. The students sat below at the narrowest of wooden desks – the originals survive and are still in place – while their servants sat at the back of the room or round the edges, ready to offer light or pen as circumstance demanded. This unusual arrangement reflected the status of the Escuelas Mayores as a training place for the children of grandees, as also for the prosperous but slightly humbler classes from whom the public officials of the future would be drawn. Recruitment from this group was at its height in the times of Carlos V and his son Felipe II.

Fray Luis de León was himself dragged off to the cells of the Inquisition where he spent five years before returning to his lecture hall with the often-quoted, but possibly apocryphal opening: 'As I was saying yesterday . . .' And it was just next door in the *paraninfo* that Miguel de Unamuno, university rector and representative Spanish thinker of the early part of this century, had his famous confrontation with Franco's General Millán Astray, ending with the general's angry shout of 'Death to intellectuals! Long live death!' – the latter sentiment the battle cry of the Spanish foreign legion. Unamuno had already been forcibly banished in the 1920s, to Fuerteventura, most Saharan of the Canary Islands; he called it 'an oasis in the desert of civilization'. Now, boycotted in public, he retired to his home, scarcely to emerge again until his death that winter, a story told most movingly in Hugh Thomas's history of the Spanish Civil War. There is a statue of Unamuno opposite his former house, hands behind his back, chin thrust vigorously forward, his coat falling away in indentations like a Cézanne landscape done in three dimensions. Whenever we pass that way, I notice Javier covertly saluting Unamuno. He loves the statue, reveres the tradition of the great lost leader – rather more, perhaps, than he reveres Unamuno's slightly jumbled intellectual contribution.

The first floor above the old cloister is reached by a stone stairway whose ascending balustrade is carved, inside and out, with identical decorations of extraordinary sprightliness. The outside, seen by standing in the stairwell, is the best preserved. It seems to be entirely secular. There are men and women dancers caught up in a swirling pattern of vine tendrils, women in high bonnets like fools' caps, a bullfight with a mounted torero (in modern bullfighting, known as a *rejoneador*), a man on the back of a naked woman and vice versa, cavalrymen with shields, mythical beasts, anything you could ask for in terms of the bucolic or playfully grotesque. It is a surprising and a lovely stairway.

At it; top, the university library, one of the most famous in Europe, runs round two sides of the quadrangle, its centre-piece a long, wide gallery with clear glass windows. The books run high up the side walls in handsome wooden shelves, which are supported on ornately carved wooden brackets. The wood is plain, with wiggly letters carved inside a rim along the top – *Philosophia Vetus*, *Pragmatici*, *Theologi Morales* and so on. Arriving with the professor, I find myself expected and the two of us are drawn into an alcove, heavily defended by modern security precautions.

Here we are shown the great five-locked strongbox that had to be opened simultaneously by the five university key-holders. Treasure upon treasure – not least, one of two manuscripts of the medieval *Libro de Buen Amor* of the Archpriest of Hita, Spanish equivalent of Chaucer's *Tales*. I touch it with a fingertip. My companion leafs through as if reading a novel.

During one of the intervals in our extended tour, Javier troops off to give a lecture. On a guarantee of good behaviour, I go with him and take a seat towards the back. The subject is the cultural background to the novels of William Faulkner and Javier addresses it with humour and modesty and none of the afflatus sometimes encountered in Spanish academic life. But when he bothers to point out to students that one of the great liberties in early American literature was the freedom from bishops and the ecclesiastical hierarchy, you realize he expects his students still to be deeply Catholic, at least in intellectual formation. They are friendly and open when I talk with them afterwards but extremely conservative in dress and hair-style and, so far as I can tell, conservative in attitude.

'That's right,' says Javier. 'In Franco's time, it was more or less obligatory to take up a liberal, oppositional position. But the students we see today are very conventionally minded. What's more, the class system is reflected in the subjects they choose. With wealth as the great goal these days, the upper-middle class goes into the money-making professions, medicine, engineering, law. Philology and languages attract the middle-middle and lower-middle classes.' Working-class students are few and far between, he adds, one of the greatest problems for the universities. Another is the sheer weight of numbers, an issue with a considerable background.

Javier believes, and one must agree with him, that General Franco's victory in the Civil War devastated intellectual life in Spain, with almost all the country's leading artists, writers and thinkers moving into exile, to Mexico City, Paris and Buenos Aires. The effects on university life were dire; intellectual pace and rigour are only just returning in the present generation. But one of the paradoxes was that Franco, not generally known for his libertarian approach, insisted on open admission to higher education for all who had matriculated from secondary school. Resources meanwhile remained minimal. The result was tremendous crowding and little education. In some subjects, such as medicine, the situation was chaotic by the time of Franco's death and it has now been necessary to restrict admission. Even so, numbers remain enormous, particularly in the liberal arts, far outpacing facilities.

'Madrid has got 130,000 students,' says Javier. 'Can you believe it? It's Babel. Imagine trying to teach English to 250 people at a time, meeting them three times a week for just two hours? Madrid used to be by far the most desirable place for lecturers. That's certainly not true any longer.'

We sit around in Javier's office, our conversation moving from education to the partial welfare state emerging under the socialist administration. Javier considers that this is coming along as well as can be expected. Certainly, he says, even the well-to-do now use the public system if they need to go to hospital or have a serious operation, an instance of Spain moving in the opposite direction to countries such as Britain or America. But unemployment pay, at a time of high unemployment, still remains pitifully poor. Great numbers still fail to qualify for benefits – one of many reasons why the untaxed, black economy remains so strong in Spain.

Remembering that Javier comes from a vast and strictly Catholic Murcia family, I try him next on the question of the Church. Several of his brothers have been Jesuits, though all have finally left the Society.

'Yes,' says Javier, himself no longer a church-goer, 'the hierarchy remains conservative, resolutely conservative. But plenty of the young priests are radical and they leave when they are finally frustrated in the attempt to get things changed. It's that, I think, more than the marriage issue.'

Many of the leftist priests in Latin America, says Javier, originally came from Spain. They were not especially committed ideologically, but they were driven by what they saw to take up extreme positions. This has fed back again to Spain itself. It is true Spain has the same drop-off in the seminaries that the Church is experiencing in other countries; many of them are closing. But religion still has a great pull on the people. The churches are full, the confessional is doing good business. Just recently the Bishop of Madrid issued a pastoral letter denouncing a piece of socialist legislation, in effect telling people how he thought they should vote. Just to be able to do that shows how strong a position the Church still occupies.

We fall to chatter on related matters. Javier points out that the special word *barragana* was used in former times to signify the mistress of a priest, the relationship being taken entirely for granted. And from here, simply to amuse ourselves, we start off on the subject of Spanish female names. Peculiarities arise from the fact that girls are often called after local Virgins, who may be the Virgin of the Rocks or the Virgin, indeed, of almost anything. When the 'María de' is left off the beginning you get the oddest consequences. Thus Pilar, 'Column' in English, a very common name for Spanish girls, comes from María del Pilar, the Virgin of the Pillar at Zaragoza. The abbreviation Inma is an attempt to escape from Inmaculada or Mary the Immaculate, a name to be married with, perhaps, but hardly auspicious for raising a large family. It has an extremely unfortunate meaning in Brazilian slang. Concha, that very pretty name, far from meaning 'Seashell', is short for María de la Concepción, Mary of the Conception.

Name-games done with, our university tour next takes us to the cloistered courtyard of the Escuelas Menores, made beautiful by what are known as 'mixtilinear' arches. These swoop down to their resting place, on rounded columns, through curves as sensuous and varied as those described by swallows in full flight. Next stop again, and we have reached the *Salamanca Sky*, start of the seminar in Renaissance thought offered by the architecture and decorations of the university.

The *Sky* consists of the remains of a ceiling painting originally in the library but removed to safety when the roof began to collapse. It shows the Sun and the planet Mercury and the zodiac signs of Libra, Leo, Virgo, Scorpio and Sagittarius. Hercules also figures while Hydra, that great snake, goes wiggling fatly across, fully seven metres of her. The whole is set on a blue field and liberally spangled with stars.

It is not that the *Sky* is so remarkable to look at, though it is certainly interesting. The questions concern its meaning and the light it may throw on Renaissance attitudes to learning, vice and virtue. The first essential in considering it is to grasp the importance of the stars.

Astrology had fallen somewhat out of favour in the early Middle Ages. St Augustine, for instance, had been severely critical. But now, as ancient Greek and Arab astronomy re-entered the intellectual mainstream, transmitted in part through Spain but pondered most deeply in Italy, astrology came along as an inseparable companion, one of the cornerstones of contemporary thought. It was often taught jointly with medicine, and a request for a chair in the subject at a university in the Low Countries, to take one example, maintained it was a discipline 'important enough to ensure men's welfare.' Salamanca had its own astrology professors by the fifteenth century and it is no accident at all that their subject supplied the motif for the decoration of the library, the very centre of the temple, or at least the palace, of learning.

There was, of course, a major problem to get over right at the beginning. For if human destiny depended on the stars, where then was Christian free will, essential prerequisite for salvation? The answer given was that free will indeed existed; it was the duty of an individual to struggle against the fate implied by his stars if these should lead down paths of vice. The study of the stars could help one to outwit a sinful fate. In a very real sense, then, the *Salamanca Sky* may be taken as an invitation to virtue, but virtue pursued through learning. For the next step in the argument is the assertion that the missing part of the painting would have shown the remainder of the planets and the zodiac and – this is the key point – the signs of the Seven Arts as well. These are frequently associated with the celestial signs in the iconography of the period and would inevitably figure, it is argued, in the context of a Renaissance university. In turn, the liberal arts were deeply associated with magic and the revelation of the secrets of nature. There was an ancient tradition that magic had been taught since the dawn of time in a cave at Salamanca. In the *Salamanca Sky*, therefore, if the iconographers are right and the signs of the liberal arts were really on the ceiling, learning and magic, virtue and salvation were bound together in a single scheme of ideas.

But if the ceiling for a library was important in stating the philosophy and aims enshrined in a university, nothing could be so important as the main doorway and the façade that surrounded it. The significance of this feature had already been made apparent, not just in Italy but in the façades of Spanish palaces and churches. How was it to be articulated here, at the university of Salamanca?

One should at the outset state that in a land of quite magnificent and beautiful façades, this is reckoned by many, myself enthusiastically included, to be the finest of them all. Enclosing the entrance to the Escuelas Mayores and providing the outer wall of the library strong-room on the first floor, it rises through a delicate elaboration of plateresque filigree. This exquisite shallow carving, here with clear antecedents in Italian design books, is laid as decorative background on to an arrangement of panels defined by columns and cornices, similar in style to the façade of San Gregorio in Valladolid but considerably flatter. In the ascending series of central panels it is easy to make out the subject-matter that rises out of the filigree: first, a large medallion showing the Catholic Kings, then the most beautiful of all heraldic escutcheons and above again the Pope and his cardinals in an arresting sculptural tableau. Partly it is the flatness that makes the façade so tender and so tantalizing, but the evenness of surface is counteracted by the fact that the sculpture grows in scale as it climbs away from the viewer in that marvellous and totally Spanish style sometimes described as 'suspended architecture'.

Discussion in the past has centred mostly on the architecture. It is only in recent decades that serious attempts have been made to unravel the iconography of the façade and tease out meaning. Much has now been hazarded on the subject and it is a matter, for the non-scholar, of finding a convincing authority. For me, that version is offered by Luis Cortés and Santiago Sebastián, the latter my iconographer acquaintance from Valencia, in a little book published by Salamanca university in 1973. Here the authors argue that the façade was designed under the Neoplatonic precept that love, the motive force through which God infuses the world and which leads his creatures to desire unity with him, stands at the centre. The detail of the façade, they argue, is derived from the discussion of an imaginary House of Vice and Virtue in the *Utopia of Filarete*, a treatise written for the Duke of Sforza in Milan in the 1460s. This concerns the Renaissance notion of *architettura parlante*, in which not only the form of the building but its sculpture, bas-reliefs and paintings all emphasize its symbolic value. Differences and some misconceptions have crept in, but essentially, the authors say, the Salamanca façade is a dialectic between profane and sacred love. The complications and entertainments on the way are endless but we are left finally with their belief that the figure framed in a doorway high on the left is Venus, her stave broken to show she cannot guard her chastity. Priapus and Bacchus, in the same vicinity, represent the animal passions. On the right, in his own frame, stands Hercules, conqueror of disordered appetites as well as more obvious foes. He was regarded as their patron by the Spanish monarchs and here mounts a protective guard above them. The whole façade, say Cortés and Sebastián, is an assertion of the superiority of sacred love and reason and a Temple of Fame with the Spanish monarchy at centre. It is, they argue, the most original expression of humanism in sixteenth-century Spain.

There is yet another symbol on the façade that is invariably pointed out by guides and people reading guidebooks out loud to one another and students showing parents round the university –

the 'Salamantine frog', up on the right-hand side, crouched on a human skull. Cortés and Sebastián have no trouble showing that the frog began its career in European iconography as a symbol of the devil, based on a text in the Apocalypse. Soon it came to mean sin, then sins of the flesh and ultimately death, but death awarded as a punishment for the sins of the flesh. Thus both Grünewald and Memling show the frog in place of genitals on rotting cadavers. Here, in Salamanca, the frog is being offered to the students, in those days mostly adolescents, as a terrible warning.

This thought is in my mind as Javier despatches me to the Convent of Las Dueñas, perhaps a quarter of a mile away across this city which throughout its history has occupied itself in tending to young people. In the cloister, architecturally harmonious and of much the same period as the university façade, the capitals on the columns, particularly on the upper storey, show an extraordinary series of macabre contortions based on themes of death and dismemberment. Figures are doubled up in torment, bound, gagged, dead. Death's heads proliferate, with at least one frog, on top of a trepanated skull. Some figures have been beheaded, others have had their arms cut off. Animals, whether mythical or realistically shown, are also in torment.

Putting all this together with the frog on the university façade and not forgetting a series of skulls adorning the front of the house next door to Unamuno's – known in Salamanca as La Casa de los Muertos, the House of the Dead – and adding also, if one cares to go so far, Millán Astray's 'Long live death', one cannot but concede the prevalence of the theme of death in Salamanca. A dreadful statement is being made time after time in the city of intellect, philosophy and youth. And from now on, in Spanish art and thought, this theme will be pursued with an intensity unknown in any other European country.

Carlos V meanwhile was dealing death on a continental scale. Fierce rivalry with France, and in particular with the French king Francis I, led to wars fought mainly in Italy. The unfortunate Duchy of Milan was the epicentre of the struggle though at one point Carlos's forces sacked the Holy City of Rome, an act that caused the greatest outrage. Later, 'in order to avoid the deaths of so many people', Carlos challenged Francis I, chivalrously but unavailingly, to single combat. In the Mediterranean, in a developing trial of strength between east and west, Carlos fought continually, but not very successfully, against the Turks and Islamic piracy. He led an expedition to Algiers in person. In the Low Countries, favourite among his possessions, the rise of Lutheranism upset him gravely. He introduced the Inquisition there and set it working with a terrifying zeal. This was the start of serious troubles in the Low Countries which, within a century, would leech away the spirit, and the finances, of the empire. Wars against the Protestant states of northern Europe also became intense as the mid-century approached.

Carlos had the highest possible sense of duty; his struggle was to save his many realms from heresy and the onslaught of 'the infidel'. In this, the concerns of the empire inevitably came before the welfare of the Hispanic kingdoms. To compound the matter, it was Spain that had to pay for his endless and prodigally expensive wars once he had exhausted the cash reserves of the Low Countries and imperial Italy. Since Carlos was scrupulous in respecting the rights and traditions of his individual dominions and since the constitution of Aragón protected it from depredations, it followed with a sad predictability that the greatest burden would fall on Castile.

At the start of this process, northern Castile was enjoying a prosperity presaged in the days of Isabel and Fernando. The great wool merchants had by now emerged; the flocks of the Mesta had reached their all-time record. But before the end of the reign personal taxation had climbed so high – with the aristocracy, of course, exempt – that young Prince Felipe, Carlos's son, was writing desperately to his absent father: 'The common people, who have to pay these *servicios*, are reduced to such misery that many of them walk naked. And the misery is so universal that it is even greater among the vassals of nobles than it is among Your Majesty's vassals, for they are unable to pay their rents, lacking the wherewithal, and the prisons are full.' Many of the poor were women; vagabonds roamed the land; the entrepreneurial spirit of the Castilian merchants little by little began to peter out, the more so as they fell into debt to foreign bankers.

There has been debate among historians as to whether or not it was still regarded as dishonourable to engage in trade, so helping to further the collapse. The Florentine envoy Guicciardini, travelling in Spain in 1512, is positive this was then the case. One thing is certain, however; following the defeat of the towns in the revolt of the *comuneros*, the Crown and the aristocracy got into bed together and the aristocracy at least were pledged to the old ideals. Carlos personally reinforced the process, importing chivalrous extravagances from the Low Countries. One of these was the order of the Golden Fleece. Another was the introduction of Burgundian pomp and pageantry to the Spanish court. And he fixed a hierarchy of rank, from the top twenty-five grandees, whom he addressed as his *primos*, or cousins, down to the lowest members of the aristocracy, known as the hidalgos. (It is worth noting that while for foreigners the word 'hidalgo' has always conveyed a sense of Spanish nobility, for Spaniards themselves a sense of comparative lowliness, and of the poverty of the lesser nobles, is also present.)

Under the rule of Carlos, then, the higher aristocracy were flourishing. But they had one special and very serious problem, new to Spain. Ever since the expulsion of the Jews, anti-Jewish racism had been gaining ground, leading to a fanatical quest for 'purity of blood', in Spanish *limpieza de sangre*. The fortunes of *conversos*, and those who had *converso* ancestors, many of them aristocrats, were deeply prejudiced in a development that was to echo on, in more and more sinister fashion, throughout the century. The Inquisition meanwhile continued with its persecution of *conversos*, meaning that nobody was safe.

As for religion in the time of Carlos, there were one or two insignificant scares over Protestantism, but generally the Inquisition had done its work too well. Such spiritual battles as there were concerned a form of pietism reaching down from the Low Countries, concentrating much more on personal relationships with God than was comfortable for dyed-in-the-wool conservative ecclesiastics. The propagators of this approach were called the Illuminists and soon, despite their great attainments, they too found themselves persecuted. The writings of Erasmus, with their similar insistence on personal religion, had an immense impact in Spain, greater perhaps than anywhere else in Europe, but for the time being, the Erasmians enjoyed the support of the emperor.

This was a strange mixed period of repression and open debate; and, given the importance of the discoveries and conquests now taking place in the Americas, it is hardly surprising that these too became a subject of debate, often conducted in the fiercest possible terms. The problems revolved mainly around the Indians. Did they perhaps have souls, some of the more radical clergy began to ask? If so, was it proper to enslave them? Could they not be saved for Christ, and spared from slavery? Bartolomé de las Casas was a landowner-turned-priest who spoke passionately for the Indians against the new landowners, encouraged in the dispute by Carlos V himself and allowed by Carlos to publish his great treatise *The Destruction of the Indies* in 1552. But already it was too late and the irretrievable catastrophe in progress. For as the conquistadors took the continent, they choked it with the blood of their violent arrival. Disease followed remorselessly. By the time las Casas published, the Indians were dying in millions and black slaves were being moved in thousands from Africa to Latin America.

One way of gaining a first impression of the conquistadors, or at least of their origins, is to travel south from Salamanca, still in Old Castile, and on down into Extremadura, the land beyond the Duero. This is the way the Christians came during the Reconquista; and Extremadura was later the home of a surprising number of the conquistadors.

The journey leads through cattle country. Holm-oak and cork-oak trees stand singly among somewhat park-like grasslands, tawny as a lion's pelt in summer. By contrast, wild and shaggy mountains give an intoxicating edge to almost every horizon. It is a countryside where hawks hang overhead unswerving, mostly red kites with strong, divided tails. Cattle bred for the bullfight stand lean and restless in the clumps of shade. Herds of grey-black pigs roam beneath the oak trees, dappled in sunlight, gaining a special savour from the acorns. Entrances to individual farms, which are really ranches, are marked by strong stone gateposts bearing the brand of the farm in question. Sometimes you see a little whitewashed bullring where men and beasts are both evaluated. Often the farms have individual chapels.

We make the journey in springtime, dallying on the Peña de Francia, a notable peak of pilgrimage and close to the little half-timbered tourist town of La Alberca. In La Alberca we meet the Housewives Union of Zamora, enjoying a pleasant outing; one of the features of modern Spain is that the Spanish themselves are wealthy enough now to have become the greatest travellers in their own land. We carry on through wilder hills and valleys, stopping to chat with a goatherd whose 400 animals, all belled, are trooping delicately across a hillside of wild lavender. A strong, sweet scent arises with the music of the bells. We divert to Ciudad Rodrigo, a little town untouched by economic advancement and hence extremely well-preserved. It is full of plaques celebrating Wellington's victory here in 1812. The city walls survive intact despite the attentions of the future Iron Duke, and you can walk the whole way round without descending; there is a parador in the castle and once a year, at festival time, bull-running through the streets like a miniature Pamplona. We watch the sun set over Portugal, then eat in a bar in the main square, El Sanatorio by name. It is a traditional port of call for those injured in the wild scenes of amateur bullfighting that ensue in the main square when the running bulls have finally arrived. The walls are plastered with photographs of gorings and near misses. But none were serious, the proprietor promises us, with an honest smile we try hard to believe. There is a publicity photo on the bar showing the tender face of a young boy and a printed caption claiming that he and he alone is the great torero the whole of Extremadura is awaiting. What he is looking for, it seems, is work in his chosen profession.

Ciudad Rodrigo is still just north of the Extremadura border. We travel down next day, crossing the Sierra de Gata by the pass of Perales. It is communal ploughing day on the northern side. Everybody seems to be at work. Some are tilling the rich-looking land with big black oxen, a few with mules. Some walk in front like Van Gogh peasants, scattering the seed from sacks. Others again are breaking the earth with mattocks. Women wear headscarves, cowled, as if the Moors had never been defeated. The European Economic Community seems very far away.

As we climb up towards the pass, the land begins to roll with white broom breaking on the slopes like waves. Gold broom presses in and more wild lavender. Higher again we encounter heather, pale green lichen on the trees and rocks and everywhere that most Iberian of shrubs, the resinous, strong-smelling *jara*, or cistus, with wide, cup-like flowers, bright yellow stamens and sometimes five crimson markings close to the heart of the flower. On the way down, we know we have reached the south. Suddenly there are olive and orange trees and vines; the villages are mostly white, with iron grilles on windows. And now at last we have entered Extremadura proper, still cattle country, still extremely wild but with just a touch of southern in it, sometimes a little desolate. For me, it is quite as lovely as the high country of Aragón, and the part of Spain where I should like to lay my bones.

Extremadura votes Socialist today, tries to care for its scattered agricultural community, worries that it is being left behind by the tide of economic progress and neglected by Madrid – 'almost an Indian reserve,' says the local paper bitterly. Five centuries ago, it produced by far the highest number of conquistadors, proportionate to population, of any part of Spain. Among them were an astonishing number of the leaders: Hernán Cortés from insignificant Medellín – he at least paused in admiration before the Aztec civilization that he overthrew; Pizarro, illiterate labourer from Trujillo, mass-murderer of the Incas and finally himself murdered; the gentler Vasco Núñez de Balboa, 'discoverer of the Pacific', from Jerez de la Frontera. All were men of astonishing hardihood and bravery, fighters thrown up by the wars against Granada and then in Italy. They served their king. They answered to an unbending religion. They had no wealth and this was what they wanted most of all. Perhaps their savagery was not so much a personal responsibility as written into the warrior society they sprang from.

We make our tour of the conquistador towns. Trujillo is most famous, for several of Pizarro's family returned here with their fortunes. Notable conquistador palaces stand on the triangular main square, an intriguing place with steps and roads at different levels round it and a huge Moorish castle high above. Here a traffic policeman assures us that Pizarro is a true Spanish hero – 'No question about that.' In the equestrian statue in front of the church, both Pizarro and his horse are abundantly, not to say absurdly, helmeted. Jerez de los Caballeros, in wild, wild country, burgeons with extravagant church towers richly decorated with ceramic tiles. The old quarter of Cáceres is honey-coloured stone and nothing else, enormously dignified, with towers in scores, large doorways with immense voussoirs and full of nesting storks. Little cobbled streets lead away down the hill with a view of the sierra at the end of them.

Of the conquistador towns Trujillo is generally the most admired; Cáceres to my taste is finest, though over-restored in spots. Then there is Guadalupe, the monastery where the conquistadors made obeisances and which Columbus visited on two occasions, having vowed at least one pilgrimage during a storm at sea. Guadalupe, with its mountain freshness and its cloisters, its numinous black Virgin and its accumulation of relics and grave paintings of the saints, is inevitably on the main tourist trail. For the monastery's Virgin has given her name to the patroness of Mexico, a country even more fervid in its Mariolatry than Spain. The Spanish monastery, for better or for worse, is regarded as the home of *Hispanidad*, or Hispanicism, the common cultural and religious ties that supposedly bind the Latin American countries to their European stepmother. Many Spaniards believe devoutly in *Hispanidad*; some Latin Americans, no matter how Catholic, would rather eat a dish of worms than enter the monastery tied so deeply into this colonialist concept.

Carlos V did a surprising thing in 1555 – he abdicated. In the great hall of Brussels castle, in one of the more theatrical scenes of history, before a gathering of his family, advisers, ministers, foreign ambassadors and dignitaries of Church and State, entirely of his own free will, he renounced the prodigious powers he had held for three and a half decades. His strength was failing him, he said, enumerating the travails and the many travels of his reign. Now he must leave them. Felipe, his son and heir, was to replace him. He wept aloud. His audience did the same.

Curiously enough, considering his long absences, Carlos had become surprisingly Hispanicized and very popular in Spain. He had an ear for languages and had mastered Castilian effectively, often using it to make a point. On one occasion, rebuked for speaking Castilian in an address to the Pope and cardinals, he had replied indignantly: 'Do not expect me to speak any other language but Spanish, which is so noble that it should be learned and understood by all Christian people.' Now, in his retirement, he made for Spain, to the conquistador country of Extremadura.

The Hieronymite monastery of Yuste is well off the beaten track, backed by wild hills with steep fruit-growing valleys and looking out southwards over a broader dip in the land. At the time when Carlos chose it for himself, mainly because of a climate of 'perpetual springtime', it consisted of a cloister with cells on the mountainside and a large Gothic church adjoining it on the open side to the south. Here, on the sunny southern flank, with a wide view out across the valley, Carlos built himself a comfortable villa, four rooms on the ground floor, four up on the first. Surrounded now by immense trees, it has the air of a prosperous gentleman's residence in the Italian style, distinguished by the ramp that led up to the first floor, allowing the gout-stricken former emperor to be carried up in his litter. Not knowing the area was malarial, or not understanding the significance of standing water in fostering the disease, Carlos commissioned a pond immediately outside his ground-floor rooms.

Even today, when it is furnished rather grimly, one has a sense that this could have been a comfortable and gracious house. Carlos furnished it with Flemish tapestries and paintings, mainly Titians. Isabel, his beloved wife, had died early, in 1539. Her portrait was here, along with other family likenesses. Carlos attended four masses daily, for his father, his mother, for Isabel and for his own health.

He listened to the singing of the outstanding choir and discussed religious texts. In winter he slept in a bedroom with a door opening on to the high altar of the church. (This is a moving room to visit; it smells strongly of incense.) He gave some attention to the details of his future burial, but not so much as has sometimes been claimed. He took a siesta daily, fished out of his window and ate and drank uncontrollably, reckless of the consequences. It is possible his appetite was urged on by diabetes. He was at first attended by a small court of about fifty people but soon the number of visitors began to grow enormously. Nor could he cut himself off entirely from his old preoccupations, offering advice and worrying continually about affairs of state. Part of his anxiety was financial. Over the decades, in his desperate attempts to raise money for the wars, he had sold innumerable annuities and borrowed inordinate sums from bankers, German and Genoese. Future income, so desperately needed for the maintenance of the empire, was committed years ahead for payment of earlier debts. In 1557, while in London, Felipe II was obliged to declare a Spanish bankruptcy.

Carlos died the following year, on 21 September, not of gout but of malaria, holding the crucifix that Isabel of Portugal had held in her last moments nineteen years before.

North-west out of Madrid, crossing a landscape of long grass and low stone walls, cattle and little rounded pine trees, you soon have the mountains well in view. There are signs of growing affluence as you draw near them, of summer houses and new developments with swimming-pools and poplars. 'Live like the kings themselves', says an advertisement hoarding outside a new estate. The reference is to the monastery-palace of El Escorial, one of the most extraordinary, certainly the most discussed, of all buildings in Spain. It stands immense and rigid, austere beyond belief or comfort, some distance up the rocky slopes, and lapped on its western side by the stern little town that has grown up in attendance. 'From the beginning of building,' says the architectural historian George Kubler, 'the mental image of the Escorial among its builders was of a granite structure on a granite pedestal in a landscape of granite.' This it became; this it remains.

The town itself is dear to me from summer visits in a kindly household. I have known the monastery since, on a school-trip in my teens, I stood with my equally grubby companions open-mouthed at the immensity and self-denying grandiosity. Now I make my way across the plains in raw winter mist, to be rewarded, just as I reach the level of the monastery gardens, by clear-washed skies and a cool yellow sunlight. The vast array of stone and endless rows of window glow almost cheerfully.

It was Felipe II, successor of Carlos V, who conceived this imperial megalith, this statement of power and virtue on a prodigious scale; and if I seem to emphasize its size, this is deliberate for in discussion of the building's role and meaning, this one overriding factor tends often to give way to the fascination of detail. Just for the record, then, and because these are the questions every visitor asks the monastery guides, there are 2,673 windows and 1,200 doors, 16 courtyards and no fewer than 7,422 holy relics.

Felipe was caught up in northern Europe for the first four years after the abdication of his father, attending to his unsatisfactory marriage to Mary Tudor – part of a grand scheme to win England back for Catholicism – to affairs in the Low Countries and wars with France. In 1557, on St Lawrence's day, the Spanish won the substantial victory of St Quentin. Felipe vowed a monastery to the saint, whence the formal dedication of El Escorial to San Lorenzo (its full name is the remarkably cumbrous El Real Sitio de San Lorenzo el Real de El Escorial). But Felipe had other motives, too. He wished to build a worthy burial place for his father and to reinvoke that traditional Castilian formula, a dwelling-place within a monastery where the king could lead a life of penitence and religious retreat. The models were many, among them Las Huelgas in Burgos, Tordesillas on the Duero and his own father's place of retirement at Yuste.

The site was chosen in 1561, two years after Felipe's return to Spain (unlike his father, he was never again to leave the peninsula). A commission, mainly of friars, had examined possibilities all round Madrid, and though they feared the wind and cold of the Escorial, they saw advantages in its plentiful water supply and forests – for both construction and firewood – and in the presence nearby of granite and gypsum. Felipe agreed the location and chose the precise spot personally. A start was made in 1563. For the next twenty-one years, in his usual painstaking style, involving endless documents and many thousands of marginal notations in his own hand, Felipe unceasingly drove on the project.

The first architect was Juan Bautista de Toledo, formerly an assistant to Michelangelo at St Peter's in Rome. He was summoned from Naples, but when his wife and daughters followed, they were lost at sea along with Bautista's books and papers. He never recovered from the disaster, became disordered and forgetful, failing even to turn up for appointments with Felipe. But he laid down the basis of the style and many of the leading concepts before his death in 1567. His effective successor was the thoroughly interesting Juan de Herrera, a courtier and soldier of about Felipe's own age, cultured and with a technical bent (his father had an iron foundry in Santander). Herrera at this stage had no specific knowledge of architecture and was not appointed architect as such for many years. (His future impact on architecture, however, was to be considerable.) He was at first more of a works manager, but a most unusual one since he maintained an important intellectual relationship with the king. Some writers have claimed that the two men had a mutual interest in the occult and that magical principles underlay the whole construction of El Escorial.

Astrology certainly features here, among the ceiling paintings in the library, just as at Salamanca university. But the Hieronymite librarian and chronicler Fray José de Sigüenza, who himself designed the programme for the ceiling paintings, insists the intention was to show that human beings need not take the consequences of their stars as being fearful or inevitable. We know that Felipe personally disliked astrology. There is a story of his angrily tearing up a horoscope cast for his son, the future Felipe III. He thought alchemy 'a joke' – this from an informal exchange of letters between himself and Herrera. But it is also true that scholars of the age believed knowledge of nature to be inseparable from the concept of magic, in the benign sense, and that El Escorial was a building well-informed by the Renaissance notion of knowledge. It is probably not safe to go much further than this.

But there were other underlying concepts, too. According to Kubler, the most important is the reverence for Order, seen by St Augustine as a fundamental principle of divine creation. This was bodied out at every stage of the iron-hard design. The style chosen to render the idea was the *desornamentado*, or unornamented, an obvious reaction to the elaboration of plateresque, as also to Mudéjar and Gothic ornamentation. Some art historians see it as part of an ever-continuing dialogue between the two great poles of the Spanish temperament, the sombre, introverted and austere on one hand and on the other the gloriously ornate, exuberant and playful. At all events, the style had precursors, both in Italy and in Portugal, where it was already in vogue. Felipe's mother and nurses had been Portuguese, Felipe spoke some Portuguese as well as Spanish and he already had an eye on the Portuguese succession. He seized upon the *desornamentado* style for El Escorial, seeking advice from Italy at many points, and projected it on to a building of unprecedented size. Fray José Sigüenza, inevitably an enthusiast, describes it as possessing 'a great majesty of a kind unusual in Spain, which for so many centuries has been buried in the barbarity, or grossness, of the Goths and Arabs.'

There has been a tendency for the building to be stripped away from its position in the evolution of architecture and made to stand as a personal symbol of King Felipe. How far it can be read in these terms remains a fascinating question, justified to some degree by the king's close attention to the project. We know, to take an uncontroversial example, that the steep-pitched slate roofs and little Flemish steeples which adorn the skyline, giving a touch of fantasy to what would otherwise be intolerably dour, were imported to Spain by Felipe for a previous project, reflecting a northern allegiance in his sense of beauty and practicality. From now on, roofs and steeples of just this kind were to play a large part in Spanish architecture. You see them everywhere, from countless late sixteenth- and seventeenth-century main squares to the huge Air Ministry in Madrid, built under General Franco.

Even more intriguing, in terms of Felipe's personal psychology, is the 'royal house' built at his command deep inside the monastery. Whereas his father at Yuste could go straight in through the front door, Felipe had to proceed through a tangle of corridors and stairs as labyrinthine as anything at Knossos. The state apartments, once reached, were severe but of a reasonable size, with good sunlight and views south-east towards Madrid. But Felipe's own rooms, and the mirroring set of rooms just opposite, were like those of a moderately well-to-do Castilian home, small and domestic, with floors in terracotta brick and a tiled dado, a style still much evoked in paradors and Castilian restaurants. Their modesty, given that this was the habitation of the greatest monarch on earth, shocked contemporaries and later commentators, particularly those in the French classical tradition. The tiny bedroom, in imitation of Carlos V's at Yuste, gives directly on to the high altar of the church.

Those who accuse the building of making a shockingly ostentatious display of introversion incline to rest their argument on Felipe's rooms as well as on the unutterable severity of the whole construction. This ignores the fact that El Escorial was intended primarily as a religious retreat. Instead of coming to El Escorial on each occasion that the king visited, the court quite often remained in Madrid, now positively chosen as capital. This helped preserve the sense of the retreat. Yet even so, one can hardly consider the self-abnegation anything less than highly ostentatious. It makes one wonder, trooping about El Escorial with a flock of fellow-tourists, just what kind of king it was who called for such an extremist monastery-palace.

Felipe was fair-haired, somewhat on the short side, neat and sober in dress; in old age, he wore only black, with the Order of the Golden Fleece dangling round his neck on a black ribbon. It is to be seen in almost every portrait of him. His features were sharp and firm except for his large lips, observed very clearly by Titian in the portrait, not much liked by Felipe, which went to Mary Tudor by way of advance information. His jaw, while large, was more modest than his father's and concealed, from the frontal view, by a short beard. He ate sparingly and travelled little – travel was thought to be one reason for his father's gout. Where Carlos V had led armies in the field, Felipe ruled through paperwork and meetings with his ministers. He complained continually at the size of the task, comparing himself to a pack animal burdened by paper, apologizing for an omission with the explanation that he had had to sign 400 papers that day. He spoke slowly and deliberately. He took decisions slowly and reluctantly. His minister, Cardinal Granvelle, said he held on to documents 'till they wilted'.

This earned him, in his own age, the honorific title of Felipe the Prudent. Gregorio Marañon, the physician–historian for whom, in the engaging Spanish habit, a Madrid street is named, has argued that on the contrary he was numbed by self-doubt. Marañon suggests that Felipe compared himself continually to his father and felt continually inadequate. J. H. Elliott, that eloquent British historian of imperial Spain, describes him as feeling a sense of safety only among his state papers, 'which he would tirelessly read, mark, annotate, and amend, as if hoping to find in them the perfect solution to an intractable conundrum – a solution which would somehow dispense him from the agonizing duty of making up his mind.' In this version, all that holds the king together is an iron will, deliberately cultivated, through which the personal is constantly subordinated to duties of state, allowing him to pursue the great objectives handed on to him by his excessively admired father: the maintenance of territory, suppression of heresy, the dispensation of justice and care for the welfare of his subjects.

There is much to appeal in this explanation, though to my eye it does not finally account for the huge bulk of Felipe's enterprises, often as great in scale and as vainglorious as critics hold El Escorial to be. Perhaps Professor S. G. Payne comes closest, descriptively rather than analytically, when he speaks of Felipe's wisdom and prudence being very much in doubt, his career consisting of long periods of caution followed by episodes in which he over-reached himself.

Of warfare on an epic scale, there was plenty, certainly. Felipe had inherited only the Habsburg patrimony and not the Holy Roman Empire; he held, that is to say, all the Hispanic kingdoms (except for Portugal), the Low Countries, Sicily and Naples and the whole of Latin America (except Brazil). Believing not only his own Mediterranean dominions but Christendom in general were threatened by Islam, he went to war on a colossal scale against the Turks. Spain's Mediterranean fleet had been on the scanty side. Now, by a combination of ship-building, use of allied forces and neglect of the Spanish mainland – which accordingly became vulnerable to attack – he turned out very large fleets for the Turkish wars. Spain, like America at a later date, clearly felt obliged to act as a self-appointed international police force. The result was the astonishingly thorough victory of Lepanto, won by his twenty-four-year-old half-brother, Don John of Austria, Don Juan in Spanish, in 1571. Felipe was brought the news in the temporary church of El Escorial, known now as the old church and closed to visitors. He heard it without a smile or any flicker of emotion but ordered a *Te Deum* at the end of the service.

Next, it was the Low Countries, where his father's suppression of heresy had finally proved unavailing. Faced by growing troubles, and finally by a fierce bout of Calvinist iconoclasm, Felipe swung into action with outright repression. This proved equally unavailing. Carlos V, at his abdication, had entered the great hall of Brussels leaning on the shoulders of his Low Countries favourite, the young Prince William of Orange. Now Felipe's policies thrust William, history's William the Silent, into leadership of the revolt, making him the most bitter and effective of personal foes. After this, nothing went right for Spain, whether the policy of the day was repression or leniency. In 1575, as a result of his military expenses, Felipe had to declare a second bankruptcy. Soon he could no longer pay his troops. Next year, in one of several mutinies brought on by lack of pay, the Spanish army devastated Antwerp, greatest city of northern Europe, burning large parts of the town and killing some 8,000. Known as the Spanish Fury, it was the worst outrage of the sixteenth century, more shocking to contemporaries than his father's sack of Rome.

And all this was little more than a prelude to Felipe's wars in the Atlantic, which again involved the building of great fleets and unsuccessful forays on a huge scale. The best known is the Armada against Britain, dispatched in 1588. Other fleets followed, all equally unsuccessful, while the English successfully raided Vigo and Cádiz, attacking both cities twice over. By the time Felipe was old and the reign was ending, he was hopelessly embroiled in unsuccessful wars in France. Spain, without enough wealth to sustain the endeavour, had willed itself to become the European superpower. The country remained immensely strong but had achieved precious few of its objectives, except to stem the Turkish advance in the Mediterranean. Felipe reckoned all his wars defensive; to the eye of history, he appears a genuine aggressor.

Financially, he continued his father's work of bringing Spain and especially Castile to its knees. The inflation that had begun in the early part of the century, fuelled by a fast-growing population and a demand for consumer goods in the new American colonies, had now become even more severe, more or less in line with the growth of bullion imports. These were mostly silver from the mines of Potosí in Bolivia, quintupling the quantities of that metal in Europe. Much of the bullion was soon being shipped straight through in payment to international creditors. Borrowing ran on uncontrollably while in Castile, particularly, the least well-off were bled white by taxation. In 1596, not far from death, Felipe once more repudiated his debts.

In the peninsula itself, he did a little better, if only by his own standards. He successfully annexed Portugal in 1581, using military force to make good his perfectly respectable claim to the vacant throne. Now, for most of several years, he lived in Lisbon, writing charming letters to the daughters of his third marriage, to Elizabeth de Valois, his cousin twice over. He was a man of widespread sexual energy, yet even so it must have been a compensation to have a wife with whom he was happy and daughters whom he loved. For Felipe had by now lost his only son under grievous circumstances.

Even before his strange marriage to Mary Tudor, the teenage Felipe had had a short-lived teenage bride, Manuela of Portugal. Manuela bore him a son named Carlos. The boy had grown into a violent and unstable adult, a danger to those around him and in continual conflict with his father. One night, a small group led by Felipe, wearing a helmet and carrying a sword, burst into the prince's room, seizing the dagger and arquebus Carlos kept by his bedhead. 'I am not mad,' screamed the young prince, 'I am desperate. Does Your Majesty mean to kill me?' Kept from now on in confinement, Carlos was in fact dead within months, though almost certainly from natural causes. This was a personal disaster but saved the realm from rule by a mentally disturbed king. It may indeed have been the supreme example of Felipe's personal self-sacrifice to public duty. Much later on, by his fourth marriage – this time to his niece, Ana of Austria – Felipe was to father another son, assuring succession in the male line.

Two major revolts occurred in Spain during Felipe's time, both springing from deep roots and leading on towards a depressing future. The first was by the Moors of Granada, now notionally converted to Christianity and known, like all converted Moors, by the name of Moriscos. Provoked by brutally unfair treatment, they launched a rebellion in the Alpujarras that took two years to quell. Afterwards, the surviving Morisco population was dispersed through Castile, Extremadura and Andalucía and, naturally, new aggravations arose. Solutions officially canvassed ranged from expulsion to castration of the males.

The other trouble-spot, inevitably, was Aragón, where political events convinced the aristocracy that Felipe was plotting to remove their ancient liberties. Certainly there was a strong thrust towards the imposition of Castilian systems right across the peninsula. Felipe was above all a Castilian. But he ruled much like his father, treating his various dominions as separate from one another, each under its own arrangements and united only in sharing his kingship. Even so, his solution at the end of the 1591 revolt involved considerable growth in central power, not to mention judicial murders and unaccountable deaths in prison. For Felipe, though in general a stickler for the legal processes, was prepared to go outside them when the security of state, in his view, made it necessary. His reign was punctuated with assassinations and imprisonments carried out on his personal, secret orders. Contemporaries observed that it was only a short distance from Felipe's smile to his dagger.

Religion, throughout, was his greatest concern, for Felipe was convinced that heresy and rebellion were one and indivisible. Right at the start of his reign, very small Protestant cells were uncovered in Seville and Valladolid. These were dealt with forcefully by the Inquisition, determined to stop any leakage of heretical ideas from northern Europe into Spain. In the ensuing moral panic, literature came under the close scrutiny of the Inquisition, now publishing their own Index, and Felipe forbade Spaniards to study abroad. A curtain of repressive Habsburg purple had fallen along the Pyrenees – breached, of course, by the demands of trade and the constant movement of armies across Europe. Behind this porous curtain, the Inquisition pursued the few remaining heretics, continued to examine the *conversos* but now turned the greater weight of religious persecution against the Moriscos. According to Henry Kamen, most recent English-language historian to tackle the imperial epoch, moral education was an even greater concern. Many of those examined by the Inquisition did not know the creed and held that fornication was a natural part of life. Meanwhile the Council of Trent had resulted in a powerful reform movement within the Church itself. And for those so minded, there was plenty to reform. In Barcelona, for example, it is known that twenty per cent of priests lived with their mistresses, or *barraganas*. In some parts of Spain the clergy were too illiterate to say mass. In Catalonia and the Basque Country they were often ignorant of the local language and unable to communicate with their parishioners.

Perhaps it was the threat of Protestantism, perhaps a response to the calls of the Council of Trent, perhaps some special intensity in the Castilian air, but Felipe's reign coincided with the greatest outburst of mysticism ever seen in Spain. Teresa of Avila, profuse in visions, is the saint best known to us, along with her confessor, the poet St John of the Cross. His wonderful religious lyrics enter deep into the same world as the Song of Songs, one where imagery and expressions normally confined to sexual love are used as spiritual metaphors. St Teresa, bride of Jesus and founder of the Discalced or Barefoot Carmelites, was no stranger to this way of thought.

Because of her saintliness and drive, Teresa entered the repertoire of religious art surprisingly quickly and one may get some idea of her presence and intensity from the many paintings of her. The best I know is by Ribera, in the Bellas Artes in Valencia. There she sits, the busy administrator in nun's garb, quill in hand, skull on her desk, looking up towards a lightly haloed dove in the top left-hand corner of the painting. The firmness with which the scene is rendered shows not a flicker of doubt about the combination of mysticism with practicality. Standing in front of this fine painting, one may well reflect that this in itself stands for a larger aspect of Spain's religious life – the easy movement from sacred to profane and back again.

In real life, where the Church's writ still runs, crucifixes dangle over marriage beds. Babies in prams are wheeled into churches at the most solemn moments. During Easter processions, a young man carrying the Virgin may duck out for a moment from underneath his heavy float, light up a cigarette, chat with his friends and then dive back again without the slightest sense of contradiction. This ease springs from the logically consistent Spanish notion that the whole of life, even its most secular moments, belongs entirely to the Lord.

For more of Teresa than can be seen in paintings, there is her autobiography, *The Life*, with its accounts of doubts and inner sureness, of submission to discipline and of her struggle to understand which of her visions were 'real' and which imaginary or deluded. Better still is to go to Avila, her birthplace, with its eighty-eight circular bastions set in vast medieval walls, the most imposing and severe of all the fortified cities of Old Castile. I have been in Avila in winter when winds tug at your coat and chafe your hands; I have been there on summer days with lightning crashing over the stony city. Extremist weather suits the temper of the place, making an appropriate companion on a tour that has to include the spot, on the far side of the river, where the search-party caught up with Teresa and her brother as they set off in pursuit of martyrdom among the Moors. The future saint was seven at the time. From here, as from at least two sides of the city, there are splendid, almost overwhelming views of the great walls.

Bad weather is less essential for a visit to the nearby Convent of the Incarnation, where Teresa spent twenty-seven years. Even so, it gave me a perverse pleasure on a recent visit to find the electricity knocked out by lightning. With light eventually restored, I set off on a tour among the faithful, nodding and genuflecting when we were shown the very spots where Teresa experienced her visions. Here, for example, says our guide, another of the keen young ladies peculiar to convent visits, is the stairway on which, looking upwards into the light, Teresa saw a child above her. 'Who are you?' the child asked her. 'Teresa of Jesus,' she replied, asking the child his name in return. 'I,' said the child, 'am Jesus of Teresa.' This was a specially big moment for the faithful.

Coming out of the convent door, again you cannot help but notice that from here also the great walls of Avila dominate the view, imposing themselves on the perception. Much of Teresa's life and many of her most intense spiritual experiences took place within the very shadow of the walls, under the immense carapace of Castilian militarism. To arrive at this unpleasing understanding is perhaps one serious aim of a visit to Avila.

Teresa's diary is in the great library of El Escorial, along with such wonders as a thirteenth-century Arabic work on chess, translated for Alfonso the Learned and showing two turbanned players sitting at the board. Teresa's hand is spidery but decided. Felipe's was almost illegible.

Visiting the monastery, one sees the impact of later generations. One internal wing was made into a residence by the Bourbons, most lightly and beautifully decorated with tapestries to the designs of Bayeu and Goya. The pantheon or mausoleum that Felipe founded for his father, a circular chamber beneath the high altar of the basilica, was decorated in the seventeenth century, a sumptuous display of marbles and ornate scroll-work identifying each of the Catholic monarchs. Carlos is buried here and so is Felipe, along with almost all their successors, hopeful the system would endure for ever so that daily masses would be said for them. There is even space for the present king, Juan Carlos, along with his Greek-born wife Doña Sofía. After that, the vault will be full up. Just outside the doorway of the pantheon is the *pudridero*, or rotting room, where royal cadavers wait for a decade or more before entombment. And stretching out under the very rooms that Felipe lived in, there now lie what seem acre upon acre of lesser tombs; a vast, composite wedding cake for children dead before baptism, the tombs of the infantas, tombs for childless queens. Don Juan of Austria lies here, his effigy wearing no fewer than sixteen rings and looking, it must be said, as if the man himself was quite a handsome devil. This is in total a true temple of death in the most morbid Castilian style and nobody who hopes to wrestle with the Christian soul of Spain should miss it.

As to Felipe himself, who can say which element of his life expresses the greater truth? His period, and within it his own conduct, marked the start of the Leyenda Negra, the black version of Spanish history, which was to have so huge a propaganda effect over the centuries. The Leyenda Negra derived from Italian hostility to Castile, from the horror provoked by the Spanish Fury of Antwerp, from the dire accusations against Spain contained in William the Silent's *Apology*, and from the atrocities in the Americas reported by Bartolomé de las Casas. Four centuries later, romantic writers were to cast Felipe as the great tyrant and to see El Escorial as the embodiment of his tyranny. Schiller made the doomed prince Carlos the tragic symbol of youth in search of freedom. Verdi echoed this version in his score of the opera of the same name. Gautier called El Escorial 'an architectural nightmare, desert of granite'.

But consider also the king inspired by an implacable sense of duty, the man of cold exterior who could still find a moment to write a loving letter to his daughters, the man who never ceased to toil and who grows old before our eyes in the grave portraits hung about El Escorial. Sánchez Coello, that admirable court painter, represents him as controlled and dignified. Then, as Felipe moves towards the end, Pantoja de la Cruz takes up the task of observation. He shows us that the king's eyes are red and rimmed by unsustainable fatigue. Felipe seems suddenly worthy of pity as well as the hate so often accorded him, more an exhausted bank clerk than an emperor. Carried painfully from Madrid to El Escorial in a sedan chair still to be seen in the monastery, he died in his bed in September 1598.

5 'Golden Age'

Art Ascendant in a Time of Trouble

EL GRECO AND VELÁZQUEZ, Ribalta and Ribera, Alonso Cano, Zurbarán, Murillo – suddenly there are giants in the land, painters beyond compare, to dazzle and amaze and, in the last resort, to humble. They range from the merely excellent to the utterly magnificent, their lesser works certainly open to criticism, but the best, however closely they are tied into their times, quite without precedent. Within their own particular styles, these paintings will never be matched again. Together they are a new Great Mosque of Córdoba, a fresh Granada, a pantheon of León writ ten times larger. The phenomenon, as commonly received, begins with El Greco in Toledo, marches for a while in step with that great Spanish genius Cervantes – equalled in his own time only by Velázquez, later perhaps by Goya – and starts to ebb a century from its beginnings with the death of Murillo in Seville. It is conventionally called, flat-footedly enough, the Golden Age of Spain.

I used to believe there was some kind of indwelling mystery here, which, if it could be penetrated, would illuminate all that is most remarkable in the Spanish psyche, from its reckless daring to its feverish concentration on death, from its potent sense of beauty, as also of frivolity, to a gravity and decorum that can be positively choking. The painting of the Golden Age, whether it shows the sombre faces of Castilian hidalgos, the gravely pacing monks of Extremadura, or smiling street-wise children from Andalucía, is profuse in the images by which we think we recognize Spain today.

It is as if there were a single inspiration at centre, a common brilliance of vision waiting to be understood. In the end though, the more one looks and reads, the more one must accept that matters are quite the other way around. Even though the painters had important truths to tell, many still relevant to Spain today, there were in fact scores of influences which impinged on them, several competing ways of thought and considerable variety in the opportunities they were offered and to which, presumably, they were responding as they painted. Many of these factors changed with time. As a result, where once my image of the Golden Age was of a brilliantly illuminated ball of light, I see it now still as a circle, but one encrusted in multiple pin-points of light, continually rolling down a gentle slope of change and development.

For me, that slope begins, as so much does in Spain, with sculpture.

In Valladolid, on the far side of the great Isabel-and-Fernando façade of the College of San Gregorio, the Museum of Polychrome Sculpture unfolds around a brilliant Isabelline Gothic cloister. The first three rooms, under their gravely coffered Mudéjar ceiling, are taken up entirely by one work. This is an enormous *retablo*, disassembled and arranged around the walls so that all its constituent statuary and some of the architectural ensemble may easily be seen. It is wooden; it is multicoloured, ringing with gold and midnight blue; and, though it may evoke anxiety as well as wonder, it is unquestionably a masterpiece.

Alonso Berruguete, son of the same Pedro Berruguete who had been court painter to Isabel and Fernando, was commissioned to execute the work on 8 November 1526 by the abbot of the monastery of San Benito (one of the features of art history in Spain is the survival from the sixteenth century onwards of many of the original contracts for ecclesiastical art-works). It was normal at this time for patrons in churches and monasteries to prescribe the positioning and nature of the various statues and busts in a *retablo*. The San Benito contract referred to a previous agreement on these matters between Berruguete and the abbot. It went on to demand that the work be 'very sumptuous and well done' and specified that Berruguete should personally paint the hands and faces of the statues and the whole of the busts. There was obviously some hope that he might be finished quickly, but at the same time realistic provision was made for four or even five years. Final payment would come only when expert arbitrators for both sides were satisfied.

The young sculptor who accepted this commission was Castilian through and through, born in Paredes de Nava near Palencia and brought up in Valladolid. What made him unusual was that he had spent more than a decade in Rome and Florence. Berruguete's Italian stay overlapped the unveiling of Michelangelo's Sistine ceiling and this appears to have had as great an impact on him as it did on his Italian contemporaries. The ancient Greek statue of Laocoon and sons, struggling unavailingly with serpents, was rediscovered in 1506 and also made an enormous impression in Italy; it is said that Berruguete was permanently enthralled by it.

On his return to Valladolid Berruguete was appointed *escribano del crimen*, or clerk of crime. In this capacity he was to take down the testimony of the condemned and tortured – torture was then a standard means of eliciting confessions as well as a punishment for serious misdemeanours. Later, when he became too busy, he tried to pass the commitment to his son. But the steady income from an official appointment, even if a fairly grisly one, was probably very welcome to begin with. Though art historians often refrain from making the connection, it is clear that Berruguete witnessed not just a sculpted Laocoon but living human beings *in extremis*.

As a painter, he was remarkable from the beginning. A Calvary intended for San Benito reveals him as the master of a style that owed surprisingly little to Renaissance ideals of beauty. The figures are twisted. Christ's legs are elongated. Flowing figures are made vivid by sweeps of brightly coloured raiment, with highlights flashing in gold and green, icy or velvety.

As a sculptor, he is still more extraordinary. The Holy Family, the saints and other blessed figures of the San Benito *retablo* cannot contain themselves. Fevered and passionate, they express outsize emotions with every ounce of their brightly painted wooden bodies.

They lean backwards, lean sideways, look as if they might fall right over, step up, step down, pivot and sway. Legs akimbo, arms outflung, they cry aloud in anguish or prophecy. Even St Christopher looks as if the small boy on his shoulders will be the death of him. The contours of the faces, male and female, swoop as dramatically as swifts. Long beards, wavy as candle flame or the edges of a Muslim sword, descend below male chins to emphasize the vertical. The Virgin Mary, once too high to see but now brought close to us, has a jaw as long as that of any Habsburg. The figure of Christ himself, with slanted head and slit of mouth and slit eyes overhung by swollen eyelids, must be one of the most painful in all of dolorous Spain.

Watching the many visitors to the gallery, it is clear they respond most strongly to the statue of San Sebastián. This saint is beautiful of body but definitely dismayed by the arrows piercing him, not gloating in the epicene, sado-masochistic fashion so often hinted at in Spanish and Italian art. For me, however, here as in remote medieval Jaca, the most powerful of the images is that of Abraham and Isaac. The young man kneels, hands bound behind his back, body bent forward, desperate. His father, tall and gaunt as any Spanish version of St Jerome, has grabbed the young man's hair to reveal the tender nape of neck where he must strike. But there is more to it, much more. The father's head, trailing its long beard, is flung right back to emit a roar of anguish at the bestiality he must commit. This is a silent cry of outrage that transfixes the museum.

It is truly an amazement to see it all close up, for as well as revealing the details of the drama, scrutiny from close at hand reveals the detail of the workmanship as well; the inside of a cuff, for example, taken from a position where it would have been invisible, disclosed as a brilliance of gold flecks emerging from beneath the overpainted greens or blues. Limbs, faces, tunics and feet are carved and painted with an extraordinary exactitude of passion.

It would have been a pleasure to report that this great work found favour with the abbot. Alas, it took Berruguete seven years to finish and ended in a dismal wrangle, with all kinds of alterations hotly demanded. These, it seems, were never made, and it was not until thirteen years from the beginning of the task that Berruguete was finally paid in full.

Berruguete went on to carve the upper portions – the *sillería alta* – of the choir-stalls in Toledo cathedral, collaborating here with another fine sculptor, Felipe Vigarny. These walnut panels, surmounting the scenes of the conquest of Granada, are far less tortured than the San Benito *retablo*, incomparably beautiful in a country where choir-stalls are often one of the greatest glories of cathedrals. He was responsible for *retablos* from Úbeda to Cáceres. He influenced the much-admired Damián Forment, who carved the *retablo* of Santo Domingo de la Calzada. Meanwhile, as Berruguete's extravagant style flourished in monasteries and churches, a different tradition was developing at court. Both styles were to flow into the mainstream of the Golden Age.

Carlos V was just a little younger than Berruguete. As emperor, he was able to choose his painters freely from almost the whole of Europe. It was quite reasonable that he should do so, for despite the magnificence of Spanish sculpture, Spain at this point could offer little depth in painting. Carlos had an eye for art, and made the wise choice of Titian as court painter. The great Venetian produced great works for the emperor. Consider the Titian portrait of Carlos after his victory at Mühlberg in 1547, properly got up with lance and armour like an old-fashioned Christian knight, horse prancing delicately beneath him. He is a splendid if isolated figure. But from close up the eyes are red and tired. Later, Titian offers us the ageing emperor, seated disconsolately in a chair (interestingly enough, despite the eating, Carlos does not seem to have grown fat). Titian brought to the Spanish court his own profound observation, and the colours, skills and preferences of Venice. For Felipe II, he went on to produce large mythical paintings of an almost explicit eroticism, a phenomenon extremely rare in Spanish art. Indeed, it may be the lack of mythical scenes, not to mention eroticism, which can sometimes make galleries of Spanish painting so forbidding, concentrating as they do, from the Middle Ages to at least the sixteenth century, on savage martyrdoms and brutal crucifixions.

The other main courtly contribution was from the Low Countries.

Isabel the Catholic had collected northern paintings. One need only
recall the brilliant display, within a few paces of her tomb, in the
sacristy of the Royal Chapel in Granada. This respect continued
under Carlos V and Felipe II, and the northern style of portraiture,
grave and unadorned, was passed on to such excellent painters as
Sánchez Coello. It is from Sánchez Coello's brush that we have the
best of our information on Felipe II, not to mention his infinitely
sad representations of the doomed Don Carlos, a child looking for
ever as if he is about to burst into tears. The sobriety of this style
exactly matched Habsburg notions of imperial reticence and under-
statement. Why, after all, should the most powerful beings in the
known world feel under any obligation to vaunt their claims? The
wintry imperial portraits, with Sánchez Coello in due course giving
way to the less impressive but still austere Pantoja de la Cruz, form
an exact parallel to the almost aggressive modesty of Felipe's private
chambers in El Escorial.

El Greco stepped into this amalgam of display and reticence, passion
and constraint, in 1576 or 1577. All of us know his work – the
enormous elongations, the ravished, moist-eyed figures, the play of
flame and lightning, the swirling robes in citrous yellow, azure,
scarlet. When I was sixteen and made my first trip to Spain, it was
not just El Escorial that impressed me. The El Greco paintings in
Toledo made me go quite literally weak at the knee. Nothing is
better suited to teenage romanticism and religiosity than the impossible yearning of El Greco's saints.

Nowadays, I am happy to acknowledge Berruguete as a thrilling
master of Mannerism in sculpture. In painting I get the greatest
pleasure, delight is not too strong a word, from the work of Luis de
Morales, known in his day as El Divino. He painted mainly in
Badajoz, one of the chief cities of Extremadura, and unfortunately a
most depressing place today. In time, he comes somewhere between
Berruguete and the peak of El Greco's achievement, a gentle Man-
nerist who interposes fewer extravagances between himself and the
spectator. There is a Morales Madonna and Child in the National
Gallery in London, and a Piedad in the Prado in Madrid, either of

which would make the case with poignant eloquence. As for El Greco, I fear I would be much less responsive than I am were it not for a growing body of scholarship which enables us to see him as rather more than simple romantic visionary and mystical colourist.

Domenikos Theotokopoulos, later called El Greco, came, as is well known, from Crete by way of Italy. In Crete, Byzantine icon painting flourished in the school of St Catherine in Candia, modern Iraklion. On the walls of the Cretan country chapels, Byzantine fresco painters were still producing a hieratic but intensely moving body of work. El Greco studied at St Catherine's and must have known the frescoes. In Italy, the young Greek met the High Renaissance and a growing Mannerism. He met formal perspective, glowing colour and contorted subject-matter. Tradition has placed him mainly in Venice. It now seems likely that he spent more time in Rome. His friends here were not only artists but people of learning in many branches of science and humane studies. Theotokopoulos became familiar with mathematics and architecture and the whole body of prints and paintings, the general stock of images on which contemporary Italians could draw. He was emerging as a *pintor sabio*, a learned painter.

He reached Toledo at an interesting juncture. Up to just fifteen years before, when Felipe established Madrid as capital and ceased the perambulations of the court, Toledo had been one of the main royal stopping places. The city still remained the religious capital of Spain, with an intense intellectual and spiritual life. On the negative side, it had experienced one of the most bizarre and disturbing episodes of Felipe's reign, the eighteen-year imprisonment of its own archbishop and the nation's primate, Bartolome de Carranza, held first in Spain and after that in Rome. Astonishingly, Carranza himself had fallen foul of the Inquisition.

In 1573, an ecclesiastic named Gaspar de Quiroga took over the Inquisition. He began by releasing Luis de León, another undeserving prisoner. In 1577, Archbishop Carranza emerged from his long confinement only to die within a matter of days. Now Quiroga himself became the Spanish primate. He bravely defended the reputation of his predecessor and meanwhile launched the reforms demanded by the Council of Trent. This initiated Spain's Counter-Reformation. Quiroga's rather more open and generous attitudes simultaneously provided a breathing space for the kind of post-Erasmian mysticism, based on a desire for personal union with God, so eloquently represented by Luis de León, St John of the Cross and Teresa of Avila. All of this favoured the artistic development of El Greco, allowing him to express his own mystical vision while painting along the theological lines prescribed by the Council of Trent. It is also true, of course, that his work departed wildly from the kind of realism envisaged as part of the process of Counter-Reformation.

El Greco's strongly individual approach was evidently linked to a developing Mannerism. There were also theological considerations of a slightly obscure kind. As a man of education, the new arrival seems to have found a place in Toledo's intellectual community (to the extent that Spain still disdainfully rejected the concept of manual labour, painters and sculptors were ranked as lowly artisans). Scholars have shown that Toledo's intellectuals took considerable interest both in Neoplatonism and in the writings of Pseudo-Dionysius the Areopagite, a sixth-century Syrian theologian and impostor, who claimed to be the very Dionysius converted by St Paul. In his work *The Celestial Hierarchy*, Pseudo-Dionysius interpreted divinity in terms of light. Light flowed downwards from the Radiant Light of God, by way of the angels who were themselves compounds of fire, to provide enlightenment on earth. El Greco possessed a Greek edition of *The Celestial Hierarchy* and it is probable that he had studied it closely. Increasingly it seems likely that the messages of *The Celestial Hierarchy* inform his work, helping to give an unearthly light to the subjects he was commissioned to paint. This seems to make up somewhat for some of the worst of his excesses.

For El Greco as a painter the going was hard to begin with in Toledo. One of his first major commissions was the Expolio, or Disrobing of Christ, to go above the altar in the cathedral sacristy. Though it led to immediate dispute, this large work still takes pride of place in the sacristy even among the many outstanding paintings there, both Spanish and Italian. The patter of passing tour guides ranks the Expolio unhesitatingly with the *Burial of the Conde de*

Orgaz as one of the two great masterpieces of El Greco's still remaining in Toledo. It is indeed an imposing painting, showing the importance Italian naturalism still had for El Greco at this stage; and except for the gormlessness of Christ's face, which once no doubt would have appealed to me, I willingly go along with the tour guides. Extremely large at the centre, Christ is clothed in the mocking scarlet robe which is about to be ripped off him. The colour dominates the picture. The executioner, hugely foreshortened, bends towards the viewer to bore a hole in the downshaft of the crucifix. The dark heads of the Three Marys are to be seen at Christ's feet and above and behind are the raging faces of the populace, the skyline raggedly topped with spears and halberds.

The dispute about this picture concerned the Three Marys, who allegedly should not have been there at all, and the positioning of the crowd, higher than Christ. El Greco replied to the complaints with the haughtiness that was to distinguish him in Spain and only agreed to make the changes after the possibility of prison was invoked. Just as with the Berruguete *retablo*, the changes were not made and in the end he got his money.

In the middle of his Toledo difficulties, however, he also encountered problems in work for Felipe II. The submission to the Crown of two small sample pictures had led to a commission for a full-size painting for El Escorial, still in place there and now known variously as the *Dream of Philip* or the *Allegory of the Holy League* – the League, that is to say, which had won the great victory of Lepanto. This work is divided into heaven and earth in the zoning system that was soon to become a trademark of El Greco. Felipe kneels on earth, just in the middle, his jaw much longer in this side view than was customary in formal portraits. The painting nevertheless found favour and its success led to a further commission, *The Martyrdom of St Maurice and the Theban Legion*. Many of the legion, so the story tells us, came to an unpleasant end because of their refusal to worship Roman gods. Greco showed the martyrdom in the middle distance while the foreground was occupied by a view of Maurice and his captains energetically debating how to respond to an order to march the legion towards the prescribed place of worship. This

Above: 18 The upper storey of the cloister of
the College of San Gregorio, Valladolid, home
of the National Museum of Sculpture. The
college was built between 1488 and 1496 in one
of the most extravagant flourishes of Isabelline
architecture. The rope-like ornamentation
reveals the style as a close cousin of Portuguese
Manueline.

Right: 19 Sculptural façade over the main
doorway of the college of San Gregorio,
attributed to Gil de Siloé: ' . . . under shield and
outsize lions, babies dangle from the branches
of a tree with all the playfulness of kittens.'

Opposite top: 20 Tordesillas and its bridge, spanning the Río Duero.

Opposite below: 21 A shrine outside the walls of Avila where the future St Teresa was overtaken by an anxious search party at the start of her childhood quest for martyrdom in Africa.

Right: 22 Cloisters at Guadalupe, with pot plants carefully tended by the monks. Until the building of El Escorial by Felipe II, Guadalupe was Spain's leading Hieronymite monastery and spiritual key to Spain's expansion in the Americas. Columbus conferred the name of the monastery on an island; the Virgin of Guadalupe is patroness of Mexico.

Below: 23 Following its dissolution in 1836, Guadalupe passed into private hands for a long spell. Today it is cared for by some twenty Franciscans, a far cry from its former days of glory. Here, one of the monks in autumn sunshine in front of the monastery.

24 Pottery kilns, once English-owned, adjoin the Seville Charterhouse and Expo site.

25 Most Spanish of details, from the rear doorway of Seville town hall.

26 A Sevillian schoolgirl dances in the street, helping to raise money for a school journey.

27 Ceramic bollards and balustrades in the Plaza de España, Seville, built for the 1929 Exhibition.

28 A lone horseman appears in the village of El Rocio, Huelva, demonstrates his skills and disappears again.

29 In Cádiz, as elsewhere in the south, ancient buildings rise in a tangle of tiles and whitewash.

30 Storks and Spaniards live in easy association.

31 Coca Castle in Old Castile, built for an archbishop.

32 The bridge of San Martín, Toledo, surmounted by the royal coat of arms. Behind, San Juan de los Reyes, originally intended as their burial place by the Catholic Kings.

visually dominating group is seen from low down and in the case of Maurice from behind, all bare thigh and gesturing hands. For reasons unknown, but possibly at the behest of the Italian assessors – one of whom got the reversal of the contract – Felipe rejected the painting. El Greco never worked for the king again, despite the praises heaped on his art by Fray José de Sigüenza in his history of the Hieronymites and El Escorial.

Toledo gained by the court's refusal. Greco's portraits are scattered all over the world but he painted saints aplenty and many remain in the city, along with a goodly number of apostles. His landscapes of Toledo are a Pseudo-Dionysian illumination, particularly the view, in the Metropolitan Museum in New York, showing gorge and city in the light of a summer storm. The sky swirls from deep black to hectic blue, with white of cloud and a tumult of grey and brown. The hills behind the city have the look of leather mysteriously illuminated from within while Toledo itself, plunging down towards the river and the bridge, is turning purple under this assault of colour. Inside the gorge, the precipitous hillsides are a pulsing green.

Other views are less dramatic but show different parts of the city. The artist's *View and Plan of Toledo*, done late in his life, engagingly raises a large building on to a cloud, so permitting a view of the Visagra gate through which Alfonso VI had come riding six centuries before. It looks here much as it does today, with the round twin towers to either side.

The principal glory of course, and here nobody could disagree with tour guide or learned analyst, has to be the *Burial of the Conde de Orgaz*. Orgaz is a sleepy little town to the south of Toledo with large church, the standard complement of outsize tractors, an arcaded plaza, a couple of sleepy dogs and little else. The count in question was a benefactor to the Toledan church of Santo Tomé for which the painting was commissioned and in which it still reposes. According to the legend, which naturally endorsed the count's munificence, his funeral was materially helped along by two saints – Stephen and Augustine – who came down specially from heaven.

El Greco's treatment of the scene is quite astounding. The nobles of Toledo, black tunics and white ruffs, some with the scarlet insignia of the military orders on their chests, have gathered at the graveside in a long row. More than any other image, it is this line of faces that has fixed in the minds of foreigners, apparently for ever, a common concept of Castilian nobility. El Greco's mourners have hollow cheeks, their almond faces extended downwards by black beards of the same shape. Their black moustaches, graceful in the mass, are actually quite long, sometimes protruding out beyond the cheeks. They are constrained, devout, immensely dignified. You cannot imagine they have ever laughed. Their grave eyes simultaneously burn and melt, inviting you to look straight in and see their immensely aristocratic, utterly Catholic souls. El Greco has placed himself in his own picture, remarkably like the rest of the Toledans, looking out at us from above St Stephen's head.

In front of the nobles, the saints have duly materialized. St Augustine, to the right, is old, with flowing white beard and bishop's mitre. You wonder if it is right for him to take so much of the dead man's weight. St Stephen is young and soft of face. The robes and copes of both are gold, scarlet and silver, with embroidered scenes let into them, the whole painted with almost Flemish exactitude. They have gathered up the body of the count, whey-faced in death but supple in damascene armour, to lower him gently in the tomb. A priest in the foreground looks up in astonishment, the black of his cassock showing through the delicate transparency of his surplice. 'Best transparency in all Spain,' a tour guide tells his Spanish flock as I sit by the picture, introducing a category unfamiliar to me but evidently commonplace to them. From now on in my travels, I am quick off the mark in assessing transparencies.

As one would perhaps expect in a major El Greco work, heaven lies above the count and saints, above the priest and noble mourners. Jesus is topmost with Mary ready just a little lower down to receive the soul of the dead man. The upper layer is separated off by a dense bank of the kind of swirling ectoplasm so characteristic of El Greco but seen more often, in our day, in horror movies. The soul, which has to make the journey from earth to heaven, is represented as a baby, just as Mary's soul is represented in Cretan versions of the Dormition of the Virgin. A flying angel gently assists it up a fissure in the ectoplasm, a kind of funnel which has the appearance, though in a much more florid style, of the cutaway of a birth canal in any biology textbook. I am sorry to say this, genuinely sorry, but the effect is entirely risible.

Francisco Pacheco, a painter from Seville, visited El Greco, now an old man, in 1611. Pacheco was a very different kind of artist, believing in old-fashioned formal beauty and moving personally towards baroque. He advocated a precise, pedantic iconography in which a crucified Christ must have separate nails through both his feet; in the Immaculate Conception the Virgin should have the sun behind her, blocking it out with her body, and her feet should rest on a crescent moon with the points turned downwards. There was a host of other symbols that had to be included. Naturally enough, there was not much common ground between El Greco and a man who thought like this. The two agreed to disagree. Later, in his *Arte de Pintura*, one of the great source-books for seventeenth-century Spanish painting, Pacheco wrote contemptuously: 'Who will believe that Domenico Greco returned many times to his paintings and revised them again and again so as to end up with different and clashing colours and leave those cruel blotches in order to make a show of bravura?' He also reported El Greco's now famous remark on Michelangelo – that he was a good man who unfortunately had no idea how to paint.

Pacheco was not the most talented of painters, but he was at this time the leading artist in Seville. He was also the centre of an 'academy', a talking shop whose members met to discuss work in progress, support one another in their projects and practise the arts of critical analysis. In this way it became a meeting point for writers, who were regarded as potential gentry, and painters, who, of course, were not. This relationship had been paralleled by El Greco's experience in Toledo, but here in Seville it was informally formalized, with considerable future consequences. Even more interesting as we look back was the identity of one of Pacheco's young apprentices – Diego Rodríguez de Silva y Velázquez.

Before taking up the story of the greatest painter of Spain's greatest period in painting, the pivot of any account of the history and achievements of Spanish art, it is worth devoting just a moment to the condition of Seville; for Pacheco's academy held its meetings in what was at this time, beyond a shadow of a doubt, the foremost city of Spain. All that it lacked was the presence of the court.

The focus was the Atlantic and America. Enjoying the monopoly of the Indies trade, the city's population had swelled hugely, with Spaniards arriving from all parts of Castile and a great growth in the number of foreigners. The Genoese had established a toe-hold here as long ago as the days of the Almohads and were now foremost among the foreign business community. There were many black faces, too, for anyone who lived in any style kept slaves. When the government in Madrid ran short of criminals to man the galleys and attempted to draft slaves to take their place, the municipality of Seville protested formally at what they saw as the theft of their possessions, stating that slavery was 'a usage generally accepted in this region'.

Spain could no longer keep up with the manufacture of the goods required by the American colonies. Inflation had made them too expensive and the trading and manufacturing cities of the north and centre – Medina del Campo, Segovia, Cuenca, for example – were in the hands of foreign creditors and scarcely able to stagger onwards. The result was the import into Seville, from more northerly parts of Europe, of all the supplies that had to be passed on to America. Between 7 October 1597 and 19 November of the same year, for instance, ninety-seven ships arrived with goods, mostly from Hamburg and the Baltic. In great displays of energy and animation the cargoes were stacked up on the Arenal, the beach along the river bank. There is a fine engraving of the scene in the Biblioteca Nacional in Madrid. A few steps from the river, and just by the cathedral, stood the newly built Casa de Contratación, designed in severe style by Juan de Herrera, the second architect of El Escorial. Here all the official paperwork for the Indies was handled. Literally scores of churches and convents and monasteries had sprung up as companions to the surviving Almohad monuments.

The Virgin Mary already held a central place in Andalusian affections and many of these foundations owed a special allegiance to her. Religious processions were numerous and much admired. But alongside the extravagant displays by merchants and ecclesiastics, there was also wretched, shameful poverty.

Velázquez was born in Seville in 1599. He was apprenticed to Pacheco in 1610 and served his master for six or seven years. Granted a licence as a painter in 1617, he married Pacheco's daughter, Juana, the following year. From his first emergence into maturity, he painted masterpieces, using the up-to-date device of strongly contrasted light and darkness. It has been argued that his perspective was shaky to begin with, even that Pacheco may not have taught it to him, resulting in tilted surfaces, in unintentionally cramped settings and, as a consequence, in the odd placement of individual figures within groups. One may, with the eye of cold assessment, see all of this in Velázquez's early work. Pacheco's standardizing prescriptions, or most of them, are also embodied in Velázquez's early Immaculate Conception.

But what one also sees, right from the beginning, is an extraordinary engagement with reality, an ability to make paint and canvas stand in for the natural world. Who can see and not be moved by the *Old Woman Cooking*, her face emerging from deep shadows, hand holding out a wooden spoon, eggs coming along nicely in the earthenware dish on top of the brazier? Who can fail to be caught up by the worn face of the Seville water-seller or by the drops of water running down the side of his great jug like beads of light? In Velázquez we suddenly confront an observation so acute that it seems to express, even in the early genre subjects, the reverence for creation that inspired his Dutch contemporaries. Here too it is rendered so piercingly, so beautifully, that it is almost painful. Right from the beginning, the simplest-seeming gestures of Velázquez, whether in genre or religious works or in the first portraits, reach out towards the emotions of the viewer in a way one may discuss to some advantage but never, perhaps, entirely comprehend.

The young Velázquez was ambitious and competitive, of that there is no doubt. Antonio Palomino, his first biographer, and another great source on painting in this period, tells how Velázquez was reproved for specializing in 'rough' genre subjects – then extremely unusual in Seville – rather than in the suaver subject-matter of the Italians. Velázquez answered that he would rather be first among rough painters than lower down the list among the smooth. It is no surprise to find him making a sortie to Madrid, home of the richest patronage available, as early as 1622.

Quite why Felipe II chose Madrid as a permanent site for the court remains obscure. In the years leading up to 1561, Toledo had been the main staging post. But Toledo seems to have had several drawbacks as a potential capital. Forty years had elapsed since it led the *comuneros* revolt, but apparently Felipe still resented this aspect of its history; within the city itself old enmities still lay just beneath the surface. Madrid, by contrast, was a tiny place, offering a clean slate. There had recently been bitter snowfalls in Toledo, cutting imperial communications. Madrid was out on the wide plains, and much less likely to be affected in this way. The site had originally been settled by the Arabs with a fortress characteristically placed where a bank of hill rose sharply above the tiny river. Tiny the Río Manzanares may have been, and much mocked ever since for being so, but all around there were excellent water supplies. Firewood was at that time abundant. There was granite not far off for grandiose building projects of the kind Felipe favoured. It was physically in the centre of the Iberian land mass (though not at all central so far as the empire was concerned).

One or several of these factors may have helped Felipe take a decision otherwise as arbitrary as the siting of Brasilia or Canberra. If Madrid were to flourish it would have to depend on lines of communication that at the time must have appeared almost endless. Even today it remains a bizarre idea that food and fuel and raw materials must be brought from hundreds of miles distance to so artificial a spot. Could Felipe possibly have dreamed, one wonders, that his chosen capital, though having a bad stutter near the start, and never achieving any striking beauty, would soon figure among the liveliest and most appealing of Europe's great cities, bursting with an atmosphere entirely its own, and still in the twentieth century as rich in its localism and peculiarities as Dickens's London?

I make my way there from Seville, and set out on a walk through the parts of town that were already built when the twenty-three-year-old Velázquez first arrived. It was, as one might imagine, not a long walk at all.

On the heights above the Manzanares in the west, just a few steps from the apse of the city's permanently unfinished cathedral, recent building works have revealed a substantial chunk of the original Moorish fortifications. Looking down from above you see stone walling with inserts of brick. There is a cluster of arches, still half-buried and filled in with masonry. It is little enough but it may serve as reminder of nine centuries of Spanish history that had come to a definitive end with the expulsion of the Moors, just a decade before the arrival of Velázquez.

The ruler who signed the order of expulsion was Felipe III, the one surviving son of Felipe II. Dominated by his father in childhood, Felipe III had little of the Habsburg sense of duty and drifted round his realm like any tourist, seemingly taking his orders from the royal favourite, the Duke of Lerma, and stopping off for months if a place seemed promising. The court meanwhile remained in Madrid. In 1601, mainly on the grounds that he preferred the climate, the young king moved the capital north to Valladolid. Madrid by now had a fast-growing population consisting largely of the nobles who attended court and the enormous retinues who attended on the nobles. Then there was the network of supply and services that had grown up to attend to all of them. The removal of the court was a devastating blow, only ameliorated in 1606 when Felipe brought it back again.

The Moors were expelled in a rolling programme starting three years later. Fought to a standstill in the Low Countries, Felipe III was obliged to sign a twelve-year truce with the United Provinces (the territory that finally emerged as modern Holland). He attempted to make up for this by signing the expulsion order on the same day.

It was intended to be a last great victory for Christendom, full stop and amen to the Reconquista. In fact, it beggared the whole of eastern Spain. In Valencia, where the Moriscos were in a majority, agriculture simply collapsed. In Aragón, where they made up one third of the population, the results were similar. There was grave dislocation even in Castile where the Granada Moors had been resettled. As for the Moors themselves, they were mercilessly preyed upon at every stage of their forced journey. Charged impossible sums for shade and water, they stumbled sick and dying towards destinations that had no welcome for them. Cardinal Richelieu called it barbarous. Opinion outside Spain agreed with him. Velázquez, however, was soon to paint a picture glorifying the episode.

Presumably, the young painter visited the old Arab fortifications. A short distance north-west along the ridge, scarcely 200 metres, there now stands the vast eighteenth-century royal palace, grand and grey, the very opposite of homely. This will require a visit later in the story. When Velázquez first arrived, however, there was a substantial *alcázar* on the site. A great heap of Gothic stone and steep-pitched roof, it was renovated, partly under his direction, during the course of the impressive career that little by little opened up to him.

Coming back now from the royal palace to the centre of the city, one walks just a short distance up pleasantly old-fashioned streets towards the Puerta del Sol, or Gate of the Sun, formerly indeed a city gate but for centuries now the symbolic heart of the capital. It is a busy place, a cream-coloured nineteenth-century semi-circle with a large official building on its one flat side. On the cream-coloured flank opposite, there stands a statue of Madrid's other great symbol, a brown bear feasting on the fruit of the strawberry tree, or arbutus.

On the way up, the walker will probably have passed the Plaza de la Villa, containing Madrid's town hall and one or two other splendid ancient buildings. Just in behind the Puerta del Sol is the Plaza Mayor, the finest monument Madrid retains from its early days as capital.

The square was built in 1619 and then rebuilt in 1631 after a destructive fire. Five storeys high, rising severe in brick above a stone arcade, adorned with Flemish pinnacles on its one grandiose façade – that of the Panaderia, or Bakery – it was the scene of bullfights and executions. Soon after Velázquez's arrival, in restitution for the out-and-out corruption of the Lerma regime, Rodrigo Calderón, one of his most hated minions, was beheaded here. But so impeccably noble was his bearing, so utterly Christian and so thoroughly Castilian that the populace at once forgave his crimes and the phrase 'proud as Rodrigo on the scaffold' entered the language. Heretics were burned a short way off, beyond one of the newer city gates.

The Plaza Mayor and the heavily buttressed streets behind it, pulsing with bars and restaurants, tourists and Madrileños, as Madrid's inhabitants are called, remains one of the most agreeable little districts in the capital. At the same time, one should remember that many of the greatest monuments of Felipe III's reign were, as it happens, literary. Cervantes's *Don Quixote* was published in two parts, in 1604 and 1614. Throughout this period, roughly in parallel with the astonishing outburst of painting, writing of the highest quality was pouring forth, a phenomenon at least as widespread and intense as the literary flood of Shakespeare's England. This book, by concentrating on the visible, can offer little space to Spanish literature. But always and everywhere the traveller does well to bear in mind that despite its many ups and downs Spain was and remains one of the great literary nations.

From the Puerta del Sol and the Plaza Mayor, roads run gently downhill to the east. At the bottom of the hill was the Prado – the word means meadow – a favourite spot for sauntering and later for promenading in carriages and arranging assignations behind cloak or veil. Wellington, though no doubt he behaved more decorously than some, came every evening during his stay in Madrid in 1812. In 1819, the recently constructed Prado gallery, originally intended for other purposes, opened its doors to show the magnificent picture collections accumulated over centuries by the Spanish Crown. These included by far the greatest concentration anywhere of paintings by Velázquez. Beyond the Prado, in the painter's day, stood the large

convent of the Hieronymites. In this area, Velázquez was to witness
the construction of a huge new palace called the Buen Retiro. Many
of his canvases were painted for it. Nowadays almost all of the
buildings are gone, but the palace gardens, known simply as the
Retiro, live on as a city-centre park. Here, you can go boating
on the original artificial lake, have your palm read by bearded
foreigners or, if you happen to be a girl of twelve years old or so, go
twirling along the gravel paths, intensely admired by parents, in
your first communion dress. Beyond again, in the sixteenth century,
lay open country.

On the evening of my Velázquez walk, from the Arab wall to the
far side of the Retiro, I am carted off to a dinner party, in a house
rather than the usual apartment, with a barking dog and all the
bourgeois appurtenances. We are a bourgeois group, it soon trans-
pires, husbands and wives each with their own careers – lawyers,
publishers, journalists, academics. Arriving from Seville early in the
day, I had seen a great inverted cup of mist and smog above Madrid.
An engineer at the dinner party explains that this is a phenomenon
of recent years, brought on by traffic and, in winter, central heating.
But, he continues, bad as it is, the real problem in Spain comes from
the industries backed by the Franco government from the 1950s
onwards. These, he says, are the kinds of industry more usually
encountered in eastern Europe or in Third World countries, with
large and messy low-cost plant, employing as many people as possible and to hell with any environmental consequences. The task of
undoing this legacy will be greater than in any other western
country.

This is serious stuff. So is the next set of exchanges, with a senior
linguist from the university. She is putting the finer points of fem-
inism as seen from a Spanish perspective. I cannot help but notice
that the writers and philosophers to whose work she appeals are all,
to a woman, French. Meanwhile, down at the far end of the table
another conversation is warming up. The speaker is a lawyer whom
I have known for years, not right-wing precisely, at times extremely
radical, but full of self-consciously traditional attitudes. He works
for a living but he does not care for it. He keeps a horse in the

outskirts of Madrid and while he practises dressage he dreams of riding, spurs jingling, on his head a cattleman's wide-brimmed hat – the *sombrero ancho*, known as a Cordoban hat just about everywhere except in Córdoba – through the vast acres of his own, entirely imaginary, cork forests. Though middle class in origin, he is living proof of the survival of aristocratic aspirations in Spain.

Just at this moment he has launched into a learned rodomontade on riding whips, comparing the Australian to the Argentinian, the British huntsman's to that of the Russian sleigh-driver. We listen, enthralled at the oddity and particularity of his knowledge. Then he is off again, telling a story about the Spanish consul in an industrial port which shall be nameless. Having too little to do and rather too high an opinion of his office, the consul requires the captains of passing Spanish merchant vessels to call on him personally to make their obeisances. A daring captain has refused to do so. As the ship sails, the consul, in all solemnity, attempts to have it detained by the host government.

The laughter that follows this little tale reminds me of Cervantes. I cannot vouch for the truth of the story or for the excellence of its telling, but the response to it, all around the table, is one of delighted, gossipy, self-mockery. Nobody could match Cervantes in his assaults on the false pride and self-vaunting unreason of his fellow Spaniards; but delight in the attempt remains a part of life in modern Spain.

In grappling with Velázquez, the time has come for a full-scale visit to the Prado. Already, in trying to understand something of Spanish painting, I have inevitably had several dips into this magisterial collection. Here, for instance, are not only some of the best of early Spanish paintings – Pedro Berruguete and Luis de Morales, Juan de Juanes and Sánchez Coello, for example – but also the incomparable collection of Flemish primitives put together mainly by the Spanish Habsburgs. Most of the Bosch canvases collected by Felipe II are here; so is Rogier van der Weyden's Deposition from the Cross. In my opinion – and not in mine alone – this has to be the most profound of early works produced in the Low Countries. Many of the Titians painted for Carlos V and then for Felipe II are here. And so it goes, on into the future, by way of Velázquez and contemporaries, both Spanish and foreign, and on again through Goya and the nineteenth century – the latter housed in a smaller building close to the main gallery – until we come at last to Picasso's *Guernica*, also in the rather stately outhouse. There are other magnificent galleries in Spain, the Bellas Artes in Valencia, of course, and sister institutions in Seville and Cádiz. The sacristy of Toledo cathedral is itself a small but dense collection of masterworks. In individual monasteries and churches all over Spain there are paintings familiar, at least in reproduction, to anyone who takes more than a passing interest in Spanish art. But in the last analysis, all pale into insignificance beside the Prado. This is the temple and we, the many thousands who pound the floors of its innumerable rooms, are the devout and sometimes exhausted worshippers. Like the Rijksmuseum in Amsterdam, this is a gallery that needs to be taken often in small doses.

There are, by my calculation, fifty-seven Velázquez canvases in the Prado, almost half of his entire known output. Velázquez was a slow painter and there were long periods of his career when he scarcely touched a brush. Even so, in discussing his work, it will from time to time be necessary to range abroad to point to particular examples. My own prescription for enjoying Velázquez is to get to the Prado if at all possible or, failing that, at least to see whatever is available close to home. London and New York are particularly well endowed and there are other Velázquez works from Edinburgh – the *Old Woman Cooking*, for example – to Cleveland, Ohio, Vienna, Leningrad and Paris. Even to see just one or two will give an idea of tone and scale and how the paint is worked. After that, since Velázquez's *oeuvre* is small enough for almost the whole of it to be illustrated in a single volume, art books serve unusually well. The catalogue of the great Velázquez exhibition of 1990 is one source. Even better is the full-scale study by the American scholar Jonathan Brown. His book *Velázquez, Painter and Courtier* amounts to a personal Velázquez exhibition easily consulted in the privacy of home.

Perhaps the most convenient beginning here will be to look at Velázquez's work from his arrival in Madrid, considering it both in its biographical context and simultaneously as a window on his times.

The first trip to Madrid in 1622 was not a huge success. Velázquez painted a penetrating portrait of Luis de Góngora, most sonorous of baroque poets. But he got no work from the court and soon returned to Seville. Within a few months, however, one of the small group of official court painters died and Velázquez was summoned back. The ruling monarch by this time was Felipe IV. He had come to the throne two years before at the age of sixteen. Velázquez, not so very much older than the king, quickly achieved the role of royal portrait painter. According to Pacheco, his admiring father-in-law, there was an agreement that only he should paint the royal portrait.

From now on, one of the great themes of Velázquez's work will be his representations of Felipe IV. There were many of these, for royal portraiture had many functions: in establishing marriage alliances, in exchanges of gifts with other courts, in amplifying and insisting on the dignity and power of the subject of the painting. No court anywhere was so dignified and formal as that of the Habsburgs in Madrid. Ambassadors calling to present their credentials encountered in Felipe IV a figure who scarcely stirred, and certainly paid them no personal attention. Contemporaries recall that when he spoke he moved no part of himself at all except his tongue and lips. There is a story of Felipe IV out on an excursion to a monastery with his much-loved little daughter. His wife, the queen, is 'almost swooning' at the antics of the child. Felipe himself has to hide a smile behind his arm in order to preserve his irreproachable gravity.

Every Velázquez portrait of the king echoes this quest for the impassive, and by the same token enters the Habsburg canon of deliberate reticence. Just as in the time of Felipe II, this was an inverted assertion of power by the king of what was still, at the start of the reign, the strongest, the most feared and probably the most hated nation on earth. As the reign progressed, in the traditional attempt to preserve his territory and interests, Felipe IV found himself almost continually at war, sometimes on a global scale, with hostilities ranging from the Pacific right the way round again to Latin America. As he grows gradually older, we see the cost and strain begin to take their toll. But what Velázquez offers is not the romantic progress of a man moving towards melancholy as his nation declines. Rather it is, as always, an updated account of monarchical formality. Even the portraits of the king out hunting, intended for the royal hunting lodges, reveal a very solemn subject.

As for the wars, Velázquez offers, naturally enough, a vision of glory. In 1621, at the end of the twelve-year truce with the Low Countries, Spain returned once more to that unwinnable and disproportionately expensive conflict. Some successes came early on, among them the capture of Breda after a long siege. One of the most familiar and elaborate of all Velázquez images depicts the moment of high chivalry when the victorious Spanish general accepts the keys of the city from the defeated Dutch. The Spanish general, actually the Italian-born Ambrosio Spínola, leans forward to Justin of Nassau. With an expression of ineffable, sweet graciousness, he reaches out in compassion to prevent his former enemy from kneeling. Beside, to the right, is the huge horse from which the Spanish general has symbolically dismounted. Behind, again to the right, are the Spanish veterans, their lances fierce and upright as a forest of burnt pines along the skyline. Small wonder that this picture is known in Spanish as *Las Lanzas*. To the left, behind quite wonderful individual portraits of participants, intent on the exchange of keys, staring right out of the picture at the viewer or simply looking down at their own hands, the scanty weapons of the Dutch are less than threatening. The picture is a *tour de force*, based not on what actually occurred at the transfer of the keys, chivalrous though it was, but on a text from a play on the subject by the great Golden Age dramatist Calderón de la Barca.

After Breda in 1625, with a few much-lauded exceptions, it was downhill all the way for Felipe IV. 1635 saw the start of a long-running and disastrous war with Bourbon France, the rising power that would eventually overwhelm the Habsburgs. In 1640 Portugal rebelled, starting the process that led to the recovery of her independence. Also in 1640, Catalonia began a twelve-year secession that threatened to tear the emerging nation-state of Spain to pieces. The region was finally reduced by full-scale military operations.

The man who ran Felipe's wars for him – invented them and prosecuted them, along with desperate attempts to sustain the economy he was ruining all the while – was the inordinately energetic royal favourite, the Conde-Duque, or Count-Duke, of Olivares. Once again, as with Felipe II, the historian J. H. Elliott offers an unforgettable glimpse of the man, hustling and hassling, voice booming down the palace corridors, his hat and pockets stuffed with state papers.

Olivares was from Andalucía and had had intermittent contacts with members of Pacheco's academy. It was he who summoned Velázquez to Madrid and through him that other members of the 'Seville connection' were shortly to reach the court. In this way, both he and the Pacheco academy made an immense contribution to the arts. Velázquez created several memorable representations of the Conde-Duque, openly asserting his power and substance, the more so as it came in question. The Olivares pictures, admirably capturing the pomp and swagger of the man, include the most forceful of Velázquez's equestrian portraits. This shows the Conde-Duque astride a rearing horse, which faces diagonally away from us towards a distant landscape rent by battle.

There is no direct allusion in the paintings but one could, at a pinch, adopt these works as a point of reference for the many schemes that Olivares sought to impose on Spain. The impulse came from Spain's progressive economic failure. As wars proliferated and the flow of American bullion diminished, debts grew at a prodigious pace. Industry and agriculture meanwhile lay wounded. The kind of people who might today write endless letters to the papers, known somewhat dismissively as *arbitristas*, schemers and armchair politicians, put forward endless explanations and proposals. Some thought the troubles had begun with the expulsion of the Moriscos. Others put them down to the influence of foreign finance. The Conde-Duque paid close attention and was always attempting, against resistance and without success, to re-order banking and taxation. His main anxiety was the unfair burden falling on Castile.

Like any representative of central government, the Conde-Duque believed that full-ranking membership of the central state, for individuals as well as the component regions, would be a mighty privilege for which all would be genuinely grateful. In this spirit, he tried to confer on Catalans, Valencians and Aragonese, as well as on Neapolitans and American colonists, the positions and privileges open to Castilians and, at the same time, to make them pay their fair share of the expenses of the enlarged Castilian concept. This was bodied out in an Olivares dogma called the Union of Arms, by which all parts of the Spanish empire would have to put up men and money, in a fixed proportion, for furtherance of the imperial wars. The Aragonese and Valencians submitted, partially and grudgingly. The Catalans simply refused, seeing no benefits for themselves in being part of a larger unit. They reckoned Olivares's schemes a gross example of Castilian imperialism. In due course, as the war with France developed, Olivares tried to force Catalonia to participate by making the Catalan–French border the main theatre of operations. Matters went from bad to worse, with vast numbers of desertions and bitter acrimony. Next, Olivares billeted the Castilian army on Catalan villages and towns. The result was a fierce rebellion, the viceroy killed on the beach as he tried to escape from Barcelona in a galley, the rebels themselves turning progressively against the aristocrats in what once again became a social revolution. Catalonia, independent and in turmoil, now looked to the French for help but found herself, instead of rescued, an economic colony of France. Twelve terrible years ensued before reconquest, after a long siege at Barcelona, by Felipe IV's more experienced troops.

Though for the moment the Catalan question seemed settled, one may certainly say of Olivares that in the short term his policies led to much suffering. And in the long term, nothing at all had been achieved except the further alienation of Catalonia. Meanwhile, in 1643, Olivares himself had fallen and the economy had taken yet another long step downwards towards its own destruction.

Olivares died, broken and mad, in Toro two years later. Felipe stayed on the throne for another twenty years. In depicting war and monarchy and Olivares, not to mention his painting of the *Expulsion of the Moors*, destroyed in a palace fire, Velázquez touched on the main themes of the century. Other issues also surface, if only by inference.

Take slavery, for instance. Velázquez had a slave of his own from Andalusian days, a man of Muslim descent named Juan de Pareja. Velázquez painted a magnificent portrait of him, depicting him as a man of dignity and worth. In the 1650s he freed Pareja who went on to become a painter in his own right. There is a fine example of his work, colourful and detailed, in the Velázquez exhibition catalogue, and several canvases to be seen in the Prado. Then there are the Velázquez paintings of dwarves and jesters, retained at court to play with the royal children, to entertain the adults and to remind their Habsburg masters of their own comparative stature and good looks. The question here is the attitude Velázquez took to them. Some think these portraits, commissioned as they were for the royal palaces, contain more than a touch of mockery. Perhaps with a little wishful thinking, I see them as clear-sighted statements of common humanity, sometimes done with humour but also sympathetically recording loss, vacuity, even a spirit of resistance.

One could continue with a long list of points at which Velázquez works throw light of one kind or another on the period. To end, though, with just one final instance, the *Rokeby Venus*, named after the English country house where she resided for centuries but also known as *Venus at her Toilet*. This is the only surviving example of a Velázquez nude (he is thought to have painted three others). It shows the back view of a woman of perfect loveliness, attended by Cupid as she lies full-length on her side, holding up a mirror to her face. Given the rarity of nudes in Spanish painting, especially of female nudes, it is interesting to learn that she was painted for the corrupt nephew of Olivares, the man who succeeded him as royal favourite, or *valido*. It is a neat example of the kind of art created for the private pleasure of wealthy men.

In working unswervingly for Crown and monied interests, there is much in Velázquez that may strike the reader as likely in one way or another to be compromised. Yet this is a response that viewers never seem to have. Reactions range from awe to simple pleasure, from an almost mystical sense of depths within the paintings to the easy appreciation of surface felicities. What is it then, one asks oneself at first, ready to join the choruses of praise but needing a little extra exegesis, that makes the work of this one painter so utterly compelling? What is it that lets him stand alone in the great century of Spanish art?

In starting to approach an answer, it is necessary first to chart the introduction into Spain of the vivid lighting techniques developed in Italy and used, in one way or another, by the young Velázquez and his Spanish contemporaries. This will have the added advantage of introducing two older painters of the age without whom the story might have developed in markedly different ways. They are Francisco Ribalta and Jusepe Ribera, the former known mostly for his work in Valencia, the latter a Spaniard resident in Naples.

Ribalta lived from 1565 to 1628. Catalan born, he first tried his luck as a painter in Madrid and the Escorial penumbra. Felipe II had imported successive waves of Italian fresco painters to decorate El Escorial and these exerted a considerable influence on Spaniards of the day. Ribalta was exposed to them for a significant period. But failing to make a name for himself in the capital, he withdrew to Valencia in his mid thirties and here, little by little, his artistic practice grew. He did fine works in parish churches, many destroyed in 1936 at the start of the Civil War, and in due course received enough commissions to establish his own workshop. This marked the start of a new period of excellence in Valencian painting. His own great moment sprang from the religious visions of a local priest.

Wandering the streets of Valencia at night, Francisco Jerónimo Simón met Christ carrying the cross. As Christ passed the priest, he parted the long locks hanging down across his face. Behind him came the Virgin Mary, Mary Magdalene and St John the Evangelist and behind again a troop of Roman soldiers blowing trumpets. Simón saw his vision several times and its intensity was overwhelming. In the grip of religious ecstasy, he finally lost consciousness and died. The event caused a great stir and though the Church was ultimately to forbid the portrayal of Simón with a halo, thus casting doubt on the veracity of the vision, Ribalta painted early versions of the scene for the Pope, for Felipe III and for his *valido*, the Duke of Lerma. There is a magnificent example in the National Gallery in London, full of dramatic light and darkness, of trumpets, suffering and revelation. A sticker on the back, now mostly obliterated, bore the handwriting of the nineteenth-century traveller Richard Ford, author of the great *Handbook for Spain*, telling how he made the purchase in Valencia in 1831.

Ribalta's last works are reckoned to show the influence of Caravaggio as transmitted by Ribera. This resident of Naples, who lived from 1591 to 1652, enjoyed a Europe-wide success. He had scarcely reached his mid twenties at the time when his style was influencing the mature Ribalta. Much of Ribera's work was for the Spanish market, which explains the excellence of the Prado's collection.

By now, in one of the major shifts in art, the baroque era was arriving, with naturalism straining heavenwards to serve ends that were fundamentally spiritual. El Greco's Mannerism had gone and instead we are offered realistic representations of the individual, in large, dramatic scenes, evocatively lit. Byron mocked Ribera for glorying in gruesome martyrdoms and certainly, in visiting the Prado, one feels there is some justice in the accusation. But this is only one of several religious themes. His Trinity is excellent, his penitent Mary Magdalene has one of the prettiest faces in Spanish painting. The effect overall, leaving aside the look in Mary Magdalene's eyes, is one of monumentality.

Ribera is unquestionably one of the giants. Velázquez as a young man in Seville would probably have been unfamiliar with Caravaggio but he would certainly have known the new and dramatic style of Ribera. Right from the beginning, deep contrasts in lighting are one of the main weapons in Velázquez's armoury along with Low Countries subject-matter for his genre paintings. With sources in both the Netherlands and Italy, Velázquez was from the start in the mainstream of Spanish artistic development. Outwardly speaking, his career consists in taking these background elements, learning much more of both and developing them in line with his times, in line with his own sensibility and with the extraordinary acuteness of his observation.

One should also say quite firmly that the relationship between his eye and hand, the faithfulness with which he was able to record what he saw – the act of vision itself – must play a large part in his ability to transcend the normal limits of realistic art. He worked, so far as can be ascertained, laboriously, certainly slowly. Clients complained continually of late delivery and there are many references to his 'phlegmatic' approach. Obviously enough, the compositions are often formal, even at times constrained, yet one feels continuously in his work that he is able to do anything whatsoever that he intends. This gives the most formal paintings an uncanny sense of freedom. The poet Rafael Alberti describes his brush as 'a loosed bird', a phrase that goes near to the heart of the mystery. Velázquez seems to show an exceptional closeness to what he observes. We receive it, subjectively enough, as evidence of love for the observed world and its creatures. But the love, if such it is, is expressed without sentimentality.

The stages of his artistic career are well defined. The first great step was his appointment as court painter in 1623. His presence clearly aroused jealousies, not to mention the accusation that he was only good at faces. To settle the dispute a contest was organized; the set subject for Velázquez and the others was the expulsion of the Moriscos. It is said the jury was rigged. At all events, Velázquez won. Soon after this came an even more important event, the three-year visit to the Spanish court, on a diplomatic errand, of Pieter Paul Rubens, greatest of Low Countries Catholic painters (Rembrandt and the Protestants were, of course, inaccessible beyond the battle lines). There is evidence that Rubens spent a considerable portion of his time with Velázquez. Possibly the highly educated courtier-painter on his diplomatic mission served as a role model for the younger man. Velázquez would have seen Rubens at work – he breached the supposed monopoly and painted portraits of the king – and seen the Lowlander's richness, fluency and invention. Even more important, Rubens seems to have inspired in Velázquez a need to study the art of painting still more deeply.

Almost as Rubens left for the Low Countries, Velázquez successfully petitioned Felipe IV for permission to travel to Italy. He was
away more than a year, in Venice and, principally, Rome. Now,
more than at any other moment, his work underwent a revolution.
Never again can it be said that there is any failure in perspective.
Indeed, Velázquez has not only mastered classical perspective but
gone far beyond, to a position where he will soon be able to play
unprecedented tricks with the representation of space. He has also
become almost at a stroke that rarity in Spanish painting, a mythology painter. Those who spend some time in the Prado with
Vulcan's Forge, one of the most elaborate of the 'Italian' paintings,
will freely acknowledge that, from a standing start, he has almost
instantly become one of the great exponents of this branch of the
art. The workmen toiling at the forge, to whom Apollo brings the
news of Venus's infidelity to Vulcan, are vivid portraits of ordinary
mortals. Paint is thinner, brushstrokes lighter, light itself more
evenly diffused in ways that at first seem simple but are, the more
one looks, extremely complex. Already, the ground is being laid for
his final mythological masterpiece, the *Fable of Arachne*, a mixture
of myth and genre painting, taking and developing a tale from Ovid
to offer a whole series of simultaneous readings on themes ranging
from social order to the status of the artist. What we witness during
Velázquez's first trip to Italy – another was to follow some twenty
years later – is not only development in technique, but a growth in
allusive power and invention.

Starting in Italy, but gathering pace on Velázquez's return to
Madrid in 1631, comes another development that has long been an
astonishment to painters as well as critics. This is a tendency to
abandon the exact depiction of surfaces, as had for centuries been
the great tradition in northern art, in favour of painting light, form
and colour as faithfully as possible to the impression gained by the
eye. This is seen clearly in the painting of court clothing, where
amazing little squiggles of highlight, combined with the occasional
element of formal pattern, still manage to convey, as if one had seen
them with one's own eyes, the essence of an extravagant brocade or
a delicate piece of embroidery. The royal portrait known as 'The

Silver Philip', at the National Gallery in London, has been offered by critics as a key example of a technique which had now entered the Velázquez repertoire never to depart. The same effect may be observed in the downward hanging swag of Olivares's sash in the great equestrian portrait or in the butterfly ornaments in the hair of the infanta María Teresa in her portrait in the New York Metropolitan.

It may be argued by those who do not automatically give their first allegiance to the Italians that, by the time of his return from Italy, Velázquez is the most complete painter ever to appear in Western art. In mythology and religious painting, in genre, portraiture and landscape, even in the still-life elements lurking within larger paintings, there is nobody before or since who can surpass him. Comparative judgements being irresistible, I go along with this. From now on, Velázquez's career is a matter of articulating his perception in forms that, by and large, have been brought close to their final condition.

There are a few exceptions. In the clown and jester portraits, Velázquez seems to have felt free to reach for new effects, in one case entirely abolishing perspective in the background, in another drawing an opaque veil right across the face he is representing. Mostly, though, the growth is in depth and complexity, in reach and sureness.

Here, there is no more striking painting than *Las Meninas*, or *The Ladies-in-Waiting*, known in Spanish till this century by the more satisfactory title *The Family*. It shows Velázquez himself to left, serious of face behind his handlebar moustache, but posed in a rollicking, Frans Hals style. He pauses in thought before stepping forward to apply his brush to a huge canvas that occupies the whole of the left portion of the picture, a painting-within-a-painting but one with its back turned to us. Across the foreground of the painting proper various figures are ranged – two ladies-in-waiting, both with teenage face and figure, a dwarf, a midget jester, a dog (no painter ever better at dogs than Velázquez). Behind stand two other royal servitors and behind again, in the depths of the painting, the silhouette of a man is stepping endlessly in or out of an open door at the top of a few steps. The centre foreground is occupied by a young princess, in silver dress with salmon-coloured flowers on her bodice, a flood of gold and silver hair and an expression of clear-eyed curiosity. She seems at once adorable and, we suppose, adored. Her look, perhaps a little challenging, is directed at her parents, the king and queen, who stand outside the picture, exactly where the viewer stands to look at it, reflected jointly in a mirror behind their daughter's head.

In the absence of the king and queen, and bearing in mind the set of multiple presences and absences within the picture, not to mention the palpable presence of Velázquez, observing his painting-within-the-painting, unseeable by us, the French philosopher Michel Foucault concludes that *Las Meninas* is the purest possible representation of representation itself. His essay, difficult but finally fascinating, almost in the end a poem, has in our own day inspired a torrent of philosophy and criticism based on *Las Meninas*. This is merely to perpetuate a tradition, for from the start it has been felt by all who saw it that here in this picture lay not just a set of time-defying portraits in a brilliant and teasing composition, but an extra dimension beyond ordinary reach. Velázquez's biographer Palomino said that the work was 'truth, not painting', echoing the opinion of an age when verisimilitude was all. At the end of the seventeenth century, in a phrase that has always seemed to hold more than a mite of truth, the Italian artist Luca de Giordano pronounced it the 'Theology of Painting'.

Painting was one thing, however, and life as a courtier another. For while painters were menials, courtiers followed the most noble calling known to seventeenth-century Spain. And for Velázquez, little by little, the second occupation replaced the first. Parallel to his painting, he had all along held posts in the royal household, accumulating wealth and some prestige. His administrative duties grew and grew. Now, in his maturity, the roles of artist and courtier were brought together by his appointment to a post that required him to collaborate directly with the king in making purchases for the royal collection and arranging them in great baroque displays appropriate to the Habsburg court. Jonathan Brown argues that these were among the most notable creations of the age, graver and less luxurious than the decorative schemes of Louis XIV but worthy of comparison. Some of the paintings, as it happened, came from the collection of Charles I of England and reached the art market through the Commonwealth sales which followed Charles's execution. It would have been unseemly for one king to be seen to benefit from the beheading of another and the paintings actually came into Felipe's hands as gifts from a private Spanish collector. Velázquez advised on the authenticity of attributions.

He made a second trip to Italy, from 1648–51, to purchase paintings and sculpture for Felipe IV. Once again, while on his travels, he painted a number of masterpieces. But his rate of production was slowing almost to a standstill and in the final years, when he was capable of producing works like the *Fable of Arachne* and *Las Meninas*, the rate had dropped again, to an average of two finished paintings a year. Presumably he thought the growth of his other activities a compensation for the meagreness in this branch of his labours.

He was also, meanwhile, hot in the pursuit of his own ennoblement. After the helpful intervention of both pope and king, he was at last received into the initially resistant Order of Santiago, and allowed to wear its insignia for the last year of his life. This, perhaps, more than excellence in painting, was the achievement of his real ambition, the true reward for all his lifelong service. The knightly symbols on his chest in *Las Meninas* were painted in retrospectively, probably by his own hand and at the king's request. Their presence in the greatest of his paintings must surely indicate a major theme in any summary of his life and works.

Juan Martínez Montañés was reckoned the greatest sculptor of his age. Contemporaries called him the *Dios de la Madera*, the God of Woodcarving. His only serious rival was Gregorio Fernández, heir to Berruguete in Valladolid. Montañés was a southerner, however. Born in Jaén in 1568 and trained in Granada, he was drawn in due course to Seville where he became an intimate friend of Francisco Pacheco, Velázquez's master. Inevitably, Velázquez the apprentice must have known Montañés the mature sculptor. In 1635, Montañés, now nearing the age of seventy, arrived in Madrid – some twelve years after Velázquez – to carry out a commission. Velázquez painted a splendid portrait of him. It is an illusion, of course, but one feels one can almost read in the gravely serene face, with its broad brow, its eyes more direct than challenging, the uneven white moustaches and spade-shaped beard in the centre of the chin, the transition made in Montañés's lifetime from Mannerism to baroque, from frenzied anguish to sobriety and realism in representation. The sculptor, dressed as a gentleman – it seems Velázquez could never leave aside his argument about the social status of the artist – stands with knife or chisel poised over the bust he is carving. Velázquez has seized on that same moment of anticipatory thought in which he was to show himself in *Las Meninas*.

The subject of this fine portrait well deserved such homage. When you come across Montañés's work unknowingly, as I did once in a small town in the province of Córdoba, you realize at once you are in the presence of something special, a Christ perhaps who may be rheumy-eyed and suffering but one who carries his suffering impressively within, rather than declaim it from the rooftops. Where Gregorio Fernández in Valladolid produced work that inclines to emotional excess – magnificent in its way and nobody should miss his famous Piedad in the Museum of Polychrome Sculpture – Montañés is weightier and more inward. Two works he created for Seville cathedral in the early 1600s, his Christ of Clemency and the Immaculate Conception, were an inspiration for a generation of painters as well as sculptors.

Montañés was also the direct teacher to one of the finest artists of the next generation, that is to say the group immediately contemporary with Velázquez. Alonso Cano, the century's great artistic polymath, was not only sculptor, painter, architect and designer but an artist of extreme delicacy and sensibility, more able to produce the swooning response than almost any other. There is one place – if there are others I have not yet found them – where the work of Montañés and Alonso Cano can be seen together, each neatly demonstrating the talents of its creator. This is the sacristy of Granada cathedral where a grave Montañés crucifixion hangs above a case containing a small-scale Cano sculpture, from late in his career, of the Immaculate Conception. In the Montañés work, Christ bears his torment inwardly, as usual, with at his hip a contrasting flurry of tousled drapery. In the Cano work beneath, we see a young girl, sweet but firm, also with a touch of inwardness, bundled in a blue-painted, off-the-shoulder cloak that gathers bulkily about her hips. Much loved by the Spanish public, she seems the very ancestress of eighteenth-century Dresden. The Cano is undoubtedly more sentimental than the Montañés, yet each is masterful, the two together a statement not only about all-permeating Catholic faith but also the great tradition of Spanish sculpture.

As well as studying sculpture with Montañés, Alonso Cano studied painting under Pacheco, joining Velázquez there as an apprentice. We know the two spent four months living in the same house. In 1638, again a good deal later in his career than Velázquez and probably through Velázquez's influence, Cano was called to Madrid in the service of the Conde-Duque, Olivares. Perhaps this was a good time to be away from Andalucía, for in the wake of the 1640 rebellions in Portugal and Catalonia, Andalusian aristocrats were also plotting an independence movement. Olivares repressed the movement viciously. He himself, however, was now nearing the end of his period of greatness, harried on all sides and with his mental health declining. His fall in 1643 was a key moment for his entourage. Cano somehow survived the crash, only to encounter difficulties of his own.

It is clear that in his personal and financial life Cano was extremely disordered. An episode in the debtors' gaol in Seville was only brought to an end when a fellow-painter bailed him out. There is no truth in Palomino's assertion that he fled to Madrid after a duel. But the critic Camón Aznar, marvelling at the discrepancy between his works and the tangle of his personal affairs, is surely right when he speaks of Cano's life as 'filled with fits of rage and disastrous events'.

The most disastrous of all occurred one day in 1644, when he returned to his home in Madrid to find his young wife dead from multiple stab wounds. Cano was tortured and found innocent and an assistant, who had absconded at that moment, was finally blamed for the murder. No permanent damage was done to Cano's good name, but his own life was clearly changed by these grotesque events. He retreated for a while to a monastery in Valencia; not in flight, as has been alleged, for he took a large library with him. He returned to Madrid for a productive spell of painting but then, unable to re-enter secular life successfully, decided to take holy orders, back in his native Granada. Granada cathedral took him on, apparently in the hope of getting art-works on the cheap. Almost at once a bitter dispute broke out, with both sides decrying one another in a marvellously documented row. The cathedral prebendaries alleged that Cano was ignorant and irregular, scarcely attending mass. Cano for his part, says a biographer, was doing all he could to annoy the prebendaries. In the end, the matter went right up to the king who gave strong support to Cano. Finally ordained in Salamanca, he lived out the rest of his untidy, upset life between Granada and Málaga.

Throughout, in a manner beyond easy comprehension, he was creating works of delicate assurance across the whole range of arts that he had mastered. During his post-Valencia return to Madrid, he produced in *The Descent into Limbo* a painting that detains even the casual viewer, even among the many masterpieces in the Prado. Firm, dignified and tender, it exemplifies the potent mixture of moods that Cano had at his command. Some critics quibble over the modelling of the figure of Christ at centre, but none could disagree with the assertion that the portrait of Eve, naked and with back to us in the Velázquez manner, is other than beautiful in her monumental presence – as well, of course, as being a great rarity in Spanish art.

In his final period in and around Granada, Alonso Cano worked on the frontage of the cathedral, designed the hanging lamps still to be seen there and painted a series of holy works, still also in the cathedral. He sculpted with great intensity. The collection of his work in the art gallery in Carlos V's palace up in the Alhambra offers a moving account of his many excellences.

*

Francisco de Zurbarán, painter of monks and monastery scenes, was the last great artist in this generation, an almost exact contemporary of Cano and Velázquez. But where Cano and Velázquez were sufficiently well-connected to have Pacheco as their master, Zurbarán received his training from a Seville painter of scanty reputation. The young apprentice came from a village in Extremadura and after three years in Seville, returned to his native heath, though this time to the somewhat larger town of Llerena. Poverty was severe in Extremadura; just a few years earlier, almost half the population of Cáceres were registered as paupers. In Llerena, in a threadbare community, he would have expected to live the life of a journeyman painter. If there were big commissions to be had, they would probably go to a painter brought in specially from Seville. Against the normal run, however, it was small-town Zurbarán who soon received a major commission for a series of paintings in a Seville monastery. How this came about remains uncertain, nor are there any known early works by Zurbarán which might offer an explanation. His first signed and dated piece, a Crucifixion painted for the monastery of San Pablo el Real, now in Chicago, is already the work of a great master. If comparisons are required, these must be with the finest religious works of the seventeenth century, with Montañés's Seville Christ or with Velázquez's Crucifixion in the Prado. Surging three-dimensionally out of tenebrist gloom, with a physical presence that was in its turn to exert an influence on sculptors, Zurbarán's soberly modelled and broadchested figure expresses huge dignity and patience in the face of suffering. Perhaps it is furthering a stereotype to speak of nobility in Spanish religious art, but it is hard to keep the concept at bay when thinking of Zurbarán's 1627 Crucifixion.

Now, in a city with so many monasteries and convents, numerous ecclesiastical commissions followed. Two years after the first Crucifixion, and mainly on the strength of it, Zurbarán was invited to take up residence in Seville. 'And the city will take good care to favour him and help him in all circumstances,' said the invitation from the town hall. This was not at all to the liking of some of the painters already living there, and it was Alonso Cano, as president of the painters' guild, who led a protest, on the bureaucratic grounds that Zurbarán had not taken his final examinations. In reply, Zurbarán pointed out to the town council that they had already shown their confidence in him as a painter and complained of colleagues 'envious of the favour that is granted me'.

Many of the images for which Zurbarán is most famous come from the next ten or fifteen years. There are large and complex paintings for monasteries with enough subject-matter to delight the iconographers. Here the palm goes to a series in the Hieronymite monastery in Guadalupe. This is the only Zurbarán series still in its proper place, though other visitors may find, like me, that they are whisked past by the guide too quickly to gain anything but a general impression of gravity and grandeur. It was commissioned by the monks to glorify their own foundation at a time when primacy among Hieronymite institutions had passed to El Escorial. Zurbarán also painted an outsize series of mythological works, 'The Labours of Hercules', for the Buen Retiro palace in Madrid. But overwhelmingly the paintings on which his popular reputation lies are his portrayals of individual monks and saints. The cowled St Francis holding the skull that reminds him of the vanity of existence, or kneeling as a penitent with the skull set out in front of him, the monks with their strong faces emerging out of darkness into brilliant highlight – all these are as unforgettable as anything by Velázquez and form one of the stock images of Spain. Here, strength and faith are bodied forth in the most dramatic intensity.

The other lasting impression is of the monks' long habits, white or cream, grey in the shadows, falling in what a French critic has described as 'snowy ranges'. Sometimes these gowns occupy a full third of a canvas. When the paintings of the monks are seen together in a series, as at the Bellas Artes in Cádiz or in the Academy of San Fernando in Madrid, one of the best galleries in Spain, the effect of their habits is revealed as something entirely individual to Zurbarán. Even in a painting like *St Peter Nolasco's Vision of the Crucified St Peter*, in the Prado, where the habit has to contend with a saint being crucified upside down, the gown may still be the most memorable part of the composition.

The French romantics saw an unearthly, thrilling asceticism in these paintings. The Cubists loved them for their ordering of planes and volumes. I suspect that today their colour has a particular appeal, along with whatever messages of our times we happen to read into them. They undoubtedly comprise one of the great achievements of the Spanish seventeenth century.

We hear slightly less about Zurbarán's female saints though the more one looks at them the more remarkable they seem. Tall, often high-coloured, and dressed in dazzling costumes of the kind today described as ethnic, they parade across the canvases like fashion-models. St Margaret of Antioch, for instance, indifferent to the dragon behind her, is carrying over her arm a sumptuous double bag, the kind that would hang on either side of a donkey's back except that it looks too expensive for the purpose. She wears a smart straw hat with a curly brim (as also does the Virgin Mary, observed during the Flight into Egypt). St Elizabeth of Portugal is even more remarkable, with dark, dramatic face and robes of almost poisonous brilliance, an image that is both quite beautiful and mysteriously repugnant. She lifts her skirt in front of her like a murderess about to tiptoe up the stairs. The darkness that surrounds her is almost absolute.

Ranking with Zurbarán's saints are his still lifes, few and sober, drawing on the Low Countries' reverence for objects and lit with Italianate flair. Another source, undoubtedly, was the work of Juan Sánchez Cotán, an ascetic Carthusian monk-painter whose work is almost as tactile as Zurbarán's. A few Sánchez Cotáns can be seen in Granada, in the palace of Carlos V. In one fine painting of his, in California, fruits and vegetables are either suspended in a window embrasure or lying in careful order along the sill, all of them, though very real as fruit and vegetables, arranged in imitation of musical notation. Sánchez Cotán is a worthy source for a greater master. And then, of course, there are the still-life passages within Velázquez's paintings.

Zurbarán, in other words, had a growing tradition of still life to draw upon in Spain as well as through his foreign sources. He took from all and created work that equals and sometimes transcends almost all of them. Take, for instance, the famous *Still Life with Oranges*. Here, a dish of lemons, a small basket of oranges and a mug of water standing on a dish with a carnation, are ranged in processional order across a table, each object in utter solemnity and spatially separated from the others. Perhaps there are particular inner messages; the blossom on the oranges may indicate perpetual life, for instance, the water in the mug, if water it is, may stand for purity. Yet one feels in the very gravity and regularity of the composition, especially in the separation of objects from each other, some deeper metaphysical impulse at work, as if a statement were being made about the nature of things. One is reminded of the creed of the American poet William Carlos Williams: 'No poetry except in things.'

Monks and saints, both male and female, and simple-seeming still lifes showing humble objects – these, for me, are the glories of Zurbarán. Others may prefer the more complex and allusive works like the series at Guadalupe. In all cases, it is clear that the subject-matter was dictated by the market and that Zurbarán was as commercial as any other painter. When new possibilities opened up, he tried to respond. As particular 'lines' became unsaleable he ceased to paint them.

Consider his expedition to Madrid where he was to paint for the Hall of Realms in the Buen Retiro, the same interior for which Velázquez's *Surrender of Breda* and some of his best equestrian portraits were destined. Zurbarán, despite his lack of preparation for such a task, obediently did his best with the prescribed but unfamiliar scenes from 'The Labours of Hercules'. His fame was by now considerable and Felipe IV came down sometimes to watch him work, vouchsafing the often-quoted remark that Zurbarán was 'painter of the king and king of painters'. But nobody could be happy with an end result in which the hero Hercules, adoptive ancestor of Spanish royalty, looked like a modern body-builder with a bad back. That was the end of Zurbarán's royal service. Had it been otherwise there might have been a thousand courtly paintings instead of a steady flow of religious works. On the other hand, after his Madrid visit, Zurbarán decisively modified his style, reducing a tenebrism that had begun to look old-fashioned and from now on painting pictures that had a more general radiance.

In Seville, there was at this time severe financial trouble, caused both by the long war with France, starting in 1635, and by the general decline of the Spanish economy. Monastic commissions ground to a halt. Zurbarán now tried, with some success, to work speculatively for the American market, dispatching paintings for sale on commission by ships' captains. These were rather general in subject-matter, suitable for as many settings as possible, workshop products, often poor in quality. At home, he continued to paint for private patrons. Here, too, a fresh approach was called for.

The Church had now admitted a number of more popular subjects into the repertoire, often drawn from the Apocrypha. With this came a tone that was less austere, exemplified in the work of the young Bartolomé Esteban Murillo, who now rose like a comet, commanding fees far greater than any Zurbarán could earn. Zurbarán's reputation had been built on gravity and austerity. Softening his style, he produced some lovely work in the new manner. But he was no longer a young man and it is clear that he was struggling. And now, to add to personal and public difficulties, there came the great Seville plague of 1649, a raging sickness that killed half the population of the city. There was no longer time for the respectable to make their wills; the poor died in the streets and lay there. Zurbarán himself seems to have lost several of the children of his three marriages. (The great number of remarriages stemmed from the horrifying mortality among women in childbirth.)

In 1658 he moved to Madrid to start a new life. In 1664, a creditor, not a debtor and in better circumstances than has sometimes been asserted, he died in rented lodgings in the capital. Meanwhile, the baton in Seville had passed definitively to Murillo.

Murillo, painter of Andalusian Virgins ascending amid puffballs of angels, of Holy Infants playing with the cuddliest of lambs, of laughing street children and smiling flower girls, was held until modern times to be one of the greatest painters ever to have lived. His reputation then suffered a disastrous decline, only now yielding to a calmer estimate of him as brilliant draughtsman and colourist, expressing better than any other Spanish painter the newly arrived mood within religion. There is also, as witnessed in the Valencia Bellas Artes, and in any venue where enough of his work is assembled, a firmer and more resolute observation, too often ignored. He was undoubtedly a painter of quite exceptional talent who offered many easily pleasing images and a few that were more austere. He lived in Seville the whole of his life, from 1617 to 1682, and his temperament seems to have been as sweet and loving as his paintings might suggest.

In his own day, indeed right up to their dispersal in Napoleonic times, one group of paintings in particular was considered his masterwork. These were painted for the extraordinary Sevillian foundation named La Caridad, the Charity, already in Murillo's lifetime the subject of legend.

La Caridad had been founded in the sixteenth century for the unusual purpose of burying the dead. The first of the legends has the founder himself cutting down the corpses of hanged men – after the regulation one week of display – or gathering the rotting bodies that had already fallen, in order to give them a decent resting place. The order experienced some decline in the early seventeenth century but was revitalized in the 1660s, partly by plague and the necessity of giving a burial to paupers but also by another remarkable figure around whom, as round the founder, legend soon accrued. Miguel Mañara Vicentelo is said to have been, and indeed claims in his own will to have been, a spectacular sinner. A stone at the church doorway tells how he lay here at his own request till moved to a resting place under the altar by the wishes of the brotherhood. Mañara's hope was that all should tread upon his anonymous remains, unworthy of a place in the temple of God, while pondering the inscription, 'Here lie the bones and ashes of the worst man who ever lived. Pray to God for him.'

It is an extravagant, luxurious self-abnegation, reminding one of Felipe II's domestic arrangements. In popular belief, Mañara was soon promoted to seducer of nuns and a duellist who mercilessly dispatched the many husbands whom he had cuckolded. He has long been held in Seville to have been the source of the whole Don Juan legend, embracing Tirso de Molina's Don Juan Tenorio and Mozart's Don Giovanni. This seems, alas, to be a mistaken theory. It is known for certain, however, that Mañara inherited a fortune in 1648 at the age of twenty-one, and that upon the death of his own young wife thirteen years later, he became a spectacular penitent. Hounded by nightmare thoughts of physical corruption, he was accepted as a member by a slightly apprehensive Caridad. Within a year, just as some brothers had feared, he emerged as the head of the order, reinvigorating the work of burying the dead and venturing into a range of other charitable work. According to Jonathan Brown, ubiquitous art historian of the period, Mañara believed that only charitable work could save the souls of sinners such as himself. This was the basis of the programme for La Caridad's new church. Murillo was commissioned to contribute to it in the 1670s.

Visitors entered the church by the main doorway, to be accosted immediately by two terrifying visions of death and decay by the painter Valdés Leal and then, advancing up the aisle, Murillo's works hung to either side, celebrating the whole range of charitable endeavour – the Loaves and Fishes to represent the feeding of the hungry, Moses Sweetening the Water for the quenching of thirst, another painting to stand for the visiting of the sick, another for ministering to those imprisoned and so on, right up to the altarpiece where the Entombment of Christ reflected the main purpose of the charity, the burial of the dead.

Though many from the original series are gone, enough remains in place to give a good idea of how the ensemble would have appeared.

The confrontation in La Caridad of charity with corruption, of grace and charm with a terrifying, creepy-crawly view of death, may stand as a powerful symbol of much in seventeenth-century Spain. Another confrontation is between the grave, ascetic monumentality of Zurbarán and the lightness of Murillo at his more relaxed, each representing a great stream of the Spanish character; El Escorial, as it were, compared to plateresque. Murillo and Zurbarán, Alonso

Cano and the other artists of Spain's great Golden Age, in all their differing and complementary ways, were, one feels, capable of looking deep into the essences of things while also rendering their visible surfaces. But high above them all the figure of Velázquez towers. Both he, as a painter, and Cervantes in the world of writing, deployed the eye that sees straight through.

6 Enlightenment and Black Reaction

Goya's Inheritance

O NLY THE GRANDEUR and apparent immutability of the
court could have blinded its members to what was happening
in the middle years of the seventeenth century. Felipe IV appears to
have understood, even while he reached for baroque glories, that his
nation's troubles were mounting uncontrollably. He blamed his
sins, sought consolation in an endless correspondence with Sor
María de Ágreda, a Franciscan nun and mystic in distant Aragón.
She, in her innocence, advised him on matters of state as well as
conscience; he repaired more often to the penitential gloom of El
Escorial, sometimes lying in the tomb that awaited his demise. In
1648, the Protestant Low Countries were granted their inevitable
independence. In 1659, at the Treaty of the Pyrenees, peace with
France was bought at the expense of Rossellón and Cerdaña, the
Catalan counties that Fernando the Catholic had recovered for the
monarchy so long ago. By the same treaty it was agreed, with
fateful consequences, that María Teresa, Felipe's daughter, should
marry the rapacious young Louis XIV of France.

The two monarchs were uncle and nephew. They met to seal the
agreement on the tiny Island of Pheasants in the Bidasoa, the river
that divided their territories as it ran down through the Basque
Country. Velázquez was there, notably well-dressed for what proved
the last of his grand official functions. He died in Madrid in 1660,
his king in 1665.

Carlos II, the feeble son of Felipe's late marriage to his niece, now came to the throne, aged four, with his mother as regent. His jaw was more seriously deformed than that of any of his ancestors, his future to consist increasingly of fits and mental confusion. Thirty-five years later and it was all over, the last of the Spanish Habsburgs dead and gone and Spain, as it entered the new century, under the rule of a French Bourbon – Louis XIV's grandson, Philip of Anjou, Felipe V of Spain.

The place to meet the Bourbons and the eighteenth century is in halcyon high country north of Madrid, at the palace of La Granja, technically La Granja de San Ildefonso and incomparably the most appealing of Spain's post-Moorish royal residences. Coming up out of the capital, you cross the Guadarrama Mountains, leaving El Escorial a short way to the west. The road now climbs through suburban-gracious summer settlements, past the winter skiing station of Navacerrada, then down again, not quite so far, through resin-scented air. Pines soon give way to elm and oak, ash and black poplar, all Spanish natives. When you begin to encounter such exotics as the maple, you are close to La Granja. When you go beyond it and look back, you can see that the palace and its un-spoiled little town are set on a sloping apron, a wooded lap beneath the green and grey of mountain. This is a soaring countryside of leaf and water, a final breath of freshness and delight before the aching countryside of Old Castile, with Segovia a stone's throw off and Avila not more than an hour's driving.

In royal terms, the site was already an old one, used as a base for hunting parties from the fourteenth century. In the fifteenth century, Enrique IV endowed a monastery on the spot, dedicated to San Ildefonso of Immaculate Conception fame. Isabel and Fernando were enthusiastic visitors. Eventually a *granja*, or farm, grew up in association with the monastery, giving the complex its modern name. Felipe V, first of the Bourbons, came here on a visit and was immediately enchanted, deciding that this was the perfect place for his retirement. He had been king for almost twenty years and longed to emulate Carlos V in his retreat to Yuste.

The years from 1700 had been hard ones. The Bourbon takeover of Spain, and Louis XIV's reported saying that now the Pyrenees had vanished, filled neighbouring countries with alarm and dread. Soon a general conflict, known as the War of the Spanish Succession, broke out across Europe. In Spain, Archduke Karl of Austria, the Habsburg champion passed over for the crown in 1700, now put himself at the head of the anti-Bourbon forces in Aragón, Valencia and Catalonia, advocating the kind of decentralized, federal state that the Spanish Habsburgs had traditionally supported (except during the unfortunate years of the Conde-Duque). With the help, among others, of the British, Karl did extremely well, twice taking Madrid though never holding it. In due course he lost Valencia and Aragón and, after his election as emperor in 1711, set off for eastern Europe, abandoning Catalonia to its fate. The French had by now also pulled back, successfully separated from Spain by the course of the war. This left the Catalans alone, and soon in possession of nothing more than the city of Barcelona. The tenacity with which they held the capital of their hopeless, ruined territory, their courage and endurance, were an amazement right across Europe. Their punishment, when the city fell in 1714, was the loss of all their traditional rights and institutions, Catalonia now following Valencia and Aragón into the maw of a centralizing state. Navarre and the Basque Country, by contrast, had remained loyal to the Bourbons and retained their *fueros*, their historic rights.

The essence of the Bourbon state, always excluding Navarre and the Basque Country, was effectively its insistence on centralization. Rightly or wrongly, many historians have praised both this and the increased efficiency of Spanish administration. Certainly, a large bureaucracy grew up. For Felipe V, though, the main preoccupation was loss of territory – most of Spain's European possessions, the island of Menorca and that thorn-in-the-flesh for centuries to come, Gibraltar. He staged huge expeditions, to little avail, to recover his lost property, but at least managed to ensure that there would be Italian thrones and dukedoms for his sons to practise on. Now, as he reached La Granja, he was tired and ready to reinvoke the monastery-palace concept traditional to the Spanish monarchy.

The first building that he ordered up was a simple *alcázar* built around the cloister of San Ildefonso. To this, according to plan, he retired in 1724, abdicating in favour of his son Luis. Within a year, Luis was dead of smallpox and the weary Felipe V had to take up the throne again, ruling for a further twenty-one years, through intermittent bouts of madness. La Granja now became the summer palace of the king and court and something rather grander than the *alcázar* was called for.

Following Felipe to La Granja to check on the results, I enter by the back door in the routine manner and find myself at once in the hands of bureaucracy. My mistake, it seems, is trying to buy a book at the ticket counter while also trying to catch the guided tour assembling all around me. The opposition comes from a clerk determined to write out a full receipt.

'Please just write "Book",' I plead with him. He writes the title, then the author's name and finally the publisher. 'Thanks,' I say, relief showing too clearly. He takes a ruler and underlines the title. 'Thanks,' I say again, patience wearing thinner. Then, to my astonishment, he picks his ruler up once more, draws a diagonal line across the page and another at the bottom and then two more, top and bottom of the total. Work done, he looks up sadly, compelled at last to pass me the receipt, and at once there swims before my eyes a memory of all those Spanish banks where you have to queue twice over to achieve a single piece of business, of all those government offices where the only questions answered are the ones you ask, meaning that if you have not asked the right ones, your forms are still as badly out of order as they were the first time that you called. This, as much as centralism, is the Bourbon inheritance, a perpetual small insult to the Spanish people as well as to crass foreigners like myself. Worked up to a fine art under Franco, it is by no means to be surrendered by loving civil servants, however great the efforts of successor governments.

Once inside the palace, all this falls away at once. Much of the décor comes from later kings and queens but there is plenty to give an impression of Felipe and his second wife, Isabel Farnese, whose taste was dominant at the time of building. Most beautiful of all, for me, is the very first impression – no corridors at this period but room leading on to room, each doorway draped to either side in a shallow arc of finest Talavera lace. What the eye takes in appears to be a receding image of the opening in front of it, lace curtain behind lace, diminishing into the distance like an image endlessly repeating in a mirror. No sombre Habsburg could ever have achieved half so pretty an effect.

Then there are the pictures of the period, mostly by foreigners, Ranc, Houasse, Van Loo. Houasse is of interest because of the influence that his cheerful outdoor paintings had later on the young Goya, Van Loo painted a vast great spread of the whole royal family (seen at La Granja in a copy) just as Goya was likewise to do. Ranc offered only moderately charming portraits of the royal children, often with rather foxy faces; and Ranc, it must be said, was definitely a mixed blessing so far as wider issues were concerned. It was in his bedroom in the *alcázar* in Madrid, following a Christmas party with his friends, that the great fire of 1734 began, destroying the whole of the building along with much of the royal picture collection. The loss of so many great works, including a considerable number by Velázquez, was irreparable. So far as the building went, however, Felipe V was probably pleased with the chance to erect a modern substitute. It was, in fact, to replace the Madrid *alcázar* that he first summoned the Italian architects who worked on the second version of La Granja.

The tour of La Granja is snap, crackle, pop, ask no questions and out of the door quickly, in the unbecoming manner of the Patrimonio Nacional, the building's guardians. But once turned out into the gardens, with no time limit before dusk, the visitor can at last see the main façade in its proper setting and experience the pleasure of garden and palace exterior together.

It is often said that La Granja is a small Versailles, built to allay Felipe V's homesickness. In fact, the style of the palace we see today is more international than purely French, having, in addition to French echoes, some of the charm of the Italian villa and some of the grace notes of contemporary German palaces. Only the gardens are truly French in style though here too, with the centuries, there have been changes, a Spanish exuberance and freedom – the other cheek, as it were, of the face that offers the bureaucracy – showing more clearly with the growth of the great trees.

Rising on hilly ground above the palace, gravelled avenues cut through the woods on an even larger scale than at Versailles, offering mountain vistas or groups of mythological statuary, formal and informal all at once. On a hot day in midsummer, I see a large patch of snow high up towards the skyline. An artificial lake feeds fountains; the fountains surge and spray, if you get there on the right day, with huge enthusiasm. They photograph wonderfully and look quite as engaging in midwinter, stilled by ice and snow. It is half frivolity, half a magnificent voyage of discovery in a taste that for me, and I suspect for others, may have been alien in younger days. Best of all is a long cascade of shallow steps, water flowing over them as they descend, with trees to either side, towards a vista of white and gleaming marble urns, formal parterres and finally the centre of the palace façade. Columns of pinkish limestone reach the whole height of it. Above, there rise an ornate, square-cut pediment, the dome of the palace church and the grey-black glint of mountain slate. This graceful building, a centre-piece of the Spanish eighteenth century, is not at first sight even remotely Spanish. But with the coming of the Bourbons, however sorry the outcome may have been for Catalonia, we have already travelled a refreshing distance from El Escorial.

For most of the eighteenth century the tale of art and architecture is still dominated to an extraordinary degree by the court and the foreign influences acting on it. To find a style that is more purely Spanish one must venture out again into the provinces in search of the secular and clerical. The first impression, confirmed in a thousand florid doorways and *retablos*, is that this was a period in which local baroque, already reaching a rococo destination, exceeded itself in a wild Hispanic suberabundance, providing an opposition of a different kind to El Escorial. The classic instance is the doorway of the palace of the Marquis of Dos Aguas in Valencia, the building that now houses the National Museum of Ceramics. And yes, there is no denying it, the doorway is a phenomenon. At the base of a frolicsome façade cloaked top to bottom in alabaster, two hunched giants support the two-storey structure of the doorway. This contains, around a central and far calmer statue of the Virgin, mermaids with pendant breasts and tortured faces, old men holding up shields, quivers of arrows, crocodile heads and who knows what besides. The giant to the left is pensive if a little sulky under his huge burden, the figure to the right seems positively alarmed. Not slackening for a moment in sustaining the uncomfortable weight, they simultaneously decant two endless streams of alabaster water, entirely suitable for a marquis named Dos Aguas. The structure flows downwards like amber clotted cream, like swirling treacle suddenly petrified. In a world of wildest fantasy, the one touch of normality lies in the little white trenches dug by rain, genuine, ordinary rain, in the hair and scalp of the right-hand giant. Many who come to see the doorway shake their heads and go away again disgusted.

Except for the image of the Virgin, the Dos Aguas fantasy is the work of the sculptor Ignacio Vergara, not otherwise especially prominent. It was the Churriguera family, containing a host of architects, whose name was borrowed to form the adjective Churrigueresque, applied to all the excesses of the period. This is a shame in two ways: first, because one comes to think that the whole of the architecture of the time was in this style, which is untrue; second and related, some members of the Churriguera family did far more sober work, creating a number of Spain's great architectural ensembles.

Here, the showpiece is the Plaza Mayor in Salamanca, designed in 1728 by the youngest of the brothers of the first Churriguera generation. One day during my journeyings, towards the start of spring, I found myself taking coffee here at an outdoor table. Next door sat a father and small son, the boy with a plate of crisps in front of him. Dancers in the costumes of local villages were performing rather perfunctorily in aid of their Easter processions, but were really more interested in chatting with one another. Passers-by joined in the chat and then joined in the dances, stepping out more boldly than the official performers, skirts held in both hands and swished aside, revealing ankles thin and sometimes very fat indeed. The performers' high boots were elaborate and dashing, the women dancers sequinned, with a gypsy air. It was a chilly day and rather windy, but I was still unprepared when a gust of gale scooped all the coffee out of my cup and sent the small boy's crisps wheeling away up past the warm stone and the repeating window embrasures of the Plaza Mayor. Salamanca's severe climate is matched, I thought, right there in the eighteenth century, by the austere dignity of a Churriguera. No wonder local people still approve the place.

Two poles, Dos Aguas in Valencia and the Salamanca plaza. Between them lies an unexpected masterpiece hidden away in Andalusian sierra. There must be easier ways to get to Priego de Córdoba than by the back-country road from Loja, a spot made famous by Isabel and Fernando's Granada campaigns. If so, I never found it. The little road wound and climbed and doubled on itself among the olive groves and scrub, with steep descents to narrow bridges followed by brisk pulls up again. Spring had come on apace, the roadside glittering blue and red with flowers, the air fresh as the season, nothing to contend with on the way except a single motor cycle, now overtaking, now falling behind. Apart from aching arms and shoulders, I would not wish to have changed places with anyone on earth.

Nor was Priego de Córdoba a disappointment, even after the pleasures of the approach. Somehow, through the patronage of the Medinaceli family and the benefits of a local silkworks, this lost little town among low mountains achieved the purest and most beautiful effects within what one might call the florid sector of late Spanish baroque. There is a small church or chapel known as La Aurora with a huge wooden doorway to let the Easter floats get in and out. You enter by the side to find white walls and a round barrel of ceiling encrusted all over with plaster fruit and flowers and other vegetation, in places a foot thick. Wherever a vantage point occurs within the decoration, out pops the painted sculpture of a face. In the central panel of the ceiling there emerges a quartet of female figures, torsos clothed in gold, vivid against white, their upraised arms clutching floral bundles, their windswept, chestnut hair tossing in abundance. You might see them going past on bicycles if you stepped outside for just a moment. On a wide ledge to either side of an archway leading to the altar, there sits a female figure dangling bare feet in space.

The young man showing me around, boy rather, son of the sacristan, assures me with excitement in his voice that the whole town is full of tunnels, Moorish ones, leading from the site of the old mosque down to the castle, this way, that, the other. His arms wave wildly as we reach the street.

I follow the course of one of his presumptive tunnels, and soon find myself, after a little bit of town that has been tarted up unduly, at the main door of the large church of the Asunción. Inside is the little-visited but much-vaunted Sagrario or Tabernacle, my other main goal in Priego. It turns out to be a hollow wedding cake, white-stuccoed on the inside, an octagon retreating inwards as it climbs, first past a balcony with gold and grey railings, up past a storey of clear windows, up and up, appearing far bigger than it is, a complex, simple-seeming exercise in light and space. It did not surprise me to be approached, as I came away again, by several young townspeople who wanted to say quite simply that they too thought their Sagrario the epitome of grace and beauty.

Travellers in Spain soon get to know that Carlos III is one of the better brandies. The king who bore this name in person, the younger son of Felipe V, was certainly the best of Spanish monarchs in the century of absolutism. Fond of hunting and mechanically minded, he grew up as the reigning Duke of Parma, necessarily separated from his parents at an early age. His mother's regretful letters still make touching reading. Carlos then served for twenty-four years as king of the two Sicilies; Naples, the capital, was his first and greatest love. But in 1759, the death of his elder brother, Fernando VI, the reigning king of Spain, summoned Carlos to Madrid. Hearing the news, he shut himself up with his lathe for a week of woodwork before he could face the future.

On reaching Spain, the palace that he chose as most like home was Aranjuez, to the south of the capital, in a riparian oasis. With murmurous stands of trees along the river, it is famous today not only for Rodrigo's Aranjuez Concierto but for early asparagus and tiny strawberries, hand-reared and picked and wildly expensive. To get there from the city, you must first cross the bare-boned plain, in this direction exceptionally dreary. Its very cheerlessness makes the arrival in Aranjuez a pleasure for day-trippers like myself, whether come by coach or car or on the special weekend train. Feeling a well-earned sense of ease, we stroll among the great trees in kilometres of riverside parkland. We enjoy a small subsidiary palace in the woods – there are a couple of these royal 'cottages' at El Escorial as well – and file through a boat-house museum crammed full of gilded royal craft. The river now runs by a milky green, ghastly to look upon, but this aside it is all extremely pleasant. There is no difficulty in imagining courtly boating on the cleaner waters of the past and the parading of bewigged grandees among the low parterres.

By comparison with the setting, the royal palace itself, accumulated over centuries in many waves of building, is generally rather blank and dull. Carlos III made it blanker still by building long low wings to reach right forward on either side, so creating a wide and stony rectangle. Crafty photographers foreshorten the bare courtyard, making it look almost cheerful. The truth is that a pot of geraniums would work a wonder. Inside, however, it is far more interesting, though perhaps I should record that here my tour at the hands of the Patrimonio Nacional took eighteen minutes precisely, with machine-gun explanations and blurring notebook. Luckily I had visited the palace previously and had a good idea what I was after now – particularly Spanish-made chandeliers and mirrors and a single room decorated entirely in porcelain cladding.

The porcelain room was easy since we ran right through it. Memory suggests, and photographs confirm, that it was made up mostly of Japanese motifs and scenery, shamelessly copied. The chandeliers and mirrors were more difficult since some were from such distant countries as Bohemia. But those that were clearly Spanish were grand and imposing. The interest in all of them – mirrors, chandeliers and porcelain – is that they were produced in royal factories founded personally by Carlos III. From now on, similar fixtures were installed in all the royal palaces, giving them a great deal of the character they have today. The mirrors and chandeliers were made at La Granja in a royal glassworks, which also turned out graceful and unpompous smaller pieces. The porcelain factory was established in the grounds of the Buen Retiro in Madrid, using managers and craftsmen brought from Carlos's earlier, Capodimonte factory near Naples. In Naples he had commissioned a porcelain room for his queen, Amalia of Saxony. The aim at Aranjuez was to please her with something similar. She died, alas, before the room was ready and for the rest of his long, chaste life Carlos used it for his most personal meetings. The room looks out (I am sure of this despite the haste) right on to the river and the island garden, originally planted by Felipe II and prettiest of all the gardens in Aranjuez.

The kind of enterprise Carlos was backing in his factories was typical of the eighteenth-century Enlightenment, now in full spate in France and other northern European countries. But where Voltaire, Rousseau and Adam Smith were ranging freely in their thought, Spanish intellectuals were far more limited. Carlos was himself extremely authoritarian, unwilling to permit any challenge to his concept of monarchy. The continuing presence of the Inquisition made it dangerous to criticize the dogmas of the Church. As a result, the leading figures of the Spanish Enlightenment were concerned almost entirely with the spread of scientific thought and practical projects for bettering the realm. Under this rather limited guise, some quite outstanding work was done.

The monk Benito Gerónimo Feijóo from Oviedo university was the first great popularizer of the science of other nations. Another even more notable Asturian, Gaspar Melchor de Jovellanos, came to the firm belief that land would be best used by independent peasant farmers who, in a simple setting, would have a chance to cultivate the virtues of family love and mutual support. All this fell neatly into the eighteenth-century context of the pursuit of happiness. It also underlay a number of interesting practical projects, particularly new land settlements in the Sierra Morena. Jovellanos refrained from any display of religious scepticism but he felt strong enough to attack the Church in the exercise of its own functions. 'What remains of the old glory [of Castile],' he asked, 'other than the skeletons of its cities, once populous and full of factories and workshops, of warehouses and shops, today peopled only with churches, convents and [religious] hospitals, which have survived the misery they caused?'

One of the features of the age was indeed the continuing poverty of Castile. But in the periphery matters were looking up. The north coast prospered, Seville and Cádiz were coming to life again. Valencia had once again become a leading intellectual centre, liberal in its attitudes. The Catalans, deprived of their ancients rights and responsibilities, were nevertheless recovering strongly from the disasters of two generations ago. Indeed, their very success marked the start of the Catalan problem as it has often appeared in modern times – a thriving, capitalist society deprived of the right to handle its own affairs by a far less energetic centre. In this new situation, as well as in past struggles, there lay the seeds of bitter future trouble. The Basques, of course, still had their rights intact and it was to be more than a century before the emergence of serious strife round Basque identity. For the moment, theirs was among the most enlightened regions of the peninsula and it was here that the first of the Sociedades de Amigos del País was founded. The great humanities–sciences dichotomy had not yet been invented and these 'Societies of the Friends of the Country' made little distinction between art and their main interest of practical self-improvement.

Perhaps the greatest achievement of the Spanish Enlightenment was in the science of botany, hugely important in the eighteenth century. Here, the sponsor was the king himself and under his guidance Spanish flora was at last classified according to Linnaean rules. Expedition after expensive botanical expedition was dispatched to the wilds of Latin America and the Philippines. Carlos's brother, Fernando, had founded a botanical garden in Madrid. Carlos himself now moved it to a spot on the Prado where it still flourishes today, lusher and more restful than the Retiro, right beside the Prado gallery. The present gallery building was commissioned by Carlos, for a future it never fulfilled, as botanical museum and astronomical observatory.

It was all part of a great scheme for the improvement of the capital. Now the avenue running past the Prado got its fountains, Neptune and Cibeles, both still grandiloquently in place. Cibeles, in front of the much later post office, fussy with spires and turrets, stands at one of the main junctions of the city. It is almost impossible to visit Madrid without being conscious of the goddess in her chariot, her lions striding through the fountain's ample basin. Eighteenth-century prints show the scene with the flesh-and-blood horses of passing *caballeros* drinking quite calmly beside the sculpted lions.

Over on the far side of town, Carlos took the Palacio de Oriente, started by his father to replace the *alcázar*, sobered the design into the great dull bulk we see today and set about decorating it in royal style. It was designed to impress rather than charm, used only for some two months a year. Mirrors and chandeliers came trundling down from La Granja on the far side of the mountains with many breakages and at ruinous expense. The Italians Gasparini and Tiepolo, last flare of colourist late baroque, produced a swirl of painted ceilings. The Bohemian classicist Antón Rafael Mengs painted stylishly correct portraits of the royals (there is a charming scene of Carlos III in youth, identifying a wild flower). The greatest surviving public works of Velázquez, all today to be seen in the Prado, were hung in some profusion, along with the royal Titians.

Here and in other royal palaces, particularly the more domestic Pardo north-west of Madrid, there was a considerable need for tapestries. A royal tapestry factory had been established earlier in the century turning out works made specially for the spots they were to hang in. At first it was almost automatic to use the works of seventeenth-century Flemish masters as models. Then, when Mengs was given artistic leadership, changes began at once. It was he who first employed Spanish painters to produce Spanish designs and it was he who summoned Francisco de Goya y Lucientes to come from Zaragoza to work for him.

*

With Goya the Spanish people at last make a full appearance in Spanish art, along with tumult, outrage, piercing beauty, colours bright as any morning sky, menace, feminine allure, masculine bestiality, cruelties of all kinds, satire, grotesquery, witchcraft, doom, despair – and then at times the brilliant light of hope and reason which shines out radiantly. It takes a while to sort it out, even in the simplest terms of what was produced when, and how this relates to the all-consuming political history of the period. But never is the willing viewer likely to forget the shock of a first acquaintanceship with Goya or the mixed repugnances and pleasure of getting to know his work more thoroughly. Even today, after thirty years of appalled and astonished admiration, there are times when he makes me hide my eyes at revisiting some half-forgotten horror or step out with new joy at a transparent loveliness. Velázquez is the perfect painter, seldom flawed. Goya is far more patchy, but he sees everything and reacts to everything as nobody before or since, with the possible exception of Picasso.

His beginnings, though, were surprisingly slow and stumbling. Goya was almost thirty when he was summoned to Madrid and more than a decade would pass before he was within sight of his best work. Luckily he lived on into his eighties, continually developing and changing and over time producing the most profound and turbulent of meditations, most of it based firmly on the realities of Spanish life. For his images, when examined, turn out almost always to be local, culturally and geographically, and if we find them universal, as is inevitably the case, then perhaps that is due in part to the depth of the concentration that he gave to his own times.

Fuendetodos, where Goya was born, is a serious, stone-built village in the serious landscape of central Aragón. There is nothing soft or yielding here; not even a stream runs down the valley. In winter, the winds wail bitterly over the sierra. In summer, hills and fields are pitifully dry and sparse, eroded, chalky-looking. Anybody living here in the eighteenth century would inevitably amass a vast store of knowledge about the hardness of peasant life, the labour and grief and sufferings of men, women, children and animals. By Aragonese standards, though, the house where the future painter spent his first few years is solid and substantial. An act of will is necessary to turn it into the humble stone cottage essential to the romantic legend. For in this still popular interpretation, Goya is the rough and ready rural genius, the suffering, isolated soul who thrusts his way forward in his art through the power of an irresistible, untutored imagination. Only a fool could question the power and originality of Goya's imagination and the huge creative force that drove him on, but obviously, for the romantic version, the lowlier his origins the better.

Alas, the painter's father was a master gilder, definitely of artisan status, and his mother the daughter of minor aristocrats. Why she came to Fuendetodos to have her baby is still unclear, but in due course the family moved back again to Zaragoza, where Francisco attended the local branch of the Escuelas Pías, the Pious Schools. The reputation for good teaching in these remarkable institutions attracted aspiring students of all classes. Here Goya formed a friendship with a boy named Martín Zapater, to whom in adult life he wrote more than 130 surviving, though probably expurgated, letters. Zapater himself was to grow into a leading figure of the Aragonese Enlightenment. He became a successful businessman and, as such, a prominent member of the local Society of the Friends of the Country (which bore, in Zaragoza, a slightly different name). He was also a founder member of the Zaragoza Academy of Fine Arts, one of several institutions across the country devised in the shadow of the Academy of San Fernando in Madrid. The Madrid Academy, recently established by Fernando VI, was to play a considerable part in Goya's own affairs.

The essential point about these early years is that through Zapater and other members of what is sometimes called 'the Aragonese connection', Goya had access from his schooldays to the rapidly developing world of the Enlightenment. Acquainted with the realities of peasant life in Fuendetodos, he would inevitably have taken part in Zaragoza in discussions about the social utility of agriculture and commerce, perhaps of work in general, for work itself was now seen as a virtue. These are all themes he will develop later. It is also worth noting that Aragón, with only the Somport Pass between itself and France, had its own strong connections with that country. It has been shown that Goya's group in Zaragoza, with whom he stayed in contact for the whole of his career, was exceptionally alert to ways of thought that were developing there.

At first all this was little help to Goya in his painting. Apprenticed to an indifferent master, he struggled unavailingly for the success that came so easily to lesser talents. In 1763 and again in 1766, at the ages of approximately seventeen and twenty, he travelled to Madrid and there competed unsuccessfully in the drawing competitions mounted by the Academy of San Fernando. The prize would have been a grant to travel in Italy. Refusing to accept defeat, Goya somehow found funds of his own for an extensive trip through Rome, Naples and Lombardy, entering a competition in Parma and doing rather better than he had at home. Along the way, he probably met Antón Rafael Mengs, already court painter to Carlos III.

By the time of his return to Zaragoza at the age of twenty-five – Velázquez by this stage already had a monopoly on royal portraits in Madrid – Goya was at last able to pick up worthwhile commissions in his own home town. The first was in a chapel in the great basilica of El Pilar; the second in the Carthusian monastery of Aula Dei a few miles north-east of the city.

Satisfied in Fuendetodos but disappointed in El Pilar, where Goya's works are very hard to see, I make the trip to Aula Dei, in the company of Tim Bozman, English resident of Zaragoza and translator of a weighty tome on Goya in old age. Tim is tall, and seemingly mild, and learned, the very essence of the English gentleman-scholar. As for the monastery, a men-only establishment admitting not even female visitors, it has its own working garden, with a pleasant stream and novices in broad-brimmed hats, like bee-keepers without the veil. Our guide is an aged monk with shaven head, his breath a shaft of purest garlic. He tells us that there are twenty-six monks today where once there were eighty but that it is true they have a few new entrants – in this, they are unlike many monasteries. Being a novice can be a terrible experience, he says, worse than prison for any beginner who lacks the true vocation and spirit of solitude. He himself has been a monk for many, many years ... My attention, I'm afraid, has wandered, not least because Tim is whispering in my other ear a tale about Aula Dei, how farmers up above the monastery were paid to tip a pig into the stream at Lent. The monks would fetch it out again a few yards lower down, with a cry of thanks to the Good Lord for sending them a fish in time of need. I don't tell Tim but I recognize the story as an archetype, told of several Spanish monasteries, and if of Spanish no doubt of Italian, too, and French and Austrian. I like the story, though; what with Tim and our monkly guide and the fictitious porker, I am enjoying Aula Dei.

The church when we reach it is covered almost entirely in Goya paintings, easy to see as a result of restoration, which has also ruined parts of some of them. The general subject is the life of Mary and in a great flourish of energy they occupy the space above the door, most of both sides of the nave and both the transepts. Our guide pulls on his specs and dispenses floods of information but in a while, when he sees we are actually looking at the paintings, decides to leave us on our own.

'We are a silent order,' he says, 'if anyone comes in, please don't say a word to them.'

Monks do indeed come in, with brooms and pails, eyeing us askance and disappearing, after very limited cleaning activities, into what seem to be unlighted cupboards. We carry on with our cultural duties for, indeed, these paintings, so often neglected even by serious male students of Goya (and necessarily by female), turn out to be a considerable pleasure. The figures are large and sculptural, with plenty of space around them – in contrast here to the angel-ridden skies of other works of the period, even some by Goya. There are fine sweeps of clothing, touching gestures, noble holy figures, servant girls who sit in that lazy, sprawling manner that causes adults to rebuke teenagers. The Circumcision is striking, with a priest who looks like a Viking in a helmet and Mary very much a presence, despite the earlier thunderings of Pacheco against her representation in this scene. The handsome Visitation comes out as my favourite. But it is here, in the background, that Tim points out a phenomenon that immediately enters my mind as a category of its own like sixteenth-century transparencies. This is what he calls 'the Goya all-purpose tree', a vague deciduous creature with sideways-reaching, lobe-like leaves, suggestive of countryside and blown by the mildest of winds. I am to see a good many more of these, even in Goya's later work, as I go in pursuit of the master. Are they really as casual and perfunctory as they seem, we wonder here in Aula Dei, a way of blocking off a bit of space, conveying a simple atmosphere without much thought? I am also troubled by the rendering of secondary faces. They are swiftly impressionistic and there is enough implied to allow the viewer to supply the rest. But are they not painted with a deliberate crudeness, as if the owners of the faces were dumb and lumpy, perhaps to be mildly despised? Some critics seem convinced that in his later portrayals of the Spanish masses, Goya's great humanity always reveals the individual, often contrasting physical beauty with the imminence of the body's destruction. This is true, I think, on some occasions, but what we see in Aula Dei is the beginning of an ambiguity in attitude with something not far off a Goya all-purpose peasant face, hardly individual, a long way from complimentary.

The next step in the quest for Goya has to be the Prado in Madrid, for here there is a superb collection of the tapestry cartoons that he painted quite profusely on his arrival in the capital in 1774, following the summons from Mengs, and intermittently for most of the next twenty years. Once used as models for the finished tapestry, they were bundled up as unimportant and lay for a century in the royal tapestry factory before being recovered. The freedom of Goya's work in this medium is prefigured in some ways in Aula Dei. It is easy-looking, and unencumbered, colourful, humorous, touching, full of observation. The faces here are certainly not types, but individuals, in images ranging from festive views of picnics and the grape harvest to the famous scene of *Winter*, where farmworkers trudge along through wind-whipped snow, heads cowled in blankets, a mule behind them with a dead pig slung across its back. The cartoons include many of the charming scenes we recognize as trademark cheerful Goya: there is that happy outdoors couple, the young man sheltering his girl under a green parasol (with quite a cluster of all-purpose trees behind); there is the cartoon of roadside pottery sellers offering floral Valencian ware to a lady observed fleetingly, mysterious inside her carriage.

By the time he came to Madrid, Goya was married to Josefa Bayeu, sister of the Aragonese painter Francisco Bayeu, himself already settled in the capital and also painting cartoons for royal tapestries. It is perfectly possible that Bayeu played some part in the younger man's arrival in Madrid and for a time, though they had a fearful row over paintings for El Pilar in Zaragoza, their work runs parallel. There is not much to choose between them, for both are excellent. The Bourbon suites in El Escorial where Bayeu and Goya tapestries are hung together show how graceful and successful were the end results. Just every now and then, though, a deeper theme peeps through in Goya's work.

The long, narrow cartoon of the 'wounded mason' is a case in point. Based on a preliminary sketch showing a drunken mason being helped away from work, this became much more serious in the final cartoon. Now the man has fallen and seems to be badly hurt. His colleagues, with sadly sympathetic faces, hoist him on their shoulders against a background of high scaffolding and dimly observed landscape far away below, suggesting height and danger. Work is glorified here as well as its perils, fitting in neatly with new work regulations promulgated by Carlos III's enlightened ministers. It was even established at this time by royal edict that manual labour of the humbler kinds would no longer be considered dishonourable or a bar to achieving hidalgo status.

But if the Enlightenment shows through even in tapestry cartoons, it gleams as clear as day in Goya's portraiture, another fast-developing element in his Madrid career. The series opens in 1783 with a not entirely successful rendering of the chief minister, the Conde de Floridablanca (not, alas, in the Prado but to be found in art books). The count is shown under an oval portrait of the king, and along with an outsize clock, symbol of princes, ministers and the regularity and good order of the realm. Goya stands before Floridablanca humbly holding up a painting for the minister's inspection. Palomino's great treatise on art lies on the floor, half of its title clearly decipherable. Most interesting of all, however, are the maps and papers on the floor and table. These refer explicitly to the Aragón Canal, greatest of Spain's Enlightenment projects and Floridablanca's personal enthusiasm.

Goya had difficulty getting paid for this picture; other commissions still remained scarce. But within a year or two, his technique is evidently a match for a deeper understanding of his sitters, and he has become virtually official portrait painter to the Spanish Enlightenment. We know that the foremost figure of them all, Gaspar Melchor de Jovellanos, now became Goya's special patron and friend and remained such as he rose to be minister of justice. It seems from a reference in a Goya letter to Zapater, back home in Zaragoza, that Jovellanos may actually have learned sign language so as to communicate with the painter after he went deaf. Certainly the two men shared a belief, fortified on Goya's part by studying and copying Velázquez, in the cardinal importance for the artist of the observation and true representation of nature. The Jovellanos portrait, fortunately in the Prado, is one of the most beautiful of all the works of Goya, in colour – a surprising lilac, green and gold – in observation of character and in its subtle array of Enlightenment symbolism. This work may stand as chief of all the many Goya portraits of reformers, from the banker who wanted to license state-run brothels, to the reformer who soon dared raise his voice against the Inquisition (Francisco de Cabarrús and Juan Antonio Llorente respectively, both in the Prado). Goya's work in this area is a great achievement. In terms of his personal and intellectual progress, it meant that he occupied a world of lively, up-to-date ideas and well-informed discussion.

Lest anyone should think, however, that Goya's career as a great but tolerably conventional painter was now, at last, beginning to flow smoothly, a concatenation of events occurred, leading him to produce score upon score of the most bizarre and disturbing images ever created in Western art. But at the same time, right through the rest of his life, he remained capable of turning out the finest and most perceptive work within more ordinary public limits.

The first of the events that affected Goya directly was the death of Carlos III in 1788 and the accession of Carlos IV. The new king seems always to have had a high opinion of Goya and promptly appointed him *pintor de cámara*, painter to the royal chamber. It is from now on, through the 1790s and 1800s, that we get the Goya royal portraits, the equestrian studies and his huge family tableau, centre-piece of the Prado's Goya collection. All are done with such piercing clarity that the observer is perpetually puzzled. How can the monarchs have accepted a version of themselves in which they often look frankly ridiculous, particularly the queen, María Luisa, with her frizzy hairdo and her silly manner? The evidence suggests that the royals were satisfied Goya was producing a true likeness and sufficiently confident of themselves, perhaps sufficiently un-selfconscious, to worry not at all. María Luisa was described by a French diplomat as having at the age of fifty 'pretensions and coquetry one would scarcely pardon in a young and pretty woman'. She writes breathlessly of how well her portrait is coming along and how much it is admired. There is no reason to suppose that Carlos IV felt differently. The royal couple were on the whole a simple, good-hearted pair. They were scarcely adequate to deal with the events now soon to overwhelm their kingdom.

These began with the French Revolution in 1789 but were brought to a head by the execution of the French king in 1793. Appalled at developments in France from 1789, Floridablanca turned a reactionary face upon the world and did his best to suffocate the progressive ideas that were flooding in. He himself soon fell and many of the earlier figures of the Enlightenment in the end found themselves in serious difficulties. Jovellanos, to take the most signifi-cant example, was first banished to his native Asturias, and later im-prisoned.

Goya's normal circle was progressively reduced. Now, for patron-age, he turned increasingly to the more liberal-minded members of the aristocracy. From the late 1780s and on into the next century he was to produce a memorable set of dukes, duchesses and their children. Some were liberated enough to buy other works of his. The Duchess of Osuna, for example, took the whole of a mocking series on witchcraft, based on contemporary stage-scenes.

As Goya painted his aristocrats, a twenty-five-year-old guards' officer named Manuel Godoy, an escort and probably a lover of the queen's, was invited to head the government. Godoy reckoned himself in the reforming tradition and did indeed succeed with some useful fiscal measures, including the sale of a seventh of all Church property and the extension of taxation to many of the aristocracy. But the Carlos III concept of professional, well-trained ministers was gone. As a throwback to the old system of royal favourites, Godoy became the most hated *valido* that Spain had known. In a land where honour was all-important but so external a quality that a man could be deprived of it by the slightest misbehaviour of his wife, Godoy's relationship with the queen enormously damaged the royal family. We know that Goya had a low opinion of the favourite as he rose to be a duke and then a prince. But his Godoy portrait, showing the young *valido* as a general at ease after a battle, is soft and sympathetic, luxuriantly elegant. It has to be the best Goya work of its period, unless one concedes that honour to the portrait of Godoy's unhappy wife, the Countess of Chinchon. This most delicate of paintings is one of many Goya works that seem to show an unrestrained delight in femininity.

From Goya's personal point of view, the most important event of all was undoubtedly a near-fatal illness, in Andalucía, in 1792, which left him completely deaf for the remaining thirty-six years of his life. During his convalescence he produced a series of paintings that he presented to the Academy of San Fernando. He had undertaken them, he wrote to a friend at the Academy, to ease a mind 'mortified by reflection on my misfortunes'. Over the years Goya had eventually achieved Academy membership, had been promoted to deputy director of painting and would finally be made director, no doubt healing the wounds of earlier rejection. In the present paintings, Goya said, he had made observations 'for which no place exists in commissioned works' where there could be little 'fantasy or imagination'.

The Romantic movement was already afoot in northern Europe, the workings of the artistic mind a proper subject for discussion. Goya himself, in notes on teaching method for the Academy of San

Fernando, subscribes to the view that there is some kind of mystery, so that even the artist who has achieved 'more than most' cannot easily explain 'how he reaches that deep understanding and appreciation of things which is necessary for great art.' He can give few rules, adds Goya, 'and is unable to say why his least careful work may possibly be more successful than the one on which he laboured longest.' Now, after his illness, the move towards personal comment and self-expression was a development of great importance, partly because it was new in Spanish painting, partly because of the strange terrains into which he immediately ventured. His gift to the Academy included a view of naked lunatics fighting one another in a jumbled madhouse scene, with a warder beating them, trying to make them stop. The action in the picture (alas, again, now in the USA) takes place in a courtyard with a weird light flowing downwards from the sky and in through a barred window to the left. It is horrible and shocking and appears to contain no message other than documentation of a horror. 'This I have witnessed,' Goya later wrote in connection with the painting.

At home, Goya was working on the 'Caprichos', a series of etchings that emerged for sale in 1799 and was then hurriedly withdrawn, perhaps in fear of the Inquisition. These are, in a sense, an extension of the madhouse painting, touching as they do on a world of horror. In this work, though, the horrors are imaginary, assembled from the crowded scenes of nightmare, with witches, now altogether sinister, cobwebby bats, humans as donkeys, monstrosities performed on tiny children. The first response of those who come to these etchings unprepared is the conclusion that Goya, in the seclusion of his deafness, has entered a private world that is almost totally dark. There may indeed be some element of personal darkness, but to his Enlightenment contemporaries, and indeed ever since to critics and art historians, it has been clear that the 'Caprichos' are primarily riddles and enigmas, satires on human ignorance, custom and folly, just as the introduction to the series says, and intended to be read for hidden meanings. They draw on a huge fund of sixteenth- and seventeenth-century emblems, on theatre, literature and slang, on almost as many sources as there are

'Caprichos'. They gain uncomfortable depth and ambiguity from the brief, often sarcastic captions that accompany them.

There is not much mystery about the title-page, showing Goya in a top hat, the corners of his mouth turned down sardonically. Nor is there much, on the face of it, in no. 43 in the series, seemingly intended for the title-page until replaced by the self-portrait. Its caption reads 'The Sleep of Reason Produces Monsters' and the etching shows a frock-coated figure leaning on his desk. He is sleeping soundly, head on arms, pen fallen from his hand. All around him swoop bats and crazy-looking owls (the species, clearly, is the horned owl, or *búho*). A black cat crouches sinisterly behind. Only the watchful lynx beside him will serve as his protector. But will her clear gaze be enough to hold the monsters back? If ever a message came loud and clear from the Enlightenment, rather than from a corner of the wounded psyche, this surely is it. Or is it? For the caption may also be read as 'The Dream of Reason Produces Monsters', in which case, quite in opposition to the first explanation, the monsters may be making their appearance for the purpose of putting the Enlightenment itself on trial.

Complications abound in most of the series. Teasing them out – with the aid of learned authority – can become an obsessive matter. In one, for example, the horned owl is used again, providing a visual pun on slang interpretations of its name. The owl may be present either in the sense of witch or prostitute. Both meanings suit the image of a hag riding off naked on a broomstick, owl hovering above her, with a younger, naked woman seated just behind. *'Linda Maestra!'*, says the caption, 'A Fine Teacher!', embracing either meaning with a snarl. Lust, vanity, cruelty, credulity, all failings and vices become targets in this series. Here, too, are the common people, along with oppressive priests and cretinous doctors, friars stuffing themselves as they ride on the backs of the poor. But while sometimes the stumbling people support the weight of Church and State, portrayed as donkeys, on other occasions it is the people themselves who are the donkeys.

In the years when Goya was working on the 'Caprichos', he was also, evidently, in love, experiencing an amorous passion for the

Duchess of Alba, described by one contemporary as the most beautiful woman in Madrid. This slim, dark-haired aristocrat was the most unconventional of creatures, eager to break down social barriers in her household and on her Andalusian estates. Goya painted her portrait and was allowed into her circle. He drew her over and over and painted her in different situations, poses and postures, some of the latter extremely sexy. One outwardly formal rendering shows her standing in open countryside with trees and river. There are two rings on her fingers. One reads Alba and the other Goya. She points downwards to the ground with her ring hand and there on the sand is written the name Goya. When the painting was cleaned the word *solo*, or 'only', was revealed before the painter's name, so that the message on the sand read 'Only Goya'. This compromising legend had been painted over and the portrait itself, as is known from an inventory, remained in Goya's studio as a personal possession.

There is no evidence one way or the other on whether his love was reciprocated. Nor was the duchess the model for those most famous of female studies, the Maja with her clothes on and the Maja naked. These appear to have been painted for the young ruler Godoy, who had a mistress as well as a wife and his special relationship with the queen. Godoy at this time had the Velázquez *Venus* in his mansion and clearly wanted further stimulation. Though Goya hated Godoy, or, even more insultingly, despised him, he sold the younger man a house he had bought as an investment and here Godoy promptly installed the mistress. The married painter's love for the Duchess of Alba may have been pure and sweet as these things go; but Goya also lived in a murky world of self-advancement.

War and chaos were by now just round the corner. Spain first opposed revolutionary France but soon, as Napoleon took command of the revolution and began his imperial onslaught, she was swept into the French camp, virtually as a vassal state. Fighting for France against the English, she lost the whole of her fleet at Trafalgar and promptly sank into the condition of a second-class power. Then, in

1808, the young Prince Fernando, hungry for power and full of scorn for his father, Carlos IV, fell in with reactionary aristocrats to stage a coup. Godoy was caught up in it and imprisoned by angry crowds at Aranjuez. Carlos abdicated in favour of his son. But Napoleon outplayed them, luring both to Bayonne, and there depriving both of rights to the Spanish crown. In Madrid, during this process, the populace erupted, falling on Murat's Mameluke cavalry in the Puerta del Sol, dragging men down from their horses and killing them with knives. Next day, there were pitiful executions by firing squad. Napoleon's brother Joseph was soon installed as king of Spain.

Goya had by this time created a resonant gallery of Madrid street life, the sultry young women on their balconies in dark mantillas, the procuress or customer lurking behind. Now, as required, he turned his hand to serving his new French masters, painting an *Allegory of the City of Madrid* for the town hall. This had a medallion in the centre bearing a portrait of Joseph Napoleon, crowned José I of Spain – known popularly, however, as Pepe Botellas, or Joe Bottles, because of his supposed taste for liquor. The *Allegory* became a weather-vane for the extreme political changes that had now begun; the medallion itself was painted over no fewer than eight times in the next sixty years as Madrid accommodated itself to varying political fortunes and regimes.

Outside Madrid, the Spanish army and the Spanish people refused absolutely to accept the French and so began the War of Independence, first and perhaps the fiercest of its kind in modern history. Briefly Pepe Botellas was driven from Madrid after a Spanish victory at Bailén. In Zaragoza, General Palafox and the citizens held out against the French in a dour and ferociously contested siege. They were spurred on by the local heroine, Agustina de Aragón, who climbed across the bodies of dead men to fire their cannon. Goya, whose personal opinions at this stage remain unknowable, accepted an invitation from Palafox to record what was happening in Zaragoza. It appears he saw horrors enough to haunt him for the remainder of his life. At one point he was obliged to take refuge in his native Fuendetodos but in due course he returned to the capital, picking up the threads of his career under the occupation.

The People's War, meanwhile, moved on slowly but irresistibly. French troops were harried and cut to pieces whenever they ventured outside their garrisons. The English sent Wellington with an expeditionary force, which manoeuvred carefully and helped to win the day. Wellington himself was showered with honours, both in Portugal and Spain. He became, among other things, Duque de Ciudad Rodrigo and a Spanish grandee and he was given several estates – some now returned to the Spanish nation, others still retained by the family. When Wellington reached Madrid, it was Goya who drew him, brilliantly, and painted his equestrian portrait with suspicious speed. The picture, which Wellington disliked and kept rolled up, now hangs in Apsley House in London, home of the Dukes of Wellington. It is almost certain that it was originally a portrait of José Napoleon in a tricorn hat, hastily overpainted with Wellington's features.

One of the most remarkable aspects of the war was the common feeling that developed between Spain's hugely separated social classes. The young Duke of Osuna, painted as a child by Goya, renounced his rank to stand in common fortune with the people. Robin Hood figures made an appearance, robbing the rich on the grounds that property should be held in common. What had begun essentially as revolution against the French became a rallying point for social expectations as far-reaching as anything the French might have proposed in idealistic moments.

It was in these circumstances that the resistance Cortes, the forerunner of the modern-day Spanish parliament, assembled in Cádiz, meeting from 1811 to 1812 in the Oratory of San Felipe Neri, as pretty a building as you could hope to find.

When at last my wife and I reach Cádiz, safe from the French out on its snake-neck promontory, we receive friendly directions from a policeman sitting astride a motor bike. There seem to be a few traffic problems. The Easter holiday has just ended, bringing to a close the season of the great religious processions. The sacred floats, which have reposed for a day or two in churches all round town, must now be taken off to garages and warehouses where they will spend the remainder of the year, rubbing up against diesel engines and crates of canned fish awaiting delivery. To carry the floats to their parking places is almost as complicated a business as the processions themselves, involving traffic diversions and armies of young men. Our policeman, it turns out, is the man in charge.

We encounter him in what must be a lull since, when we linger, he begins to explain the technicalities of carrying Easter floats. Teams called *costaleros*, or 'barrow boys', shuffle along under their massive burden with a sniggly little step that causes the float to jiggle back and forth as they move it forwards. The policeman climbs off his bike to demonstrate the step. Then there are other teams called *cargadores*, or porters. Their speciality is a step that rocks the float from side to side. Like any watcher of Spain's Easter processions, I have seen this beautiful movement many times, whole huge floats with their groups of holy figures, illuminated with a thousand candles, swaying perilously round corners in towns and villages. I had not realized there was so much to it until, again, the policeman did the step.

It turned out that he was from Galicia, up in that north-west corner of Spain where tiny landholdings are a guarantee of poverty and where there is precious little industry to offer alternative employment. The Galicians are the Irish of Spain, not only Celtic in stock but perpetual exiles seeking work where they can find it. The policeman, another of those well-read Spanish autodidacts, had now been in Cádiz for many years and shared an interest in the events of 1812. For in that early year the resistance Cortes meeting in the Oratory devised a constitution based on universal male suffrage by indirect householder's vote, with a single legislative chamber, and offering the king no more than a veto on legislation. The delegates who wrote this document placed themselves consciously in the tradition of the sixteenth-century *comuneros* and the Spanish liberties that they believed had been snuffed out by centuries of Habsburg rule. Their ringing declaration of intent was promulgated on the day of San José, St Joseph's day. Pepe, of course, is the nickname of all those called José. But since a constitution is feminine in Spanish it was promptly dubbed La Pepa, in noble counterpoint to Pepe

Botellas. It had the political effect, however, of immediately dividing the nation into progressives and reactionaries, those who were for it and those who heard it as a death-knell. 'Not too clever, really,' said the policeman.

Discussing all these matters, our friend now parks his bike definitively and leads us into the Oratory where the debates took place. The interior is blue and white and locket-shaped. You look up into a narrowing oval, with three tiers of galleries all round, fenced in with slender railings. The public sat in the galleries, the deputies on the lozenge of floor. Journalists sat in a shallow side chapel behind a hoop of marble railing, and backed by a cluster of *mouvementés* nude angels. The policeman genuflects before the main altar, almost curtsying. Silver handcuffs bounce on one buttock, his pistol on the other. A walkie-talkie, stuffed somehow into a pocket, blares away disregarded. And now it is the turn of the ancient sacristan of the Oratory, a friend of the policeman's. He shuffles forward amiably, gesturing upwards to a Murillo Immaculate Conception, coppery-russet in a gilded *retablo*. Do we know, asks the sacristan, that the painter based the image on his younger daughter, soon to become a nun? And on he goes, with sacred stories to match the political. One involves an image carried in the Easter procession in Seville. The sculptor, says the old man, modelled it on the face of a gypsy dying of knife wounds in the doorway of the cathedral. 'It's tremendous and terrible,' he says. 'You are looking on the face of death itself.' My wife gives an obliging shudder. 'But that's how it has to be,' he says with Spanish gloom, 'you take the bad along with good and that's the way that all of us are going.'

On the notion of Goya as untutored genius, concerned only with the exploration of his own brooding subconscious, limits are once more placed by the Cádiz Cortes. For as its debates progress, and are reported in the anti-Bonapartist press, so Goya's notebooks show him taking up their themes. Torture as an official means of punishment and for the extraction of confessions is discussed and then condemned; Goya is at work on terrible drawings of torture, bitterly captioned. The Inquisition is discussed and Goya paints a strange and frightening Inquisition scene. This now hangs in the Academy of San Fernando, along with the Godoy portrait, a scene of prisoners reminiscent of the struggling madmen and a famous popular scene called the *Burial of the Sardine*. In fact, for an intense, encapsulated view of Goya as a painter, though not as an etcher, there is no better place than the Academy, comfortable in its grand old mansion just by the Puerta del Sol.

But it is to the Prado that one must return for Goya's record of the events that had taken place in the Puerta del Sol on 2 May 1808 and the executions at Moncloa on the following day. For now it is 1814, the war is won, the French are on the run and Goya has received an official stipend to celebrate the heroic and disastrous happenings surrounding the French take-over. The pictures he produces are unforgettable, with first the wild assault on the Mamelukes, a painting often known as *May 2*. (Streets and restaurants sometimes also have this name.) Then comes the execution scene, *May 3*, in which the young man at centre, wild-eyed, his shirt a brilliant, sacrificial white, flings his arms high above the terrified figures who crouch round him and the dead lying in pools of blood. Remorseless, the firing squad still point their rifles.

This is one of the most astounding pictures ever painted, the strongest and clearest denunciation of state violence inflicted on a simple people. It might have presaged many other plain statements from Goya but again, almost on the instant, as if there were no mercy or hope for Spain, the political situation darkened and Goya's public voice was silenced.

The key event was the re-installation of Fernando VII, considered even by so calm and judicious a historian as Professor S. G. Payne the 'basest' monarch ever to rule Spain – 'cowardly, selfish, grasping, suspicious, vengeful . . . unmoved by the enormous sacrifices of the Spanish people to retain their independence and preserve his throne.' Fernando came back on a tide of bitterest reaction, welcomed by a Madrid mob shouting 'Long live the absolute monarch' and even 'Long live chains'. In a document which incidentally complained that the public in the galleries at Cádiz had terrorized the deputies, robbing them of free expression, he cancelled the constitution.

During the years of the first Fernandine repression, Goya was called upon to paint the king on several occasions. One of these portraits, now in Santander, contains a ridiculous, misrepresented lion, either a ghastly failure by the painter or intended to be ridiculous. The most interesting, because of its destination, was done for the board of the Aragón Canal. It now hangs in the Fine Arts Museum in Zaragoza, showing the new sovereign very clearly – at least to retrospective eyes – as the perfect image of the tin-pot dictator. At home, meanwhile, Goya's energies were now going into another series of etchings, eventually published, many years after his death, as 'The Disasters of War'.

Even in the long career of this extraordinary artist, the 'Disasters' are unparalleled. Those who cannot abide horror would do well to avoid them altogether. Those prepared to witness a people in its utmost extremity will look at them and shudder, then puzzle at the bitter counterpoint of caption and engraving and begin again, as with the 'Caprichos', to ferret out the meanings implied in the total. There is a small Goya museum in Fuendetodos, a step away from the house where he was born, in which both sets of etchings are displayed in full and it is possible to wander among them, comparing sequences from the pre-war 'Caprichos' with the much later 'Disasters'. As you do so, it becomes apparent that the imagery for most of the more satirical portions of the 'Disasters' was already in place before the coming of the French. Not so, however, for the images of war. These are entirely terrible.

Trying to think back calmly to Fuendetodos, it seems to me that Goya thrusts in front of us not merely a Spanish people savagely abused – raped, decapitated, hung on trees like rags, begging for mercy, bayoneted too grossly for description, their corpses heaped in piles, and on and on in all the scenes that Goya had imagined or observed – but also a people who progressively become indistinguishable from the soldiery. Who is doing what to whom in this intolerable parade, and how, and why become entirely immaterial. As Unamuno wrote: 'In how many ways (Goya seems to have asked himself) can human beings be shown meeting their death?' What we are witnessing is a tempest, a cauldron rendering down humanity to its basest components. The Goya all-purpose peasant face is back again and there are plenty of characters who wear it, whether expressing lust or demonic hatred, greed or simple, unabatable violence. One reels away from this indictment, thankful at least that in the few images of peace and reconciliation, the Light of Reason still spreads its spokes across the dark. But simultaneously one is forced to ask, as with the lynx in the *Sleep of Reason*, whether even this bright light is light enough.

Goya worked at the 'Disasters' over a long period. In 1820, in a fresh political convulsion, the so-called liberal Triennium began. In response to the Fernandine violence, a 'leftist' military coup took place, the 1812 constitution was invoked and Fernando was for a time obliged to act as constitutional monarch. Goya, now in his mid seventies, played little part in the ensuing liberal years, which undoubtedly led to some excess, with revenge killings and other disorders. After a second grave illness, Goya himself had moved to a house on the far side of the Manzanares, with seventeen acres to farm and close to the site of his well-known cartoon, the festival of San Isidro. The new residence was called the Quinta del Sordo, or House of the Deaf Man, and on the walls here Goya painted a series of decorations. These are the 'Black Paintings', the last great sequence of his career, and like the 'Disasters', a set of images to astonish and appal. Detached from the house walls and somewhat enthusiastically restored, these too are in the Prado. They include flying witches, a dog drowning in an expanse of rain and fog and a kinder image, of Leocadia Weiss, the estranged wife of a banker, now sharing her life with Goya (Josefa Bayeu had died some years before). But there are at least two other paintings that, once seen, are never forgotten. One shows two men, up to their knees in mud or quicksand, slowly cudgelling each other to death. The other shows Saturn devouring his child, vast mouth agape around the pitiful, bleeding figure, clenched in his two hands. Is this an image of humanity? Or is Goya still drawing on local impulses to make a universal image? Is Saturn, perhaps, as has been powerfully suggested, a portrait of absolute monarchy?

Fernando VII threw out the liberals in 1823, backed by a French army now dedicated to legitimacy. Soon, intense repression began, with arrests and executions. Goya hid for three months in the house of an Aragonese priest, eventually obtaining royal permission to take the waters in France and heading, full of fears, real or imaginary, towards the border. Though he made one journey to Paris and two restless forays back to Madrid, the last period of his life was spent among the many exiles in Bordeaux. With him were Leocadia Weiss and her children, one of them probably his own daughter. And here, as he entered his eighties, he continued to study new techniques, paid visits to the circus and the madhouse and worked away until the end, still producing memorable paintings. Not long before his death, he captioned a sketch '*Aun aprendo*', literally 'I am still learning'.

7 Art and Politics

Nineteenth-Century Madrid and Barcelona

THE RHYTHMIC CLAPPING and the castanets; the dancer, heels drumming, hips forward, spine like a drawn bow; guitars and daggers; dalliance and danger; gypsy faces shading into Moorish in the shadows – all these are classic images drawn from the early nineteenth century. For the French, who had recently devastated Spain, reducing the country to a new and painful poverty and undoing every step towards improvement taken in the century before, now set about romanticizing their exhausted neighbour. It started with the Napoleonic conquest and the removal of great numbers of Spanish paintings. When these were exhibited in Paris they caused a tremendous stir. But the writers were never far behind, soon spreading their appreciation into the Anglo-Saxon world. The notion of an exotic Spain, based almost entirely on the south, spread with a vivacity beyond the reach of Spain herself. In 1829 Washington Irving made, as he wrote, 'a rambling expedition from Seville to Granada with a friend, a member of the Russian Embassy at Madrid.' From this journey, along with a serious historical study, there came his compulsively romantic *Tales of the Alhambra*, first published in 1832. In 1835, Richard Ford, another lover of the south, published his massive, intelligent and quirky *Handbook*. Equally effective in setting up the romantic backdrop was Prosper Mérimée's novel *Carmen*, published in 1846.

So it began; so it continued. Even today, there is much in the south that causes a quickening of the pulse; and it would be a rash traveller who tried to challenge the stereotype. The trouble is, though, now as then, that simple images leave out too much. To nineteenth-century Andalucía with the carnation in its teeth, it is clear that one must add a landless peasantry, rapacious landlords and a political situation that allowed them to be so. Considering the whole of Spain, there is almost a duty to recall the endless drudgery and poverty of village life, the thin-faced men with their lined foreheads, squinting in the great heat of midsummer, the women with gnarled fingers gathering firewood on icy mornings high on the *meseta*. Spain in the nineteenth century is now a backward land and the fuel-gatherers are lucky if they have a mule between them. Even when the railways go in, there is little at either end of the glistening tracks for any economic miracle to feed upon. Only around the north and north-east coasts, in the Basque Country, Catalonia and Valencia, is there any real prospect as the century moves ahead of significant material development.

For Spaniards themselves, the nineteenth century has often seemed a source of shame. The Prado's published notes on Goya, for example, speak of the 'invasions and civil confrontations which so regrettably characterized the nineteenth century in Spain.' The word 'regrettably' is offered as something beyond dispute, based on an understanding not specifically acknowledged: eighteenth century good; nineteenth century bad. This, certainly, was the way official historians liked to look at things during the Franco epoch, for in praising Carlos III and his enlightened despotism they were covertly justifying the Generalísimo; and in deploring the nineteenth century they were falling in behind the explicit wish of Franco himself to purge from Spanish consciousness, except as a dread warning, all memory of liberalism. For Franco and his generals, the struggles of nineteenth-century politics were dangerous, incoherent and ultimately a national betrayal. Few nowadays accept the Francoist view but, unfortunately, the habit of seeing the nineteenth century in self-deprecating terms has stuck. Even for today's liberal Spaniards, it appears to be little more than government succeeding government at a pell-mell pace, wars and civil wars, coups and *pronunciamientos*.

It is a pity, though, to view it just in this one perspective, for there exists the possibility of a marginally more heroic version in which the observer might descry a country starting in an extremely disadvantaged situation and striving, in a slightly more open manner than in the eighteenth century, to find a solution to a multitude of contending interests, a saucepan boiling away with the lid at least half off the pot. If the solutions remained as elusive as a workable democracy and the end result was a pair of dictatorships in the twentieth century, well, perhaps that may be taken not so much as a justification for dictatorship as an indication of the need to do things differently this time round in a newly and more truly democratic Spain.

The trouble is, the nineteenth-century story is a rather long and complicated one, bristling with people, parties and ideas that were important in their day but not exactly memorable over a longer time span. History books on the subject often weigh in, quite literally, at kilos. Wondering one hot day in Madrid how to gain an instant overview, it occurred to me that the streets of the capital could themselves make a symbolic guide to the period, much as one uses counters in a board-game in place of bona fide money. Many of the main figures of the period, at a time when Madrid was expanding rapidly, have important streets or avenues named after them and I was sure that anyone else I needed would be represented somewhere, if not in a street, then in a roundabout or circus or, if the worst came to the worst and one had to fall back on the absolutely obvious, then surely in a proper, public monument. Might it not be fun, I wondered, to draw up a short list of essential people and walk the whole way round the lot of them?

Since the nineteenth century becomes as fascinating as any other once you take the plunge, the list itself was not too hard at all. Nor were the more obvious streets and monuments. But some of the lesser figures were on the awkward side. You can never tell with Madrid street directories whether a public person's street will be listed under surname, first name, military rank or similar. Just spotting them on the map took most of an afternoon. And my walk, when I came to it, took over twenty hours, morning to evening on two successive days, in an egg-shaped sweep around the city, at a temperature that varied between forty and forty-four degrees, through neighbourhoods of every class and condition. It was, in short, one of those stupid undertakings that one treasures retrospectively. I loved the walk, but would not wish it on a dog.

Mendizábal – Juan Álvarez Mendizábal Street – lies near the south-west edge of town where Madrid comes suddenly to an end with a steep hill and the Río Manzanares and out beyond them both a large tract of one-time royal hunting ground that has never been built over. This open land is the Casa de Campo, literally the Country House, quaintly named perhaps but a true green lung for the city. The royal palace gets a specially good view of it; Mendizábal is tucked away inside the city, tall, narrow and graceful, a prosperous place of residence for the more old-fashioned kind of folk. Just a short walk from the Plaza de España with its tourist-delighting statues of Don Quixote and Sancho Panza, Mendizábal's outstanding feature is an old-fashioned grocer's shop with age-old shutters, tall and thin as the street and laden with countless coats of grey, flaking paint.

Mendizábal came to power not so very long after the death of Fernando VII, the capricious, autocratic king of the post-Napoleonic restoration, whose shocking ways had done so much to frighten Goya. Fernando had also contrived, one way and another, to lose virtually the whole of South America to the so-called Liberators, people of Spanish descent who believed they could manage more effectively without Madrid. After Fernando's death, the situation at first got even worse, with full-scale civil war in Spain over the succession. Fernando left a tiny daughter named Isabel, who now became queen, again with a young mother as regent. But Fernando's brother Carlos believed the crown was his, not Isabel's, on grounds that the Bourbon dynasty, by virtue of the Salic Law, could not permit succession through the female line. Technically, he had a point, since Fernando had been trying to revoke this constitutional assumption in order to help his daughter's chances but he had not quite succeeded by the time of his death. In practical terms, this meant that forces even more conservative than those represented by Fernando were now unleashed in the name of Carlos. From the most bigoted and ferocious reaches of Navarre and the Basque Country, with support from mountain dwellers in Aragón and Catalonia, there now emerged the ultra-Catholic, absolutist, backward-looking creed named Carlism, an intransigent anachronism breathing a wild romance through every pore. The creed survived through two long and bloody civil wars during the nineteenth century and another in the twentieth, as much a family tradition as a political programme, and remained a constant element in the balance of Spanish forces right up to the 1970s. It may, for all one knows, still linger among the homesteads of the high valleys, ready to be called upon once again should circumstances, in the eyes of the mountaineers, require it.

Naturally enough, given their background and entrenched beliefs, the Carlists were extremely doughty fighters, particularly in defence of home terrain. Their bayonet charges were a byword and once, in 1837, they came within a whisker of taking Madrid.

María Cristina, the cheerful young regent, struggled to hold her daughter's inheritance together at a time when the reactionary forces of the Carlists had almost found their match among the Progressives of Madrid, extreme anti-clericals who turned a blind eye to the mob murder of monks. Looking for an opening leftwards to save the political order, she appointed Juan Álvarez Mendizábal her prime minister. Mendizábal was a financier from Cádiz, a tree-trunk of a man with a successful business career in London behind him. Short of cash for waging war against the Carlists, and finding international credit hard to come by, he hit upon the satisfying scheme of dissolving the monasteries and selling their huge properties.

The arguments on this subject still rage today. Unquestionably, the Church had too much land. Unquestionably it was right to return it to the nation and had this not happened, at least in part, the anti-clericalism that was to be such a feature of Spanish life, with church burnings and priest slayings, at its most extreme in the twentieth-century Civil War, might have been still more fearful than it was. Yet, in common with many privatizations, it was the wrong people who got the pickings. As Church land sales progressed over decades, there were frequent shifts from genuinely liberal to more reactionary administrations (the latter known euphemistically as *moderados*, or moderates). But the limited 'political classes' who brought the administrations into power were fundamentally the same, mostly already landowners and now poised to acquire the lion's share of the new lands according to whether or not it was their particular friends who were in power at the moment. This crude division of the spoils, especially in Andalucía and Extremadura, along with the old aristocratic landholdings of earlier centuries, produced the pattern of land tenure which has been such a devastating, if picturesquely seigneurial, encumbrance to twentieth-century Spain.

And then there was the question of the artistic treasures of the monasteries. Many went into private ownership and were soon scattered across Europe and America. Contemporary polemicists still maintain that Mendizábal did more to damage the Spanish patrimony than ever the French invasion could have done. On the other hand, a great many of the very finest paintings came in due course into the possession of the Prado, greatly strengthening a picture-holding that was already hard to match in any other gallery, anywhere in the world.

It seems to me, you pays your money and you takes your choice. Mendizábal broke the monasteries; and in the end the war with the Carlists was won. A general named Espartero made the peace – on generous terms – and was soon in his turn appointed head of government. Like most of the Spanish army, formed in the resistance to Napoleon, this son of a Castilian wheelwright believed his patriotic duty lay with the liberal cause and his administration, like Mendizábal's, was essentially liberal. This did not prevent him from establishing the first of Spain's military dictatorships, using the title of *caudillo*, or leader, made more familiar by Franco some ninety years later on.

Faced with total loss of power, María Cristina abdicated, leaving young Isabel on the throne in case a queen should still be needed for the future. Espartero had no particular programme but soon fell into deadly struggles with the periphery, stripping the Basques of their *fueros* and bombarding Barcelona. The Basques got their rights back again but lost them, finally, later in the century. Espartero lasted just three years, and got an equestrian statue, not a street.

From Mendizábal to the Espartero statue, the hot way lay along the Gran Vía, a main street carved at an angle through the old city later in the century, with huge disruption and considerable civic pride. There is a lively *zarzuela*, a very Madrileñan form of comic opera, on the subject. The street itself is rather grey and dour, though it comes to life a little when it passes close by the Puerta del Sol, with cinemas and a handful of department stores. Then on downhill to debouch close to the fountain of Cibeles with its steady lions and the post office, sarcastically described as 'Our Lady of Communications'. From here, the way leads up again, through the handsome Puerta de Alcalá to the top end of the Retiro. Six lanes of traffic whizz where Espartero sits astride his horse.

This is a matter of regret; to Madrileños the horse is particularly important. A person of courage in Spain's macho capital is said to have '*mas cojónes que el caballo de Espartero*' – more balls than Espartero's mount. And here I am, dripping with sweat, suffering for the sake of self-improvement, and I cannot even see the underbelly of the beastly animal. Suddenly the frustration boils right up and I am dashing like a lunatic across the burning roadway and up on to the floral island where the statue stands. Cars swerve and hoot; pedestrians on the pavement stare in blank surmise. Have I shown, I wonder, the necessary courage? Earned myself comparison, however fleetingly, with the great stallion? On the subject of the horse itself it seems indelicate to say too much, but the general has a fine, sharp-bearded chin, and holds his cocked hat down at the full extent of his right arm.

Next stop now, Narváez. At a time when the political vacuum was a standing invitation to the soldiery, every party had to have an *espadón*, or 'broadsword', its very own strong man in the army. General Ramon Narváez, so-called Espadón de Loja, was strong man to the moderates, a swaggering authoritarian with a few passably liberal beliefs in his right-wing repertoire. In 1844, as premier soon after the fall of Espartero, he set up the Civil Guard, reviving memories of Isabel and Fernando's vicious Santa Hermandad. Narváez's model, though, was French, a rural police force acting under military discipline. One of its rules was that its members should always serve away from their own home districts. With the quaintest of tricorn hats, now generally phased out in favour of forage caps, and a self-protective system of going everywhere in well-armed pairs, they soon became a familiar part of every country prospect. Though kind to foreigners – as I have often discovered to my benefit – they have traditionally been tough to the point of ruthlessness with their own people. There are signs, though, that some softening is underway. If occasionally you come across a newspaper report of a terrible beating doled out by the Civil Guard, usually in Andalucía where the Guard have systematically supported landed interests, then that in itself may be taken as a new openness to public scrutiny. And the Guard are earning real sympathy from sectors of the Spanish public, mainly outside the Basque Country, in their role as official, on-the-spot opponents to militant Basque terrorism.

Narváez himself was a great one for executing people – some 200 radicals during his tenure. Asked on his deathbed to forgive his enemies, he said he had none, he had killed them all. His street is not too far from Espartero's horse, rebuilt during this century in dullest style, but lined with acacia trees, another of the trademarks of Madrid, shaking out a glossy yellow in the springtime. One end of Narváez is on the poor side; children with runny noses scrabbling round the roots of the acacias, mothers in aprons, arms folded, down in the street to sort them out. A little higher up Narváez, an apron would be unthinkable.

Perhaps at this point, at about 1850 and at one end or other of Narváez according to personal predilection, with a left-wing period and a right-wing period, a civil war, a military dictatorship and an abdication already behind us, it is worth pausing for a beer or mineral water in order to reflect in the broadest terms on what is happening in the Spanish body politic. It seems to me, though any generalization will be vulnerable, that we are witnessing a more or less continuous effort to evolve some kind of working constitutional monarchy, supported by a Cortes with a very limited franchise, which will allow the possessing classes to govern Spain in an approximation to the national interest while simultaneously enriching themselves. Some political groups incline a great deal more towards 'the people' than do others so that the franchise and accompanying constitutional arrangements are constantly manipulated up or down. There are genuine leftists about, though generally they need to come to power by a coup, involving frequent recourse to the politics – and violence – of the street. In general, political activity is limited, conducted by formally attired gentlemen in rather fussy drawing-rooms. Lacking any firm power base outside their own social sector, they are not enormously impressive in their political role. As a result, a civic-minded army often feels obliged to join the fray, producing many of the most effective and decisive politicians. They come to power through conspiracies and coups backed up by force but far more often through that most Spanish of devices, the military *pronunciamiento*, or pronouncement. In this, after taking any soundings that seem prudent, a military commander merely sits in his base and announces that such-and-such a policy must change or that he himself will now take charge of the government. If the army rallies to him, he has won. If not, he is disgraced and will probably end up in exile. It is a simple, almost elegant method of achieving change, often more meaningful than nineteenth-century elections. Generally, a military ruler manages to live within the party structure, accommodating to queen and Cortes. Even Espartero, when he came to power again in his old age, did so as a constitutional premier. The great snag, though, is that the army began to see itself as the true repository of the national will.

For a time in the middle of the century the right wing was making rather more ground than the left. It had a theorist of sorts in the person of Juan Donoso Cortés, an aristocrat from Extremadura. His street is in the west of town, a long canyon cutting down towards the principal university, with a view of open country out towards the sunset and what used to be at least a glimpse of open sky at the other end, clear through, the whole way back across the city to the east. Donoso Cortés thought that Fernando VII had brought true peace to Spain and that Mendizábal was the next best thing to Satan. Government, he believed, must rest on the superior intelligence of the governing classes; dictatorship was perfectly justified in the event of trouble. Really, he does not deserve too honourable a placing in my list – a Spanish friend describes him as 'a black reactionary, the sort we were taught to admire at school in Franco's day' – but I lived in his street a quarter of a century ago and curiosity has brought me trudging back again.

The views of distant country to the west are still in place, though naturally that countryside is more built over. Back to the east, I see no hint at all of sky at the far end of the canyon, only a dull haze with buildings disappearing into it. There is little left of the sensation of freshness and openness, the awareness of wind stirring the heat in summer, or biting sharp in springtime – the famous Madrid wind said to be capable of killing a man without so much as snuffing out a candle. Though physically the street looks much as it used to, long and grey and unremarkable, six storeys high on either side, the old wood merchant has departed along with the glimpse of eastern sky; he used to occupy a cranny, axe hafted in hands with fingerless mittens, splitting his logs no matter what the weather. The coalman has gone too, his open basement closed to view. So has the shop where a pair of cows were stabled, struggling to provide the neighbourhood with milk. I cannot find the café where everyone played chess. The ancient ironmongers are still holding out, thank goodness, dusty among the dustless car showrooms (entirely new), and neat little video shops. The bar on the corner where the television was always tuned to boxing or bullfighting now strives for elegance as a *mesón*, a Castilian-style restaurant with open oven, dark wood décor, ceramic tiles and fancy prices. Money, parasitic style and smart accessories – such are the gods invoked these days by lower-middle-class Madrid.

Too much complaining. Travellers have been saying for centuries that Spain is losing its character. Yet even if parallels with northern European materialism are evident, every step I take during my long, hot march is a reassurance about the deep individuality of this city, the liveliness of the men, the impossible, elegant beauty of the women, not to mention their delightful style of walking – also remarked on over the centuries by travellers. No street more full of elegantly dressed and elegantly walking women than the Calle Serrano, named for yet another politician who started as a general and who was then in and out of office for many years, this time in the progressive cause. Serrano runs up right through the middle of town, from close by Espartero's horse to the northern sector of the city, parallel all the way to the broad avenue of Castellana, the principal north–south axis. It starts with elegant nineteenth-century architecture, with quiet and orderly, plain-spoken frontages rising above smart flower shops and banks whose names are written in Arabic as well as Spanish. Up past the smaller women's clothes stores runs Serrano, up by establishments with elegant-looking sweets or stockings, till after a mile or three it becomes residential, wealthy still but of no special interest except by comparison with the street that brings me down again next day in a long and shallow arc on the far side of the Castellana.

It is breakfast time when I begin, still on the Serrano side of the Castellana. Water sprinklers are hard at work on little lawns with cypresses and oleanders. Men in silk suits with briefcases hurry their suited wives by the elbow to pick up BMWs and Mercedes. Up at this altitude, not far from the clangorous roundabout called the Plaza de Castilla, starting-point for Burgos and the north, we are in ultra-modern Madrid. Shopping malls and American-style office developments bid fair to make this the new city centre, leaving the Puerta del Sol and the Plaza Mayor stranded far away south in the old city.

But as I cross the Castellana and head off just a little further north, it is suddenly all change in every respect. The first clue is a set of law courts, with a crowd of gypsies waiting patiently outside. The men wear straw hats at a rakish angle, leaning weightlessly on long, thin sticks like cattle drovers. Within a moment, I am in a district that the map calls Almenara, nothing at all to do with nineteenth-century politicians. Steep little streets tip down into a cleft of valley, lined with single-storey houses, grey and grim. There are iron grilles on windows in Andalusian style, with roller blinds let down behind the grilles to give each house a closed and sightless look. Not a soul appears to be about, except for a woman struggling home with plastic shopping bags that stretch out ominously and cheaply at the handles. A man goes by carrying a roll of esparto grass; another sweats heavily under a sack of peanuts. Otherwise, little moves except for the odd dog. The place is shut up, lost and dying. I go into a bar for breakfast and find that the impression is a true one.

According to the proprietors – frying up pork crackling in a cloud of grease drops, joshing with henna-haired local women who stop by for coffee and a brandy – their little valley is to become a modern avenue and has been caught in planning blight for years. You cannot sell your home; you cannot make a living; there is nothing here, no hope at all for the young people. The lady of the bar has lived here all her life; so has her eighty-year-old mother. They remember the district when it was a village, full of animation. Most houses kept a pig and chickens. Most people worked in the rag and bone trade, the men heading off each morning with horse- or mule-drawn carts to pick up refuse from the big houses in town, then sorting it out at home, to sell off anything of value. It was, she says, a different kind of life, poor and hard but livelier and happier.

A breeze stirs the plastic stripping in the doorway. '*Viene de mi tierra de Segovia,*' says her husband, the barman – 'It's coming from my home country in Segovia.' The sausages he sells are also from his Segovian village, one more example of the intense localism still deeply structured into the whole of Spanish life, loyalty going first to one's own *patria chica*, or 'little fatherland', next to the district, after that to the region and only then, often at the last gasp, to Spain itself.

The street that finally carries me south, sweeping down on the west of Castellana to within a mile or two of the old centre, is again nineteenth-century political, named for Bravo Murillo, a strong administrator who came soon after Narváez and ruled by decree instead of through the Cortes. His street contrasts with Serrano on the other side in being full-out Madrileño working-class almost the whole of its length. At one point on the way I run into a television team doing street interviews on immigration – universally assumed in Spain to refer to people from North Africa. The team has found Bravo Murillo residents strongly opposed, worried about competition for jobs and housing. These, they say, are standard working-class objections, in Spain as in other parts of Europe. Middle-class people are generally more tolerant, being less threatened, but they haven't found many such in their straw poll down Bravo Murillo.

The northern end of the long street is fairly horrible to look upon, with grey, dilapidated buildings and the odd modern construction, often in shiny brick, standing out like one false tooth among decaying neighbours. In parts its inhabitants are plainly suffering. I pass a woman with a bandaged leg, the blood showing right through. And in this land where the family still holds sway and babies are continually held in their mothers' arms, I pass a baby-minding establishment advertising that it will look after children from seven in the morning to seven in the evening, accepting infants from the age of two months up. Mothers from this part of town who need to make a living – as many do – must evidently be separated from even the tiniest of infants. And yet in places, too, it is a cheerful, bustling street, a good deal better off than it used to be, with the occasional luxury like a comfortable café or a crowded shellfish bar – Spaniards of all classes are tremendous fish and shellfish eaters. In terms of the total Spanish population, I have to assume that Bravo Murillo, in its contrasts of poverty and growing plenty, must represent a greater portion of the truth than smart Serrano or aspirant Donoso Cortés.

As premier from 1849–53, Bravo Murillo was profuse in public works. At the Plaza de Castilla and right through this part of town, there is copious evidence of nineteenth-century waterworks, all constituent parts of a system called the Canal of Isabel II. The coming of this fresh supply of running water enabled the growing population to wash more frequently. Sales of personal linen leapt while laundries sprang up all around.

The canal makes a very pleasant monument to Isabel, Fernando

VII's daughter, who had eventually come of age. Other monuments are to be found in almost all the royal palaces, for Isabel emerged as a person of distinctive taste and there grew up around her a style named Isabelline – heavy and very ornamental, not too dissimilar from mid-Victorian style in Britain. The music room in La Granja is a good example. Another is her bedroom in Aranjuez, a palace where one may also see her putting on so much weight between one portrait and the next that her eyes begin almost to disappear inside her face.

In her personal life she was unfortunate, married for reasons of state to an aristocrat of decidedly effeminate temperament. But she was energetic in her love affairs and went on to produce seven children, most probably all by fathers other than her husband. In policy and statecraft, she was capricious like her father and, like him, obliged to follow an erratic course. After Bravo Murillo, a 'liberal biennium' was ushered in by popular revolution, with days of street fighting in Madrid. Now the ancient Espartero was once more placed nominally in charge. Under O'Donnell – another more-or-less liberal general – Spain actually won the century's one and only military victory, in the Spanish back garden of Morocco. O'Donnell's street crosses Narváez and runs on down beneath the television tower, blank and uninteresting. And then, in 1868, General Juan Prim, the hero of Morocco and a resolute liberal, led a revolt of both army and navy. His street is a sober, nineteenth-century affair running up off Castellana just a short way from Cibeles. His victory, though he himself was soon assassinated, led to Isabel's abdication, the end of the Isabelline era and the end of the last of anything approaching the old-style, unrepentant Spanish Bourbons.

Prim's assassination was a greater loss than that of the *ancien régime*, for if anyone showed signs of being the century's great liberalizer it was he. Before he came to power, not very much had been achieved. The Church had been somewhat restrained; a slightly more modern basis had been laid for public administration; new laws put through during the liberal biennium had encouraged the middle classes to enter business. Prim, in two brisk years, opened the suffrage to all males over twenty-five and wrote into the Spanish law and constitution the great bulk of the civil liberties required for an escape from the dark age of capricious absolutism. These included freedom of association, much sought after by the swelling industrial work-force in Catalonia. Prim also imported a new king, Don Amadeo from the House of Savoy in Italy. But with Prim dead and factionalism in the ascendant, Amadeo soon gave up his hopeless task.

There now emerged, tumultuously and suddenly, a brand new republicanism. Having only a short history, this so far had little philosophical background; though from now and into an ever more complicated future, republicanism was to be one of the main strands of Spanish thought. The First Republic lasted for the single year of 1873, getting through four presidents in that brief period. The most striking aspect of the year was the way in which municipality after municipality declared for total independence and autonomy, a theory of Swiss-style cantonalism fragmenting into ever tinier constituent parts as the *patria chica* asserted itself in general suspicion of Madrid; the great reversal came when Emilio Castelar, third of the presidents and the century's great orator, brought in the army to restore central control. The death of the republic came when a Civil Guard general burst into the Cortes and brought its deliberations to an end.

Now it seemed scarcely the twinkling of an eye before a young officer named Martínez Campos pronounced for a Bourbon restoration and back came Isabel II's son, the admirable, if sickly, Alfonso XII, pledged to good behaviour as a constitutional monarch. The Carlists had once again embarked on a small-scale but ferocious civil war; somehow, painfully, first the republic and then the new monarchical regime defended themselves. Spain settled once more to rule by politicians but under a more responsive Crown. For the next fifty years, elections were grossly, shamelessly manipulated to establish a system called the *turno*, with alternating conservative and liberal governments. It was the classic period of *caciquismo*, boss rule, when rural bosses simply told the people how to vote – and whipped them half to death if they disobeyed. Even so, except for those like the republicans who were root and branch opposed to the whole system, the cumulative achievements over a decade or two were reasonably forward-looking. Cánovas for the conservatives was the mastermind of the restoration, holding the fabric of the system together; Sagasta for the liberals was an episodic reformer. One great danger for the future, however, was the return, in force, of the Spanish Church, which now consciously sought, and soon attracted, a devout and passionate following among the wealthier sections of society. The Jesuits, many times banned, were back again; so were the monks and nuns. In the rural south and the industrializing east, the poorer people, unchurched and alienated, became more and more hostile to the clergy. Radical intellectuals in the cities took up the same position.

By the 1890s two new developments were taking place. Industrial Catalonia was becoming desperately restless, and simultaneously the political system of Madrid was failing and stagnant. Crisis, clearly, was once again approaching. But this time, when it came, the difficulty was international – from the 1895 revolt in Cuba, last substantial holding of the Spanish empire. In 1898, as is well known, following the mysterious explosion of the battleship USS Maine, the young United States sided with the Cubans. Military Spain, old-fashioned, creaking at the seams, advanced upon the contest as a matter of honour, only to see her ancient ships go down in minutes, her armies perish of disease. No greater shame than 1898 had ever previously afflicted Spain, even in the days of Felipe II's foolish Armada or when the colonial liberators seized back Latin America during the 1820s.

There soon arose in Spain, in a response that released decades of emotion, the so-called Generation of '98, a number of writers dedicated to diagnosing their country's ills. Unamuno was among their impassioned number and so excellent was their work that the period is often called the Silver Age of Spanish literature. Outside their magic circle, the Aragonese thinker Joaquín Costa, son of a peasant family, called unrealistically for the participation of the unpoliticized lower-middle classes and much more urgently for *escuela y despensa* – education and more to eat. Ominously, he called too for 'an iron surgeon' to remedy the country's sickness.

Naturally enough, these dramas of republic and restoration, Carlism, the *turno* and Cuba, lured me on in my historical tourism, though now thoroughly footsore, to corresponding streets and monuments. Emilio Castelar, so briefly president of the First Republic, has a pompous monument at a roundabout in the Castellana. It shows him, risen oratorically to his feet on a high plinth, hand raised, forefinger lifted to make an impassioned point. On stone steps to one side of him, the public or perhaps his colleagues – clothed in togas – listen in humble admiration. But to the other side there is a group of naked ladies and up above him, topmost in the monument, three naked Graces make a tender circle. What Castelar is actually saying, according to approving Madrileños, is *Las de arriba estan mejor* – the ones up top are better.

With proper even-handedness, Martínez Campos, who restored the monarchy, is immediately adjacent. His street runs down to Castelar's roundabout, with three surviving mansions in the Spanish equivalent of late Victorian or Edwardian style, ample and comfortable, the kind which used to cluster all around the Castellana. With gardens, driveways and welcoming windows, they are hugely more interesting than the dull twentieth-century blocks that have otherwise replaced them – though, of course, the mansions housed only a handful compared to the hundreds who now live in the apartments or swarm into the office premises that jockey with them along the Castellana. One of the old houses in Martínez Campos belonged to Joaquín Sorolla, the turn-of-the-century painter of Valencian beach scenes. His naked boys – rather a lot of these – and ladies under broad umbrellas may be seen here in an excellent display, essentially of genre scenes illuminated with the brilliant light of the Levant.

As for Sagasta, his street is not far off, solid residential with a lot of traffic pouring through. The statesman-like, conservative Cánovas in a sense does better since to him has been awarded, under both his surnames (Cánovas del Castillo), the large roundabout or circus by the Prado, with Carlos III's Neptune fountain in the middle. The only problem is that every citizen and taxi-driver knows it more familiarly as Neptune. Joaquín Costa's street, right up near the top of Serrano, is one of the most boring in Madrid, certainly not worth the blisters.

Cánovas was assassinated in a resort in the Basque Country, by an Italian anarchist, in reprisal for his attempts to repress terrorism in Catalonia. His place in the conservative hierarchy was eventually taken by the dramatically austere and arrogant Antonio Maura; his street, as grand and as starchy as his personality, lies behind the post office at Cibeles. As the twentieth century developed, Maura governments began to alternate with those of José Canalejas, eventual replacement for Sagasta on the left. Canalejas has a circus just by the Puerta del Sol, rat race for traffic but possessing a wonderfully old-fashioned sweetshop where everything is either scented with violets or decorated with them and prettily stacked up in baskets tied with violet-coloured ribbons. For both these men, Maura and Canalejas, until the assassination of the latter in 1912, also by anarchists, one of the problems at the top of the list was precisely how to deal with the anarchists. Both men will feature in the story once again but since it was Barcelona, not Madrid, that was home, hearth and nursery of Spanish anarchism, it seemed that my walk in Madrid had come to a natural conclusion.

Barcelona, seaboard city, great capital of a tiny nation of six million, speaking a language of its own, but believing itself open to every wind that blows, enabling it, in its own myth, to be entirely European while still intensely Catalan; a capital that, in my personal opinion, is serious, generous, genial and excessively self-approving all at once; smaller than its arch-rival in the centre, yet by any reckoning more of a city than Madrid, more metropolitan and more organic. For me, Madrid is closer home, and I confess I love it more, but going to Barcelona is always the adventure.

I am holed up in a hotel on the Avinguda del Paral·lel, with a view on to the greenery of the big hill of Montjuïc, home of the Olympic stadium, a fun-fair and stupendous galleries of Catalan art and artefacts. It was up here on Montjuïc that George Orwell and his fellow soldiers practised marching at the start of the Civil War. Down below, at the nearest corner, there is a cluster of theatres and entertainment halls and one or two 'porno' establishments (there has been trouble lately with a protest from animal rights' defenders over an act involving a donkey). Popping down in the evening for a beer I find myself among the performers from the entertainment hall, large, blousy, blonde women attended by small men, all enormously polite and talking away about the children's schools and how to get spots out of carpets. There is a little statue of a flower girl and every day, as like as not, someone will put fresh roses in her basket.

I have come to Barcelona for the atmosphere and the anarchists, of course, but not for them alone. For it was in the nineteenth century, the era I am visiting at present, that Barcelona witnessed the rebirth of serious regionalism, the little-nationhood, that gives it so much of its present quality. Out of this, in due course, there grew the extraordinary and brilliant phenomenon of Modernista architecture, by far the most exciting development in the arts in nineteenth-century Spain. This in turn presaged an artistic future that was to launch not merely the young Picasso, on his way through from Málaga to Paris, but later, as the nineteenth century gave way to the twentieth, Miró, Dalí and Tàpies. Even without its contributions to the history of politics, intense but not always agreeable, Barcelona would still be a world-class city all the way.

Because the present clamours so insistently in Barcelona, I have a date at the university to discuss the current state of Catalonia and Catalanism before I launch myself upon the past. I make my way there just a little circuitously, starting down by the harbour and the high Columbus column – perversely sited, perhaps, considering that Catalonia was banned from trade with America. Beside the column stands a huge and pompous customs house, evidence of energy in trading wherever the Catalans were actually allowed to trade. Behind, in equally huge warehouses, there is a glimpse of Easter floats, laid up until next year.

Anyone who knows the city will realize I have come this way for the pleasure of striking straight up the Ramblas, one of the most famous and still the most delightful of European thoroughfares. The Ramblas – one street, really, but known by different names in different places and hence obtaining a collective plural – climb gently up towards the heart of town, the ample central pavement shadowed by plane trees, dappled with sunlight, planted out successively with cafés and newspaper stalls, flower shops and finally a bird market with parrots and fantail doves and even a few guinea pigs in cages. It's seedy, it's decrepit, it's completely fascinating, with everything from prostitutes and pimps (low down on the Ramblas, rough and tough of a winter's evening), to a grand opera house, the Liceu, spiritual home of the bourgeoisie. The people stroll and flow, often fantastically dressed, watch buskers, watch each other, watch their handbags very carefully. I pass a woman with a bowler hat, a rigid smile and heavily veined legs. She is tap-dancing fiercely, alone amidst the crowd. A clown with whited face performs a trick that makes me laugh out loud. Before I know it, he's embracing me.

The houses are rather stern (or would be without the trees that brush against them), five or six storeys high, flat-faced with stiff little iron balconies and wooden shutters, mostly brown and peeling. You could use a walk along the Ramblas, if you felt inclined to, as a coat-hanger for a visit to the ancient city that mostly lies immediately to your right, with its deep little shadowed streets giving way to open plazas and chunks of truly monumental masonry, a warren that never ceases to beguile. There is the arcaded Plaça Reial, full of African street traders and young people with guitars. The whiff of drugs is almost tangible. Then there is the Barri Gòtic (or Barrio Gótico) with splendid cathedral and the broad and high-arched Tinell Hall where Columbus reported to the Catholic Kings after his first and greatest voyage. (He rode beside Fernando through the city, an event that pleased him almost as much as opening what he believed was the western route to Asia.)

University-bound today, I cannot linger. At the top of the Ramblas are the wide, open spaces of the Plaça de Catalunya, ringed by banks and department stores, traditional dividing point between the old town and the nineteenth-century extension – *ensanche* in Castilian, *eixample* in Catalan – where most of the Modernista architecture was erected. The university is not far off, itself a stately nineteenth-century building. Its main entrance hall is decorated with all the appropriate symbolic statues: Alfonso X the Learned;

Averroes in a turban; the great Catalan humanist Lluís Vives; and, best of all, Ramón Llull, key figure of the Catalan Middle Ages – originally knight at arms, then a composer of novels and innumerable treatises, a polymath and missionary, and quite one of the most extraordinary figures in peninsular history. A work of his on navigation, written in 1295, was still in use at the time of Columbus; he was also probably the only European to have studied Islam sympathetically and fully.

There is a conference in progress at the university – linguistics, cybernetics, something incomprehensible – the voices all about me American, French, Castilian, Catalan, their owners wandering in gossipy groups like characters from a campus novel. This could be any big university, anywhere. The man I am about to meet fits into the pattern, well-known nationally in his discipline, even internationally. But when he comes he seems to have a furtive look about him and he draws me along with him, not to his office, but to a bench in the university garden as far as possible from the conference clientele. He will talk to me, he says, certainly he will, and I can make any use I like of the material, except that I must not quote his name or identify him in any way and if I do, he will deny he ever met me. It is not a reflection on writers or journalists, he says, merely a matter of self-protection.

So there we sit, in shade, on a summer's day, in a sweet-smelling garden in central Barcelona, wrapped in deepest secrecy. I find it hard to conceal my astonishment. Nor is there much, it seems at first, to justify the precautions for my companion opens his remarks by speaking of his pride in Catalonia and its current achievements, its dominance of the national theatre in Madrid, the excellence of Catalan novelists. We talk of such universal figures as Llull and Josep Trueta, whose method of bandaging and draining wounds has saved literally millions of lives during our century. My companion adds that he certainly welcomed the return of Catalonia's own government, the reinvented medieval Generalitat, after the great repression under Franco. (Catalonia is now an 'autonomy', with wider powers than most and using them vigorously. The British journalist John Hooper speaks of it as a 'state within a state'. A

Spanish diplomat tells me, hardly concealing his irritation, that in setting up trade delegations in foreign capitals Catalonia is effectively running its own diplomatic service.)

Those in charge of the Generalitat, says my academic friend in Barcelona, quite naturally want more than they have under the autonomy, federal status, perhaps, but certainly something short of total independence. It is true there are separatists and they do indeed pursue a policy of violence, but incidents are few and public support for them is nil.

So what, I wonder, is the problem? Why the secrecy?

'Language,' he replies, with passion. 'It is all a question of language. Look at me, I am a Catalan. Catalan is the language I use when somebody steps on my toe. I pray to my God in Catalan. But nowadays when the Catalanists say we are a nation – *Som una nacio* – and talk about "normalizing" the use of our language, that's just an excuse for imposing it on everybody at all levels. We are actually doing what Franco did when he suppressed Catalan – using language as a political weapon.

'In universities, there is no requirement to teach in Catalan but there is great pressure. Am I doing a student a favour if he or she can't write a decent essay in Castilian? Three hundred million people speak Castilian, six million Catalan. What if students should want to work abroad when they have graduated? University application forms used to be in Castilian. But instead of waiting till they were finished, thousands and thousands were secretly destroyed, at a cost of millions of pesetas, so that Catalan forms could be substituted right away. Universities should be above this kind of fighting over which language to use, we should remember the universalism of the university idea. Catalonia was great when she opened herself to the world in the thirteenth and fourteenth centuries. So why should we try to enclose ourselves now? It's irrefutable that we are the European part of Spain – and the rest of Spain, it's true, looks at us with a certain kind of envy and admiration. We work hard, we have ideas, we have connections. Why spoil it through linguistic regimentation? The Catalanists call themselves "patriots" but when one group wants to impose a definition of something, entirely leaving out what others think, well, that's simply fascism. It has no other name.'

Everybody knows the work of Antoni Gaudí, the elastic flow of his apartment blocks, the cursive lines that are almost animal, the glittering, absurdist tentacles of the unfinished mega-church of the Sagrada Familia or Holy Family. Fewer know the depth of Catalan architecture at the end of the last century and the start of this, with scores and scores of surviving buildings sometimes comparable to Gaudí projects, sometimes strongly opposed to them, all supported by a multitude of decorative sculptors and furniture-makers, of gifted craftsmen working in wrought iron, stained glass or ceramics. It is a world of startling invention and bounteous oddity, thrilling to discover, far more profuse than one could possibly imagine before one has paced the streets of Barcelona.

The origins of this and other cultural phenomena of the period in Catalonia are usually traced back to the 1830s. In line with the romantic discovery of southern Spain by foreigners, Spaniards themselves were beginning to discover the pleasure and singularities of their own native regions and landscapes. Out of this there arose the so-called *costumbrista* school of writing, literally 'writing about customs', better translated perhaps as folkloric or genre writing. In Catalonia the *costumbrista* movement coincided with strongly renewed interest in the language. This, like Portuguese or Galician, or for that matter Castilian itself, derives from early medieval Latin. It was spoken in the ninth century, written by the twelfth and had for long periods of time been the official language of Catalonia. The eighteenth-century Bourbons suppressed it in the name of centralism, but it appears merely to have gone underground, remaining sufficiently strong to lend itself, in the time of the *costumbristas*, to a widescale cultural revival known as the Catalan *renaixença*, or renaissance. Indeed, the promotion of the language became the animating principle of the *renaixença*. Catalan flourished at every level, from the revived troubadour contests, or *jocs florals*, of the educated classes to choral singing among the working people of the quickly growing towns.

Catalonia had regained its sense of self and cultural identity. Now other things began to happen fairly quickly, a number of them related to new building projects. From 1854, the walls of the medieval city began to be dismantled. In 1859 a plan was adopted for the construction of a new *eixample*, up beyond the Plaça de Catalunya, basically in square city blocks, or *manzanas*, but pierced by a great angled throughway – today's Avinguda Diagonal. In 1875 a new School of Architecture was established. Now, a new class of self-made industrialists began to commission mansions in the *eixample* and sometimes in already existing parts of town.

One of the earliest and most brilliant of the professors of the new School of Architecture was the Madrid-trained Catalan, Lluís Domènech i Montaner. In 1878, still in his twenty-eighth year, he called on fellow-architects to join him in 'the search for a national architecture'. By 'national' at this stage it seems that he meant Spanish, but at the same time he pointed colleagues towards Catalan Romanesque and Gothic as natural sources. He himself went on to become deeply involved in the politics of emergent Catalan nationalism, twice representing Catalonia in the Madrid Cortes and figuring prominently in the Catalan Lliga or League. This powerful political grouping grew up to represent the industrial establishment, so paving the way for limited Catalan self-government by a revived Generalitat.

Domènech's buildings seem from the beginning deeply Catalan, at least in the sense that they are in the style which we now call Modernista (though this itself was originally the Spanish word for Art Nouveau or German Jugendstil). Though most of the work of the Barcelona architects is in the city itself, they also erected buildings in other parts of Spain, giving a touch of the new Catalan gaudiness to many surprising places. There are clusters of Modernista buildings on the Cantabrian north coast and Gaudí worked as far afield as Madrid, Astorga and León. Of Domènech's buildings, the most spectacular and most often cited is firmly in Barcelona, the Palau de la Música Catalana of 1905–6, slightly buried among small streets in the old town but a majestic exercise in colourful excess. It was built in brick – Modernista theory came to favour this local material – with archways and flying buttresses buried in the fabric and series of round columns brilliantly decorated in ceramic cladding. Inside, with riotous sculpture and stained-glass walling, the palace is even more of an astonishment, exemplifying the other Modernista tenet that all the decorative arts must work together to form the totality. Another Domènech building that made the same point was the elaborately castellated, distinctly Moorish-looking Café-Restaurant erected for the Great Exhibition of 1888 – a key moment for Barcelona in staking its claims to international regard. The exhibition was held in the park of the Ciutadella (erected by Felipe V and torn down by the Barcelona people as a symbol of hated centralism). After the exhibition the Café-Restaurant was left in place and became a communal workshop, under the guidance of Domènech and the architect Antoni Allissa, for many of the leading craftsmen associated with the Modernista movement. Today it has changed function once again, doing duty now as a zoological museum.

But if these buildings are the best known face of Domènech, there are at least two others of equal worth that show him in rather a different light. They have the added advantage of being in the *eixample*, and might serve as motive for a first stroll among its broad and elegant avenues. The first-constructed was originally a private house in a now-famous block called the Manzana de la Discòrdia (*manzana* meaning apple as well as city block), which contains teasingly contrasting yet wonderfully complementary work not only by Domènech and Gaudí but also by Josep Puig i Cadafalch, third in the trio of great names of the period. It is sited in the Passeig de Gràcia, foremost of the grand avenues of the *eixample*.

The Domènech house was actually a remodelling, undertaken for Albert Lleó, the doctor son of an industrialist, and his wife Francesca Morera, whence it acquired its name, the Lleó Morera house. It has been somewhat knocked about outside, though it has an interesting arrangement of balconies, galleries and windows, with strangely Gothic–Moorish touches. The deepest interest, however, lies within, once again making the point about the totality, both of the architecture and its decoration. In the Modernista totalist approach, there were clear borrowings from William Morris and the Arts and Crafts Movement, as also from continental Art Nouveau, seen particularly in serpentine and floral patterns in stained glass (just as there were to be borrowings in form and structure from Charles Rennie Mackintosh in Glasgow). But the way the combinations are put together, and the extra sources that are drawn upon – both broadly Spanish and specifically Catalan – together with the colossal inventiveness of the Catalan artist-craftsmen, give the best Modernista buildings a feeling of being totally *sui generis*, a new species.

In the first floor of the Lleó Morera house, which was formerly inhabited by the family and is now, by happy chance, the headquarters of the Barcelona tourist board, thus easy to penetrate, there is a gallimaufry of coffered ceilings and inlaid woodwork, of mosaic floors and *azulejos* dados. The dining-room, most famous part of the house, has stained-glass windows showing geese, ducks, chicks, hens and roosters, all in a slightly vapid countryside. The internal walls of the dining-room are decorated with arcadian mosaics, said to have been worked up from photographs, showing the family picnicking in the country, with carefully disposed ladies in long dresses and gentlemen standing to pour the wine. In another sylvan scene, a woman servant arrives from nowhere with a tray of tiny cups and coffee for a young couple, no doubt Lleó and his wife, both seated at ease on the ground, she under a parasol.

It is a charming, rather ingenuous interior, to my eye less remarkable than another feature of the house, also created to order in the same very personal fashion – a series of sculptural scenes told over doorways and arches from the entry of the apartment, down the corridor half-way to the dining-room and back again to the front door.

The story is an ancient Catalan lullaby. It tells of a king and queen who go off hunting; we see the king first, cup in hand, being offered an overflowing dish of fruit. Above the next doorway, the king and queen, clear-profiled, young, are in the country, accompanied by dog and huntsman. Birds fly obligingly about. Meanwhile back at the palace – and here the real drama starts – the wet nurse is giving her left breast, Madonna-like, to the royal infant. The baby's head is so gently rounded that you have to love it. The nurse, with long triangular face and hooded eyes – closed, perhaps, in the luxury of giving suck – has a tall medieval coif. It is so tender a scene that unless you know the lullaby you can scarcely imagine what comes next. The king and his party are all right, thank you. A young man blasts an arrow clear across the corridor at a boar pursued through undergrowth by rampant hounds. But, ah, at home, the nurse, the nurse – to soothe the child, she lights a fire, then drifts away to sleep, as sweet and elegant as ever. But when she wakes – oh horror – the cradle is engulfed by flame, the poor baby a burning brand. Now, in her dismay, the nurse prays hard to the image of the Virgin ... Please, please, make the baby well and I'll give you two crowns, one for yourself, one for the Infant Jesus. The Virgin at once obliges, the baby is whole again and now the nurse's friend – whoever he may be – produces a bag of gold to pay the craftsmen who will make the crowns. Off-stage, the hunting's done, a good catch, by the look of it, with a bit of hawking on the side. The king and queen come home all innocence – you never know what the baby-sitter has been up to – and happily receive their child. On the very last panel, much wider, over a door and window, the pretty nurse looks on, arm over a parapet, while two artist-craftsmen actually make the crowns.

Within this charmingly told drama – the sculpture is the work of Eusebi Arnau, and not entirely sentimental – there seem to be several messages. They include the importance of the artist-craftsman, the redeeming love of the Virgin and the unreliability of the underclasses, all articles of faith in Catalan bourgeois ideology. It is also the case that the doctor and his wife had themselves lost a baby, named Albert like his father. When they had a replacement child, they gave him the very same name, and perhaps it is really the story of a miraculous rebirth that is being told so touchingly in the Lleó Morera house. Optimism based on religious faith is a considerable feature in the Catalan cosmogony.

Dr Albert Lleó, father of the baby, worked, when Domènech had finished building it, in the great Barcelona hospital of Sant Pau (St Paul). As a busy city institution, this is not exactly on the tourist trail but it is surely worth a visit, for it incorporates another set of ideas that were widely held among the Catalan bourgeoisie, charity and service to the community and a little bit of self-congratulation at meeting the financial cost. (Significantly, the words 'I love you' in Catalan are *'te estimo'* – literally 'I count your worth'.) Physically, the hospital is again a remarkable place, Gothic, Byzantine, brick, just as one has now learnt to expect from Domènech, with individual wards and specialist departments set out as separate buildings round a large inner courtyard. Here, in balmy weather, patients in pyjamas wander with their visitors under the shady trees, passing, to take one example, the vascular surgery department, decked out harmoniously but surprisingly with spires and cupolas. Above the street entrance to the accident and emergency department, there is a gilded mosaic of the founder signing the will that endowed the hospital.

Domènech was accessible, eclectic, fecund in discussion, an optimist like Dr Lleó and wife, definitely one of the Catalan Europeans. Some twenty or so lesser architects are cited as his collaborators and followers and they produced a great volume of work, much of it surviving in the *eixample*. Gaudí, born in 1852, was narrow, rigid in ideas, a puritan, one of those who believed the Church had a duty to check the growing looseness of society. He drew around him a tight group of like-minded conservatives; perhaps reactionaries is the fairer word. They were disciples more than collaborators, and almost all belonged to the Cercle Artístic de San Lluc, a society controlled by a paternalist Catalan priest, Josep Torras i Bages, who later rose to be a bishop. The label Modernista, with its implication of up-to-dateness and mild suggestion of *fin de siècle* decadence, was applied retrospectively to architecture and it is an irony that Gaudí's group are regarded as the epicentre of a movement to which they would emphatically have denied allegiance. Yet it is they in particular, with their cranky, soaring, wonderful and sometimes quite repugnant inventions, whom we recognize today as the freest spirits of the age, true creators right across the range of architecture and its associated arts.

For Gaudí, the notion of the Church stood at the centre, architecturally as well as spiritually. This means that the Sagrada

Familia, taken over by Gaudí when he was already fifty, and occupying him right up to his death in 1926 (he fell under a tram outside the church and was taken off to die unrecognized in hospital), is nevertheless a useful place to start. You do not have to like it – personally, I hate it – to realize that in its vast, stiff, skyward reach, it is one of the great phenomena of our century, an apt summation for a city that has never been afraid of fantasy. Nor is it a surprise that the church-burning revolutionaries of 1936 took so much pride in it that they spared it, leaving it standing there half-built, a perpetual source of argument as to whether and how the attempt should be made to finish it.

In terms of Gaudí's relationship with the Modernista movement, two main points emerge from the Sagrada Familia. One is the sheer height of the transept towers, great cellular-seeming prongs climbing up and up, endlessly inscribed with the word 'Sanctus', to end in a ceramic coxcomb, out-Disneying Disney ahead of time. These lofty constructions are actually quite small compared to the central spire envisaged by Gaudí but never built. The point here is that the Modernistas, including Gaudí, exploited modern materials like concrete, brick and iron to the full. They trusted their static calculations; they had no fear at all; they were thus able to achieve unprecedented shapes and contours.

The other main point concerns the sculpture, which is organic, seemingly part of the structure. For if one takes the west end of the church as representative, what one sees is stone made liquid, tumbling down in a waterfall of mythological invention, a little reminiscent, though the scale is infinitely greater, of the baroque fantasy of the Marquis of Dos Aguas in Valencia. What sets Gaudí and his followers apart from their Barcelona contemporaries is the way they liberated themselves from historical precedent, despite their intellectual conservatism, to achieve an astonishing free flow. Perhaps the only comparisons are twentieth-century music or the experimental novel.

To reach this freedom, Gaudí travelled a considerable distance in his own life, working his way through earlier Spanish styles. There is a fascinating Gaudí building – the Casa Vicens – a short way up the hill that rises over the *eixample*. These lower slopes were not particularly fashionable (they climb right up to the friendly presence of Monte Tibidabo, splendid outlook point over the city) and the house is somewhat more modest than other Gaudí blocks. The interest is that it is largely Moorish or at least Mudéjar in style, with green, yellow and white ceramics, stepped arches, *ajimeces*. Owing to Catalonia's early recapture by the Franks, there is no Mudéjar building to speak of in the region, an indication that Catalan architects were not narrowly national but looked across the whole of Spain for inspiration. Gaudí, on the other hand, refused to speak Castilian.

He had no qualms at all about the use of Gothic, which seemed to Modernistas, as it seemed to the English architect Pugin, free and agreeably untrammelled by the constraints of classicism. The best of Gaudí Gothic may be the Palau Güell, built for his principal patron in a narrow street off the lower Ramblas. This is a forbidding medieval fortress, mildly Scottish in appearance, though surmounted by fantastical chimneys with pointed hats like toadstools. The greatest feature of its façade is the ironwork, which characterizes not only this but many Gaudí buildings, offering no simple shape like round or rectangular, to which you might attach a regular adjective, but swirling or spiky, lumpy or drawn out. You may come across a Gaudí gateway, say, with the wrought iron pulled out in an attenuated mass like a bird being gutted. Here, on the Palau Güell, the main piece of ironwork is topped by the most dreadful, scrawny, scraggy bird imaginable, flapping for a take-off it will never achieve.

The building houses a museum, so providing public access to the interior, a wild mixture of the threatening, dark and low, and of considerable loftiness, composed, as always, of surprising shapes. It even features an internal colonnade. The supporting detail of furniture, carved panelling, stained glass and coffered ceiling – and at one point the end of an iron beam with rivets like something from a railway bridge – combine to make the interior weirdly, stirringly spectacular.

The best of Gaudí, though, because the freest, lies in monuments such as the city block informally known as La Pedrera – the Stone Quarry – not far up from the Manzana de la Discòrdia on Passeig de Gràcia. This has surging concrete forms and wildly, jaggedly, swirling wrought-iron balcony railings (railings is too prosaic a word for these works by Gaudí's collaborator Josep Maria Jujol). Looking at them, you begin to think their proper use might well be suicide by impalement. And absolutely the most genial of Gaudí works – genial both in the English sense of good humoured and the Spanish sense of possessing genius – is the Parc Güell, high on the hill above the city, intended as an architectural open space for a private housing venture that never happened. Only two houses were built and Gaudí lived in one of them; in comparison with other works of his it seems a little on the dingy, certainly on the spartan side. But the park itself is a delightful treat. Gaudí and Jujol together were among the earliest makers of collages, encrusting everything in richly coloured, broken-up ceramics, generally abstract and in the Moorish style (special orders for the Modernistas breathed new life into Manises). Here, where Gaudí's sculpturally modulated crypts and pillars are combined with the long swirl of running benches by Jujol, brilliant, almost comical with their ceramic dressing, the visitor to Barcelona encounters the Modernistas at their happiest.

Josep Puig i Cadafalch was almost twenty years younger and fell in behind Domènech, not Gaudí. Puig, like Domènech, was also an art historian and became a great expert on the Romanesque. In the remote Pyrenean churches of Catalonia there existed a body of Romanesque art that was comparable in excellence to the painting of the León pantheon, cumulatively a good deal more extensive, grave, austere, magnificent, but sometimes, too, erupting with emotion. By the early twentieth century, the churches were in ruins and the paintings were either perishing or being spirited abroad. Puig was involved in the rescue of great numbers of frescoes and painted wooden panels. Today they are exhibited up on Montjuïc in the Museu d'Art de Catalunya (itself housed in a huge great clump of palatial masonry erected for the city's second great international exhibition, in 1929). For Romanesque enthusiasts, one of the best reasons for visiting Barcelona is to spend time with these paintings.

Puig also erected a host of buildings. His extremely spiky Casa Terrades, Oxford-college-Gothic-crossed-with-Rhineland-mystical, and the Museu de la Música almost opposite, with its crossed medieval-Moorish interior, give some idea of his range. His best known single work is probably the earlier Casa Amatller in the great terrace of the Manzana de la Discòrdia, where he collaborated with a host of decorative artists. Its stepped façade and particularly its noble mock-medieval staircase might well put one in mind of Keats and the sumptuous richness of his *Eve of St Agnes*. But in the end, being more narrowly historicist than either Domènech or Gaudí, Puig in my view is a less interesting architect.

As a Catalan public figure, on the other hand, he was even more notable than his mentor Domènech, rising through the politics of the bourgeoisie to become, from 1917 to 1924, the second president of the Mancomunitat, an early version of today's 'autonomy'. It is in this capacity that we will next encounter him, facing a major crisis in the name of Catalonia.

The Catalan industrialists for whom the architects carried out most of their large commissions, including some purely industrial projects, were by no means model employers. The work-force laboured long and hard for its modest living and took no part in the Catalanist politics of the bourgeoisie. What was achieved in terms of separate or special status was achieved, almost by definition, without their support or interest. There was crossover in terms of language and popular entertainments. But the one and only point where the urban proletariat makes any connection with high art or the bourgeoisie, in anything other than inferior status, is in the work of the Modernista painters.

The two leading artists to whom the name Modernista is attached were Santiago Rusiñol and Ramon Casas, both wealthy sons of bourgeois families. Both enthusiastically embraced bohemianism, passing long periods in Montmartre (Paris, of course, had overtaken Rome as the one place that artists had to visit).

The first signs of serious regionalism in Catalan painting had come a little earlier through local landscape painters. These took their native heath as subject-matter while borrowing tone and composition from the robuster work of the Barbizon school in France. Rusiñol and Casas, who were friends of the Impressionists, followed the trend in borrowing quite heavily from France. But their work, in a range of media from oil painting to poster graphics – a great Catalan speciality – was of a different order to that of the landscape painters, justifying a visit to the Museu d'Art Modern in the Ciutadella Park, and anywhere else that keeps a representative selection (the nineteenth-century collection in the Prado has some good if somewhat sentimental Rusiñol, for instance).

Rusiñol painted a number of portraits but, more than anything, he was a specialist in mood, with a touch of the Celtic fringe about his work. Also an impassioned theorist and poet, he set up a studio in Sitges that made this seaside town, then not much more than a village, the recognized 'Mecca of Modernism'. He had bought two El Greco paintings in Paris and he and some friends carried them through the streets in full solemnity as a substitute Easter procession. They staged dances in boats offshore to be admired by watchers on the beach, again with utter seriousness. Surprisingly, it was Rusiñol who was first to turn to political matters, with a sketch (1893–4) of eight men on trial for an anarchist outrage. It is hard, though, in this sketch to see anything other than straightforward reporting.

Casas was far more sensitive than Rusiñol to the implications of the present moment, profuse in charcoal sketches of leading contemporaries, including Domènech and Puig. Later in life he was to turn to the portraiture of bourgeois women, which he managed admirably. But in 1894, in his twenty-eighth year, he exhibited in the retrospectively famous Sala Parés a painting called *Garrote Vil*, showing the public execution by garroting of an anarchist named Aniceto Peinador in the presence of a large crowd in the prison yard. In this painting, with its muted indication of horror at the victim's fate, Casas counterpointed the scarcely visible action with the soft tone of winter tree trunks and the surrounding buildings. Though one visitor to the Sala Parés fainted when she saw it, the evidence suggests that *Garrote Vil* made rather less of an impression than a genre scene of two years earlier, by another hand but also shown at the Sala Parés, of an old man on a donkey being publicly flogged at various stations round the city in pursuance of a medieval punishment still practised in Barcelona up until 1816. For us today, of course, knowing what happened later, it is the far more subtle Casas painting that has particular significance.

From their first arrival in Spain in 1868, brought by the Italian engineer Giuseppe Fanelli, the anarchist ideas of the Russian revolutionary Bakunin became a beacon of hope for the Spanish poor, far outweighing the attractions of Marxism. Urban Barcelona and intensely rural Andalucía both became strongholds of the doctrine, not regionalist but internationalist in their approach, believing in worldwide brother- and sisterhood, particularly of the workers. Bakunin himself called his approach collective, rather than anarchist, believing that men and women need only be freed of the repressive and self-serving power of the state to emerge as fully cooperative beings. Humans were social, Bakunin thought; they had no existence outside society and even if they were not fundamentally good, then the norms and practices of society would ensure that their behaviour was cooperative. There was no need for a political hierarchy, with some to give orders and others to obey. Quite on the contrary, all action should come from below. Revolutionary action, the first purpose of Bakunin's movement, should only be taken when the time seemed ripe to those actually taking it.

Fanelli's poverty-wracked journey through Spain, and the power he exercised over audiences, though speaking only in a foreign language, have been brilliantly described by Gerald Brenan, along with the fierce in-fighting between Marx and Bakunin that left Spain out on a limb, together with parts of northern Italy, as almost the only corners of the world where anarchism took proper root.

Fanelli came to Spain in 1868 to take advantage of the unstable situation presented by Prim's rebellion against the Bourbons. He immediately found followers. Anarchism played some part in the local separatism of the First Republic of 1873 (though a greater part was played by the Catalan federalist, Pi i Margall, who became the first of the republic's four presidents, pledged to cantonalization). The anarchists were cruelly persecuted in Andalucía and for a time became almost invisible, re-emerging in Barcelona in the 1890s, with a theory of 'propaganda by deed' and under the slogan that a single act is better than a thousand pamphlets.

The first Barcelona bomb was thrown in 1891 at the employers' headquarters during an industrial dispute. The following year an attempt was made on the life of Martínez Campos, of restoration fame, now captain-general in Barcelona. His attacker was caught and shot. In vengeance for this shooting, the young anarchist Santiago Salvador, leaning forward over the gallery of the Liceu during a performance of *William Tell*, lobbed a bomb that killed twenty people, mostly women. He and others were executed for the deed. A later bomb, which killed a number of the poorer members of a religious procession, became the occasion for the famous Montjuïc trials, with suspects tortured to death and international protests. It was in reprisal for Montjuïc that Cánovas was assassinated in 1897.

And so it went, with Barcelona now established as Bomb City and an emergent republicanism feeding into anarchism and vice versa. The notion of perpetual disturbance must, however, be a myth. For this was the very period when Modernista building was at its height and Catalan industry was prospering mightily. In the following year of 1898, however, the loss of Cuba finally proved to the local bourgeoisie that Madrid was bankrupt of ideas as well as money and that they must now pursue a purely Catalan path to self-advancement. The impression we should therefore carry in our heads is one of a city basically at peace, perhaps like London in the present era, with a possessing class intent on its own business and only from time to time the shocking interruption of a terrorist outrage or a public demonstration angrily suppressed. There were two cities side by side in Barcelona, the city of the industrialists and Modernistas and that of the labouring poor, with a leavening of militant anarchists and millenarian republicans. So far, only Ramon Casas, in *Garrote Vil* and a brief series of other protest paintings, had paid attention to both.

*

Pablo Picasso blew into the café of Els Quatre Gats – Catalan for the Four Cats – like a hot wind from the south. The year was 1899. Jaime Sabartés, the writer and close friend who later on in life became Picasso's secretary and helper, recalls the suspicions aroused in Barcelona by the mere word 'Andalusian', anybody answering to that description presumed by the prosperous classes to be 'a bull-fighter, a gypsy, a "wide boy"'. But the dashing and energetic young southerner, still in his late teens, enchanted the young companions whom he found in the café and soon it was he whose arrival was most ardently awaited, he who was most discussed when he was absent.

In lighting on Els Quatre Gats, Picasso had found exactly the right place. This remarkable establishment had been set up in the ground floor of a house in the old town, newly built by Puig i Cadafalch, all beams and Gothic arches, steel rivets and ceramic dados. It is still there today, looking very much as it does in photos taken in the 1890s. Rusiñol was a founder member, so was Miquel Utrillo, father of Maurice. Utrillo laid on puppet shows. There were exhibitions, readings, concerts of the work of Catalonian contemporaries such as Albéniz and Granados (many of Granados's scores and personal items are in the Domènech-designed Museu de la Música in the Avinguda Diagonal). Ibsen, Wagner, Maeterlinck, Nietzsche – all these favourites of the Modernistas came in for discussion. Ramon Casas was another of the older *habitués* and he had done a painting of himself and the proprietor, the tall, lugubrious-looking Pere Romeu, cycling along most earnestly upon a tandem, both men with large black beards. This hung on one wall. (The painting here now is a replica; the original is in the Museu d'Art Modern.) Other walls might have the work of younger regulars pinned up on them. Picasso soon did exactly this himself, producing a series of charcoal drawings of his friends and sticking them up in Els Quatre Gats as a frontal challenge to Ramon Casas, then entirely dominant in the city as portrait-painter and maker of portrait-sketches. Nobody much came in to look at them, however, so that it was Picasso and his friends who sat there in diminishing hopes of aggravation and diversion, drinking endless cups of coffee.

For a young man of his age – we see him in a sketch by Casas, wide-brimmed, high-crowned hat, loose jacket, trousers loose at thigh and tight at ankle, emulating the style of the anarchists – Picasso had already done a lot. He had been born in Málaga in 1881 to a charming and entirely supportive mother – his first words, she recalled, were 'piz, piz', short for *lápiz*, or pencil. His father was a slightly sad art teacher, driven in due course from Málaga to La Coruña, then on to Barcelona by the need to keep up his income for the growing family. At every stage of his childhood, the young Pablo Ruiz Picasso (he later called himself Picasso only, dropping his father's surname in favour of his mother's) produced work that seems quite literally marvellous, a visual equivalent to Mozart's childhood musicianship. In 1890, still in Málaga, he manages a brilliant set of amatory, pouting pigeons. On the same sheet but the other way up, a bullfighter is being tossed by an athletically out-stretched bull, in front of a crowd whose individual members are either lightly sketched or indicated by squiggles. In Barcelona, in his early teens, he did in a single day, for admission to a higher class in his father's art school, a drawing for which a whole month was allowed to students older than himself. The outcome is a triumph of realistic observation. By the age of sixteen, for admission to the Academy of San Fernando in Madrid (which he scarcely bothered to attend once he had got there, the academicians having little or nothing to teach him), he had done a huge scene called *Science and Charity* in which a doctor – his father sat for the part – takes the pulse of a sick woman. From the far side of the bed, a nurse holds a child in the crook of one arm, with the other holds out a mug of liquid to the patient. It is a fairly soppy scene, but you cannot imagine it being better done by anyone else of the period, whether in France or Catalonia.

Miracle on miracle: paper cut-outs from infancy, expressive sketches and paintings of mother and father, of his sister Lola; academic studies from his Barcelona art school, beach scenes that could have been done by a Barbizon or Hague School painter – Barcelona is extraordinarily fortunate to possess in its Picasso Museum, housed in a castle-mansion a short walk from Els Quatre

Gats, the near-complete works of the young Picasso, as well as a good deal else from the rest of his long life.

Hardly has Picasso hit upon Els Quatre Gats, however, than he is off to Paris, now producing the street and night-life scenes Toulouse-Lautrec had made so fashionable. He goes once, he goes twice to Paris, spending most of his time there with Spaniards and Catalans, all of them enduring hardship and poverty in their chosen studio and attic lifestyle. This is a period when art and suffering are believed to be inseparable. Picasso is still only nineteen, and temporarily in Madrid, when he hears that his close friend Carlos Casagemas, with whom he has spent the summer in Málaga, has shot himself to death in a Paris café, despairing at his impotence within a love affair.

Picasso at first shows little reaction but as soon as he returns to Paris, a curious blue tone drops over all his work. This is the style he uses for a portrait of his friend Jaime Sabartés, observed unawares in a café, alone and separate. Then comes a most curious work, split in two, in conscious deference to El Greco, with earth below and a mystical sky above. Robed figures gather round a body on the earth, while a white horse, possibly a circus horse, prances heavenwards. Its rider is almost hidden by the naked body of a woman kissing him. Naked women look on from the right, naked prostitutes in stockings look on from the left, as if to banish any thought of sentimentality. This picture is catalogued as *Evocation* but to Picasso's friends it was always known as *The Burial of Casagemas*.

Some believe that the Picasso Blue Period, with its disturbing portrayals of despair and alienation, of blindness, poverty and loss, was triggered directly by Casagemas's death. Some see a connection with Picasso's poverty in Paris; he was very cold each winter and one year burned many of his drawings to keep the fire alight. Both of these suggestions no doubt contain some element of truth. We know, on the other hand, that most of the Blue Period work, some of it shown in the Picasso Museum in Barcelona, was done during a long spell back in the city and that Picasso seemed personally cheerful throughout, indulging with his friends in the usual round of cafés, concerts, music halls and bullfights, as well as plenty of hard work. Of course, it is more than possible for personal upset to go along with extrovert behaviour, but it is equally possible, and in my opinion probable, that Picasso was painting to a more widely thought-out programme than the purely personal, deliberately articulating a general concept of human distress and separateness.

If so, he was in line with the second generation of the Modernista movement, represented by two fine painters, Joaquim Mir and Isidre Nonell. Mir at this time – he went on later to become a landscape painter – was strongly involved in documenting social miseries. Nonell, to my taste, is the more striking figure. When Els Quatre Gats first opened it contained an exhibition of Nonell paintings, of imbecilic goitre patients in a Pyrenean village. From that point onwards, his work becomes continually more painful, and in 1901 he turns entirely to the depiction of Barcelona's gypsies, catching their poverty and misery in a strong expressionism that won him little favour at the time. These harsh, upsetting works make an impressive parallel to Picasso's Blue paintings.

In 1904 Picasso moved permanently to France. Nonell died in 1911, at the age of thirty-eight, and was given a gypsy funeral in Barcelona.

To understand how Spain proceeded so briskly now to the first of its twentieth-century dictatorships – that of Primo de Rivera, installed in 1923 – it is necessary to follow progress in three separate but continually overlapping theatres. The first is Catalan regionalism; the second covers central government and Crown; the third is worker politics and the republicans. All can be dealt with either in many chapters or briefly by referring to the principal events. It is, of course, the second option that must be adopted here and if the result begins to sound like a history lesson, then I must put on my schoolmaster's voice and beg a moment's concentration, hoping the reader will find it worthwhile in the end.

Catalan political regionalism, as opposed to merely cultural and linguistic regionalism, began with books and pamphlets in the 1860s and 1870s. Its first solid public step came in 1885 when business leaders and intellectuals presented the Madrid government with a set of formal complaints and a demand for regional recognition, the so-called Memorial de Greuges. The underlying, unromantic problem, as often in Catalan affairs, concerned the level of tariffs. The Catalan textile industry had not done well enough to make itself competitive internationally and always needed protection, mainly against Manchester. The demand for higher tariff rates was a continuous concern in Catalonia, one of the main reasons for its alienation from Madrid.

In 1892, Catalan intellectuals and professional groupings published a manifesto called the Bases de Manresa. This called for thoroughgoing regional autonomy within the Spanish state. As throughout the history of Aragón and Catalonia, the authors also wanted to establish definite limits to their obligation for military service to the Madrid government. This was another central theme in Catalan nationalism.

The disaster in Cuba in 1898 brought matters to a head, partly because Madrid seemed so incompetent, partly because, in Cuba, Catalonia now lost its last remaining captive export market. Almost at once, regionalist politicians began to be returned in place of those drawn from the established parties. In 1913 the Madrid government was obliged to concede a consolidation of the powers held by the four Catalan provinces within a single body in Barcelona. The unit so composed was called the Mancomunitat. This was not really such a huge matter; the powers were very limited, not nearly so sweeping as those demanded by the Bases de Manresa, but at least they covered the single area of historic Catalonia. The Catalans now exploited them efficiently and imaginatively, achieving a great deal in education and public services. With the coming of the First World War and Spain's successful neutrality policy, Catalan industry – and Valencian orange production – went into overdrive, adding considerably to local wealth and self-confidence. The Mancomunitat itself appeared set fair. But this, though it pleased the bourgeois interest, was no solution for the emergent, full-blooded separatists who wanted more than limited liberties licensed by Madrid. Progressively, those on the left of Catalan regionalism began to feel the only way ahead might lie with the republicans, which would, of course, be bitterly resisted by the centre. Perils evidently loomed.

Nor was there any cause for self-satisfaction back in Madrid within the central government. Following Cuba, there was a general understanding that national 'regeneration' must be sought. There was, however, no clear means of seeking it. Antonio Maura, the dominant conservative, believed in 'revolution from above', a creed that did not impress the anarchists with their belief in revolution from below. His attempts to clean up local government and to abolish *caciquismo* were so high-handed that he alienated everybody. As for the liberals, after various administrations under Sagasta and others, Canalejas from 1910 attempted serious reforms to the tax system, trying at last to benefit the poor. This has to be reckoned on the credit side. Slightly more doubtful was the arrival in 1902, after yet another long regency, of a new king. Alfonso XIII was still only sixteen but showed considerable charm, more charm perhaps than political ability. His acquaintanceship with the realities of Spanish life was limited and his love of hunting and that marvellous new invention, the sports car, combined to keep him on the margins as he matured, devoting such time as he had left from entertainment mainly to wooing the generals.

Within this unpromising context, it was military affairs that produced the first great crisis. In 1909, following attacks on Spanish mining interests in Morocco, Maura attempted a military call-up and ran headlong into deep difficulty, as was inevitable, in Catalonia.

At this point, it is necessary to look back quickly to the background in worker politics. The anarchists were already well-established in Catalonia and were reinforced by the republicans under their inflammatory leader Alejandro Lerroux. Marxist trade unions and a Marxist political party set up national headquarters there in 1888, but found the going hard and transferred to Madrid the following year. It was the anarchists, therefore, who were still in the ascendant in Barcelona at the time of the 1909 call-up. They and the vast majority of the working class resisted. The result was La Semana Trágica, the Tragic Week of Barcelona. Over one hundred workers died at the barricades, great numbers of churches and convents were damaged or destroyed, and Maura, when the week was over, set about accusing the wrong man of provoking the trouble. The trial and execution of Francisco Ferrer, head of a free-thinking school in Barcelona, set Europe alight with hostility to Spain, evoking once again the bleak Leyenda Negra. Far from easing up in their endeavours, anarchists and republicans now prepared for a long struggle.

The next major item requiring the attention of Madrid was colonial affairs, again a problem with a military dimension. At this time, France was attempting to dominate Morocco, and her ambitions were regarded by Madrid as an intrusion into family affairs. It was Canalejas who fought back, successfully claiming the northern five per cent of the country – rugged, inhospitable, essentially ungovernable – as a Spanish protectorate. A puppet caliph was installed in Tetuan, in a palace that backed on to the residency of the Spanish high commissioner. In the Atlas mountains, though, the people were left to their own pursuits with little interference from either Madrid or Tetuan.

Predictably, it was Morocco that was in the end to do the damage. From 1913 onwards, the Madrid party system collapsed, although monarchy and politicians survived. In 1917, Marxists and anarchists combined in a general strike and even though parliamentary government languished, the system still survived. In 1921, however, the Spanish army was humiliatingly crushed at Anual, in the mountains of Morocco, by a brilliantly led guerrilla rising. During two years of debate and anguish after Anual, the politicians found no answer, no way of restoring national or military pride. On 23 September 1923, Miguel Primo de Rivera, captain-general of Barcelona, announced in a *pronunciamiento* that he would now take over government. The king accepted the ultimatum. Political democracy, under a constitutional monarch, perished on the instant, not to be seen again till 1975. For the next fifty years the pattern was to be dictatorship, republic and dictatorship yet again.

8 Days of Death and Dictatorship

Spinal 1923–1982

FIT ALL TOO OFTEN for the brush of Goya, Spain has been sacrificed on many altars during our century. The dictatorship of Primo de Rivera was not exactly one of them, since it proceeded on no clear premise and, initially at least, with more than a measure of goodwill towards the public. Nobody was ever executed under Primo for political reasons and he came to power full of good intentions, such as an improvement in the lives of women and the conditions of the workers. It sounds like nineteenth-century liberalism all over again. He was, however, a dictator and of the most personal, potentially irresponsible kind, believing that he and he alone, by virtue of his native common sense, his undoubted ability to get things done and his deep communings with the Spanish spirit, could lead his nation back to its true self. It was the politicians who had carried Spain astray and his one key notion was to manage things without them. In his first government, for instance, all senior municipal posts were occupied by army officers. He saw himself as Costa's 'iron surgeon', ready to implement Maura's 'revolution from above'. Lacking all other theory, Primo was no fascist, but politicians, as a class, he definitely did not care for.

His achievements were substantial – real advances in labour conditions, a vigorous programme of road building and rural electrification, large hydroelectric projects (easy for dictators who need pay no attention to those whose land is flooded) and many other useful enterprises. He set up a state oil monopoly and, when the Western companies complained, shipped in all his oil from Russia. He supported the international fairs of Seville and Barcelona, both in 1929. Until the fall of the peseta in that same year, the country was rather more prosperous than usual. His greatest success was in Morocco where he first completed a politically daring withdrawal and later, when circumstances changed, with equal daring won back all that had been lost.

His was a nanny state, however, with Primo, the bluff Andalusian, prodding at every shoulder. Garrulous and bossy, continually 'rectifying' his policies, he sat up late at night to write long letters to his people. In the end he drove them mad, alienating sector after sector.

The Catalans were the first to lose all sympathy for the dictator. Matters here had undoubtedly been difficult in the years before Primo's arrival. In the crisis of 1917, a strong bid for autonomy had failed, helping to undercut the bourgeois leadership. By 1919, the anarchists were in the ascendant in Barcelona. In that year, they staged the hugely successful *Canadiense* strike, following it up with other strikes when their leaders were imprisoned. Repression brought reprisals and soon there were death squads on the streets, police versus the anarchists and anarchists gunning down resistant workers. By 1922, still fiercer military repression had quietened the city. Perhaps seeing some advantage in the helping hand of the military, the conservative-minded Catalan Mancomunitat, under the leadership of Puig i Cadafalch, the Modernista architect, gave its support to Primo. Primo's record certainly suggested he supported Catalan regionalism but to the surprise of Puig and friends, he promptly abolished the Mancomunitat and forbade the official use of the Catalan language, even in church services. These actions were to affect Spanish history profoundly, deepening Catalan regionalism even further and swinging it strongly leftwards, into alliance with gathering republicanism.

And so it went – Catalans, conservatives, even, in the end, the army, utterly fed up with Primo. It had been his intention when he took over to hand the country back to non-political civilians, but he never found the men and never found the moment. One morning in 1930, in a fit of discouragement, he asked his generals if they supported him and when they equivocated he resigned.

Alfonso XIII, the king who had legitimized the dictator, was by now also extremely unpopular. He brought in another general to hold the fort, but Berenguer, old, infirm, conservative, delayed in calling an election. By the time municipal elections were held in April 1931, the Catalans had done a deal with the republicans, the San Sebastián pact, by which, in return for autonomy, they would support the republican ticket. When the election results were declared, the republican–socialist bloc had swept the cities. Alfonso, decisively rejected in his role as monarch, preferred to leave the country rather than risk civil war.

If even Alfonso quailed, why then were the generals ready to take that risk just five years later, and never to repent at having begun a struggle more bitter, savage and destructive than any Spain had ever faced? Since an answer must embrace both the failure of the Second Republic and the origins of Franco's long and critically important period of dictatorship, this is perhaps the single most important question of Spanish twentieth-century history. The literature on the subject, virtually inseparable from that on the Civil War, is immense even in English and often enthralling. The interested reader can turn not only to many of the best writers of the day but also to more recent contributors such as Hugh Thomas and Raymond Carr. Given the accessibility of these riches, it seems unnecessary here to set down more than a few of the main facts about the Second Republic, as an *aide-mémoire* and not as a systematic interpretation.

It is important to remember at the outset, and no doubt readers will, that between 1931 and the start of the Civil War in July 1936, the republic passed through three distinct phases. For its first two years it was a liberal bourgeois republic, not socialist but of socialist inclination, which nevertheless severely scared the right. In its middle phase it was at first mildly right-wing and then extremely so, more than capable of harsh repression. Finally, in its last six months, it was pure left-wing republican but unable to command, with the result that politics passed back to the street with mutual violence between left and right. And it was at this point, in defence of order and the honour of the army and with a good deal of grandiloquent rhetoric about Spain, that the generals finally rose.

To understand at least some of the implications of the rising, it is necessary to look briefly at each stage of the republic's ill-starred life. (It lived on, of course, wounded and with limbs progressively chopped off, until its final military defeat in 1939.)

In its opening phase, the republic carried out a number of reforms that only the malevolent could have objected to – the continuing reform of labour laws, for instance, and the improvement of wages, especially in the countryside. This was carried out, moreover, against a background of orthodox finance and balanced budgets. The troubles lay with matters that were traditionally far more divisive, with Catalonia and with the Church and army.

The concession of Catalan autonomy, just as agreed in the pact of San Sebastián, was a red rag to those many traditionalists who saw the Spanish destiny as one and indivisible. (Basque autonomy was also granted, but later and far less enthusiastically; the Basque Country was more conservative than Catalonia and the Basque nationalists enjoyed the strong support of the local clergy, a definite black mark.) Meanwhile, through the whole of Spain, the Catholic Church was separated from the State on terms that seemed to Catholics to remove from them the liberties deemed so essential for others. Religious processions were banned, for example; the Orders were restricted and forbidden to teach. As for the army, Azaña, then the defence minister, and later the prime minister, retired half of the swollen corps of officers. It was obviously a prudent measure and they went out on full pay, but accompanied by jibes the army would never forgive. At the same time, under this same government, twenty-five anarchist workers had been shot dead in the course of a small-town revolution.

The cumulative results were dire, particularly on the right. Carlists, inflamed over the religious issue, began to ship in arms, over the same Pyrenean passes that had brought the Enlightenment to Aragón. They started in 1931, right at the beginning. The first military revolt, a poorly organized affair, took place in Seville in 1932. At the election of 1933, Azaña was defeated.

After the election, and now into the second phase of the republic, one of the main forces on the victorious right was a proto-fascist party, of dubious loyalty to the republic, led by the young Salamanca law professor Gil Robles. The president of the republic refused to allow Gil Robles into a government that nevertheless needed his support in order to survive. In 1934 he withdrew that support, wanting tougher treatment for Catalonia, already partially stripped of its autonomy. When Gil Robles was finally admitted to the government, it was the turn of the workers to stage a revolution.

The 'revolution' of 1934 caused barely a ripple in Madrid. In Barcelona, it was swiftly overcome. In Asturias, however, the tough and disciplined coalminers actually captured the whole of the coalfield and the industrial area of the province, including much of Oviedo, and held on for a fortnight, anarchists, communists and socialists collaborating effectively. It was a spectacular affair, with Asturian dynamiters dynamiting and allegations of atrocities. Oviedo university was badly damaged along with parts of the town. The response of the right-wing government was draconian. General Francisco Franco, already with a reputation for personal courage, leadership and effective organization, was called to the Madrid War Office to take charge, along with General Goded, important once again at the start of the Civil War. They brought in the Foreign Legion and Moroccan troops and put the revolution down with atrocities that far outweighed those that had gone before. The shape of the future was becoming visible.

Given the Asturian repression, given falling wages, given the treatment of Catalonia, it was no surprise that the leftist Popular Front carried the elections of February 1936. Numerically, the majority was not so great, with mainly the cities voting for the left and the Castilian heartlands voting for the right, but the vote translated into a large left-wing majority in the Cortes. Now the right wing progressively took to the streets and was met there, with enthusiasm, by the left. The anarchists, of course, had taken no part in government in all these years, believing bourgeois republics just as bad as anything that had gone before. Now they were joined by the socialists, progressively disillusioned with the republic. Their old labour leader Largo Caballero, soon to be prime minister of the republic at war, was making speeches that were distinctly revolutionary in tone. Youth parties grew on both sides, especially among the communists and Falangists. Death squads were operating in Madrid. When the right wing killed a republican lieutenant, government security forces killed Calvo Sotelo, formerly Primo de Rivera's finance minister, now the most louring of the proto-fascist leaders. The generals, whose plot was well advanced, were able to receive this as a call to action.

My journeyings, one or two of them retrospective, begin again with the Civil War. In hopes of staving off a rising, the republican government had moved the three most threatening generals – Goded, Mola and Franco – to out-of-the-way commands. Franco had been sent the furthest, to Tenerife, way down in the Canary Islands. By a variety of ruses he got himself to neighbouring Las Palmas and was there picked up by an English aeroplane chartered out of Croydon. This plane now ferried Franco to Morocco.

In Santa Cruz, the capital of Tenerife, there is a statue down at the far end of the front that sums up one aspect of the war. It shows a young, romantic General Franco – he was actually 5 foot 3 inches in height and soon developed a paunch with a curiously low centre of gravity. Here, though, he stands erect and handsome, looking towards the mainland. He holds a crusader's sword in front of him, pommel in his hands, tip on the ground. But the ground he is standing on is actually the back of a huge, winged angel, thrusting forwards. Franco, departing for Morocco in the plane from Croydon, was leaving on God's business. The Church, in the face of fearful persecution, would soon pronounce the rebellion a just war and dignify it with the title of crusade. And Franco, slightly to everyone's surprise, would soon become the chief of the crusaders. For him and his fellow rebels, this war was a second Reconquista.

The point of Franco's journey to Morocco was to collect the Spanish Army of Africa, battle-hardened under himself and General Sanjurjo, and convey it to Spain. It was by far the most efficient of Spain's fighting forces and this of all risings was no mere *pronunciamiento*; the generals had resolved right at the outset that if the republic did not crumble, then they would fight until they gained the victory. For this, the Army of Africa was the crucial instrument.

In the late 1970s, not long after Franco's death, I spent a holiday with the Spanish consul and his family in Tetuan in Morocco. The consulate is the former Spanish residency, the building from which the protectorate was effectively governed. With its high walls abutting the kasbah on one side and the caliph's palace on the other, it was hard not to see it still as the town's principal building, a purpose-built palace in the Moorish style, with coffered ceilings, arabesque walls and Islamic *azulejos*. Much of it was by then disused, shadowy backroom retreating into shadowy backroom, dim pools of twilight full of rusting bridles and discarded papers, forgotten corners that nobody had entered for decades. Out in the front, there was space and to spare for the thirty or so clerical staff busy with the pensions of the Moroccan volunteers who left to fight with Franco. And it was here, in this very house, that Franco planned the invasion of the Spanish mainland. The desk he worked at was now in the consul's dressing-room and my friend the consul, retiring of an evening, would empty out car keys and loose change from his pockets on to its shiny surface. Even under newly democratic Spain, even with teenagers and their friends, with swimming towels, straw hats and picnic baskets, the whole of the strange house was still brimful of echoes, the deaths envisaged at that table, pacing along the corridors and in and out of the dark little private chapel.

It was Franco, seen in retrospect as unquestionably the most able of the generals, who had negotiated in advance with the Germans and Italians. Now, as he calculated how to move his men across the Straits of Gibraltar, the Spanish navy declared for the republic, the men killing those officers thought unreliable (eventually, up to a third of serving officers were shot). At this critical juncture, Mussolini saved the day for the nationalists by sending planes to ferry the troops across.

By now it was late July, 1936. The Spain in which the Army of Africa arrived had fallen into two clear zones. The republicans held the east, the centre and the south, including Barcelona, Valencia and Madrid. They also held the industrial north coast, though from the start this was cut off from the remainder of the republic. The nationalists held Galicia, Castile, León, parts of Extremadura, Navarre and parts of Aragón, a great wedge of conservative old Spain, solid, serious and Catholic, east to west across the upper half of Spain but with no access to the Mediterranean. They had also taken individual cities by storm or ruse, including leftist Seville. Importantly for Franco, they held the land behind Gibraltar.

His personal emergence, leading in due course both to his *mando único*, or unified command, and to his acclamation as Head of State, came about as the end result of events that took place in the early days. General Goded, arriving from the Balearics, failed to take Barcelona, was captured and later executed as a rebel. General Sanjurjo died in an aircrash and General Mola, up in the north, got hopelessly bogged down round San Sebastián. Franco sailed up the centre towards Madrid, picking off republican militia columns as he went and simultaneously emerging as the power in the nationalist land, a position later reinforced by his domination of nationalist headquarters. Now, though, if he could take the capital at a first dash, the war would be virtually at an end.

What happened next is, of course, well known. Depicted very crudely, it falls into three phases, just like the history of the Second Republic.

First comes the nationalist failure at Madrid. The militarily disordered republicans mounted a brave and brilliantly conceived defence, which brought the nationalists to a halt for several months. Early in 1937, the nationalists attacked Madrid again, coming down through Jarama to the north of the city. They were held again, but the volunteer International Brigades, which had by now joined the republic, were severely mauled in badly thought-out counter-attacks. The next assault on Madrid was made by Mussolini's troops, through Guadalajara, site of the Infantado palace (mostly burnt out in the fighting). To the humiliation of the Italians, they too were held outside Madrid and badly beaten.

Frustrated in the centre, the nationalists spent much of 1937 mopping up the north, including the Basque Country with its iron ore and precious steel-making capacity. Success in this second main phase of the war now gave decisive strength to the nationalists. But before any major new campaign could develop, the republicans counter-attacked in the east, first at Belchite, south of Zaragoza, hoping to disrupt the Basque campaign, then at Teruel with its Mudéjar towers, in the winter of 1937–8. Franco responded in force to the Teruel attack.

As a result, the war shifted to the east for its third phase and final year. Despite yet another republican counter-attack in the summer of 1938, in full force across the Ebro, the war was eventually won through Franco's capture of Valencia and Barcelona. In Madrid, in the last days, republican communists and non-communists fought one another until resistance simply collapsed. Hundreds of thousands of refugees fled across the Pyrenees before the arrival of Carlist troops who closed the border.

Behind this simplified, schematic version, there were, of course, not only a host of military complications but also one other stream in the flood of events that must be outlined before military, and ultimately political, events make any sense at all. This is foreign intervention, already touched upon.

Essentially, the nationalists were helped throughout the war by the Axis powers, Hitler's Germany and Mussolini's Italy. They committed themselves early, hoping to gain a future ally at small cost. But even when the war turned out to be a long one, they felt it would be a sign of weakness to pull back. The Germans supplied tanks and other munitions, planes and flyers, and extremely efficient training. Italy sent planes and men. The men were ultimately withdrawn – of these, Franco had enough and the Italians proved none too useful. But the planes remained vital till the end.

On the other side of the equation, Britain and France were too deeply attached to appeasement of Germany to take an open part. Reluctantly they allowed the formation of the International Brigades but their policy of non-intervention worked dramatically against the republic. This was not just a matter of failing to help with military material. It also had the effect of making the Madrid government, soon moved to Valencia and then to Barcelona, politically dependent on the Russians. Looking back today, it is hard not to feel that the republic, and particularly the Spanish communists, many of them stalwart and admirable idealists imbued with a deep love of their country, were shamelessly duped by their political masters. Stalin supplied planes, tanks and weapons, political commissars and a political police. But because he was interested in establishing an alliance with the Western powers, he supported the outward appearance of a pluralist, even bourgeois republic. When his alliance with the West failed to materialize, he dropped the republic altogether, as if the fate of Spain were immaterial to him. The side that lost the war had barely a suspicion of air cover as it battled its way across the Ebro and disintegrated in the face of Franco's last attack on Barcelona. This was perhaps the most cynical, and cruel, piece of *realpolitik* in Europe in the first half of the present century.

Another conditioning factor for the whole of the war was the initial terror waged on both sides of the lines. The emergence of nationalist and republican zones owed as much to accident as to political allegiance. In some areas, for example, the Civil Guard had stayed loyal to the republican government, thus delivering whole towns, essentially right-wing, to the left. Exactly the reverse had happened in other places. Thus on either side of the lines there were plenty of potential enemies. The nationalists saw the intellectual left and the workers' organizations as hostile. Behind the republican lines, there were whole classes – the clergy and the landlords – whose almost every action had served to build up hatred through the course of centuries.

The nationalists picked off their enemies with some efficiency, first by Falange murders, then by military tribunal. The terror in the republican zones attracted more attention since at first it seemed much wilder. Perhaps 5,000 members of the clergy died in scenes that were often grotesque. There is a surviving photograph of the skeletons of long-dead nuns propped up casually outside the doors of a Barcelona convent; the Catholic mass was parodied, vestments worn in mockery. Blood ran in simple vengeance. In due course, the political parties won back the streets, successfully restraining even their 'uncontrollables' and from now on the killing became more functional. Historians believe the numbers who died were probably about equal on both sides. But from the start, and especially at the start, it was a war in which the physical elimination of an enemy appeared the proper course. This was a measure of how deeply and how brutally the bitter history of Spain had separated its people from one another.

Luis Bolín was the London correspondent of the Spanish monarchist paper *ABC*. It was he who hired the aircraft that carried Franco to Morocco and he soon took charge of the foreign press corps covering the nationalist side of the Civil War. Later, he was to put out the story that Guernica, bombed into fragments by the Germans in 1937, had in fact been fired as a propaganda deed by the republicans, a clever canard that took decades to undo. I met him in London in the 1960s while pursuing a story about the foreign press during the Civil War, notably Kim Philby, already a communist agent but working under the cover of *Times* correspondent in Franco's head-quarters. Bolín, a charming Anglophile in tweed, dispatched me on my way with a list of the young nationalist officers who had worked for him, escorting foreign correspondents to the battle lines and making sure they did not see anything they were not meant to – a style which Bolín had modelled exactly on British practices during the First World War.

These men, when eventually I tracked them down, turned out to have had highly successful careers. One had been an ambassador, one was a general, one was Enrique Marsans, head of the Marsans travel agency, a name familiar to most who travel in Spain today. They must originally have been selected for their languages and sophistication and they had lost none of this. Marsans particularly I talked to over a long lunch; the waiters could not believe I was in the chair and brought him the wine to taste and bill to pay. I doubt if Marsans was or remains a political animal, but his effortless urbanity and considerable style put me in mind that day, and still do now, of another man, also young at the same time – José Antonio Primo de Rivera, languishing in a republican gaol in Alicante as the war broke out (and interviewed there, as it happens, by the American journalist Jay Allen). For if there was one thing José Antonio possessed, among a great many disputed qualities, that thing was a high style and a knack of elegance.

José Antonio Primo de Rivera, the son of the old dictator and known in Spain just by his Christian names, founded the Falange in 1933, eventually swallowing up another body with similar aims, the JONS, or Juntas de Ofensiva Nacional-Sindicalista. He was a fascist in the Spanish style, which included a great deal of social radicalism and cloudy economics. Dreaming of a Spain that would abolish class warfare and genuinely incorporate its working people, he poured out a torrent of poetic rhetoric that proved irresistible to university students. This was the very class that Bakunin had seen as the probable torch bearers of anarchism. Yet it was Spanish proto-fascism that took them out on to the streets, in a truly murderous romanticism.

The Falange grew swiftly in the dangerous days at the start of the war, making it a force to be reckoned with by the time José Antonio was executed in the prison yard at Alicante on 20 November 1936. His death presented an opportunity to Franco, for here was a movement that could itself be taken over and used as linchpin in the new political structure Franco was designing.

Expecting a short war, the generals had devoted little thought to the politics either of their endeavour or of a future Spain. José Antonio himself, in notes he wrote in prison, had described them as 'abysmal political mediocrities'. Franco, however, soon began to realize that his emerging military dictatorship would need some kind of structured political system in order to function. When José Antonio's successor as leader of the Falange put up resistance to a take-over, he was thrown into prison and remained there till 1947. The rest of the leadership, while protesting undying loyalty to Franco, were disciplined too. Meanwhile Franco was also cajoling the Carlists, known officially as the Tradicionalistas. They were rather a tougher nut to crack, being ardent monarchists and associated, too, with smaller groups of monarchists, but in due course all were combined into the single party which became the mainstay of the regime.

Franco's headquarters were first in Salamanca, where the marriage of the parties was accomplished. He then moved to Burgos and it was here that the first congress of the newly created party –

the bulkily named Falange Español Tradicionalista y de las JONS – was held. Extraordinary as it may seem on the face of it, but absolutely the reverse as one considers the implications, their congress was celebrated in the Chapter House of the monastery of Las Huelgas. Here, in this Catholic sanctuary of the Castilian kings, hung with a Moorish tent flap from the battle of Las Navas de Tolosa, and the banners of Christian ships from the battle of Lepanto, delegates heard Franco and his councillors pledge 'service and life in holocaust to one Spain, imperial, great and free'. That Spain, as Franco saw it, was the natural successor to Isabel and Fernando's authoritarian monarchy – willing to kill to impose a Catholic orthodoxy – and to the stern imperialism of Felipe II. He saw them also, a little inaccurately, as the apostles of a centralism that was at the heart of the new crusade.

We are at a table in a crowded bar in Zaragoza – myself, Tim Bozman, who had taken me along in an earlier age to see the Goyas at the monastery of Aula Dei, and a cluster of anarchists from a local splinter group. In Aragón and Catalonia today, that grand old grouping of the early anarcho-syndicalists – the CNT or Confederación Nacional de Trabajo, the last word meaning 'work' – has finally split in two and, what's more, over the perennial issue of whether or not to participate in other people's political structures. The older anarchists, survivors from Civil War days, have held fast to the CNT and absolute non-participation. The younger people have mostly left to form a new association, arguing that support is now so small that nothing at all will be achieved unless they participate in union elections in factories. In all of Zaragoza and Huesca there are just 200 members, not labourers but white-collar workers – teachers, bank clerks and so forth. So much has the movement declined.

The group in the Zaragoza bar are claiming that their new anarchist 'confederation' is the real power, unrecognized by the press, in a current hospital strike in Barcelona. This is interesting enough; even more interesting is that all of those with us in the bar are women. Ana Carrera, for example, is Aragón secretary-general of the new group; Lola Viciosa Montiel is treasurer. Ana explains how she became an anarchist.

As the daughter of a peasant family, from a village near Soria in Castile, she had found herself working in a sausage factory at the age of fourteen. There, she says, she learnt the nature of injustice. Being always a rebellious child, *'una cría rebelde'*, she knew by the time she was eighteen and came to Zaragoza that 'we had to do something'. Ana became a nurse, began to attend Christian workers' seminars and through the seminars arrived at the texts of the early Spanish anarchists. Reading these, she knew at once that she had found her home. She soon became a full-time anarchist worker.

'The old CNT was an organization that had the power to change society and introduce a new life. Being an anarchist was a daily practice.'

They were against bullfights and cockfights and in favour of Esperanto, she says, trying to give us the flavour of it. Literally thousands of militants knew Esperanto.

'Political parties change structures,' says Ana, 'anarchism has tried to change people. Nowadays people understand everything intellectually but nobody wants to change anything.'

Another of the group leans forward to pat Tim on the knee. 'Anarchists have to be tolerant and willing to share, even in amorous relations. It's difficult,' she says, 'but you have to try.'

After the bar and the present-day anarchists of Zaragoza, it's our intention to revisit the past and in particular to hear what we can of those extraordinary phenomena, the anarchist collectives of rural Aragón. They flourished for thirteen months in 1936–7, until they were suppressed by the communists – supposedly the allies of the anarchists on the republican side. Soon after that, their lands were captured by the advancing nationalist army. It was a short-lived experiment, paralleled to a lesser degree in other republican zones, but at its most intense right here in rural Aragón. More than any other aspect of the Civil War, it is the collective movement that has lived on in the annals of the European left, and may perhaps continue to attract admirers, even after the worldwide collapse of communism. For the brief and inconclusive story of the collectives, smothered before they had the time either to succeed or fail, demonstrates that at least for some, in 1936–7, there was another way.

The story begins, like most of the major events of anarchism, in Barcelona. While over on the far side of the country, in Burgos, Salamanca and such places, Franco was stitching together his alliance of army, Church, Falange and monarchists, behind the republican lines, quite on the contrary, the social and economic revolution that had been so long foreshadowed was finally occurring. Nowhere was this happening so forcefully as in the great, autonomous city of Barcelona. Here, with the generals' rising and the defeat and capture of Goded, the Catalan regionalists had gone into alliance with the CNT. Barcelona itself became a workers' metropolis in workers' clothes, vividly described by Orwell in his *Homage to Catalonia*.

In the initial formation of the war zones, the nationalists had taken most of Aragón. Now anarchist militia columns, some from Valencia, most from Barcelona, pushed back into the high ground of the old kingdom. In the republic's one and only successful military advance in the early part of the Civil War, they recaptured most of the Aragonese countryside, though failing to take the cities of Jaca, Huesca, Zaragoza or Teruel. These lay in a straight line north to south and this became the frontier, a settled one for the time being since the main fighting was first in central Spain, then on the north coast.

Durruti, most famous of anarchist commanders, led one of the divisions that came up to Aragón from Barcelona. Antonio Ortiz led the 25th. Luis Muñoz, now aged eighty-one, was a captain in the 25th under Ortiz. We meet him in a Zaragoza café, dignified in button-down shirt, neat jacket and with trouser seams as sharp as the corners of an iceberg. In conversation he takes you warmly by the shoulder, and he speaks modestly, with self-deprecating humour. He reminds me of nothing so much as the privet tree, symbol of Aragón – hard, spare, able to endure bitter weather – as he tells how, with the advance of the militia columns, private property was abolished and collectives began to form in the villages, established by assemblies of the people.

Now, this is a critical matter for historians, for what happened essentially is that the anarchists emerged as champions of the landless peasants and have been accused of brutally coercing small proprietors. When the communists suppressed the collectives, they did so for many reasons – not least, as they saw it, the need to establish a centralized and hierarchical war machine – but they did so in the name of the landowning peasantry, extraordinarily enough considering events in Russia, and justified themselves, again with absolute hypocrisy in the light of the Russian situation, by bringing the charge of forced collectivization against the anarchists. The communists themselves, therefore, successfully created a new Leyenda Negra, this time about the dark deeds of the anarchists. In a subsequent war of polemic and partisan historiography, waged out on the left, the anarchists have spent the past fifty years trying to rebut these charges. Anybody coming new to the subject has to realize that almost everything said by a representative of one side or the other is said as part of this consuming argument – which makes it, as Tim and I progressively discovered, extremely difficult to get the feel of what it was actually like on the collectives.

In Luis Muñoz's account, there was not enough time to establish 'the perfect situation'. But those who didn't want to join could work 'as much land as they could manage personally. The determining force in those moments was the arriving columns and most people came in voluntarily.' At all points, says Muñoz, it was a matter of below–upwards decisions and the columns helped the collectives, especially with the harvesting, when military affairs permitted.

'One thing we did not want to do,' he adds, 'was to set up dictatorships like the communists.'

With its implicit admission that some of the collectivization may have been forcible, but also with its strong suggestion of idealism at work as well, Muñoz's account sounded extremely plausible. It tallied well with lessons we had been taking along the way with Julián Casanova, a notably non-partisan historian at Zaragoza university, and a leading authority on these matters. According to Casanova, collectives were most likely to have been spontaneous where the CNT had been strong before the arrival of the columns. In the areas that were actually occupied by the columns, in an atmosphere of armed men and potential threat, they were least likely to have been so. It seems that in many of the Aragón collectives – 275 in February 1937, with almost 150,000 people, rising to 400 before they were wiped out – private proprietors survived, working their land individually. Almost all the collectives, however, had as their germ and kernel the expropriated land of the larger owners. Another point that Casanova makes very forcibly is that much of the impulse came from city people. A few local anarchists, those, that is to say, with experience of rural conditions, had been to Valencia or Barcelona and had there acquired their knowledge and political theories, but mostly the ideas now came directly from city-dwellers in the militia columns.

Luis Muñoz was an exception. An Aragonese, born into a family of eleven children with a strong political tradition – his mother was put on trial when he was just fourteen – he had learned all his anarchism in Zaragoza itself. His ideas, as he expounded them to us, were pure Fanelli out of Bakunin, reminding us of the importance that Spanish anarchism always gave to culture and learning. 'It would be much better,' he said, in the last words of our long talk, 'if all of us spoke a universal language.'

It was the notion of anarchist learning that set us off on the trail of Félix Carrasquer, autodidact, blind from the age of twenty-five, teacher of anarchists. Carrasquer had grown up in the substantial village of Albalate de Cinca. Warned not to read at the age of six because of his weak eyesight, he nevertheless read and read in a great thirst for knowledge. In 1936, as a young man in Barcelona, he was arguing that the anarchist movement desperately needed people who could at least read, add and subtract. As the militia columns moved into his native Aragón, he established a school at the village of Monzón, to service the collectives. Some of this is recorded in Ronald Fraser's *Blood of Spain*, one of the most outstanding works of oral history yet composed. Other parts come from Carrasquer's sister, Presentación, also a teacher, whom we called upon in her tidy little house in Albalate, a stern-seeming village closed up tight at lunch-time. As the nationalists moved in, in 1938, Carrasquer moved the school to Gerona, closer to Barcelona, and finally took the children across the border into France. There he lived for a while in a refugee camp with his sister and his own family.

'It's strange,' says Presentación, 'but he made our time there one of the happiest of our lives. He was full of projects and competitions to keep us alive and interested. He absolutely brimmed with vitality and optimism, he wanted to believe the best of all the world.'

Not long afterwards, blind as he was, Carrasquer returned to Barcelona, clandestinely, to carry on the struggle. He was caught, of course, not once but twice, in Franco's new police state, and served twelve years of an even longer prison sentence. Now, she said, he was living in Barcelona, aged eighty-four, in far from perfect health, but still with great internal vitality. Since I was going in that direction she would give me his address and telephone number. When it came to it, though, I never telephoned him, preferring to leave him as I had seen him on a video shot for a research project – sharp and alert and, if I may use the word, entirely noble in his dedication to an ideal.

Albalate is on the river Cinca at the edge of a *huerta* full of bamboo and apricots, peaches and eucalyptus. 'Yes,' says Presentación, 'Alcolea, Albalate, Zaidin – these are all Arabic names. The Arabs worked La Cinca. We still use an irrigation network originally laid out by the Moors.' As Tim and I cross the river to leave by Alcolea, we pass a wood-mill where the eucalyptus is pulped. Then it is up out of the valley on to a bare, brown plain, under an implacable sun. 'It's what the Spaniards call *un sol de justicia*,' says Tim, 'a sun of justice. I suppose that's because there is no escape from it.' There are pale, burned thistles on the roadside, faded flowers, mostly brown and yellow, and faded butterflies. Hoopoes flash their barred tails at us. A great bird of prey, we are not sure what species, rises from the undergrowth, feathered thighs extending downwards, electricity pylons upside down. Off in the distance, reddy-brown whirlwinds dash about. It is a countryside that is almost terrifying. Yet the Aragonese, says Tim, when they

33 Costa Brava means the Wild Coast, a name whose origins are well explained by rockscapes south of Aiguablava.

34 Modernista roofscape, Barcelona. Part of the Manzana de la Discòrdia city block. Left is the Casa Amattler by Puig i Cadafalch, to the right is Gaudí's Casa Battló.

35 Ironwork over the door of Gaudí's Palau Guëll, in the old quarter of Barcelona.

36 More Gaudí fixtures and fittings from the Palau Güell.

37 Balcony in Gaudí's famous apartment block, the Casa Milà, known also as La Pedrera, the Stone Quarry.

38 The Miró Foundation, designed by Josep Lluís Sert.

39 Sitges parish church.

40 Francoist memorial outside the *alcázar*, Toledo. The symbols of Catholicism are yoked to the Falangist cause with no embarrassment.

41 Statuary and giant cross at the Valley of the Fallen, Franco's supreme Civil War memorial.

42 The Generalisimo himself ordered that the Aragonese town of Belchite should remain in ruins.

Above: 45 November in the Plaza Mayor, Madrid. The vivacity of the couple crossing the square is a shorthand for the extraordinary animation of so many Spaniards, young and old. In this same square Rodrigo Calderón, exemplar of Castilian courage, was executed in the seventeenth century.

Right: 46 Symbol of Madrid, the bear feeds greedily from the arbutus or wild strawberry tree. The statue stands in the Puerta del Sol, symbolic centre of the city.

Opposite top: 43 Statue and fountain in the riverside gardens at Aranjuez, first planted by Felipe II.

Opposite bottom: 44 The first impression of El Escorial is one of forbidding vastness, but linger in the town and more intimate perspectives slowly present themselves.

47 A family outing provides the excuse for a jaunt with horse and carriage in Seville.

48 Goatherd and charges near Isla Cristina, province of Huelva.

travel to England, cannot abide the confinement of a countryside with trees and hedges and long to be back in the bare sweeps of Aragón.

He explains that the land in these parts is divided, clearly as night and day, into *huerta* – anything well-watered or irrigated – and *monte*, or *secano* – mountain or dry land, the two words being synonymous in this context. If you are buying *huerta* you pay up to twenty times more than you do for *monte* or *secano*. The point here is that some of the collectives were very much richer than others. If the movement was to work, and not simply perpetuate the old divisions, some way of equalizing wealth would have to be found. To try to solve this problem, the anarchists of Aragón had set up a body that they called the Council, the Consejo de Aragón, not as a government but as a clearing-house for assembling and exporting the produce of the collectives and buying in the staples that were needed. Aragón had olive oil, almonds and saffron. It needed beans, condensed milk and salt cod.

Since Zaragoza was on the wrong side of the lines and therefore closed to the anarchists, some body such as this was desperately required for purposes of trade. It might, if it had functioned well and if the republic had won the war, have proved to be a critical part of any expansion of the collective system. In fact, it worked extremely badly, since its members got swollen heads and believed they were the sole representatives of the popular movement of Aragón. They set themselves up in Caspe – the only real town in the anarchist zone, though not at all a big one – and proceeded to earn at least some of the obloquy that the communists heaped upon them. Before the council was dissolved, it was thinned out with members of other political forces.

Caspe is an interesting place historically, since it was here, in the famous *Compromiso de Caspe*, that a deal was struck in 1412 that brought a Trastámara to the throne of Aragón, so paving the way for the marital alliance of Isabel and Fernando. The town had its own collective during the Civil War and Tim and I are on our way now to an appointment with Antonio Gil Gambau, baker to that cooperative during his teenage years. Surely, we think, we will find in the one-time baker somebody who can convey some of the atmosphere of those enthusiastic days.

The start of our interview is unpromising, however. Gil Gambau, a real bull of a man, eyes sunk deep in flesh, suspicious, ready to be hostile, is deeply involved in putting across a particular view of history. He has accumulated huge manuscripts of his own and does not at all like the idea of losing control of any portion of his memories. He complains of endless misreporting. 'It is very difficult,' he says, 'when we have a clear responsibility towards our times and our companions.'

As a journalist I have heard this many times and frankly doubt my own ability – and possibly willingness, depending on what he says – to tell the story as he wants it. But more and more, as I grow older and sadder in my trade, I have been forced to respect his view as reasonable and prudent. Tim, I think, feels equally abashed. But we hang on, in the bare little house outside the town, devoid of any ornament except a typewriter and beside it a copy of the anarchist weekly, feebly protesting our sympathy, integrity and truthfulness.

Angrily, Antonio Gil Gambau begins to fill in the background to the Caspe collective, then little by little softens to the task. Listening to him there, voice hammering in the great heat, a Pyrenean mountain dog panting outside in a tiny patch of shade, we begin to feel we are hearing it exactly as it was. 'I have been a CNT militant,' he begins, 'for more than fifty years.' For myself, as I sat there, I was watching a man whom I had disliked intensely during our opening exchanges – the sort, I felt, who disagrees on principle with everything you say – slowly reveal himself as one of the most remarkable people I had met in thirty years of travelling with a notebook. All I can do is attempt a summary of what he said, in the order that he said it and in the expectation that in some way or other I will accidentally traduce him, and that, however I express it, he will probably disagree.

Caspe, said Antonio Gil Gambau, was a community living exclusively from its agriculture. It had 4,000 hectares of *huerta* and 11,000 of *secano*. There were half a dozen big landowners and a series of small proprietors. Then came *la clase humilde*, the humble class, workers who had no more than a single animal and that animal often in only middling condition. He calculated there were 1,400 members of this class since it was known that there were 1,200 farm-carts, giving a minimum of 1,200 *agricultores* and then allowing for a few more.

The very limited attempts at land redistribution made under the republic had achieved little, since the only land available was the *secano* (the laws were complex and redistribution very limited because of lack of funds for compensation*). The *secano* was a long way off and there was no machinery. And the land was *muy ingrato*, very thankless. If you sowed wheat for five years, you might have one good harvest, two that were mediocre, two that were terrible. Olives, the staple of the area, require ten years of watering while they are young. So there were many agriculturalists who were discontented (he never once, that I recall, used the word *campesino*, peasant). The discontent was somewhat hidden since they lived 'within a closed circle of autarchy' and subscribed to non-revolutionary parties and organizations. 'With just 300 members, the CNT was the smallest party of all.'

This was the situation as Caspe moved into the political vacuum created by the generals' rising. Gil Gambau, the son of a stone-breaker, most pitiless of occupations, turned sixteen the following week. He had been educated by Franciscans, and had done well at school, the sort expected to be a *santito*, a little saint. But he already felt *inquietudes* – literally anxieties, uneasiness, but more often meaning the restlessness that drives a man forward – and though his parents begged him to stay out of it, he began to attend political meetings and mix himself up in what was happening.

'When the generals' rising came, it was the CNT who answered it. The republicans were in a false position, discredited on the left and the object of a fascist rising on the right. This turned the people towards the revolution. The people sympathized with us. The breakdown of military and civil government gave us the chance to put our ideas into practice. There is discussion as to whether or not it

*This and the other parentheses that follow are my personal contribution.

305

was a good thing, but I who have known Caspe all my life can tell you this. Those who were always hungry had enough and there was work for those who never had any.'

The decisive meeting was held in the Teatro Goya; it still exists today, grey but strangely ornamental, pockmarked by bullets. The communists were there. (So were the socialist UGT, the Unión General de Trabajadores, at least as important for Spanish history as the CNT.) The communist plan was to divide the land and distribute it to the poor peasants. But it was collectivization that seemed the logical solution and won the day.

The collective had a hundred families by October/November of that first year, with many more joining after that, partly because it was successful, partly because of the arrival of newcomers from fascist-controlled land. Naturally they had no work and were anxious to join. Numbers were up to 240 or 250 by Christmas.

Here it became clear there was a bitter dispute between historians and the Caspe veterans over numbers. Gil Gambau says he is certain. He remembers clearly that they baked three sacks of flour a day, each of 100 kilos, and that would bring the numbers exactly enough to the figure he was quoting. (There were two bakers and two boys to do the work.)

It was only now, having given us what he saw as the minimum background, that Antonio Gil Gambau was ready to turn to the intimate organization and lifestyle of the collective.

First, the matter of money. This, so far as possible, was abolished. (Julián Casanova at Zaragoza university says this happened in part because there was very little left in rural Aragón – certainly no credit, with the Zaragoza banks on the far side of the lines.) Members of the Caspe collective were paid weekly 'in a kind of certificate worth one peseta, divisible into strips, each worth twenty-five centimos.' It was, says Gil Gambau, personalized money, with your own name on it. There were shoemakers, tailors, carpenters and bricklayers in the collective (not to mention a threshing-machine). For using shops outside the collective, which might be done if there was need, you were given a voucher that you presented to the shop in question. The shop later presented it to the collective for payment. (The collective as a whole, of course, was a trading organization that did possess real money, if only a minimum.) Payment for one day a week was also in real money, allowing members to go to the cinema or café. 'We did not want our people to be hermits,' says Gil Gambau. (It is a matter of historical record, though, that in most of the collectives alcohol and tobacco were used far less than previously, especially at the beginning.)

Wages were paid according to size of family, five pesetas a day per head as a standard rate. Women were paid according to the difficulty of the work, more for gathering olives or packing merchandise, less for staying at home and doing housework. (According to Casanova, this was not so much a reflection of inequality between the sexes as an indication of the huge regard for work itself – the animating principle of the collectives. We are a long way here from the mental habits of the Castilian aristocracy.)

The collective itself provided a free distribution of basic foodstuffs. 'Vegetables, carrots, olive oil, wine – there was enough to eat.' The ration was 50 kilos of pig meat per person per year. An individual would probably consume about 20 kilos of olive oil a year. Broad beans were the first vegetable of the season, followed by potatoes and kidney beans. Antonio Gil Gambau had his own rations delivered, too, though he was the only member of his family who had joined the collective. What the collective was doing, he says, was to issue food for the year in traditional form and quantity.

Social behaviour changed a good deal as well. 'Customs here were very archaic,' says Gil Gambau. 'But now religion came to an end. The church was burned the first day. All the priests but one were shot. [In total, according to Gil Gambau, historians believe that almost eighty people died in Caspe. This was mostly on the basis of ancient grudges against rural policing.] The town had risen, it was a revolution. Young people saw a new future for themselves. There was a tremendous liberation.'

Girls and boys went swimming together, whereas before 'we lived in the heights of modesty. The older people took a worse view of us than they do of drug addicts today. Now men and women could set up house together, no church weddings, no signatures. It was a big liberation for women. Girls used to dress just like their mothers, skirt and blouse, all home-made, hair up on top and never cut. Now they dressed like people from the cities and cut their hair if they wanted to. They could wear one-piece dresses if they liked.' Even so, he adds, it was not libertinism that had broken out, but something rather different. 'There was more comradeship between the sexes.'

Work, of course, stood at the centre of it all. The collectivists worked together, men and women, in teams of four, five or six, depending on inclination and the task in hand. There were no hierarchies among them, though one of their number would be chosen as team delegate to the weekly meeting of the organizing committee. The committee's function was to plan the work for the next week.

'Up to now, people had been overloaded with labour, working *de sol a sol*, from dawn to dusk. Now they worked an eight-hour day and it was more coordinated because we had a plan. Shirkers were thrown right out of the collective.'

The one exception to the eight-hour day was harvest time.

'We had sown our own seed. Now we were gathering our grain to make our own bread. It was like a fiesta. Everybody would go out, even those unused to the fields. For me, the memory of it has never changed. It was an apotheosis of joy. It was based on sharing.'

'Look,' he says to Tim. 'You are a professor, right?' He gestures out of the window towards an imaginary worker in the fields. 'That man could be a professor, I could be a professor. It all depends on education and access to knowledge. Suppose you were rich and wanted to become a doctor. Well, you would buy that knowledge and use it to make yourself richer. But in my opinion as an anarchist that knowledge comes from society, belongs to society, and should be returned to the society we live in.'

During the summer of 1937, the communists were preparing themselves to dissolve the anarchist collectives and at the same time capturing the essential mechanisms of the republic from the socialists (this included replacing the prime minister, Largo Caballero, with the more sympathetic – to them – Juan Negrín). Franco's army was meanwhile recovering the vital north coast. Up in the Basque Country, which had remained loyal to the Spanish republic, the Basque nationalists had made heroic efforts at the start of the war to prevent a terror and protect the priests who, in any event, were sympathetic to the young Basque republic. The military defence in 1937 was critically weakened by mutual suspicion between anarchists and the Basque nationalists and on several key occasions anarchist forces withdrew unpredictably, with disastrous consequences. Nor did the Basque's defensive 'Iron Ring' around Bilbao prove in the slightest degree effective.

As the Basque front collapsed, the Germans gave a hand to Franco by raiding Guernica. This little town, though it possessed the remains of the sacred oak where kings had sworn to uphold the *fueros*, was and remains a deeply ordinary little place, tucked into a shallow valley a few miles behind the sea, mostly rural but dotted nowadays with light industry. The German planes came in waves, more and more on each occasion, machine-gunning and dropping incendiaries as well as conventional bombs. It was a clear act of terror, directed at morale. Up until now, the bombing of local populations had mainly been carried out by the British, and that in the Middle East and Afghanistan. Nobody in Europe had paid attention. From a Europe-centred, Western point of view, therefore, Guernica was perceived at the time to be a clear first. Though complicated as an issue by nationalist counter-propaganda, it was immediately taken as an outrage, doubly horrifying as the work of fascists in a contest that seemed to be between democracy and fascism.

Pablo Picasso, who had now lived in France for more than thirty years and had been for some while not only a millionaire but by far the best known artist in the world, still felt himself deeply Spanish. When the Civil War broke out, in a nominal gesture that nevertheless moved him profoundly, he was appointed Director of the Prado. Then, some months before the attack on Guernica, he was asked by the republican government to paint a work for the Spanish pavilion at an international exhibition in Paris. Inevitably this would be seen as an important statement. Picasso accepted the commission but did no work on it, as if requiring time for an idea to mature or perhaps simply having no idea. Within a fortnight of the news of Guernica, he set to work at a ferocious pace.

To understand the wider background in the arts, it is necessary to look back for just a moment to Catalonia from the turn of the century. After the Modernista movement and the meteoric passage of Picasso, Barcelona had remained at the forefront of Spanish art, with a modern classicism called Noucentisme now succeeding. Many outstanding works were done in this manner, particularly in sculpture and architecture. Come the First World War, Barcelona, now troubled enough itself, became a major place of refuge for members of the international avant-garde displaced from Paris. The Dadaists were there along with a scattering of enterprising Russians and late Cubists. Picasso came in 1917, following Diaghilev's Ballets Russes and notably Olga Koklova, its lead dancer, with whom he was in love and whom he was soon to marry. He painted a clear and handsome portrait of her, in a mantilla, in a style which, if not exactly Noucentiste, was certainly a far cry from the Cubism that had preoccupied him in the years running up to the First World War. There were other works in representational style as well, a cityscape with the Columbus column in it and a mildly sentimental, pastel-coloured *Harlequin*. All of these works, including the portrait of Olga, are in the Picasso Museum in Barcelona.

But Picasso was no longer alone as a major Spanish artist. Dalí was a forceful presence, and the young Joan Miró (Joan is Catalan for the Castilian Juan) had already emerged as a strong painter, touched at this time by a modern classicism yet, like Picasso himself, ready to change and shift dramatically. By the later 1930s, with the Spanish skies darkening, Franco ascendant, war made or in the making, all three painters were engaged in it in one way or another. Dalí, who supported Franco and was never forgiven by Spain's artistic community, painted his celebrated *Premonition of Civil War* otherwise known as *Soft Construction with Boiled Beans* in 1936, a surrealistic piece showing a great quadrilateral of distorted limbs, with open sky seen through them, the limbs surmounted by a barbarous, tortured head. The landscape, which is mostly ravaged desert, has indeed been infiltrated by boiled beans. Miró, deeply engaged by that time with the repulsive, painted his luridly lit *Man and Woman in Front of a Pile of Excrement* in 1935. As the art historian Marilyn McCully has pointed out, it communicates, in common with other Miró works of this period, 'the nightmare quality of burning landscapes at night'. Picasso had done two sets of little etchings in January 1937, under the title, 'The Dream and Lie of Franco', numbers one and two. Most of the eighteen images, especially the first nine, are in cartooning style, representing Franco as a fat hairy worm, mounted either on a horse (sometimes disembowelled) or on his own genitalia, and engaged in all kinds of despicable pursuits, from the slaying of women to the worship of money. From a painter who had up until now been purely apolitical and purely a fine artist, these scabrous propaganda etchings, sold in sets to raise money for the republic, were a new departure.

They may perhaps have conditioned thinking about the enormous work that Picasso now produced, under the title of *Guernica*, for the Spanish pavilion. This painting, grey and white and black, monochrome in appearance, with a woman holding out a torch through an open window over a scene of wild confusion, with upright bull and dying horse, and fallen warrior or artist, and an untold and incalculable number of other incidents of grief or extremity, has become the best known single work of our century. This is no place for a lengthy disquisition upon *Guernica* but it is perhaps worthwhile to make just one or two simple points.

First, though it was triggered by Guernica and contains a house in flames and a woman in agony, the painting is not in any exact or literal way a representation of the events that occurred in Guernica. Early viewers seem to have taken it in something of this sense, however, helping to give the picture its huge propaganda success. The fact that it continues to disturb fifty years further on must surely rest on the way it functions, obscurely yet dramatically, not as representational art but as a collection of symbols. The question then arises of how we read the symbols. Here we may well be misled by Picasso himself, who had a visceral hatred of explanations and often gave silly answers when pressed. In the case of *Guernica* he told one interviewer (Kahnweiler in 1945) that 'the mural is for definite expression and solution of a problem and that is why I used symbolism.' Horse, bull and so on, said Picasso, are all symbolic, allegoric.

Anybody who has watched the growth of Picasso's myths and images, however, will know that they are enormously flexible, staying in one form for about as long as the characters in a Welsh shape-changing poem. Thus the bulls that frequent his work are sometimes fierce and sometimes friendly, with even greater ambiguity attached to the Minotaur who makes such spectacular appearances in the etchings of the Vollard suite and the extraordinary *Minotauromachie* of 1935. Undoubtedly, in Picasso these are associated at some times and in some ways with familiar legends and the meanings that they carried in earlier art. Yet now Surrealism, and notions such as contact with the subconscious, have separated the images of art from the old-fashioned meanings that iconography could comfortably make out in them. Almost all the images in *Guernica* exist in one form or another in earlier work by Picasso – many approaches can be seen in Barcelona in the Picasso Museum – and many totally defy any straightforward explanation. In the end it may be the very unreadability, combined with the powerful suggestiveness of image, that plays a major part in giving *Guernica* such uncanny, ugly resonance. Certainly, in looking at the many preliminary and parallel drawings and paintings that Picasso used for the evolution of *Guernica*, and in the photos of the work at different stages, taken by Dora Maar, his mistress of the moment, one feels that what is changing is not the plan of composition so much as the nature of the symbols themselves. It is a strange and dream-like process.

Critics, of course, also approach the painting in a far more painterly sense, seeking out elements that may be classical or neobaroque, pointing out that the definition of space is done in cubist style and so forth. The employment of such practices, evolved during Picasso's long years of experience as an artist, may make some contribution to the work. Yet another possibility is to look at sources that Picasso knew and may have borrowed from; these, in turn, may yield some messages if their own internal iconography is studied. This is the method followed by my happily-met acquaintance, Santiago Sebastián, the art historian from Valencia; he makes impressive mileage with a comparison between *Guernica* and Rubens's *Horrors of War*, of 1638 or 1640, painted with reference to the Thirty Years' War.

What all of these approaches rest on, deep down inside, is a well-justified belief in Picasso's visual memory. To the end, he could recall the colours of each item of clothing people were wearing when black and white photographs were taken almost a lifetime before. It is clear from his own work that he never forgot an image of his own and carried with him the memory of works by others that he may have seen long ago or only fleetingly. What he had at his disposal was not only his own extraordinary gift of invention but an enormous, possibly unparalleled stock of pre-existing images. What he brought to bear on the emotions stirred by Guernica was not so much the bombing as the whole of himself and the whole of his visual experience. The painting became the property of the republican government and after that government's defeat in the Civil War spent many years in the Museum of Modern Art in New York. It was returned to Spain after the death of Franco and now, behind heavy protective glass, continues to dispense its messages in the Prado annexe.

In the spring of 1937 there was open fighting on the republican side, communists contending with non-Stalinist Marxists – notably the Catalan Trotskyist party called POUM – and with the battle spiralling to include the anarchists themselves. Armed struggle with the anarchists was not what the communists had wanted, not at that moment at least, but they fought the battle hard and won. The leaders of POUM were tortured by Russian interrogators and Andrés Nin, foremost amongst them, murdered. Up in collectivized Aragón, the harvest was unusually good (much better than in small-holders' Catalonia, a fact often taken by supporters as proof that anarchist agriculture worked). Once the harvest was safely in, the communists arrested the anarchist members of the Council of Aragón and closed down the collectives. Luis Muñoz in Zaragoza had said that the greatest joy of his life, after so many years of fighting for it, was to see the arrival of 'libertarian communism'. Now he saw it disappear again.

Hoping to interrupt Franco's onslaught on the north, and perhaps to divert attention from their own internecine politics, the republicans now started a surprise offensive at key points along the Aragonese front, driving towards Jaca, Zaragoza, Belchite and Teruel. The biggest piece of territory taken was around Belchite, but only after a heroic resistance by nationalists holed up in the town. Belchite was reduced to rubble, and Franco, in a morbid post-war gesture, decreed that it should never be rebuilt.

Today, the people of Belchite live in a modest new town just beside the ruins. These, you enter by a high brick gate, to walk down streets of eerie emptiness, houses fallen in or falling, crows pecking in the emptiness, dust rising where a shepherd moves his flock out through the ruins to pasture on the other side. Only the cemetery is tended, a shock of flowering shrubs behind another gate, this time a locked one.

It is hot in the ruins, hot enough to make you faint. In the dead main street I meet a man, slim as a rake, who tells me proudly he is sixty-six years old, was thirteen when the nationalists came to Belchite and fourteen when they left (though only briefly, as it happened). 'We were 30,000 anarchists in Aragón when the war began, but after that it was all one – anarchists, communists, socialists, they measured us all with the same stick. I can tell you, there is a lot that isn't in the history books, Belchite people up against the wall, right here in this street, and shot.'

But what about the siege, I ask, and he replies that what he remembers most is heat, terrible, unendurable heat, just like today but worse. The defenders, he said, 'with nothing but death before them' asked continually for water. Local people were sent out to get it. Meanwhile nationalist planes, Spanish and Italian, were dropping bombs on the lines of the attackers, sometimes badly aimed. 'We listened for the planes,' he said, 'with our mouths open to the sky.

Aviation was not like it is today. You could hear the planes coming from far away and that gave you time to hide. And the bombs didn't just drop, you know. They fell diagonally, coming forward all the time and spinning just before they hit the ground. That gave you a bit more time as well.' In the end, when the republicans arrived, they fought from house to house, breaking in cellar doors to kill the nationalists like dogs.

I am not myself a great one for battlefields, feeling the evil in them sufficient for the day the battles happened. But now the Ebro beckoned in an inclusiveness of horror and I made my way there, an hour or two by road, still in the great heat.

The main event between the siege of Belchite in 1937 and the Battle of the Ebro, fought right through the summer of 1938, was the republican offensive against Teruel in the winter of 1937–8. The attack on Teruel, conducted in the bitterest of winter weather, was typical of the best efforts of the republic – a successful assault and the taking of territory that, for reasons of fundamental military weakness, could not then be held against the inevitable counter-offensive. Franco left no republican advance unpunished and each republican offensive led on at once either to a lost battle or to a slow war of attrition in the locality.

By February 1938, after fearful fighting, Teruel was nationalist again and now, in a decision much disliked by some of his generals, Franco pushed down towards Valencia through wild, rough territory. The Ebro, flowing from the gorges north of Burgos to the distant Mediterranean, follows a gentle south-easterly curve most of the distance. In its final stages, before emerging at the sea half-way between Valencia and Barcelona, it turns to run due south, partly through deep defiles and partly through more open country, rich in vineyards, extremely beautiful under high limestone peaks and ridges. The rougher parts of the country seem almost impassable and everywhere there are commanding heights to complicate movement below. The nationalists had taken up positions along this north–south stretch of river, and the republicans, hoping to divert them from the assault upon Valencia, embarked in late July of 1938 upon what proved to be their last offensive, a massive river crossing, at many different points, along a front of well over a hundred kilometres.

As often before, they made good progress to begin with, capturing a large pocket of land and all the high ground in it. They were halted before Gandesa, a wine-producing town with the loveliest of mountains up behind, dewlapped with folds of limestone and with limestone slabs lying like immense tabletops at forty-five degrees.

I come in from the north by Mequinenza, a dead little new town on a stretch of reservoir, aghast at the heat, aghast at the steepness of the land. Was this really what they fought in – this heat, these heights, climbing, running, wounded, dying? Trucks and troop carriers, where they existed, rumbling past in a dull thunder, others stricken and abandoned? Artillery atrocious on the ear? Above all, the irresistible air power of the nationalists? At Fayon there is another new town, built to replace the destroyed original. Lower down the river, I find a little place, huddled and grey, hardly destroyed at all. A ferry, flat pontoon on a double hull, pushes out across the stream to a far bank graceful with poplars and bamboo. At Gandesa itself old men sit vacantly at pavement tables. Outside the swimming-pool, women stride jauntily in bathrobes, boys run by with towels round their necks. There is an ironwork cross here under a Gothic canopy, a modern monument made of small plates welded together, and up on a high hill three or four kilometres to the north, a monument to mark the spot from which General Franco directed operations.

The opposition monument, planted a year or two back by a group of aged republicans in berets, is an enormous iron jackboot, two-dimensional, outside the ruined church in the neighbouring village of Corbera. Corbera had the misfortune to be caught in crossfire, shelled by both sides and bombed by the nationalists. The old settlement on top of the hill was simply abandoned afterwards, a kind of natural Belchite, while the population moved down to the newer scrap of settlement below. Intermediate between the two, a bulldozer is working, thick clouds of dust going up in all directions. Right there in the dust, beside the bulldozer, two men in their late fifties are digging a deep ditch with spades.

We have an odd little conversation about the bombing, their childhood memories of being hurled clear across the room and deafened with percussion. We are in Catalonia here and they are struggling a bit, they say, not having spoken Castilian for years. But all the same we get to politics.

'It was just like anywhere,' says the one with the best Castilian. 'There were two classes, the rich and the poor. The rich were nationalists. We were the poor and as you see yourself, that is just what we still are today. The reason is that we are honest men. Only the dishonest make real money.'

Imagine an uncertain number of the losers, upwards of 40,000 and maybe very many more, shot as war criminals after Nuremburg, rather than the handful who actually died. This will give some measure of the fresh, quasi-judicial terror that occurred in Spain during the years immediately following the Civil War. With no more Russian arms to meet those still supplied by Italy and Germany and with the French frontier now closed against them, the republicans lost Barcelona in January 1939. In Madrid, in the last gasp of war, internal struggle brought resistance to an end. Now Franco's peacetime governance began, in a spirit of blood and vengeance, of victors and the vanquished. He was never to abandon this point of view, never to seek reconciliation with those whom he believed were the worst enemies of Spain. When later we hear of 'the peace of Franco' or 'the peace of the Caudillo' it is always worth bearing its origins in mind.

The atmosphere in this exhausted country, proclaiming itself Catholic, imperial, great and free, must have been quite extraordinary. Schoolchildren began the day with the fascist salute. The 'reds' were mostly dead or in prison or in trouble of some other sort; in school their children were openly mocked by classmates. Land reverted to its previous owners. Priests in their vestments were seen again on every corner. If today in midwinter you should pass a group of them on the cathedral steps in Burgos, black cassocks, flat black hats on their heads, black scarves pulled across their mouths to keep out the Castilian wind, then, give or take a little for the region and the climate, you should imagine similar scenes in every Spanish town and village. For the Spanish clergy were among the victors along with the army and the Falange, the Carlists and the monarchists.

But all this was peripheral to a greater and more immediate matter, desperate poverty and in many places hunger. Some say there was more suffering in Spain in the ten years after the war than during the war itself.

Not all was the result of the Spanish conflict. Much is attributable to the World War which immediately ensued and to Spain's subsequent pariah status as the one surviving nation that could be described as fascist. This was bad luck in a way, for Franco had watched the war begin, confident that at the end of it Spain would take her place in a new and friendly fascist order. Spain was generally well-disposed towards Germany during the war but the country was too exhausted and Franco too canny to allow her to be drawn in. Hitler wanted to march across Spain to take Gibraltar; Franco pitched his price impossibly high. (Hitler spent a day with him in a railway carriage at Hendaye and compared it to a visit to the dentist.) Spain did send nearly 20,000 volunteers, the División Azul, or Blue Division, to fight the communist foe on the eastern front, but they were pulled back again in 1943. For Franco was nothing if not a Spaniard and even if it was interpreted through an archaic and authoritarian mentality, he was animated in the deepest sense by patriotism. As he saw the Axis effort failing, he brought Spain over into a neutrality more favourable to the Allies. The Spanish people were hungry and had it not been for Allied grace and favour, allowing the import of oil and food, they would actually have starved.

After the war, at Russian instigation, the poverty was dragged out by a United Nations trade boycott, accompanied by the withdrawal of UN ambassadors. There was no such thing as Marshall Aid for Spain, of course, only international condemnation. Franco's government responded by trying to produce everything it needed in its own factories, a policy of import-substitution, and by trying to clean up its image. The fascist salute was dropped in schools and there now began a period of what has been well described as 'cosmetic constitutionalism'. Little by little Franco's rule was institutionalized and the country was declared a monarchy; one that happened to have Franco, however, as its lifetime regent, head of state and head of government.

This might have had scant effect had it not been for the Cold War now developing and America's new willingness to fold to its bosom Europe's stoutest anti-communist – even if it had to be agreed that his other credentials were questionable. In due course the ambassadors came back and the trade boycott was lifted. In 1953, Franco accepted a loan in exchange for permitting the Americans to establish air and naval bases on Spanish soil. The money was still a good deal less than Marshall Aid but Spain was back on the road towards international acceptability. This must have been a satisfying moment for the Caudillo.

Compared to these great matters, my own arrival in Madrid in the early 1960s was of little significance to anyone except myself. But it was a time when it was impossible not to be aware of human dramas in progress all around. For while Franco piped away in his high little voice and proved himself an excellent manipulator of the 'families' or clans of which his governments were composed, essentially the different groups of victors along with an increasing contingent of 'technocrats' from the civil service and the universities, an enormous movement of population was also, unstoppably, occurring; a million rural Andalusians were abandoning the poverty of the countryside and pouring into Spain's industrial cities. They came with slicked-back hair and suitcases of wood or cardboard, in collarless shirts and blunt-looking country jackets and they built themselves – since they had no option – Third World shanty towns round all the greatest cities. These, thirty years on, have mostly been transmuted into the bleak, cliff-like apartment blocks that ring the cities today. They are inhabited now not only by Andalusians but by rural Castilians, Galicians and Aragonese, also forced to leave the land by the same lack of work and growth of mechanization.

In a sense, the early rural emigrants were harbingers, for the

Spanish cities, in the 1960s, had embarked on what is often called Spain's 'economic miracle'. Income, though starting low, increased three times over in a decade and all the other indices showed comparable results. Some put this down to the new technocrats whom Franco now brought into his cabinets (many of tnem were members of a Catholic 'freemasonry' called Opus Dei, which had made the recruitment of the élite its special mission, so much so that the word 'technocrat' itself became a euphemism for Opus Dei). Other commentators believe the economic changes would have happened anyway.

The miracle was founded on three things and two of them have proved double-edged to say the least. First was foreign investment, posing no greater problems than elsewhere; the second was cheap mass tourism, with wild land speculation, unregulated building and the ravaging of hundreds of miles of coast; and the third, at least as painful as the tourism, was mass emigration not just to the Spanish cities but beyond to Germany, France and Belgium. Those who went were mostly rural labourers; it was their cash remittances in foreign currency that helped, first to rescue those at home, and then to make it possible for Spanish wealth to grow.

I remember that sense of growing wealth and ease, of course, and the sexual *frisson* that arrived with semi-naked tourists. This made a great impression round the Spanish coasts. But what I remember even more are two quite contradictory aspects of life under Franco. At one extreme, there was a sense of total bureaucratic stuffiness. Much of it flowed from the rebarbative, often quite meaningless rhetoric of the National Movement, the country's sole political organization. (Soon after the war, the Falange itself had been absorbed into it.) *ABC*, the newspaper for which Luis Bolín had long before been London correspondent, used to print page after page of new statutes and economic regulations relating to the Movement and to unspeakably dull government enterprises, all set out in wide grey wedges of officialese, a kind of cotton wool that was a deadening, and ultimately quite frightening, insult to the spirit. It stood as a symbol of the whole of public life in Spain. Yet on the other hand, coexisting with it, there was an almost total private liberty. You could keep your neighbours awake all night with the Beatles – then just entering their kingdom – and nobody would say a word. You could spit. You could shout. And as long as you respected the sexual decencies and showed no interest in politics you enjoyed a personal freedom of a kind unknown in northern Europe, realm of by-laws.

Serious opposition to Franco was by now beginning, though. Six or seven years ahead of the student movement elsewhere, brave spirits willing to risk a beating began to demonstrate in the universities in Barcelona and Madrid. I lived just near the university and friends would come rushing in, breathless with tales of water cannon and broken heads. In Asturias, in 1962, those same redoubtable miners who had fought so hard in 1934 were waging a bitter strike, with every prospect of long prison sentences, and those who sympathized with them too openly were also getting into trouble.

Less than a decade later, when I was coming back as a journalist, it was possible, with precautions, to make a round of an impressive array of opponents to Franco. Catholic workers had combined with communists to set up illegal trades unions, parallel to the official semi-fascist structure of vertical syndicates. They were achieving industrial victories, too, with employers happy to come to terms so as to push on with profit-making. The Workers' Commissions, as the illegal unions were called, were happy to talk to the foreign press. So were the socialists, also operating in clandestinity. Basque nationalists were pleased to receive the occasional visit. I remember one trip round the *ikastolas*, country schools where teaching was actually in Basque despite the prohibitions; they struck me, leaving the language issue to one side, as the epitome of up-to-date educational method, with local priests, alert and open-minded, almost invariably behind them. The repression of the language had proved ineffective and as Franco grew old and ill with Parkinson's disease nobody in his government had the heart, or perhaps the gall, to stamp out the *ikastola* movement. In Catalonia, too, the language was back in force, still banned in public life, of course, but practised so vigorously in private that, looking back, one sees there was a new renaissance in the making. And it went along with public protest, too. Jordi Pujol, a doctor, after that a banker and now the leader of the post-Franco Generalitat, was one of those arrested for singing the Catalan anthem in the Liceu in the presence of Franco ministers.

Perhaps the most surprising phenomenon of all was the change in the relations of Church and State. This came about as a result of Vatican II and that brief period of Catholic liberalization, now swept away again, not just in Spain but in the whole of the Church hierarchy. For a time, under the impulse of Vatican II, Spain had a positively liberal primate and this so infuriated the right that he had to have police protection from Catholic terrorists, the so-called Guerrillas of Christ the King. Franco might have preferred to see him in gaol instead, for before the regime came to an end there was one Basque bishop under house arrest and nearly 200 priests in prison. Little moments of *apertura*, 'opening', had alternated with periods of return to the old authoritarianism and the latter was in the ascendant in the mid 1970s.

Franco died a protracted death in 1975, victim of every possible contrivance to keep him longer in this world. For many years he had been in possession of the mummified arm of St Teresa and now he clutched it unavailingly. Remembering the strange accounts of this affair, I make a pilgrimage to the two monuments that seem to me best to express the essence of his rule. One is the police computer centre at the base of the Guadarrama mountains, not far from El Escorial. With its towers and searchlights, walls and protective fencing, it inherited all the records kept over thirty-six long years by a police state. Whether or not these should be destroyed has been a matter of lively argument. You see the establishment quite clearly from the road in passing; and when you think about it, it makes you shiver.

The other monument, almost next door, is the Valley of the Fallen, el Valle de los Caidos. On top of a rocky hill cupped in the mountains, and visible from many miles away, there rises an enormous cross, 150 metres high, steel encased in rusticated granite. Beneath it, with an enormity of scale that must have been intended as some kind of parallel with El Escorial, the whole of the hill has been hollowed out to make a vast cavern, a memorial cathedral. Technically it is a church, but cathedral is the word that best expresses its size. It was dug for Franco, in the aftermath of war, by his political prisoners and quite apart from any associations this fact may confer, it is notable as being one of the least attractive architectural enterprises in Spain. Crossing a barren open space like a parade ground, you enter the hill through a barren portico of rock. The church itself is simply a tunnel, writ enormous. Passing through ranks of pews, you ascend to a circular crypt with a tall, thin crucifix at its centre, positioned immediately beneath the cross on top of the hill. In front of this crucifix, under a plain stone slab, lies José Antonio Primo de Rivera, the founding father whose movement was so thoroughly hijacked by Franco. Around behind the crucifix, still exploiting José Antonio, even in death, lies Franco.

But visitors to the Valley of the Fallen, pondering the strange history of these two men, should now raise their eyes to the mosaic dome above. Here they will make out the black flag of fascism, along with the national flag of Spain. The fasces, grim inheritance from Isabel and Fernando, gleam in gold. There is a field gun, a bunker, men in helmets and battledress. As they mount the side of the dome, their military garb gives way to robes and then, a little higher up, to loin cloths. The uppermost human figure, floating aloft in athletic middle age, has actually sprouted wings. So far as I can see, he holds a laurel wreath impaled on a drawn sword.

Most dictators die and a power-struggle follows. Franco arranged for the perpetuation of his regime, naming his successor in 1969. This was the young prince Juan Carlos de Borbón y Borbón, grandson of Alfonso XIII and son of Don Juan, the rightful heir. Franco took a very dim view of Don Juan and in any event the new monarchy was intended as a Francoist installation, not as a restoration. Franco had been responsible for the education of Juan Carlos from boyhood and had made him take an oath of loyalty, both to himself and to the National Movement. It looked as if the pass had been sold long in advance and that nothing at all would change. Nor did anything much happen for some months; perhaps a good thing in retrospect since after the old man's death the principal public emotion was fear. Probably a majority of Spaniards had supported him in the latter years; the worst that anyone could imagine now was a return to social strife and the intervention, once again, of generals and army. For the moment, then, Spain had a king instead of Franco – not widely liked or trusted, but at least safely in existence – and the old, closed system of Francoist politics.

The country had misjudged Juan Carlos. Privately, he had decided some time before that when Franco departed the system must shift in its entirety; and when the king moved, he did so decisively. In July 1976, with the resignation of the old Francoist prime minister, Juan Carlos left his nation open-mouthed by choosing, from a carefully rigged short list, a Francoist bureaucrat, aged forty-three, by name Adolfo Suárez. Suárez had previously been head of broadcasting, rigidly excluding anything sexually suggestive, according to the whims of Franco's wife, and had then gone on to head the National Movement. His appointment seemed completely backward-looking.

But the king and the new prime minister already had a plan and Suárez, to the frank astonishment of both the Spanish public and the opposition, moved with extraordinary speed to reform the regime. The essence of the trick was that he reformed it from inside, with vigorous arm-twisting and the surprised support of the old Francoist institutions. Had continuity been broken, the king would have betrayed his oath to Franco and, in a land where honour counts for something, he would therefore have lost his claim to legitimacy. This, in turn, would have invited a rebellion of the generals. But Suárez was simply too quick for everybody.

By late in that first year he had engineered a reform of the Cortes and had it blessed by a referendum. In February 1977, he legalized the Socialist Party. By now, he was a man canoeing in the rapids, no way back, one false movement and he would be over. In March, he legalized the trades unions. In April he nearly lost it all, his legalization of the Communist Party infuriating sections of the army who believed that he had promised to consult them first. Paddling at frantic speed between terrorist attacks from the extreme right and extreme left, both, for different reasons, trying to stop the political opening, he actually abolished the National Movement.

It was a thrilling process and when a centre-right party formed itself to contest elections called for June, Adolfo Suárez himself stepped forward and neatly took it over, emerging as prime minister of the first genuinely democratic government ever to be elected under a Spanish monarchy.

With his clean-cut good looks and well-cut clothes, Suárez had wooed the public like a lover. So had another young leader, one Felipe González. His party was the PSOE, the Spanish Socialist Workers' Party formed in the late nineteenth century. Under Franco, as a proscribed organization, it had gone to ground; González, a labour lawyer from Seville, captured the leadership in 1974 in a secret conference held in France. In the 1977 Spanish election, his slightly chubby good looks were a counterpoise to Suárez's leaner jaw; and when it emerged that the Suárez party lacked a clear majority, González for the socialists was ready to deal with him. The voters, who believed they had exercised a genuine right to choose, now saw Suárez and the opposition come together in a deal called the Moncloa Pact. There were two results: one was the writing of a non-partisan and liberal constitution; the second was widespread public *desencanto*, a rapid disillusionment with the new democracy.

It is true that Suárez won one more election but now that a thoroughgoing reform of society itself was needed he appeared to have no programme. His centre-right group split at the end of 1980 over the legalization of divorce; and Suárez, saviour of Spain, fell irrecoverably. It was on 23 February 1981, while voting was in progress for the investiture of a successor, that an event occurred which threatened to reduce all that had been achieved to the condition of a mirage.

On an open television channel, transmitting everything to the Spanish nation just as it happened, a Civil Guard lieutenant colonel, Antonio Tejero, swept into the Cortes with a posse of his men. It seemed a re-enactment of the Civil Guard attack on the Cortes which had brought the First Republic to an end. Absurd in tricorn hat and vast moustache, but terrifyingly for every democrat, Tejero waved an automatic pistol with an exaggerated gesture. His men loosed off their sub-machine-guns at the ceiling and forced the Cortes deputies to the floor. General Gutiérrez Mellado, soon to prove a staunch army reformer, ordered him to stop and was bruisingly roughed up; Adolfo Suárez sprang to his assistance – two men of old-fashioned courage and dignity seen to behave with both these qualities on every television set in Spain.

Tejero had been acting under the broad direction of Major-General Alfonso Armada, the king's one-time tutor and the former secretary-general of the royal household. Tejero and a third conspirator, General Jaime Milans del Bosch, the captain-general of Valencia, believed from Armada's nods and winks that he was acting for the king. In fact, in a complicated, two-faced game, Armada hoped to start a coup by pretending he was with the king and then, when events were already in motion, to induce the king to join. In Valencia, soon after Tejero's entry to the Cortes, Milans del Bosch brought his tanks out on the street, one at least with its guns trained on the local PSOE headquarters. He announced that he was awaiting the orders of the king.

The situation at this moment was that the deputies were Tejero's prisoners, in one provincial capital the tanks were on the streets and in other parts of Spain strange troop movements were occurring. Then, for hours, nothing at all happened. Friends of mine on the left in one provincial town – by now, I'm afraid, it was the children of my friends who were the activists – began to think it was all over, that the dark night of pistols and bicycle chains and lists of those to be killed had come. One by one, they quietly slipped out of town and into the neighbouring sierra.

Juan Carlos, from the Zarzuela palace near Madrid, either immediately or after a short delay – still a matter of speculation – attempted to rally the captains-general and defeat the coup. It was not a simple matter. The military commander in Seville stood ready to follow Milans del Bosch. There was every chance the Brunete tank division outside Madrid would move on the capital. Some of the generals came over to the king at once. Others havered, in touch now with the Zarzuela palace, now with Valencia, waiting to see which way events would go. It was not till 1.15 am the following morning, eight hours after Tejero entered the Cortes, that the king went on television to say he would not tolerate an assault on the Constitution or the democratic process it embodied. Tejero surrendered later on 24 February; Armada was arrested the next day. It was the king in person who had begun the move to democracy and the king in person who had moved, with courage and command, to save it.

The Spanish public, realizing how close they had come to losing their new liberties, swiftly recovered from their *desencanto*. When the next election came, in 1982, it was clear to all that the centre-right had been unable to handle the army. The electorate now raised the stakes, electing the socialist Felipe González, though on a programme greatly watered down and on a party constitution purged of Marxism. The night the election results came in, in 1982, was the night that a deeper democracy began in Spain, the night that Franco really died. It was this above all I had been pondering in the Valley of the Fallen.

9 From Coast to Coast

Travels in Spain Today

WASHINGTON IRVING RODE through Andalucía with a Russian diplomat. I find myself one of a group of journalists being lugged around the south-west of Spain in a large bus. In Seville, we get an earful from the man in charge of Expo 92, successor to the international fair of 1929. He talks like a Texan, making it sound entirely emblematic of his city, something that might be taken quite for granted, that Seville has been the subject of eight operas. It probably deserves a few more, he implies.

One of our group, no Russian he, but the closest thing available, is a literary critic from Finland. Like many Finns and Swedes, spending their holidays in Spain and cultivating the thought during the winter, Markku is a flamenco enthusiast. More than that, he is something of an expert, with contacts in the flamenco world and an entrée to the flamenco clubs, the local *peñas*, all along our route. In Seville, quite late at night, he drags me up to the north of the city, to a working-class area with big and soulless apartment blocks, and then along an unmade, dusty road. Given the city's tally of the alienated, the unemployed and desperate, it is exactly the kind of place tourists are told to keep away from.

We are welcomed warmly to a large wooden cabin set out like a theatre, with little chairs around a low raised dais. The audience is entirely Spanish working class or gypsy, fathers with tots on their shoulders, big, heavy gypsy women, hair drawn back so tight it looks quite painful. One has a white carnation in her hair; many are eating Russian salad or fried potatoes out of grey cones of greasy paper. There is an atmosphere of chat and expectation. The entertainment, when it comes, is deadly serious.

Singer and guitarist are seated in small straight chairs behind a round tin table. The guitarist strikes a note, then strikes another, then a ripple, then his guitar is thundering or tiptoeing alternately, feeling for the complex rhythm which soon descends upon him, settling him, a spirit recognized. There's an *olé* or two to spur him on, to show we have belief in him, a readiness for the voyage. Next, after the long introduction, it's the singer's turn to come alive, to follow where the guitarist leads. The singer is tall and lanky, bright red cheeks, looks like a footballer. 'Ay, ay, ay,' he cries experimentally, then, piercingly, voice lifted to the roof, he wails 'ayee', a sound of purest grief. *Olés* from the audience, 'Spanish' and gypsy, and after a little more fine tuning of his spirit, the descent of *duende*, or inspiration – one of the deepest and most trusted concepts in flamenco – and the song takes off in a roughened slip and slide across the notes, undulating, ululating in steps smaller than quarter-tones or semitones, with major and minor keys rolled into one, no sense at all of do-re-mi or tidy octaves. Sweat pours down the singer's face, sprays sideways when he shakes his head. The guitarist's hand slips over the strings in a cascade of moisture.

Together they are making a long riff of sound plucked out of inwardness and precedent. It is instantly recognizable, even to an ear so inexperienced as mine, as the music of the people of poverty, a music of loves and jealousies, of passion and betrayal, of saints, mothers and murders, of bitterness and sometimes, even, of happiness. It is strange, earthly, unearthly. It brings you out in gooseflesh, raises hair along the forearms and down the back of the neck.

In Huelva, in Columbus territory, now given over to petrochemicals and fertilizer factories, we visit a more prosperous kind of *peña*. The people here, again all working folk, are eating plates of shrimp and drinking sherry, or whisky pale as sherry in the largest measures. But the music, once again, tells the same tale of grief and struggle. It is more of a show here, more clearly an entertainment, with a range of different singers and accompanists and several little troupes of dancers. Even so, it is a million miles from the flamenco shows I used to go to in Madrid or the displays laid on in tourist hotels. If there is a mystery here, and sometimes I think there is – a kind of privacy to real flamenco – then Markku has led me straight through the barrier.

The dancers start with one arm raised above their heads, the hand turned down, in a kind of delicate pickiness. The other arm defines a small barrel shape in front of them at chest level. When the moment comes, they stamp and twirl, parading the fine vigour of the fandango. Spines curve alarmingly. Fish skeletons and cigarette stubs grow in heaps. Fans flicker, cigars are sucked into a glow. It's hot, even hotter than Seville. One of the club members moves to open the door. 'Close it,' says the president firmly, 'we don't want the *duende* to go out.'

Markku sometimes commissions flamenco singers to travel up to Finland to display their art. He maintains that flamenco is the opposite of opera, in the sense that opera singers look for purity and roundness of tone, struggle to supersede the limitations of the human voice, make themselves into an instrument. 'In flamenco the word roughness goes to the essence. You don't want to purify your voice or hide things. You go right down, deep down inside yourself. It's the same difference between ballet and flamenco dancing. In flamenco, there's no challenge to gravity. You dance with all your body. You collect your inspiration from the earth.'

Flamenco belongs to gypsies and the gypsy world, no doubt about it. Even so, there is huge debate about the origins of their music. The theory that it is related to the Hebrew liturgy is not heard much these days, nor do people tell you, as much as they used to, that it comes from India (though there are certainly strong parallels in the hand movements of dancers). This, then, leaves Arabic music as the likeliest major source, and flamenco as one of the greatest parts of the Moorish inheritance. But many of the rhythms are actually quite new, mostly nineteenth-century, and modern music plays a part as well. There are, for instance, flamenco rumbas, tangos and *colombianos*, all modified by Latin American rhythms – 'mail returned to sender with a little change,' says

Markku. In Spanish they are called *cantes de ida y vuelta* – return-ticket flamenco styles.

There is no doubt that *flamenco puro* is alive and well, sung in the *peñas* where we have heard it, at weddings and open-air parties (the famous *juergas* of Andalucía). Or perhaps some rich person may commission an evening's entertainment. It has not always been so, for after the eighteenth and nineteenth centuries, regarded by enthusiasts as the golden age, it seemed this form of music might be swept away entirely along with much else that was genuinely of the people. Lorca and the composer Manuel de Falla tried to help, organizing a great flamenco competition in Granada. Hollywood attracted some of the best performers, dancers mostly, but naturally enough they were swept up into showbiz. By the 1950s *flamenco puro* was really on the ropes. It was just at this time, possessed by a sense of its imminent collapse, that French musicologists began to take recordings, encouraging the flamenco community to remember their tradition. In Madrid, in 1958, a great recording session was held for the Hispavox label, bringing together many of the old masters of flamenco. It lasted for eight days and nights before thirty-three songs and their accompaniments, representing all the grief and loss and love of the Spanish gypsies, and all the principal rhythms, were safely captured, along with that strange mixture of rough self-pity and barely concealed virility. 'Pure flamenco is very difficult to record,' says Markku, 'it can't just be done to order. The singer chooses what to sing, has to wait for the *duende*, may need encouragement.' Extras were brought in, to shout *olé* at suitable moments, and no doubt a glass or two of wine as well. The catalogue of the Hispavox anthology, still on sale and still very popular, tells how the *saetas*, a form of flamenco sung during Easter processions, were re-enacted in genuine-but-fake processions through the night streets of the city, complete with the eeriness of muffled drums.

'*Jodel gusta más que comel.*' In standard Castilian the phrase would read '*joder gusta más que comer*' and it means, not to beat about the bush, 'fucking is even better than eating'. A friend of a friend has seen it written in large letters on a bridge in Extremadura and now, back in Madrid, it is the subject of some comment in the *tertulia*. (The *tertulia*, or informal discussion club, is the very essence of old-fashioned Spanish intellectual life, a café-style encounter reflecting sociability and an unquenchable pleasure in discussion, not necessarily too well-informed.) The general theory now emerging is that the graffito was probably written by an adolescent, certainly someone in the grip of his first experience of active sex (male authorship is assumed, I don't know why). But it is the comparison in the slogan that is so intriguing, for if the best experience in life is to be compared to the experience that has up to now seemed best, then it is evident that this phrase springs from a culture of hunger. If eating well enough is something that you take for granted, goes the argument, then you will hardly use it as a yardstick for describing the first joys of sex.

The best known individual in Spain to spring from the culture of hunger is probably Manuel Benítez, El Cordobés. This extraordinary bullfighter, raw and brusque in gesture but with a quality of courage and a willingness to try experiments that were quite undreamt of – among a dozen other horrors in his repertoire, he would go down on his knees with his back to the bull – began his life in utter poverty. An orphan, he worked, or didn't if there wasn't any work, as an occasional day labourer in a dead-end town near Córdoba, took off on the road for months at a time, stole chickens, and knew the taste of beatings from the police a good deal better than the taste of prawns. There was never enough food, never a sense of plenty. One of his first acts on making a little money was to buy himself a whole *serrano* ham, that is to say, a raw ham cured in the sierra, the rough but exquisite equivalent of northerners' smoked salmon. As he and his manager drove in a battered car from fight to fight and stayed in the shabbiest of lodging-places, El Cordobés took his ham with him everywhere. He slept with it beside the bed and took a slice from it, night or day, whenever and wherever he felt like it.

El Cordobés was the bullfighting phenomenon of my youth. He came to Madrid preceded, quite properly, by tales of reckless courage and survival from impossible taurine encounters. But now the build-up was colossal, embedded in it the cunningly deployed rumour that the one thing he was scared of was Madrid itself, the ultimate testing ground for all toreros. Seats at Las Ventas, the great Mudéjar bullring, went to the rich and clever. Naturally, I wasn't there. But I watched the happening in a bar, on television, in a more than usual state of agitation. There had been a cartoon in the morning paper showing a group of people sitting on a sofa watching the fight. In the crowded scene, it took a while to see the joke – one man absent-mindedly biting the fingernails of another.

Most people, whatever they think about it, probably have a mental image of the bullfight. In the circular amphitheatre, shade on one side, sun beating down on the other, there is a buzz of noise, a smell compounded of those three great Spanish odours, eau-de-Cologne, cigar smoke and brandy on hot breath. The fight is closer to a ritual than it is to pugilism, conducted in distinct acts and to the sound of paso dobles and cracked bugles. First come the bull-fighters and their teams, gorgeous in suits of lights, gold thread and scarlet, whatever the colour may be, crossing the sand of the wide ring to make their obeisances to the day's president of ceremonies. There will be two bulls to each of three bullfighters, all the bulls to die and the bullfighters themselves to pass through moments where it is possible they may be killed. Some are, every season. It is regarded as an art and reported on the arts pages of newspapers by 'critics'. There is an element of sacrifice to it (the worship of the bull in Spain seems to have been almost as long-standing as the bull rituals of Crete) but also, for the crowd, there is the same sensation that draws the public to Grand Prix racing – the fear and anticipation of a horrible upset.

After the bull comes roaring in first time – an enormous animal, pure muscle, bred for ferocity – there are fast, exceptionally graceful passes to try him out. These are done with the widest of capes and though spectacular are dangerous to neither man nor bull. It is the next phase that is always most upsetting, along with the later death of the bull, sometimes choking in its own blood; a horseman with a lance, the picador, enters now and leans the lance down into the humped shoulder muscles of the charging bull, working away until the neck runs a mess of blood and some of the proud strength goes out of the animal. The horses are well-padded but sometimes, even so, hurt horribly. Picasso's disembowelled horse, symbol not just of horror but of gentleness betrayed, comes from this stage of the bullfight. (When young he used to paint more cheerful bullfight scenes, not at the bullfight but the day before, so that he could sell them to the crowd and buy a ticket for himself.) After the picador comes the banderillero, deft and daring, to plant his grievous little darts in the bull's wounded neck. After that, and after a flourish of music, the bullfighter himself comes out for the penultimate set of passes, a dance of danger in which, continually deceiving the bull with a cape that is still quite broad, he draws the animal whirling round him or straight past his chest, breathtakingly close, sometimes leaning on it as it passes, his suit of lights a gory mass. His work during the fight is known, in total, as the *faena* but it is the final stages of the *faena* on which public judgement rests. The bullfighter arches his back like a flamenco dancer, thrusts his hips forward, exposing himself to the bull, male against male, the weaker potency of man made greater, in the false logic of the bullfight, by his cunning. At last he takes a small cape and a sword and again establishes his dominance over the failing animal, through a series of passes specific to this stage of the encounter. Finally, he positions the bull most carefully, feet together so that the shoulder blades will lie apart, allowing a width of some three inches for the sword to enter. The thrust must pierce deep down inside the bull to strike the heart. The bullfighter takes his sight along the sword, leans in and reaches over, the inside of his upper thigh exposed above the beast's right horn – and plunges with the sword. This is the moment when toreros die, a suddenly lifted horn severing the femoral artery as the bull tosses them. Then, as they fall to earth again, the bull returns to savage them, growling like a monstrous terrier, working and working with its knives of horn on the rag-doll figure sprawling on the sand.

El Cordobés was caught by his first bull. It was in a last belated pass before the kill, at the end of a *faena* so brilliant and dangerous that not just those at the ring but every viewer in Spain – 20 million watched television that day – must have been begging him to bring an end to it and kill the bull. It hoisted him by the inside of his thigh, seemingly right in the groin, dealing a wound eight inches long. Though it missed the artery, he nearly died. Less than a month later, pale and limping, he fought again in Andalucía to prove his courage. When he returned to Madrid I actually had a seat and was there to watch him triumph. I don't remember the details of the fight but one small incident sticks in my mind, along with his boyish bearing and his flashing smile. Often during the *faena*, enthusiasts throw down flowers. El Cordobés handled his bull quite near the protective barrier, not right out in the middle as he had done on that first occasion. Roses and carnations rained down around him. I saw his right heel move back crunching a pearl necklace in the sand – fake pearls, no doubt, but a sight to carry in one's stock of images.

Whether the bullfight is an abomination that should be abandoned, I am by no means certain. Whenever I am away from Spain, I think so; when I return I begin to doubt again. The bullfighter I most admired was not El Cordobés but a far more classical fighter named El Viti. Serene and tragic, he was continually in profile, a man whose every move was a meditation on death. Leaving Spain, though, I discovered for the first time that I felt like Isabel the Catholic when she told her confessor that she would never, so long as she lived, watch a bullfight again. Twenty years later, as I made my present journeys around Spain, I found myself in Madrid at the time of San Isidro, the major bullfighting festival of the year. Deciding to try the state of my emotions, I found myself sitting at Las Ventas with a group of tourists. All of them were horrified, disgusted. But I felt my own history stir inside me to the *olés* and the bugle and recalled a description, written by an English observer in the eighteenth century, of a bullfight held in Madrid to celebrate the arrival of Carlos III.

In those days, bulls were fought, always in the Plaza Mayor, by knights or gentlemen on horseback, with only their auxiliaries on foot. (Bullfights and bullrings as we know them now began to develop at the end of the eighteenth century.) After describing the scene – the liveries of the fighting teams were 'Moorish habits of silk' – and the events of a hot and crowded afternoon, the writer goes on to reflect on a custom whose 'Moorish or perhaps Roman barbarity' he cannot deny. It will not 'bear the reflections of the closet,' he says, nor 'the compassionate feelings of a tender heart.' Yet in it, nevertheless, he sees a hardness of manhood, the exercise of a ferocity in our natures that must not sink into cruelty nor be diverted into effeminacy. It is bravery that is most applauded there in the Plaza Mayor; it teaches scorn of danger and that the best way for us to overcome our fear 'is to look it calmly and stedfastly [sic] in the face'. This passage, reprinted in Hugh Thomas's anthology on Madrid, is scarcely an adequate defence of bullfighting but it tells us a great deal about Spain, even modern Spain, and the intensity that still abides in this archaic spectacle.

The true gods these days, as they have been for almost forty years, are footballers. The rise of Real Madrid ran parallel to the mass migration from the land (real, of course, means royal), offering some kind of pabulum to the new arrivals in the city as well as to its long-time residents. Success in Europe, for the country that had been so isolated and despised, was more than mere success in football. There was an attacking style known as the 'Spanish fury', proudly reinvoking the name that had been a badge of shame at Antwerp in 1576. In Barcelona, to make an impressionistic judgement, the passion was (and remains) still greater than in Madrid. Franco had looked benevolently on the game, never missing the main match of the week on television. There was a theory that apathy was the sign of a healthy population and football, for a time, appeared to syphon energy away from politics. One of the great contemporary discoveries is that football and democratic politics are actually compatible.

The same may be said of cinema. Spain under Franco had more cinema seats per head than any other country in Europe. If football was the circus, cinema was intended to be bread for the masses and they flocked in eagerly, myself often among them. Dubbing was compulsory, for it would never do to leave the uncensored script to those who knew foreign languages, definitely potential agitators.

Kisses were cut along with amorous exchanges so that in love stories marriages and close alliances arose with what always seemed to me a shocking lack of preliminaries. Married in her film identity, Grace Kelly falls in love with 'another man'. This would be adultery, except that the dialogue has been altered so that her husband is presented as her brother. Mysteriously, she shares a room with the 'brother' – the censors either quite incompetent or more concerned with marital appearances than with the sin of incest. It was all most wonderfully absurd. Even so, there was no disguising the consumer goods tucked away in the background, in US movies in particular; and it was the cinema which gave a first inkling that there were smart cars and low-cut dresses, something quite different from the stuffiness and poverty of life under Franco. Dubbing still persists, an unshakeable national habit and a profitable industry for actors, but the cinema has endured as a popular entertainment, even with the rise of television.

Though it sounds a little odd to say so, undoubtedly the most exciting event for arts and entertainment has been the death of the dictator himself. Spain's cities suddenly became champagne uncorked. I remember a trip to Oviedo to report on the phenom-enon. Half the young people in town appeared to be involved in a wild experimental ballet (both literally and figuratively). In the old town, where the bars were, pot smoke billowed out of doorways. It was all intended to shock the older generation, assumed to be deeply respectable, but most of them were too busy to notice, energetically catching up on light pornography. Anaïs Nin appeared to be in vogue in Oviedo.

It has steadied down since then, of course, it had to (though perhaps one should here log Spain's developing difficulties with hard drugs). But the renewed vigour of the visual arts has been a treat for the occasional observer. And while it is still too early to judge contemporaries, or to sort out the arguments about the vali-dity, or lack of it, of the Madrid biennial, one can at least record that the work of some of the older performers has found its proper place. In Barcelona, already burgeoning as a great city of style, the Joan Miró Foundation threw open its doors during the 1970s. There is a large collection of the master's work (he died in 1983), as well as a round of visiting exhibitions and all the apparatus of a full-blown centre for contemporary art. The building, by Josep Lluís Sert, once upon a time a Noucentista architect, is also a delight, white and light, with a touch of Bauhaus but full of interesting shapes. Best of all is the roof, for the Foundation rides high on Montjuïc and here, from a vantage point among bright-painted works of sculpture, one may look out across the great metropolis under the mountain of Tibidabo.

The other excitement lies down below, among the traffic and the Modernista buildings. A Modernista factory just in behind the Manzana de la Discòrdia, that famous block incorporating the work of all the Modernista stars, has been made over into an Antonio Tàpies foundation. By starting in the basement and moving up among its well-like galleries and slim wrought-iron columns, far less fussy than much Modernista work, one may make a chronological tour of Tàpies, from an iconoclastic pen and ink self-portrait of 1947 – including a vulva lightly disguised as a balloon – past a rolled-up mattress in bronze and a pair of trousers slung over a reversed canvas, and up again through wonderful displays of colour and texture, to a final wardrobe spilling out its clothes in stiff abandon. It is much graver work than it sounds in a description and peppered with crosses too, as if he is working out, Buñuel-like, some deep, dark set of feelings about Catholicism. But you can certainly see at a glance why art students fall in love with Tàpies.

For myself, for many years, I have had an affection for the work of César Manrique, now also one of the old performers, his age allowing him to be seen in at least a reasonably ample perspective. Manrique was brought up in Lanzarote, in the Canaries, among the lunar landscapes of an island that is entirely volcanic. Little white villages lie on tides of lava. The houses have round bread ovens protruding from the walls, tall little chimneys shaped at the top like onions and square black pigeon-holes punched into the walls. Wood-work is always blue or green, using paint left over from fishing boats invariably decorated in these colours. Out in the fields, vines might be planted in individual hollows in the lava, miniature craters dug specially for each of them. The method hangs on the properties of the lava grains which, in a rainless climate, gather in moisture from the night and release it slowly during the day. Around the land actually farmed, there lies *malpaís*, the badland, jumbled volcanic rocks, in places deeper than a man, bristling in black or red. Above the badlands rise the volcanoes proper, some still glowering with internal heat.

Urged by his father to do something that would bring in money, architecture for example, the young Manrique nevertheless set off for Madrid to make himself into an abstract painter. He flourished in New York before returning to his native island in search of 'purity and solitude'. His painting these days is full of the textures of the land, as rough in surface as any Tàpies and actually incorporating fragments of the earth. There is a suggestion of natural forms within it, but only a suggestion. 'I don't paint things,' he says, 'that are reconcilable with literary anecdotes.'

For many years he has been successful with his paintings, especially in Germany. This is what he takes most seriously.

For me, however, the best of Manrique lies in the more functional open-air constructions, somewhere between landscaping and architecture, with which several of the Canary Islands, especially Lanzarote, are now liberally endowed. There is a lido in Puerto de la Cruz in Tenerife, a set of swimming-pools incorporating all the colours of the Canaries – the green of palms, the aquamarine of the pools themselves, the dazzling white of the walkways, the black retaining walls of lava. Almost all Manrique projects have these colours; almost all are about the creation of interesting space.

I find myself in Lanzarote for the opening of a new Manrique project, a cactus garden set in an amphitheatre of volcanic rock, its shape like something out of ancient Egypt. I'm a day ahead of time and peeping through the gate I see him far off in a whirl of final preparations, a man in his seventies, short in stature, slight as a teenager, buzzing from spot to spot to speak to gardeners and labourers, gesturing, calling out loud, breaking into a run as he and his men struggle to ready the garden for the next day. Watching the man, I have that same impression, which I often have in Spanish art, of enormous, underground energy continually welling up. Later, when I settle for a talk with him at a more leisured moment, he expounds his central theory of the necessary symbiosis of art and nature right through from actual works of art to architecture and town planning. What impresses me most, however, is something that he says about his childhood.

'When I was very small,' Manrique said, 'we used to go to the beach of Fámara in the north of the island. That's where my father took us for holidays. I remember running naked on the sand, meditating as I peered at rockpools, at the tall cliffs, at sunsets, at the fish. I drew and painted from the earliest age. Ever since infancy my great master has been observation of nature and direct contact with the natural world.' Manrique and Goya are about as different as painters could be, but Manrique's comment puts me in mind of Goya and his comment, a frequent one, according to his son, that nature was his mistress.

Returning to Lanzarote from the USA in 1968, Manrique saw at once the poverty and isolation of his island, its desperate need for some new money-earner such as tourism. But the warning signs were already there, written very clearly, just across the water, on the walls of Tenerife and Gran Canaria. In Spain, whether on the mainland or in the islands, wherever four or five new developments and a cluster of monster hotels are gathered together, the resulting phenomenon is known as *masificación*. A landscape like that of Lanzarote's would be ruined by *masificación*, Manrique reasoned. 'This is a tiny island, not a continent. We will ruin the marvellous image that we might have had and then who will want to visit us?'

As a benchmark, he compiled a weighty book of photographs of island architecture and set to work with his schoolfriend Pepín Ramirez, then head of the island's far from powerful local government. One of the real problems of Spanish law was that each tiny *ayuntamiento*, or municipality, acted as its own planning authority, dedicated to pleasing local businessmen and improving revenues by building almost anything it could. There were seven *ayuntamientos* on Lanzarote alone. But by diligent persuasion and shame-making pronouncements, Manrique and Ramirez induced them to agree to voluntary restrictions – no houses over two storeys, no hotels over four or five, all woodwork to be green or brown or blue, no advertising hoardings anywhere. For a while, the whole of the tourist building boom was conducted under the Ramirez–Manrique rubric and most of it in the local styles recorded in the photographic inventory. This was true in the resort of Puerto del Carmen even though it soon became a pleasure strip running for miles along the coast. And then, just as land speculation was reaching its most intense, Ramirez died. Could one man on his own, an artist, not a politician, continue to hold back the tides of *masificación*? 'There is,' Manrique says, shaking his head like a man defeated – and what's more, like a man with local enemies – 'no law against speculation.'

It was with these words in my ears, and in the consciousness that cheap mass tourism is the most visible part of the Franco legacy, that I set off on a journey along the whole of Spain's mainland coast, Atlantic and Mediterranean, to see the state of play. The great tourist expansion had been embarked on in a hurry, in desperate need of foreign currency, and depended on selling off what Spain had plenty of already, sunshine and also, as the Civil War receded, cheap food and abundant wine. Numbers of foreign visitors soared to 34 million a year, then to 35 million. But now the market had given a sudden wobble, badly frightening the tourist authorities and entrepreneurs. Was the golden goose already dead, killed off by concrete? Had it brought disaster with it before its possible demise, disaster both human and ecological? Large questions, these, requiring serious study, but at least, I felt, by simply taking a look, I could gather a few impressions.

The verdant north still seemed in reasonable shape. Because it rains up here, it is harder to sell to foreigners. Spaniards pack it out in summer, though, and the beaches of the bigger towns are almost impossible to move about on, especially at the weekend. I had observed this during a summer visit to San Sebastián (Donostia in Basque, one of the chief cities of the Basque Country) and in such pressure spots as Gijón, neighbour to Oviedo. Now it was late spring again and my journey, though extremely wiggly, became an undiluted pleasure, except where I came up against the harsher social realities. What struck me most was not so much the tourism – *masificación* being scarcely present – as the threat of future tourism. For as the Mediterranean falters, one hears of alarming plans to 'develop' this coast. My journey, then, became a cataloguing of treasures, collected against a growing awareness of the fragility of the environment and the differences in atmosphere between the constituent regions of the coast – Basque Country, Cantabria, Asturias and Galicia. It is not until you travel systematically that you realize how great these differences are.

San Sebastián, my starting-point, seemed a kind of shorthand for the Basques, dignified behind its near-perfect circle of bay, the epitome of a late nineteenth-century town (this was the period when the Basque resorts were first developed), but gritty and scruffy in its older parts, scrawled all over with graffiti. Just looking at the walls you know you are in politicized terrain. The Basques have a great reputation for gastronomy and there are dining clubs where the members, all male, do their own cooking. The outside wall of one of these, when I passed it, was deep in feminist slogans, including the self-professedly 'antipatriarchal' allegation that 4,000 children a year are killed by adults. Up until now, there has been a comfortable theory in Spain that acts such as child abuse or even killing are a speciality of the cold hearts of northern Europe. If Spaniards are just waking up to the fact that they themselves are sometimes also guilty (though surely not to the extent of 4,000 deaths a year), then nowhere will this guilt be more pressingly articulated than in the Basque Country. There is an uncomfortable sense of justice here as well as a sense of potential violence, a subject to which I will return before my journeying is done. (Perhaps it should be said at this stage, though, that foreign visitors pass through, so far, with perfect safety.)

The Basque coast is the noblest in the north, though you would never imagine so if you just drove down the motorway and saw the tangle of light industry in valleys climbing up contrariwise to pure, unfettered hill. The coast has cliffs and capes and inlets, small rivers running down to meet the tidal waters, packed out with fishing harbours, linear as miners' cottages in South Wales. Many of the houses have *solanas*, shallow glass-covered balconies rising the whole height of a façade and common all along the northern coast. I have always found them intensely romantic, still do as I make my curvaceous progress east to west.

From the fishing harbour of Lequeitio, I head inland towards Guernica, Gernika in Basque (one of the principles of travelling both Basque and Spanish coasts is that there is always something of huge historical importance just behind). Here, when I ask my way to the sacred oak, I find myself on the receiving end of another of those strange impromptu speeches, delivered with an innocent dignity, that I have previously encountered among the anarchists and on the Ebro battlefields. This particular speech was not about the bombing but about the identity of the Basques, and I give it as I heard it from a man aged, I suppose, about thirty. It is condensed a little but all the words recorded here were spoken.

'We are a decent, hard-working people,' the man began, 'but we have a message for Spain. We walk to our borders and we plant a spade in the earth and here we say "No further. This we will defend till our last drop of blood." Our women are the most important people. They receive our pay and distribute it according to need. They hold the community together and it is our mothers, in front of fires fed with oak branches brought down from the mountains, who tell us our duty to the Basque Country. We are not expansionists or imperialists. It is not we who have expanded beyond our frontiers as the Spaniards expanded into the New World. Then, having stolen everything from America, they came back here to take what they could from us. It is true that Franco tried to dilute the Basques through immigration from the south, but it is the half-and-half children who become the activists. They bear a double burden, evacuation from their homelands and now, on top of that, they bear the sorrows of the Basques.'

The blasted oak tree, though well attended by a party of Basque pensioners from Bilbao, seemed only a small event after this speech. Bilbao itself, as I passed by it soon afterwards, was giving vent to smoke and fumes and vapours on a prodigious scale, still, despite a civic-minded effort to clean up, a herculean instance of pollution. Cantabria appeared a much gentler place, both physically and temperamentally, with an apron of bright green descending peacefully from higher hills to meet the ocean. There is a little *masificación*, especially at Laredo, which gave its name to a town which gave its name to a famous cowboy song. But Cantabria on the whole is rural and peaceful, softer as cow country than America's Wild West. Some of the little towns are full of heraldic doorways, reminding the visitor of a clever north coast dodge of earlier centuries: to declare the whole of the population noble so that no single citizen would have to pay his taxes to Madrid. Santillana del Mar, though not on the sea, is a beauty spot visited as much as anywhere in the Cotswolds or Provence, jam-full of heraldic houses. Comillas, a little seaside place, has a whole collection of Modernista buildings, including a spiked fantasy by Gaudí.

Next comes Asturias, land of cider, with coal-mining valleys and industrial townships to avoid unless you have business in them (they are a melancholy, grubby grey, and living through hard times; those familiar with this kind of place may find they induce a sad nostalgia). There are plenty of fishing villages as well, some, like Tazones, within striking distance of the Picos de Europa. These are often both severe and pretty. For me, though, aside from the early Asturian churches, the greatest architectural beauty lies in the little barns called *hórreos*, built for storing maize (arriving from America, maize became a staple crop here in the seventeenth century). These sweet little wooden structures, balconies in front for hanging out the orange corn cobs in the autumn, are mounted on granite pillars to keep the rats at bay. They were prefabricated, even in the seventeenth century, and trundled along by cart to be erected on the farms. The *hórreos* in each district have a distinctive little circular wooden pattern showing somewhere, rather like the markings on a butter mould. So do the three-legged clogs that lift the farmers just a mite above the mud, the northern mud that rises round the ankles everywhere in winter.

Asturias has its misty estuaries – the Eo just on the modern border with Galicia is mistiest and prettiest – but it is Galicia that is positively famed for its long inlets, known as the *rías*. I reach them in due course – they are right out in the west – but, as usual, there are intriguing matters on the way. One of my Enlightenment heroes is Antonio Raimundo Ibañez, first Marquis of Sargadelos and subject of a Goya portrait now in the USA. Though he was an Asturian, he lived for many years at Ribadeo on the Eo estuary – in Galician territory, that is to say. Just a little inland and further to the west of Ribadeo, he set up a ceramics factory and a steelworks. These were intended to provide an opportunity for work in an isolated rural area and seem to have been entirely meritorious. Even so, after the French invaded Spain in 1808, Ibañez was killed by the mob for being too Frenchified, too *afrancesado*. The ceramics factory has been restarted, turning out work that I have always found irresistible, though also rather too expensive for my pocket. What moves me, unfailingly, is a characteristic blue, already quite a deep one, that shades without a break into a far deeper blue, aquamarine at midnight.

It is Sunday when I pass by the factory and everything is shut. But it doesn't matter, for this is a pilgrimage requiring no recompense, merely a chance to see where Sargadelos porcelain originates. But I am in luck, as it happens. Plenty of shapes and colours that I haven't seen before can be made out if I press my nose to the windows of the exhibition hall and, in the office window, I can see a manifesto. This factory, it says, entirely rejects Mannerism and looks for purity of concept. It rejects the notion that copying old forms is a maintenance of tradition. Nor, on the other hand, should 'alien evolutions' be slavishly pursued. The Sargadelos factory works for originality with meaning, both in form and in what it represents, leaning on the tradition (straight eighteenth-century enlightened thinking, this) of industrial planning. You cannot travel far in Spain, even in modern, supposedly materialistic Spain, without encountering idealism in many manifestations.

My other great diversion, naturally, is Santiago de Compostela, goal of proper pilgrims. Here I linger to admire magnificence in stone, stand back to get a view of the great eighteenth-century façade of the cathedral, known as the Obradoiro. I bump heads with Master Mateo's sculpture of himself in the older doorway hidden protectively just inside (this is the Portico of Glory), and climb up behind the altar to kiss the pilgrim shell on the back of the raiment of the effigy of Santiago. For just a few pennies in a box I am handed a small paper token. I am a little saddened, being neither of the faith nor having covered the route arduously or penitentially, and I feel this keenly when a group of boys come past, pocketing their tokens and giving the victory sign. Proper religious pilgrims, meanwhile, go round the back and get a proper signed certificate from Don Jaime, presiding genius of the place.

It's June but this year there are already plenty of tourists in Santiago. We move in a special little area (it is probably a good idea that we are so confined) where tourist expectations are met by titivation and by shellfish, always pricey. Beribboned student bands called *tunas* strut the restaurants, singing very pleasantly. I go so far as to buy a tape of one of their performances. It is beautiful and even entertaining, but disturbing too, and a relief to escape back into the countryside. Here the question of voyeurism at once arises, for rural Galicia is among the poorest parts of Spain. Oxen bring in the hay in heavy carts. These have solid wooden wheels. The women labour with pitchforks beside the men, some in very old-fashioned straw bonnets. Others, it must be said, are wearing baseball caps, a sign that many emigrants return for summer and often settle here again in their old age. There are plenty of new houses built for them, jostling up sometimes against Galician *hórreos*. These are quite different from the raised Asturian barns, being long and thin and made of granite, set on short stone legs. You notice, too, the impact of Galician nationalism. Castilian road signs are painted over, daubed with the Galician version, sometimes incorrectly written. There is little sense that local nationalism is as strong here as in the Basque Country or Catalonia, but it is clear that the language – a Romance tongue not far from medieval Portuguese – is much in people's minds and on their lips.

And so, by way of Cape Finisterre – Fisterra in Galician, stern and jutting its chin towards America – to the Galician *rías*, upper and lower (north and south, that is to say). The *rías* are sometimes, misleadingly, compared to fjords. The coasts around them are generally lower than the word fjord suggests, and visually more sedate, with maize and vines, in places cultivated to the water's edge. They are island-studded, rich in beaches, prodigal in shellfish. Some are little touched by tourism, others have a few small hotels, others again have quite large cities on them and a suburban traffic tailback in the summer. I have always loved the *rías* and in La Toja – a visitors' islet which has given its name to many a Galician restaurant in exile – I watch the quintessential *rías* scene: hundreds, literally hundreds of local people, some in waders, some leaning over the edge of boats, sifting the low-tide sand and mud for shellfish. There is an ageless look to the procedure, a sense of men and women still in communion with their environment. It is picturesque but also, quite evidently, back-breaking work. And herein lies the dilemma of Galicia.

As Mediterranean tourism starts to stutter, hotel groups and other speculators now have their eyes fixed on Galicia and the *rías*. Tourism, if it is backed by local money, brings profits to the locals; and wherever the money comes from, there are likely to be jobs for Spaniards, easier jobs than digging shellfish from the sand or bringing home the hay in wooden carts. That is exactly as it should be. What guarantee exists, however, that the Mediterranean experience of intolerable overbuilding will not be repeated here in gentle Galicia?

Spain's Mediterranean coast appears a sorry sight, *masificación* the watchword. The Costa Brava at the French end still has some coast that is *brava* – the word means wild in Spanish – with pines and rock and cliff-scapes. As usual, the countryside behind is full of interest. Catalan landscapes are dramatic; the weathered stone of medieval buildings lies grey on green against well-tended farmland or forested hill and mountain. Empúries, a quarter of the way down the Costa Brava, is a major archaeological site, going back to the Phoenicians, Greeks and Romans. It offers more than a glimpse of the antiquity of Rose Macaulay's 'fabled shore', the palimpsest, the parchment written on over and over. But the resorts, the newest message on the palimpsest, rise up wherever the terrain is easy, in solid concrete wedges, loud and cheery once you are within their walls. Visually, they are a devastation.

Down at the other end, on the Costa del Sol, coming back east-wards now from far Gibraltar, through Estepona and Marbella, there are, to my surprise, distinct pockets of smartness, an intermit-tent effort to ape the equally concrete-ridden elegance of the French Riviera. The marina and purpose-built township of Puerto Banus, all different levels and cunning colours, is one such attempt. The many acres of new golf-course play a part and so does the tendency for the newer and more expensive villas to be built well back, towards or in the fine sierra that rises up behind.

One of the most interesting of the smart ventures is the very first – the five-star Meliá Don Pepe hotel. José Meliá, Pepe to friends, began his career as a Barcelona travel agent. Flourishing in the Franco years, he decided to build a flagship hotel in Marbella. Among the first regulars were Franco's senior ministers. The smell of power brought in the Spanish aristocrats, helping to launch Marbella as *the* smart place. They brought their international cousins with them. Then came the Arabs; it was an Arab royal who put up money for the unlikely project of housing local gypsies. Now the Franco ministers are dead, at least politically speaking. The aristocrats and the Arabs have moved on, leaving a gap for the hotel to fill. This is achieved, by and large, by bringing in business people from northern Europe, well-to-do swingers of shiny golf clubs. The crisis, if there is one, does not extend too easily to include the rich.

But overall, and especially when I get to Torremolinos, I cannot blind my eyes to the fact that much of it looks tatty – too quick an expansion and too cheap, back in the late 1950s and 1960s, the often shoddy buildings now worn down by use.

In a sense, the British are to blame as much as any Spaniard, since they were the first and most numerous clients for cheap sun and wine and it was the British tour operators who fought for the lowest prices and the cheapest deals. But this is only the half of it, for one of the extraordinary features, as you travel the whole coast, is to see that the Costas are still being constructed, hand over fist, regardless of apprehensions for the future. Cranes swing from north to south, from east to west, mostly installing the latest of the scourges, low-rise, high density estates, white carpets of construction, wall touching wall, terrace to ground-floor terrace, carpets spread across the flatter ground of Murcia and Alicante, wasps' nests hanging inside the little valleys of the Costa Brava. Nor can one cavil excessively, for many are destined for Spanish occupants, a car and an apartment on the coast still being part of the Spanish dream. Who could deny this dream to Spanish workers from the cities?

The question is, what should now be done, given the blotting out of natural beauty along so great a part of the Mediterranean coast and the fact that the concrete is increasing rather than receding? Many people, both in the government and in the tourist industry, are coming to believe that the one way out is the serious improvement of what exists. Some would like to improve their goods and sell more dearly to more expensive people (always assuming this were possible). Others see it as the function of a democratic Spain to provide a decent fabric right across the range, serving up holidays for foreign visitors of all social classes. But what one notices during the course of a long journey is that the wished-for improvement seems actually to be beginning, with hotel refurbishments and cleaner water, with new promenades behind the beaches, special tourist police to handle trouble, and so on and so forth. There is a new law forbidding building right beside the sea, not terribly frightening in its terms but better than nothing. Considerably more promising, however, is the fact that the autonomies are beginning to seize planning powers from the small *ayuntamientos*, opening up the possibility that tourism will at last be developed in the wider interest – and perhaps that Galicia and the north may still be saved. I am not myself optimistic; I merely record the possibility.

In all discussion on these problems inside Spain, one notices that scarcely a hostile word is spoken about tourism as such. Perhaps it is lack of environmental awareness. Perhaps it is because this industry implies a million summer jobs. Perhaps it is because the participants remember, as I do from my youthful travels, how pitiful the poverty once was.

I can't delay it any longer. I report to Benidorm in August, with several days in hand, to put my questions to the test. Is Benidorm a vision of the future, a place where true professionalism ensures the pleasures of the public, justifying, if it can be justified, the huge outpouring of cement, and bringing home the bacon for the locals? For while lesser resorts may languish, this one at least is full, suggesting that plenty here is being done just right. Four million tourists come to Benidorm each year, and keep on coming even when chill winds blow in other places. Benidorm is also meant to be a byword for vulgarity, a Blackpool of the south. I suppose another of my questions is whether it is gross.

This massed resort has an international feel today, quite different from my memories of a trip a few years back. Then, the British were in a clear majority. Now, at 3.00 am, with the streets much busier than in the afternoon, Norwegian girls blip by on motor scooters; Italian cars jostle with one another; young Britons rove on foot from Lennon's to Rockerfeller's, from Loch Ness to The Marathon; Spaniards and Belgians, Portuguese and Germans all swim in the animated current of the pavements. Car engines roar, there are cries, murmurs and music. The late night world in August belongs entirely to the young. Locals use the word Guirilandia for the part of town where most of the nightlife happens. It is an interesting usage, derived from *guiri*, a nickname for the Civil Guard. These being always brought in from outside, the name suggests a land belonging to aliens.

I poke about in Guirilandia and catch scarcely a whisper that drugs are circulating. There is plenty of drink, though. Outside a bar I hear one English boy say to another, 'What do you think, Neil? Have I had fourteen?' A girl from Scotland tells me Benidorm is not at all like Stirling. 'Everyone drinks a lot but they come out happy, not staggering out of the pub like at home.' A man in the travel trade says that excursions and evening entertainments are no longer sold on the promise of booze. 'A few years ago the trade used to believe that the number one thing was alcohol. But we are finding that the youngsters don't necessarily want to get bombed out of their heads.' What people do instead, I discover from my Scottish friends, is try to stay up all night, every night. They go to the all-night pub in packs. They have learned no Spanish words, eaten no Spanish food, had no experience that strikes the enquirer as particularly Spanish. But they have had some wonderful times, with singsongs about oral sex and farting. Coy looks and elbow nudging suggest another entertainment – plentiful sexual activity along with the drinking. It seems to me that Benidorm in August is bawdy rather than gross and I begin to think that the days of the British lager lout, if they ever existed here, may really now be over, confined perhaps to places where there is either less to do or less of a chance of doing it. As to whether it is just the British who can tear the place to pieces, I discover that this year there are more anxieties among the locals over the *tifossi*, Italian hooligans. It is a drunken Norwegian who has dropped a bottle off his balcony, laying open the head of a passer-by below, another tourist, naturally. (There are 42,000 residents to service the quarter of a million visitors present at any one moment.) 'That little incident won't make the papers back at home,' says one of the pressmen in the town hall. 'But it might have done if he'd been British. Why do the British continually wound themselves?'

Conversations in the town hall make it clear that nobody is selling Spain, as Spain, to foreigners. Rather the reverse. They are selling familiarity and value for money and offering as little as possible that might surprise or prove distasteful. That is the real meaning of Benidorm. And it goes down just as well in winter as in summer, for the town has a season that lasts all the year, catering for older people from autumn through to spring. Huge efforts and large sums of money have gone into the infrastructure. The sea, when I swim in it, seems crystalline. I learn from the 'holiday professionals' that there is a large new sewage system that ensures there is no leakage to the sea. The beach, which is visited by 160,000 people every day in summer, is purified all night, raked through to a depth of several centimetres by large machines like dustbin lorries. In short, the town, with its plethora of concrete blocks and naked flesh, is run like a huge machine.

This is what the mayor is proud of, I discover, when I have a session with him. He is proud of serving Benidorm's own chosen market with precision and he does not care a bit that it has got an urban feel or that it could be held to be the leading mainland instance of *masificación*. 'There are people,' he says, 'who like a more bucolic tourism with landscapes and mountains. Switzerland is the place for them. Other people come to Benidorm and like it and we have had no protests. You could say that Toledo and Granada are prettier than New York. I like them too. But I am also one of those who like New York.'

Manuel Catalán Chana, a sharp and humorous man, is a long-serving mayor; he hopes to be re-elected on the basis of achievement. This is a town, he says, where most of the businesses are small and run by local individuals – a special feature of the Costa Blanca, not duplicated on the Costa del Sol. 'What you need is a good programme and good management so that you can attract the voters, whatever their basic attitudes. The important thing is creating the conditions in which businesses can thrive. That's the only way that people can have jobs. Benidorm has the highest income per head in Valencia and that puts it in the national top ten. As a member of the Socialist Party, it gives me the greatest pride to say that.'

Another source of pride for both the Mayor and his assistants is that Benidorm provides a refuge for many Spanish pensioners as well. 'I wish my grandfather had been able to come here,' says one of the assistants. 'I know the cultural level of many of our visitors is not what you would call the highest. But these are the people whose hard work created modern Spain.'

All of it, somehow, makes me think of Antonio Gil Gambau, baker to the anarchist collective, another pensioner, back there in Caspe.

José Carlos belongs to the Order of St John of God, San Juan de Dios, founded in Granada in 1537. In the glittering age of supposed materialism, he has taken his vows of poverty, chastity, obedience and care for the pilgrim and the traveller. Now he works as maintenance man and night-watchman in a camping site back from the beach in the province of Huelva. We are taking our own holiday nearby, not far from the little town of Isla Cristina, almost on the border with Portugal, and we go piling into town with José Carlos.

Mostly, it is a flat landscape. Pines behind the long beach make a canopy of brilliant green, each tree a shiny mushroom, an emerald umbrella, wild flowers growing straight out of the sand beneath. Behind the pines lies a fast-moving road, behind the road lie strawberry fields. Isla Cristina, once an island but now joined firmly to the land by vigorous in-filling, is surrounded by marsh and tidal estuaries. There are creeks right in behind it, with hundreds of wooden stakes stuck haphazardly in the mud and little open boats used for collecting shellfish. Tide out, they lie at crazy angles on their sides. Most of the high ground we see in front of us, beyond the marsh, is Portugal.

The town has turned its back on the main road, a long blank strip of dingy white. Reaching the end of it, defined by a broad creek, glinting in April sunlight, riffling under the wind, we turn towards the sea and bump along the cobbles of the quay. Here there are all kinds of craft for serious fishery, from trawlers that can be away six months to boats that don't stay out much longer than a night. There is a fish market on the front. It deals with shellfish in the morning, then in the afternoon with wet fish. These travel to Seville and Córdoba by road and overnight on ice the whole way to Madrid. Long white nets lie across the cobbles; late in the night there are still men unloading fish-boxes, deeply shadowed under arc lights.

José Carlos is disposed to take a mid-morning glass of wine and *tapas*, those little bar-snacks said to be a legacy of the Moors. We try skate with green pepper and titbits made of the fatty skin of tuna, a local passion. Then José Carlos takes us on a tour of sardine canneries and salting factories. The latter smell quite terrible, deep, browny troughs of brine, from which the salted fish emerge impeccable, then disappear again into their wooden barrels. Dogs – all down the quay there seem to be as many dogs as people – wander in and out of the salteries, looking bored and sulky. In the tiny alleys leading back towards the town, shellfish are being cooked, giving off delicious odours. Later in the day, if it gets hot again, there will a noisome smell from puddles of shellfish residue among the cobbles. The other local industry is tuna fish processing, mostly into cans; the thin strip of fillet along the backbone is wind-cured and salted, however, and under the name of *mojama* becomes as great a delicacy as any *serrano* ham, and very expensive too. Tractors go beating past, with tunas on their waggons. Wide, whale-like tails bounce sadly in the sunlight.

José Carlos himself is from the small town of Lepe some miles back along the coast. Lepe is the butt of jokes in Spain as Poland is for continental Europe, but lately, having spearheaded the strawberry invasion, it has had at least the penultimate laugh, becoming one of the wealthiest communities in southern Spain. In the process, as I had learned months back on television, the levels of nitrates in the water-table have become so high that the local water is undrinkable. But many Lepe people, it appears, think this is a reasonable and proper price to pay for their new wealth.

With or without the nitrates and give or take the strawberries, José Carlos, *patria chica* deep within him, declares that he is honoured to come from such a place as Lepe. We in our turn are honoured by his kindness, but we fail to realize that it is the young people in our party, not ourselves, who will make us socially acceptable, even quite famous, here in Isla Cristina. There are two girls, aged nearly twelve. There is a young man of seventeen. Between them, to our shame, they speak only a few words of Spanish, and we fear for their social prospects. But in a town little frequented by foreigners, it turns out they possess a quite incomparable asset, something that everybody wants – easy dominion of the English language. Never have three people been so popular for what might seem so effortless an achievement.

The girls are gone at once, in a swirling tide of bigger girls, aged at least sixteen or seventeen, trying out English questions, puzzling at the answers. So is the boy of seventeen, smothered with female attention. Trembling for their safety, we see them off almost immediately to the secondary school disco. On other days, we see them riding past on bikes or sauntering with their friends. They talk to us occasionally in passing, smiling even, but really we have lost them. We, meanwhile, are now known as the adults who belong to the English children and we find ourselves welcomed to the most interesting places, the back of tobacconists' shops, even the Civil Guard barracks – where life, so far as we can tell, is homely and familial. People whom we don't know at all nod to us like old friends, scores of youngsters come up to address us. We feel as if we must have been on television in our sleep.

Slowly, in the midst of the sociability, we discover there is quite a little town here, separate from the fishing. It has a market and a supermarket but it is also very poor in patches, full of what the Germans call Tante Emma shops, tiny neighbourhood establishments selling just a little of this and a little bit of that. For some reason still unfathomed, the town is also full of Modernista wrought-iron benches.

One evening, while we are still getting to know Isla Cristina, we borrow our young people back again and make our way to a shabby neo-classical building, a cultural club where a *saeta* competition is being held. *Saetas* – the word means arrows – are those flamenco cries recorded in the false procession in Madrid, the songs thrown skywards during Easter celebrations, often, it seems, as if to pierce the side of God himself.

Because of the young, we find ourselves seated next to the president of the club. His wife whispers across to us that all the competitors are working people, fishermen, carpenters, electricians. There are not, as it turns out, too many of them, this being the semi-final, and they step forward shyly to the microphone, faced by a video recorder and with the technicians of the local radio station lurking, lights twinkling on recording gear. The competitors have thin faces; their eyes are inclined to swivel under the stress. They sing without much evident *duende*, the ululations nevertheless astonishing the girls.

Slowly, with the women competitors, matters change. The first is polite and tuneful, better than the men but not by much. The second has grey hair, a young fresh face and she is wearing jeans and trackshoes. We have dubbed her the American teenager. Also unaccustomed to performance, she sings at first with her hands in her pockets, but gradually inspiration seizes her and so her hands emerge, climb up to shoulder height, clutch at the air as her voice goes soaring weirdly heavenward in wails. She leaves the microphone with a self-deprecating giggle, puncturing her moment. It is the third competitor, a large, square woman, in white blouse, black skirt, high heels, on whom both showmanship, or rather showwomanship, and raw *duende* have descended simultaneously. She holds us in her outstretched hands from the beginning, building herself up, building up the tension. Her voice goes sliding upwards with her passion, in anguished tremulousness. As in the *peña* in Seville, it is tremendous, hair-raising, spine-tingling. I peep at our young trio and see they feel the same. The square lady invokes the agony of Christ and then at last, her own. 'I am alone, alone in the world. Help me, mother of God.'

We borrow the girls again for an excursion to Seville and ride, blessed and excused at last by their company, through the María Luisa park in a smart horse-drawn carriage, under tall trees grown from seed or sapling brought home from America an age ago. We go to the Museum of Arts and Costumes to see how the mantilla is worn, black lace falling over the face from a tortoiseshell comb, which itself is mounted on an extravagance of glossy hair, pinned high.

For the Easter processions, though, we make sure we are back in our adopted home, and night after night, right through Holy Week, we follow the developing story in Isla Cristina. Innumerable sights and scenes, with a certain similarity from night to night, remain inscribed in memory . . . the large *paso*, or float, its porters concealed beneath, emerging from the church door, bobbing respectfully, then setting off for a tour of town. The polychrome wooden figures of the display – usually Christ or Mary, in varying states of emotion depending on the stage of the story – are as they have always been, figures of sorrow and passion, intentionally inducing both emotions, illuminated by a thousand candles. One night the processing devotees wear hoods and surplices of a particular colour, scarlet or mauve for instance, next night another, giving the procession a forbidding unity. It is the tall dunce's caps, with eye slits cut in them, that are most frightening, symbol once of the Inquisition, now of the Ku Klux Klan.

Often, during the procession, the long train comes to a halt. If you are there to watch them, in some quiet backstreet, whitewashed and mysterious, you will see the tall bonnets halted, gathering, nodding together in the dark like crows. Marshals flit up and down beside the ranks, bats among the big black birds. Ahead, a sound like a football rattle, sinister in the darkness, indicates the column must move on. (The rattle is a special church instrument – no bells are tolled during the period between Christ's death and resurrection.) Bands march behind the *pasos* playing their strange dirges – we have seen and heard them practising in the fish factories. Now we see them for real, same hairdos, same spotty faces among the teenage bandsmen, same instruments night after night. In the more crowded streets, our friends from the *saeta* competition, the square lady, the American teenager, the thin-faced men, step forward, tilt their faces upwards and loose off their arrows of song, reedier and more plangent in the open air, as the *paso* slowly passes. We see the shuffle, shake and sway that we have taken lessons in in Cádiz. We see the tall float bearing Christ ducking under electric wires. My favourite is the Friday night procession of penitent ladies. They are wearing cocktail dresses and mantillas. Their faces lit by candles, they tell their rosaries ostentatiously. 'It's a film,' says our seventeen-year-old, 'it's a dream sequence from a film.'

Every now and then during the hours of watching, one of our young Spanish friends has come up to us. 'José Luis is under that one,' they might say, or 'I think the whole thing is rubbish.' We have watched one man give the fascist salute to Christ, but by and large, the religious emotions appear to be uppermost, at times quite painfully intense for the participants. Socialist friends in the Levant have told us that Easter processions are a mockery, reinvented under Franco to keep the people quiet. In Isla Cristina, as in Seville, they have outlasted him by the best of two decades.

At the end of each procession, with the easy Spanish slide from sacred to secular, all the young people head for the town discos. We have learnt by now that the girls who have become the friends of our girls, those of sixteen, seventeen or so, are extremely well-behaved. They tell their parents where they are going and agree what time they should be back. There are various danger spots in Isla Cristina: the cemetery gates just out of town where prostitutes wait for pick-ups, one end of the beach that is a hang-out for drug takers, one little square where drugs are sold and where somebody has been beaten up during our stay. The girls, and most of the young men, too, avoid these places. We hear that they also avoid going 'too far' in their relation-ships. Most of the girls belong to a Catholic group that believes in positive action as well as piety and is currently campaigning for better sports facilities. There is nothing here, one would think, to worry a parent, but how long will it be, they must surely ask themselves, before the young begin to crave a wider lifestyle? Tourism, major agent of change along the coast, is now approaching fast – the bulldozers are churning behind the house that we are staying in. English, soon, will be no rarity. And then there is the question of new wealth.

In a town that seemed to us quite poor at first, we have little by little noticed signs of change. One set of parents in our gang are doing well enough to send their daughter to a convent boarding-school in Huelva. They have a butcher's shop and a fashion shoe shop and they have moved the family to a modern estate outside Isla Cristina for the greater quiet, so they say, and 'in order to breathe a clearer air'. Each and every one of the girls, moreover, is doing science subjects and planning to try for a professional career.

Cristina has been a particular friend to us. One indication of where the sciences might be applied emerges when her father invites us to his *finca*, or estate. On the way we pass by strawberry fields, each tummock swathed in plastic and individually watered from within. Here, pickers of the late April crop are taking their lunch under the trees, a troop of women bright and garrulous, some from nearby villages, others from the closed-down mining towns of the Río Tinto. We dally in full-grown orange plantations, American in scale. Finally, we find ourselves on Juan Dasí Aloy's property.

In a landscape of open heath, under an infinite sky, enormous earthworks have recently taken place. There is a large-scale system of reservoirs, slopes rising round them in shallow terraces. A network of pipes extends from the reservoirs. From these flow lesser pipes and from the lesser pipes flow rubber tubes, tentacles reaching out hundreds of metres and delivering drop by drop – *gota a gota* – water and other nutrients to tiny orange trees. The earth itself appears to be composed entirely of broken stones. 'It is a simple scheme,' says Juan Dasí. 'There is absolutely no nutrition in the soil. We take the sun and light of Huelva, we add the nutrients and convert the sun and light to vitamins.'

He has another scheme as well, already underway in a large plastic greenhouse: to ship in tiny mango plants by air from Venezuela, transport them from Madrid in refrigerator trucks and grow them to maturity, right here on the estate, in his plastic greenhouses. If he can make it work, he says, it should be a real winner, with an insatiable European market.

Juan Dasí is a Valencian from the great *huerta* of the Levant, a horticulturalist with proper training and years of experience in Latin America. His partner is a Catalan. They have a computerized office in Barcelona. He tells us the story of it all in a futuristic barn on top of the highest hill in his domain. Outside, peeping through the window, we see the cottage of one of the labourers. There are chickens scratching in among the beans and a donkey waiting patiently to start the afternoon's proceedings. This is Isla Cristina, this is Huelva, this is half of modern Spain; donkey and computer-driven business side by side. Well may the girls of Isla study science.

Lidia Pinilla Perez, working for pin-money as a housemaid after bringing up a family. Lidia Pinilla, mother of three, married to a successful carpenter, with partners and employees. Lidia Pinilla chatting as she irons on a hot, hot afternoon in an apartment in Madrid. She and her husband own their own home, own their own car. They might perhaps be taken as representative of that rising middle class which some believe to be the backbone, and the guarantee, of political stability in Spain. Typically, both have roots in country villages. Untypically, perhaps, Lidia talks with considerable openness about sex, religion, money, happiness. She does not mind when I jot down a few of the main points.

Antonio, her husband, was born in a village in Córdoba to a family that wasn't too badly off at all. He came to Madrid at the age of eleven and never had to live in a shanty town or anything like that. Lidia's family still live in a village in the province of Toledo, a big village, *cabeza de partido*, head of its district, with a prison and a judge. Its name is Nava Hermosa, 'beautiful valley in high ground'.

Antonio was always studious and likely to get on. 'Myself,' she says, 'I did two years at college, but I wanted to get out of the village so I went to Toledo. I never studied there, I hated it, it didn't inspire me at all. I was the adventurous type, I used to like to go shopping, go out with my girlfriends, get away from my parents. So I came on to Madrid, but soon I was crying every night. I was on my own and I missed my mother and father terribly.'

Lidia found a place with a family as a live-in maid. Somewhere along the way she and a girlfriend did a summer job in Tarragona, and like good Catholic girls, one day they went to church and both confessed. 'But the priest wanted me to go out with him, he wanted to seduce me. My friend went into the confession box right after me and she came out shaking her hand as if she had burned it. "*Vamos, vamos, que tío,*" she kept on saying, "For heavens' sake, what a fellow!" He had said just the same things to her as he had to me.

'I still think the church itself is all right, but I don't think anything at all of the clergy. Our village is full of stories about the priest who lifted a dying man's head and made him nod so that the money in the will would all go to the church. I don't know how my mother goes on believing in them, she goes to church two or three times a day, she does just what they say. The older people in our village are really frightened of the priests. They are frightened of the richer people, too, because they think that they know more. My *pueblo* is like that, very backward in that way. The young people are the same, even though they have had a better education.'

Lidia moved up the housemaids' scale, with better paying jobs in richer households. One couple used to take her to visit her parents, another took her on holiday, to Vigo in Galicia. That gave her a taste for travelling; she has taken her own family to Galicia twice and once to Alicante.

Most of their struggle in the early days was economic. All Lidia's savings went into their mortgage and she remembers every figure involved – the size of the debt, how much they had to pay, the year that it was finished. A little while back, they bought a plot of land to build a house on. 'But building would have meant borrowing and when it came to it we couldn't face that. We would have been like newly-weds again.' Now she is only working for the entertainment of it, to get out of the house. The money isn't vital. The minute she is bored she'll stop, as she did before to have a family.

One of the joys of her life, she says, is that in a country 'really full of machismo', her husband is 'not like that at all'. He lets her go off on her own or with the children, confident that she will do nothing to hurt him. She has had her offers, she says, and she could have taken them up easily, without anybody knowing; 'But that is not my style.' She does wish, though, she had had sex education in her youth, instead of an absolute ignorance about the pill and condoms. Her ignorance made her frightened to let boys get any-where near her. She is bringing up her own daughters quite differ-ently, she says. She and her husband both agreed to let the elder one, just seventeen last year, go camping with her boyfriend. She wishes she had also had a wider general education. She reads but she tackles only the shortest books. 'I get tired with the long ones. But I'm very fond of history. I love to find out what it was like in the *pueblos* long ago.'

Listening to her I suspect that outside her children, her greatest joy is still her *pueblo*. She and her husband go there once a fortnight. They shut up shop in August and go for the whole month. 'Ah,' she says, 'the feast of San Bartolomé, that's the time to be there. We have fireworks and all sorts of fun – like sack-races and bullfights. Girls dress up in local costumes. At night we dance in the plaza and never go to bed, we just have chocolate and *churros* in the village.'

And the elder daughter, does she go to the village too? 'No, not much now,' says Lidia sadly. 'She doesn't like it any more. She hates to be away from her boyfriend.'

Perhaps it is in the second generation, as the new middle class become real city dwellers, that the strong, warm bond between the towns and villages will finally disappear. And this, just as it is in Lidia's family, will be a little tragedy for Spain.

Some of Spain's more solid citizens believe their country is in danger, or certainly losing its gravity, when Andalusian style is in the ascendant. It has been, though, for most of the years since Franco died. Apart from the natural attractions of the southern mode, most of those years have been occupied by a socialist government with a preponderance of top politicians from Seville. I notice, when I meet a journalist friend for lunch, still in Madrid, that the venue is an Andalusian fish restaurant on the ground floor of a smart new office block. There seem to be a lot of these about.

We have gathered here, my friend and I, to work through a quick check-list on the economy and the army. Spain at this time is in a delayed post-Franco boom. How long it will last, nobody dares guess. What happened, says my friend, was that in the first years after the old man's death, with a series of minority governments, nobody could take any political risk, least of all suggest belt-tightening, for fear of losing out in the next coalition. It was a matter of buying industrial peace at all costs. But when the socialists got a clear majority in 1982, they threw all caution to the winds, went for a non-socialist policy of monetarism, endured a period of terrible unemployment (three million out of work, a quarter of the whole labour force), and then came out on top again with a fast-growing economy. By the time Spain joined the European Common Market, she was slimmed right down and able to respond to the stimulus of external competition. 'Spain always does worst when she is most protected.'

So what about the army? Is there any chance it will erupt again and undercut recent advances, economic and political? 'Well,' says my friend, 'there have been some very significant changes. In the seventies a normally informed person would know the names of the generals, the way you might have heard of a prominent banker or recognize a TV personality. Promotions were news and you knew the political colours of the top officers. Their speeches were reported when they took up new appointments. Now we don't hear anything about them. That is quite indicative of the real state of affairs.'

He argues that Tejero's attempted coup in 1981, known as the Tejerazo, has had a salutary effect. 'It made the military look stupid and it made the army look at itself, especially with the long trial afterwards. We went into NATO right in the middle of the trial and NATO membership itself has made a huge difference. When the socialists came to power, they upped military pay, increased defence budgets, bought in new weaponry, established promotion by merit and slimmed down the officer corps.

'In the nineteenth century, the army only acted when there was a vacuum of power. Produce a strong government and they will return to barracks, play with their toys and draw up contingency plans. They have some very nice toys now, not at all the outmoded tat that Franco gave them.' The army have made a solemn vow that they will never act against the people and I get a strong feeling that my friend believes them, always excepting problems in the Basque Country. If he is right, it is 'unserious' Andalucía that has tamed the dragon.

Arriving unannounced in Barcelona, my wife and I have nevertheless been asked out by Xavier Domingo, a Catalan commentator famous in my eyes for writing simultaneously on subjects seldom paired – politics and gastronomy. As befits the gastronomer, he takes us off to a fine fish restaurant in Barceloneta (this district, just by the sea and rather rough at night, was built in compensation for the Ciutadella district, razed by the Spanish Crown to build new fortifications for holding down the city). We tuck into a heady spread, though many of the marine creatures on offer, from eels to squid, seem rather on the small side. 'Yes, yes,' says Xavier ghoulishly, eyes on my wife, testing for reaction, 'tonight we are eating babies.' Meantime, he fills us in on everything that's happening in Barcelona, including the drug problem, and the gypsies who have converted to

Seventh Day Adventism. (It's certainly true, this latter claim. I meet one of them later, a garage attendant, formerly an international flamenco impresario, full of delight at the growth of the Adventist congregation.) Then Xavier tells us about his latest exploit. It happens to be National Non-Smoking Day and having been on television that morning, he had made sure that he was smoking a very large cigar. This is *individualismo*, the God-given right of every Spaniard, or every Catalan for that matter, to do exactly as he pleases and probably to general applause as well. It helps explain why every Spaniard feels that he should pay no taxes and why he believes the government has made special efforts to rob him personally. It establishes clear entitlement to all forms of minor illegality. You see *individualismo* everywhere, though on the surface it is hard to reconcile with the heavy conformism that exists in tandem. For just as it is important to practise *individualismo*, so it is for many folk a positive obsession to be *decente* too, to do the proper thing, behave with full decorum.

Passing, then, to a broad consideration of Hispanic traits, it is evident that another one is hospitality, the kind of easy generosity lavished on us in Barcelona. It is dangerous in Spain to be too admiring of anything in a person's house or anything that person may be wearing, like a brooch or a wristwatch. You will probably be given it, and in a manner brooking no denial. But there is another side to this as well – the lorry driver who forces you to have a drink with him and will clearly take offence if you refuse, or the person who has bought you a meal ten times before but even so, to your embarrassment, will never let you pay for anything. One wonders if it isn't a power-play, an assertion of personal honour at the expense of someone else's. I have a friend who traces it all back to Spain's North African connection. 'There you are, in your own oasis, and up comes a stranger. What do you do? You overwhelm him with hospitality, you tell him you are more powerful than he is and he had better be on his way. There is a lack of solidarity in Spain. Every man is an enemy to every other.'

I love the Spanish openness of hand and lack of calculation and hate this negative explanation. Surely it can be seen as simple generosity, only on occasion perverted into a manipulative bid for dominance? Surely there must have been real warmth when the world was emptier and the arrival of a stranger a point of interest and a time for celebration? That is certainly how we felt, as a family in Isla Cristina, when local people made so much of us; and surely that is the real nature of the welcome in the oasis, whether or not it was the Moors who introduced it into Spain.

In discussing Spanish attributes, of course, the question of the Moorish inheritance inevitably looms large. The tendency towards seclusion of women in the home has a Moorish history. Then there is the cruel trap by which a woman may have to work outside the home but feel it wrong to do so. This is a conflict growing at least in part from a Moorish seed, and it is very much alive even in the twentieth-century economy. But there are other points where behaviour that may well be mainly Spanish is blamed unjustly on the Moors (just as the French invasion of 1808 is credited with every failure in the conservation of art and architecture). The nasty little phrase *ser un moro* – literally, to be a Moor – may be a give-away, indicating an offloading of guilt. It means, to treat a woman badly.

Another consequence of the former Moorish presence is the continued celebration of the battles of the Moors and Christians, in bright and noisy, often very charming, pageants all over Reconquista Spain. We find ourselves in the Valencian town of Alcoy, known to students of political history as the scene of the longest-running anarchist-tinged revolution of the late nineteenth century. But what is it that they celebrate in Alcoy? Why, Moors and Christians, naturally, they are famous for it – though we noted that the 'Moorish' army in the procession got easily the biggest cheer as they marched by. This seemed fair enough since they had the liveliest fancy dress (Spaniards love dressing up) and the greater share of personal pulchritude. But is there really anything serious beneath these holiday displays?

In my view, yes there is, symbolically at least, for what the Reconquista represented in its latter stages was pure extremism, blamed on the Moors because of their existence but also – as has been demonstrated by the rest of Spanish history – a characteristic endlessly observable in Spaniards, with or without the Moors. What else was Franco's willingness to go to war? What else was his refusal to forgive all those who stood against him? Nor can one entirely disapprove, much as one would like to, for it is in the division of the world into light and darkness, black and white, this very Hispanic extremism, that there lies a willingness to go right to the brink and on beyond; and in that willingness may lie the roots of a courage that appears so admirable. (As a footnote, it should also be said that the Spaniards are no more sanguinary than anybody else. Even with the terror and the post-war killings, the numbers who died in the Civil War are now being continually revised downwards by historians, to the point where it seems that fewer may have died in Spanish conflicts during this century than in any other major European nation.)

Linked to courage, of course, is honour, and this, as a commanding concept, presumably derives in equal measure from Moors and Christians. Both admired it. One suspects a further linkage here, onwards to the strong sense of personal worth that lets a man work as a waiter and not be humbled (though that may be linked again to the Castilian notion that every true Spaniard is an aristocrat, with a dignity that may on occasion overcome the menial, however distasteful; or even to the abundant love proffered so unstintingly by Spanish mothers). Like courage, though, honour can be a two-edged weapon. Far too often it is no more than *amour propre* in disguise. One neat historical example occurred in 1905. Army officers in Barcelona felt their honour to be so deeply wounded by a mildly anti-military cartoon, in a comic paper at that, that they ransacked the paper's offices and then persuaded a frightened government to grant the military legal jurisdiction over everything said about them in print. This absurdity endured right up to the Second Republic. Afterwards, under Franco, to voice even mild criticism of the army was once again to take a considerable risk.

It is a different matter, but people ought to know that insults to the king are received with equal gravity, even in the new parliamentary monarchy. One day on my travels I happened on a newspaper report about a young man doing his national service. Writing to his girlfriend, he had stamped his letter and then extended the portrait of the monarch down across the envelope, showing him with his trousers down, exhibiting his private parts. The young man was now on trial and though he said he had done it thoughtlessly, to amuse his girlfriend, not to make any kind of political point, the prosecutor was icily demanding six years in prison.

Individualism and conformism; hospitality and honour; the sanctity of the state in the person of its head – all these are useful concepts when thinking about Spanishness. The two most useful of all are actually Catalan, the words for them invented to describe specifically Catalan qualities. They do so admirably but they also have a certain relevance for Spain as a whole. The first is *seny*, described by the Catalan sociologist Salvador Giner, in an essay on Barcelona, as an untranslatable word that 'simultaneously evokes common sense, prudence and wisdom' and refers to 'a sense of proportion in everything'. Coexisting with *seny* is *rauxa*, defined by Giner as 'naïve and euphoric improvization'. Once you have these ideas at your disposal, and acknowledge their coexistence, you begin to understand not only how Catalan bankers lived in Modernista houses, but the apparent paradox of *decencia* and *individualismo* and the means by which Spanish democracy has managed to survive so far in a land of scarcely modified extremism.

I have been pondering all these matters because at last I have a chance for a personal meeting with Salvador Giner. He is Professor of Sociology at Barcelona university, and it is a profession not yet discredited in Spain by politicians who find its results uncomfortable. He also heads the National Institute for Advanced Social Studies here in Madrid; a friendly civil servant has routed him out for a chat about the Spanish.

The three of us meet, inevitably, in a restaurant. I've come straight from the Prado and find Giner as full of opinions as I am about painting, more than willing to advise me on what to put into a book. 'You have to say a lot about it,' he declares, joking, but not absolutely. 'It is our painting that has saved our national honour on more than one occasion. Who could say that Spain was finished when we could still turn out a Velázquez or a Goya?'

'And by the way,' he says, 'talking of national honour and your book, I should personally be very grateful if you would do that one about the frank and classless man-to-man speech of Spaniards – you know, the sense of inner dignity that leaps over every boundary. That always goes down very well in Spain. Indeed I'd go so far as to say it is our favourite foreign observation.'

I feel a bit ashamed since, on the whole, I'm ready to believe it, even if it means believing Hemingway, but I am also beginning to get the measure of what turns out to be a jolly knockabout session, opinions tossed in the ring in quick succession, half to amuse, half to point up truths deeply believed in. The civil servant turns out to be another lively provider of opinions. I quote a few from both of my companions.

Giner on painting. He believes that Velázquez's *Vulcan's Forge*, with its common men as models, and all the hammering and heating up of iron, is actually a glorification of the working class, an antecedent of Goya's wounded carpenter. Both are 'great working-class masterpieces'. On the question of how it was that Goya was able to paint the royal family so 'ruthlessly' (Giner's word), he is convinced it was a mixture of stupidity and slavery to fashion. Goya is meant to be the best painter of the day. You hire him to paint your portrait and, hey presto, you are meant to have something that is a credit to you so there the matter ends.

Snippets on localism, both contributing. Localism is something we share with the Italians. We believe in our country through our own locality. But Spain is a very old kingdom. All this about a break-up is nonsense, there is not the slightest danger of it. On the other hand, there is nothing comic opera about regionalism. It is absolutely serious.

On ways of looking at people. I hear one of them say confidentially to the other: '"X" is all right as a minister, he's pretty good, but he's a first-rate intellectual.' The values are neatly reversed compared to those of the English-speaking world – being a good intellectual is more important than being a good minister. 'A waste of good horseflesh,' the civil servant explains in an aside.

On Spanish hospitality (reflecting the fact that most entertaining takes place in public places). If people come into our houses we have a way of saying '*esta es su casa*', this is your house, my house is your house, but then we go to great lengths to stop them ever coming back again. For a Spaniard, his house really is a castle.

On sexual mores and the nation's leaders. We very much admire people who have a lot of lovers. In fact, there is grave doubt as to whether our prime minister even has a mistress. We are very worried about him. But not even our gutter press would dare to say a word about the king, whatever he did or did not do.

Up comes the (true) story about an early Buñuel film financed from the lottery win of an Aragonese anarchist. 'Typical Aragonese high finance,' says one of my companions and now, to my surprise, there ensues a lengthy episode of jokes about the Aragonese and their reputation in other parts of Spain. I am reminded irresistibly of a letter from Aragonese Goya to his Aragonese friend Zapater. The painter has just delivered a new work to Carlos IV. The king expresses himself well-satisfied, 'putting his hands on my shoulder and abusing the Aragonese and Zaragozans'. Old customs die hard.

So what is worst about Spain, I ask, and what is best?

'We are devoured by envy,' says Salvador Giner. 'We cannot allow anybody, whether it's a politician or a singer or a footballer, to stay on top for a single moment. Somebody will always pull them down.

'But we have a compensation for envy in our belief in friendship. This is a country of fierce loyalties. Spaniards will kill themselves for their friends – what the Romans called *devotio iberica*. If somebody speaks badly of your friend, you get up full of pride and say "But he's my friend". Then it is the duty of the other person to say "Sorry, sorry" and take back everything he said. Really, I mean it. No joking. Spaniards believe in friendship; Spanish friendships are profound.

'It's a ridiculous country,' says Giner, 'but I have no other. It's ridiculous and I love it.'

If Andalucía is in favour, it is the Basques, and not the Aragonese, who are in disgrace. A restaurateur I have been talking to just lately, an elderly man, recounts how he was woken from his siesta by the telephone. It was a woman's voice asking him if it was true his restaurant served Basque dishes. Yes, indeed, he replied, being a Basque himself. 'You make me vomit,' said the woman. 'You literally make me vomit,' and before he could even begin his reply – that the things about the Basques that made her sick made him feel sick as well – she had slammed down the phone, leaving him in a terrible state of anxiety.

It is as well to be quite clear about the hostility now felt by Spaniards towards most things involving Basques and especially, superabundantly, towards the Basque militants and terrorists, known among their own supporters as Basque soldiers. For myself, I am on my way to the Basque Country to try to face these issues and I shall be staying in a highly political context, as the guest of a left-wing intellectual who writes a column in *Egín*.

Egín is a newspaper which is openly sympathetic to ETA, the Basque terrorist group. It is said to be funded by ETA and it refuses to condemn violence. It publishes ETA manifestos and communiqués as these are issued. It is close to Herri Batasuna, the political party which speaks for ETA.

ETA itself was founded in 1959, as a split within the Basque nationalist movement. The group quickly absorbed both Marxist–Leninist principles and a commitment to the 'armed struggle'. Their first action was the attempted derailment of a train carrying Francoist veterans. The result was arrests, torture and long prison sentences. Later, in the first major assassination during the Franco years, they killed the police chief of one of the Basque provinces, a known torturer by the name of Melitón Manzanas. Reporting on this episode for a British paper, I found the Basque Country full of joy. The name 'Manzanas' means 'apples', here as in Barcelona's Manzana de la Discordia, and everywhere you went, except in the presence of policemen, you could hear people singing a refrain: 'Rotten apples are falling from the trees'. In 1973, ETA managed to assassinate Franco's prime minister, Admiral Luis Carrero Blanco, blowing his car right over the top of a Madrid church.

More recently ETA has divided and divided once again and the targets of terrorism have become widespread. 'They strike wherever it will most offend and wound,' a non-political Basque has told me. There have been kidnaps and murders aimed at capitalism, regarded as an oppressor like the state. There have been bombs let off in tourist resorts, Benidorm among them. There have been bombings of the utterly uninvolved – most notably, in a supermarket in a poor part of Barcelona. ETA say that a warning was not transmitted; people outside the Basque Country speak of ETA as 'the kind of people who kill the poor in supermarkets'. At the structural level, ETA consider themselves to be at war, both with the military and above all with the Civil Guard. Far from slackening their efforts with the death of Franco, they have redoubled them. If there is a threat to Spanish democracy, it comes from ETA. If there is any likelihood of a break-up of unitary Spain – the single factor most likely to provoke an army intervention – then that, undoubtedly, must be attributed to the bitter and dirty struggle waged between ETA and the Spanish authorities who have as few qualms as ETA in their handling of hostilities.

Pablo Sorozábal, *Egín* columnist, may well be the gentlest person whom I know; and I claim him, in the Spanish sense, as a true friend – though it is also true that he has lost the closest of his friends by writing for a paper that refuses to condemn violence. I have known Pablo for decades, watching him emerge from the shadow of a famous father, a composer of *zarzuelas*, with the same name as his son, one known to almost every Spaniard. Little by little the younger Pablo Sorozábal has been logging up achievements – passionate lyric poetry, a prize-winning novel, translations of German literature, film music, an opera score. His settings of war poetry for soprano voices – left-wing Civil War poetry, that is to say – pierce as deeply and as passionately as any *saeta*. Now, with *Egín*, he has found a following. When I speak to those who read the paper, I discover that he is regarded as one of the intellectual pathfinders of the Basque far left.

Pablo lives partly in Madrid, partly in a few rooms in a tumble-down house in Aya, a hill-village a few miles back from the Basque coast. He welcomes me to Aya, in heat almost unknown in the

Basque Country, to crumbling plaster ceilings, old-fashioned, brown-painted doors and shutters and to floor-boards almost the width of a man. The elderly couple who live downstairs speak no Castilian; leaning out of the window we see a wide, deep valley, the hills above pine-clad. Mist tangles in wreaths about the upper slopes. Around us the village houses stand up steep and tall above gardens with onions and maize, cabbages and hydrangeas. The valley in between is dotted with *caseríos*. These are huge farmhouses, with broad-spreading Alpine roofs, seldom more than ten or fifteen acres of land, built to house people and animals. As used originally, they would be occupied by an extended family, perhaps four generations, with any number of single aunts or elderly grandparents and probably a young maid or two as well. It was in the *caseríos*, no longer shared with animals in these parts, and now quite likely to be the home of people working in the towns or the industrial valleys, that Basque culture and the Basque language were originally transmitted.

This language, as is well known, contains what may well be the most ancient linguistic elements in Europe, easily antedating Indo-European and with mild affinities, though no proven link, to languages of the Caucasus group, most notably Georgian. Some archaeologists suggest a possible continuity between the modern Basques and the palaeolithic inhabitants of the north coast, the very people who painted the bison of the Altamira caves. Linguistically, it sounds at least possible, with the word for knife, for instance, coming from a Basque root indicating stone. The tantalizing thought that Basque may actually be a Stone Age language is linked, however, to its unhappy status as a 'preliterate', rural tongue. To survive, it has had to adopt Latin words, perhaps as many as two-thirds of its whole vocabulary, transmuting them to such an extent that they are barely recognizable. Even so, the vocabulary was too limited and it has recently been necessary, with Basque as with other minority tongues for centuries used mainly in the home, to adopt neologisms to cover the modern range of technology and thought. All this arouses scorn in those who are hostile to the language and even gives pause to its potential friends. One keen linguist in Madrid has been demonstrating to me, rightly or wrongly, that the Basque words for peace and forgiveness both have Latin roots. 'The language is wonderful, a real linguistic jewel, but it is extraordinarily primitive, they could not even forgive each other until the Romans came.'

What is certain is that Basque was once more widely spoken than it is today and that it was the influence of Basque that determined the particular evolution of Castilian, distinguishing it in key particulars from other Romance languages. There are innumerable Basque place-names in Castile, showing that the Basques played a large part, along with more obviously 'Spanish' pioneers, in the Reconquista and settlement of this part of the peninsula.

These considerations, fascinating to linguists and historians, are, however, almost an embarrassment to Pablo Sorozábal. For one of the early features of Basque nationalism (which began in the 1890s, much later than in Catalonia) was a quite clear element of racism, based on Basque blood and language. Modern, left-wing nationalists, though they love the language, are anxious to disavow these origins.

'I am fiercely against racist ideology,' says Pablo. 'To the extent that some Basques have this racist element, I hate it with all my heart. But there is an extent to which ethnicity helps to define a nation, giving it recognizable national characteristics. Many of the immigrant workers who came here from southern Spain in the fifties and sixties have been absorbed to a great degree. Herri Batasuna (the political party speaking for ETA) believes that anyone who feels himself or herself to be Basque and identifies with the problems and aspirations of the Basque Country has a right to see himself or herself as Basque. Many prominent HB activists lack Basque surnames, they may have names that reflect family origins in places like Andújar in Andalucía.'

So what does it mean to feel yourself a Basque and why should anyone, whether of Basque or Andalusian blood, be ready to risk life and limb by joining the small minority that ETA seems to represent and going to war, inside a democracy, against the democratic state – and also be prepared to kill, if ordered to, not only

Civil Guards but ordinary men and women, people with no personal involvement?

Listening to Pablo, writer and supporter of Herri Batasuna, I hear him over and over again protest how he hates violence and fears it and how, in his opinion, it is wished on the Basque people by the state. Little by little, I begin to get some picture of what it is that has driven him and others to their extremist stance.

First, you have to feel the Basques are different. Then you have to feel that they are victims – victims of history, victims of the state and victims, now, of capital, both economic and geographical. It is also necessary to see the supposedly democratic, post-Franco state as a deceiving sham. Only if you adopt each and every one of these views can you begin to feel sympathy for ETA. And because these staging posts of opinion run contrary to the views and precepts by which most Spaniards live, including, very importantly, the Basque bourgeoisie, the actions of ETA remain a total mystery to almost everybody, seemingly wilful as well as hateful and threatening.

Wandering with Pablo among the high lanes and through the flowering meadows of his country, I hear the historical argument, starting with the loss of the language in Navarre even though it was a kingdom on its own. This, in his belief, was because the interests of the ruling classes were international, dynastic, not purely Basque. In the coastal districts of Vizcaya and Guipúzcoa, the lack of a Basque political structure, says Pablo, not only disempowered the culture in favour of Castilian but confined the Basque language to home and countryside. It was the failure to allow the Basques to be themselves politically that stopped their language from developing over the centuries – allowing its enemies today to argue that poverty of the language is a proof that being Basque means very little. On the contrary, says Pablo, being Basque today means undoing centuries of history.

As for the question of the *fueros*, their long existence so often taken as an indication that the Basques got good terms from the Castilian state, that was in Pablo's view a matter of advantage mainly to the bourgeoisie. The continued existence of the *fueros* right up until the latter part of the nineteenth century, far from being of help to the working classes, represented a system of control mutually agreed by the ruling classes both in the Basque Country and Castile. Control by the ruling classes oppressed the rural Basques. With the rise of Basque industrialism in the late nineteenth century, both the Basque industrial workers and the early immigrant workers from Andalucía (so hated by the first Basque nationalists) entered this same system of oppression. It was the bourgeoisie who were the main supporters of the original, right-wing nationalism intent on recovering the *fueros*. This interest is still represented by the PNV, the Basque Nationalist Party, who today hold most of the seats in the parliament of the Basque autonomy. The left must forget the *fueros*, just as it turns its back on the racism of the early nationalists. What is required is nationhood, not special exemptions.

As for the modern state and the inadequacy of its democracy, Pablo believes quite simply that the army rules the roost. It was they, he says, who dominated the 'so-called democratic transition', effectively establishing the terms on which a nominal democracy would be allowed to flourish. As for the Basques, he points to negotiations a few years back between the socialist government and ETA. All appeared to be going well. A joint communiqué was issued. Then, suddenly, the government withdrew. What else could possibly explain that blunt and unexplained withdrawal, Pablo asks, except a warning from the army, dedicated to 'the sacred unity of Spain'? While I am staying with him, a socialist minister declares at an academic conference that all the problems of the 'nationalisms' must be resolved within the existing structure of the autonomies. There will be no such thing as self-determination (outlawed, in any event, by the constitution). What is he saying, I ask, is that a simple statement or a negotiating posture? 'Neither, really,' says Pablo, 'I see it as a reassuring message to the generals.'

So what does Herri Batasuna want? It wants, says Pablo, self-determination, whether or not the constitution provides for such a thing, and hopes that the result will be a call for full, independent nationhood – like Portugal, he says, or any other small country. The mechanism must be a referendum, but one to be held only after a period of 'free' debate inside the Basque Country, without the distorting presence of the Civil Guard and army. 'Then the population may say, "We are Spanish, we love flamenco, bullfights, the Guardia Civil and especially the Spanish language." Alternatively, they may say, "We are Basques and we want to build a sovereign state just as Lithuania wants to."' Pablo says that Herri Batasuna, if defeated, would accept the will of the majority, declared in conditions of freedom.

ETA and Herri Batasuna are always accused of having no programme. As outlined now by Pablo, these demands, which he says are endlessly repeated, sound remarkably like the beginning of a programme. They are ingenious, too, in their implication that opinion cannot be freely formed under present 'democratic' conditions. This position helps excuse the fact that Herri Batasuna usually get only about fifteen per cent of the vote in the Basque Country. Equally it makes the most of another well-attested fact: whenever a policeman dies, the population is relatively unmoved; but if the police catch or kill one of the young Basque activists a wave of revulsion and hostility towards the state and the police sweeps through the cities, the towns and villages of the Basque Country. Secretly, perhaps, and this is what the activists believe, the people are more in favour of ETA and Herri Batasuna than the ballot-box reveals.

It is strange but true that in four days of discussing these issues, with thoughts of violence and death as a constant undertow, Pablo and I are living a kind of idyll. It is the heat, perhaps, the depth of the countryside, hydrangeas in the gardens, doves and swifts above the *caseríos*, the music, the poetry, the looking-up of texts from Lenin, the talk about the lighter side of the Basque nature – the betting and pelota playing, good food and drink, the mountaineering. In the end, though, it is a matter of metaphorical arm-wrestling.

How can one person, whatever the provocation, kill another for the sake of a language and for small-country nationalism?

Pablo once again makes his position absolutely clear. 'I refuse to label as violence the response that comes from the repressed. Of course, when the repressed use violence it *is* violence and moral wrongdoing. But it must be remembered that the violence of the oppressor came first. This is not always clear to those who don't take the trouble to study the question fully and stop at the appearances of things.'

Next, to get a new perspective on the question, we head down to the coast to speak to a woman of late middle age whose husband has been murdered, under horrifying circumstances, allegedly by agents of the police. It is a painful meeting and she, as well as Pablo, argues passionately that since it is the 'forces of order' who began the violence, then they must take responsibility for it. As for the guilt, she spoke as follows and I quote her as exactly as I can: 'We have lost so many of our own Basque soldiers and so many of the enemy have died that it would be a terrible thing for us to go on fighting unless we positively knew that we would win. It will not be in my time, but deep inside me I know one day the Basques will be a nation.'

I think of the Basque friend in Madrid who has said to me, wearily passing his hand across his eyes, 'I would rather the language died than another single human being.' After one more walk with Pablo, high on the hill in Aya, I pack my bags to leave, my Spanish journeys ending much as they began, among green hills and with the friendly smell of cattle. Yet this time it is easy to imagine the smell of human blood and fear the future.

I cannot bear to leave it quite like that. Another kind of memory to end with. One Sunday morning in El Escorial, in mid July, coming downhill into the town on foot, I hear the noise of fireworks, then a brass band, jaunty as can be. Outside the little convent of the Barefoot Carmelites, the order founded by St Teresa, a neighbourhood festival is in progress. In the steep little streets, on a terrace outside a café, a crowd has gathered, men and women, tidy, soberly dressed, even on a holiday. They are intent, watching something in the street below them. Approaching, I see it is a children's game. Strung across the street at head height, in complete absurdity, there runs a cord with a half-dozen chamber-pots dangling from it. The children stand waiting quietly in a queue and as they reach the front, they are blindfolded, handed a big stick and spun around three times. The cord is jerked so that the height of the chamber-pots must be a guess. The children raise the stick – and thwack. They miss it or they hit a chamber-pot and if they hit, the broken shards go flying everywhere, to wild applause from the public and a dance of triumph from the child. The blindfolded children spinning there like tops, the upraised sticks, the steady parents, sunlight pouring down – it is a Goya cartoon, nothing else, the people's game, a serious delight.

Select bibliography

WHILE CONCENTRATING ON major English language sources, this bibliography also indicates Spanish titles I have found especially helpful or thought-provoking. For ease of reference, the titles are divided into five broad categories: Guidebooks, Art & Architecture, History, Travel Writing & Anthologies, and Contemporary Spain.

ROAD-MAPS

Single sheet Michelin SPAIN AND PORTUGAL sheet 990, scale 1/1,000,000, works well in combination with ESPAÑA MAPA OFICIAL DE CARRETERAS, MOPU (Ministerio de Obras Publicas), in extended book form, 1/40,000. A wide variety of regional and tourist maps is available, together with Spanish Ordnance Survey maps (not all sheets are obtainable; most easily bought through Stanfords, 12 Long Acre, WC2).

GUIDEBOOKS

In all cases refer to most recent editions.

Bizagorena, Francisco de. *Salamanca: Su Historia, Su Arte, Su Cultura*, Guia Turistica, Gráficas Ortega, Salamanca, 1984.

Blue Guide, *Spain: The Mainland*, Ian Robertson, A. & C. Black, revised edition 1989. Extremely learned but conveys little of the feeling of a visit.

Boyd, Alastair. *The Essence of Catalonia*, André Deutsch, 1988. Excellent introduction to Catalonia, by an author who had earlier displayed

Castilian sympathies yet here proves himself sufficiently open-minded to see the best in Catalonia as well.

Castejón, Rafael. *Medina Azahara*, Editorial Everest, León, 1977.

Companion Guide, *Madrid and Central Spain*, Alastair Boyd, Collins, revised edition 1988. Ranks with this author's guide to Catalonia, as the best contemporary guidebook.

Everything Under the Sun/España series, *Spain*, Tom Burns, 1988. More than twenty individual cities are covered in slimline versions of the same series. Useful and intelligent.

Grunfeld, Frederic V. *Wild Spain*, Ebury Press, 1988.

Hidalgo Monteagudo, Ramon, et al. *Madrid del Siglo XIX: El Ensanche*, (Recorridos Didácticos por Madrid), Ediciones La Librería, Madrid, 1990.

Insight Guides, *Spain*, Kathleen Wheaton, APA Publications, Hong Kong, 1988. Good as preparatory reading, heavy to carry around.

Michelin (Green Guide), *Spain*, Michelin et Cie, Clermont-Ferrand. Updated regularly. Surprisingly selective.

Principado de Asturias/Consejería de Educacíon, Cultura y Deportes. *Hórreos Paneras Cabazos Y Graneros de Asturias* (leaflet), 1989.

Rough Guide to Spain, Mark Ellingham and John Fisher, Harrap Columbus, revised edition 1989. This title, and this series generally, is addressed with the enthusiasm of youth to the enthusiasms of the young. Well-informed and perceptive, the present volume should not be neglected even by those who may not care too much for the cheap meals and lodgings recommended.

ART & ARCHITECTURE

The Arts of Spain by José Gudiol and *Art and Architecture in Spain and Portugal 1500–1800* by George Kubler and Martin Soria in combination provide a general introduction to Spanish art and architecture. There is, however, no single, satisfactory, up-to-date work.

Baticle, Jeannine. *Goya d'Or et de Sang*, Découvertes Gallimard, Paris, 1986.

—— *Zurbarán* (with essays by Jonathan Brown, Yves Bottineau and Alfonso E. Pérez Sánchez), the Metropolitan Museum of Art, New York, distributed by Harry N. Abrams Inc. New York, 1987. Excellent essays and illustrations.

SELECT BIBLIOGRAPHY

Brown, Jonathan. *Images and Ideas in Seventeenth-Century Spanish Painting*, Princeton University Press, New Jersey, 1978. Stimulating work by an outstanding art historian.

—— *Murillo and His Drawings*, Princeton University Press, New Jersey, 1977.

—— *Velázquez, Painter and Courtier*, Yale University Press, New Haven and London, 1986. A great work of art history, luminous and accessible; hard to recommend too highly.

Brown, Jonathan and Pita Andrade, José Manuel (eds). *Studies in the History of Art 13/El Greco: Italy and Spain*, National Gallery of Art, Washington, 1984.

Calvert, A. R. *Moorish Remains in Spain*, Bodley Head, 1906. Monumental volume with splendid period illustrations.

Camón Aznar, José. *Alonso Berruguete*, Espasa-Calpe, Madrid, 1980.

Chabrun, Jean-François. *Goya*, World of Art Library, Thames and Hudson, 1966. A somewhat romantic view, common in bookshops but not highly recommended.

Collazos, Oscar. *Royal Palaces in the National Heritage of Spain*, Patrimonio Nacional/Lunwerg Editores, Barcelona, 1988.

Comisión Nacional Organizadora del Bicentario, *Carlos III y La Ilustración* (2 vols), exhibition catalogue, Ministerio de Cultura, 1988. A glorious mine of information on the Enlightenment.

Costa Clavell, Xavier. *Picasso*, Picasso Museum, Barcelona, Escudo de Oro, Barcelona, 1989.

Davies, David. *El Greco*, Phaidon, 1976.

Domínguez Ortiz, Antonio, et al. *Velázquez*, Museo del Prado, Ministerio de Cultura, 1990. Excellent catalogue to a fine exhibition; ranks with Jonathan Brown as a sourcebook on Velázquez.

Foucault, Michel. *The Order of Things*, Tavistock, 1970. (Original French title *Les Mots et les Choses*, published by Gallimard, 1966.) Contains a brilliant essay on Velázquez's *Las Meninas*.

Gallego, Julián. *Zurbarán 1598–1664*, Secker and Warburg, 1977.

Glendinning, Nigel. *Goya and His Critics*, Yale University Press, New Haven and London, 1977.

Goodwin, Godfrey, *Islamic Spain*, Architectural Guides for Travellers, Penguin, 1991. Up-to-date and useful.

Gudiol, José. *The Arts of Spain*, Thames and Hudson, 1964.

—— *El Greco 1541–1614*, Ediciónes Polígrafa, Barcelona.

—— *Goya*, Ediciónes Polígrafa, Barcelona, 1986.

Hilton, Timothy. *Picasso*, World of Art Library, Thames and Hudson, 1975. Excellent short introduction, though demanding close reading.

Hopkins, Adam. *Crete: Its Past, Present and People*, Faber & Faber, 1989 (first published 1979). Supplies background on early El Greco.

Kowal, D. M. *Ribalta y los Ribaltescos*, Diputación Provincial de Valencia, 1985.

Kubler, George. *Building the Escorial*, Princeton University Press, New Jersey, 1982. A specialist work, full of fascinating and unexpected information.

Kubler, George and Soria, Martin. *Art and Architecture in Spain and Portugal 1500–1800*, Pelican History of Art (hardback only), Penguin, 1959.

Licht, Fred. *Goya in Perspective*, Prentice-Hall, New Jersey, 1973.

Lozoya, El Marqués de. (Edición corregida y aumentada por Concha Herrero Caretera.) *Palacio Real de la Granja de San Ildefonso*, Editorial Patrimonio Nacional, Madrid, 1985.

Luca de Tena, Consuelo and Mena, Manuela. *Guide to the Prado*, Silex, Spain, 1988.

MacLaren, Neil (revised by Allan Braham). *The Spanish School*, National Gallery Catalogues, 1988. A specialist work, like Kubler's, and also full of fascinating and unexpected information.

McCully, Marilyn (ed.). *Homage to Barcelona* (exhibition catalogue), Arts Council of Great Britain, 1985. Wide range of essays and illustrations make this the best English-language introduction to Barcelona.

McKim-Smith, Gridley. *Examining Velázquez*, Yale University Press, New Haven and London, 1988. A technical work, but fascinating.

Mendoza, Cristina y Eduardo. *Barcelona Modernista*, Planeta, Barcelona, 1989. Liveliest general work on this subject so far in Spanish.

O'Brian, Patrick. *Pablo Ruiz Picasso: A Biography*, Collins, 1976.

Penrose, Roland. *Picasso: His Life and Work*, Granada, revised edition 1971 (first published 1958). A friend writing about a friend but with great perceptiveness.

Pérez Sánchez, Alfonso E. and Sayre, Eleanor A. *Goya and the Spirit of Enlightenment*, Bulfinch Press, Little, Brown and Company, Boston, Toronto and London, 1989. Places Goya thoroughly and soundly in his historical context, with proper reverence for his art but a commendable absence of the mawkishness this painter too often evokes.

Rahlves, Friedrich. *Cathedrals and Monasteries of Spain*, Nicholas Kaye, 1966. Useful but sometimes questionable in its conclusions.

Rice, David Talbot. *Islamic Art*, World of Art Library, Thames and Hudson, 1975. The classic general introduction to its subject.

Royal Academy of Arts. *Bartolomé Esteban Murillo*, 1983.

Sabartés, Jaime. *Picasso: An Intimate Portrait*, W. H. Allen, 1949. Sabartés was a friend of Picasso's youth and later became his secretary. Especially good on early days in Barcelona.

Sebastián, Santiago y Cortés, Luis. *Simbolismo de los Programas Humanisticos de la Universidad de Salamanca*, Universidad de Salamanca, 1973. Arguments abound on this subject, here treated in the light of information collected from wide-ranging sources.

Wethey, Harold E. *Alonso Cano*, Princeton University Press, New Jersey, 1955.

Williams, Gwyn A. *Goya and the Impossible Revolution*, Penguin, 1986. Extremely stimulating and ignored at its peril by the art-historical establishment.

HISTORY

Arnold, T. W. *The Preaching of Islam: The Propagation of the Muslim Faith*, Darf Publishers Ltd, new edition 1986 (first published 1896).

Brenan, Gerald. *The Spanish Labyrinth*, Cambridge University Press, 1943. Subtitled 'An Account of the Social and Political Background of the Spanish Civil War', this subtle and measured book was the first to offer serious explanations and remains a key text covering many creeds and issues.

Carr, Raymond. *Spain 1808–1975*, Oxford History of Modern Europe, Clarendon Press, second edition 1982. There is no other book on the period to rank with this fine, capacious work. Repays many readings.

Carr, Raymond and Fusi, Juan Pablo. *Spain: Dictatorship to Democracy*, Allen and Unwin, second edition 1981.

Casanova, Julián. *El Sueño Igualitario*, Institución Fernando el Católico, Zaragoza, 1988.

Cohen, J. M. *The Four Voyages of Christopher Columbus*, Cresset Library, 1989 (first published 1969).

Corral, José del. *Madrid 1561: La Capitalidad*, Biblioteca Básica de Madrid, Ediciones La Librería, Madrid, 1990.

Defourneaux, Marcelin. *Daily Life in Spain in the Golden Age*, Stanford University Press, Stanford, 1979 (first published 1966, in French).

Elliott, J. H. *Imperial Spain 1469–1716*, Penguin, 1990 (first published 1975). Remains unquestionably the greatest English-language work on the period and an unfailingly good read.

Fernández Alvarez, Manuel. *Charles V: Elected Emperor and Hereditary Ruler*, Thames and Hudson, 1976.

Fernández-Armesto, Felipe. *Ferdinand and Isabella*, Weidenfeld & Nicolson, 1975.

Fletcher, Richard. *The Quest for El Cid*, Hutchinson, 1989. A wonderful book, and a model of accessible scholarship.

Fraser, Ronald. *Blood of Spain: The Experience of Civil War 1936–1939*, Penguin, 1988 (first published 1979). Another English-language contribution of great weight and depth. Oral history at its best.

Fuson, Robert H. (trs.). *The Log of Christopher Columbus*, Ashford Press Publishing, 1987.

Gibson, Ian. *The Assassination of Federico García Lorca*, W. H. Allen, Penguin (first published 1973); *Gabriel García Lorca: A Life*, Faber & Faber, 1989; and see below under 'New Publications', p. 387.

Glick, T. F. *Islamic and Christian Spain in the Early Middle Ages*, Princeton University Press, New Jersey, 1979. Useful and perceptive though written in unpalatable jargon.

Haliczer, Stephen (ed.). *Inquisition and Society in Early Modern Europe*, Croom Helm, London and Sydney, 1987.

Hillgarth, J. N. *The Spanish Kingdoms 1250–1516* (2 vols), Clarendon Press, 1976.

Hopkins, Adam. *Holland*, Faber & Faber, 1988. Supplies background on the Low Countries wars.

Kamen, Henry. *Spain 1469–1714: A Society of Conflict*, Longman, London and New York, 1983. Dense, but takes account of recent scholarship, bringing the historiography up to date; makes a useful supplement to Elliott, above. Kamen has a good ear for the telling quotation.

Lewis, David (trs.). *The Life of St Teresa of Jesus* (written by herself), Thomas Baker, 1904.

MacKay, Angus. *Society, Economy and Religion in Late Medieval Castile*, Variorum Reprints, 1987.

—— *Spain in the Middle Ages: From Frontier to Empire, 1000–1500*, New Studies in Medieval History, Macmillan Education, 1987 (first published 1977). A pithy and observant work, deservedly admired in Spain.

Menéndez Pidal, Ramón. *Obras de R. Menéndez Pidal Vol. VIII, Orígenes del Español*, Espasa Calpe, 1986.

SELECT BIBLIOGRAPHY

Parker, Geoffrey. *The Dutch Revolt*, Penguin, 1990 (first published 1977). A fine book that inescapably arouses some anti-Spanish feeling.

Payne, S. G. *Falange: A History of Spanish Fascism*, Stanford University Press, Stanford, California and Oxford University Press, 1962. A little kinder to the Falange than one might wish to be today.

—— *Spain and Portugal* (2 vols), University of Wisconsin Press, Madison and London, 1973. A major work from America, frequently – and wrongly – omitted from British bibliographies. Though necessarily dense, it is the most useful single work on Iberian history. It was written while Franco was still alive and should be treated with increasing caution as it approaches modern times.

Peláez del Rosal, Jesús (ed.). *The Jews in Córdoba (X–XII Centuries)*, Ediciones el Almendro, Córdoba, 1985.

Pierson, Peter. *Philip II of Spain*, Thames and Hudson, 1975.

Preston, Paul. *The Triumph of Democracy in Spain*, Methuen, 1986. A specialist work, presenting solid facts while retaining the drama.

Read, Jan. *The Moors in Spain and Portugal*, Faber & Faber, 1974. Still useful but too firmly rooted in scholarly works that have dated.

Reilly, Bernard F. *The Kingdom of León–Castilla Under King Alfonso VI 1065–1100*, Princeton University Press, New Jersey, 1988. A scholarly work with a great deal of flavour.

Sánchez-Albornoz, Claudio. *Una Ciudad de la España Cristiana Hace Mil Años*, Ediciones Rialp, 1988 (first published 1965). Semi-fictional account of early León, carefully sourced in contemporary documents.

Sarrailh, Jean. *La España Ilustrada de la Segunda Mitad del Siglo XVIII*, Fondas de Cultura Economica, Mexico, Madrid and Buenos Aires, 1974. Originally in French; still regarded by Spaniards as a key work.

Señas Encinas, F. 'Desembarco y Estancia de Carlos I en Villaviciosa de Asturias', Boletín del Instituto de Estudios Asturianos, no. XXXIV, Oviedo, August 1958.

Smith, Colin (compiler). *Moors and Christians in Spain* (chronicles vol. 1), Avis and Phillips, 1988.

Thomas, Hugh. *The Spanish Civil War*, Penguin, third edition 1977, reprinted with new preface 1986 (first published 1961). This monumental book, now updated, remains as compulsive as when first printed. Paired with Fraser, it brings its complex subject-matter magnificently to life. Dismiss all criticism as jealousy.

Watt, W. Montgomery. *A History of Islamic Spain*, Islamic Survey 4, Edinburgh University Press, 1965. Short as it is, still the outstanding

English-language work, broad in scope and wise – even as a guide to contemporary Islam.

TRAVEL WRITING & ANTHOLOGIES

Brenan, Gerald. *The Face of Spain*, Penguin, 1965 (first published 1950).
—— *South From Granada*, Cambridge University Press, 1988 (first published 1957). Any work by Brenan should be read and treasured – he is surely the best British observer of twentieth-century Spain.

Cela, Camilo José. *Journey to the Aljarria*, Granta Books, 1990.

Ford, Richard. *Handbook for Spain 1845* (3 vols), Centaur Press, 1966. This prodigious work is the outstanding British source of the nineteenth century, with depths and singularities concealed by a modest title. Absurdly enough, it is seldom cited in academic bibliographies.

Irving, Washington. *Tales of the Alhambra*, Miguel Sanchez, Granada, 1987 (first published 1832). A fine work in the romantic idiom, it helped to 'fix' the dagger-and-carnations view of Spain.

Lewis, Norman. *Voices of the Old Sea*, Penguin, 1984. An elegiac evocation of a simpler Spain caught up in the first onslaughts of tourism.

Macaulay, Rose. *Fabled Shore*, Oxford University Press, 1987 (first published 1949). A book more interested in the past than people, it nevertheless catches the Spanish coast in the final years before the tourists came.

Michener, James A. *Iberia: Spanish Travels and Reflections* (2 vols), Corgi, 1983 (first published 1968). Huge and informative, if sometimes tedious.

Morris, Jan. *Spain*, Penguin, 1986 (first published 1964). Brief, vivid and highly wrought, this remains one of the best introductions to Spain.

Morton, H. V. *A Stranger in Spain*, Methuen, 1955.

Orwell, George. *Homage to Catalonia*, Penguin, 1991 (first published 1938). A classic work.

Pritchett, V. S. *The Spanish Temper*, Hogarth Press, 1984 (first published 1954).

Thomas, Hugh (ed.). *Madrid: A Travellers' Companion*, Constable, 1988. Excellent anthology, covering the whole of Madrid's history.

Walker, Ted. *In Spain*, Corgi, 1989 (first published 1987). Walker offers a real Spain, with grandads and grandmas, village festivals and everyday concerns. Highly recommended.

SELECT BIBLIOGRAPHY

CONTEMPORARY SPAIN

Collins, Larry and Lapierre, Dominique. *Or I'll Dress You in Mourning*, Simon & Schuster, New York, 1968. Biography of bullfighter El Cordobés. Journalistic style allied to interesting subject-matter.

Giner, Salvador (ed.). *España: Sociedad y Política*, Espasa Calpe, Madrid, 1990. Huge and informative.

Hooper, John. *The Spaniards: Portrait of the New Spain*, Penguin, revised edition 1987, new edition planned (first published 1986). Careful and enthralling to those with an interest.

Sastre, Alfonso. *El Camarada Oscuro, Tierra Roja*, Gakoa Liburuak, Donostia (San Sebastian), 1990. A playwright's tour through the contemporary history of the Spanish left.

Zulaika, Joseba. *Basque Violence: Metaphor and Sacrament*, University of Nevada Press, Reno, 1988.

NEW PUBLICATIONS

A great many new works on Spain, including the present volume, first appeared in 1992, the year of the Columbus quincentennial, the Seville Expo and the Barcelona Olympic Games. Some of the most interesting are listed below.

Boyd, Alastair. *The Sierras of the South*, HarperCollins.

Gibson, Ian. *Fire in the Blood: The New Spain*, Faber/BBC.

Gilmour, David. *Cities of Spain*, John Murray.

Hughes, Peter. *Barcelona*, Harvill

van Hensbergen, Gijs. *A Taste of Castile*, Sinclair-Stevenson.

Index

Academy of San Fernando (Madrid) 203, 224, 225, 231–2, 239, 279
ajimeces 101, 103, 104
alamedas 52
al-Andalus 12–17, 18–25
Albalate 301–2
Albox 100
Albufera de Valencia 66
Alcoy 365
Alfonso VI, King 50–51, 55–8, 63, 64, 65–6, 77
Alfonso VIII, King 75, 80, 110
Alfonso X, King 85, 114
Alfonso XIII, King 106, 283, 287
Alfonso the Chaste, King 6, 7, 9
Alhambra 98, 100–105, 119, 134, 135–6
Alicante 349
Aljafería 60–61
Allegory of the City of Madrid (Goya) 235
Almanzor (al-Mansur) 25–6, 33
Almería 97
Alpujarra mountains 97–8, 161
al-Rusafa 21–2
America(s) 124, 148, 165, 178
anarchism 260, 276–7, 283–4, 286, 289, 297–308, 313–14
Andalucía 11–17, 18–25, 362
Aragón 33, 60, 130–31, 161, 182, 212

Aranjuez, palace of 218–20, 256
Arévalo 90
aristocracy 32–3, 63–4, 92, 114–15, 147, 161, 184–5
Arlanzón, Río 51, 52, 109
Arnau, Eusebi 269
astrology 59, 142–3, 155–6
Asturias 1–11, 17–18, 26–40, 127–9, 289, 344–5
Aula Dei (near Zaragoza) 225–7
Aurora, La (Priego de Córdoba) 217–18
Avila 163–4
Aya 371–2

Badajoz 171
Barcelona 26, 33, 95, 212, 260–84 *passim*, 286, 299, 337–8
Basque Country 10, 11, 221, 288, 309, 321, 341–4, 369–77
Bautista de Toledo, Juan 155
Bayeu, Francisco 228
Belchite 314–15
Benidorm 350–52
Benítez, Manuel *see* Cordobés, El
Berruguete, Alonso 167–70
Berruguete, Pedro 109
Bierzo Mountains 48
Bilbao 114, 343–4
'Black Paintings' (Goya) 241

Bolín, Luis 295
botany 221–2
Bozman, Tim 225–7, 297–308
Brown, Jonathan 186, 197–8, 208
Buen Retiro 184, 203, 205, 220
bullfighting 332–6
bureaucracy 213, 320
Burgos 50–56, 64, 76, 109–12, 296–7
Burial of the Conde de Orgaz (El Greco)
175–7

Cáceres 202
Cádiz 115, 236–8
Café-Restaurant (Barcelona) 267
Calle Serrano (Madrid) 253
Canary Islands 123, 290, 339–41
Cangas de Onís 5
Cano, Alonso 166, 199–201, 202–3, 208–9
Capdevila Orozco, José 11–12, 15
'Caprichos' (Goya) 232–3, 240
Caridad, La 207–8
Carlism 247–8, 257, 288, 296
Carlos I, King (Charles V) 85, 87, 105–
6, 127–53, 170–71
Carlos II, King 210–11
Carlos III, King 218–22, 244
Carlos IV, King 230
Carlos, Don (son to Felipe II) 160–61,
165, 171
Carmen (Mérimée/Bizet) 84, 243
Carrasquer, Félix 301–2
Carrera, Ana 297–8
Carrión de los Condes 48
Carrizo ivory 35–6
Casa Amatller (Barcelona) 274
Casa de Campo (Madrid) 246
Casa de Contratación (Seville) 82–3, 178
Casa de los Muertos (Salamanca) 145
Casa Terrades (Barcelona) 274
Casa Vicens (Barcelona) 271–2
Casagemas, Carlos 280
Casanova, Julián 300–301, 306, 307
Casas, Ramón 274, 275–6, 277, 278
caseríos 372

Caspe 303–8
Castile 34, 50–51, 62–3, 131, 146–7, 160,
182
Catalonia 95–6, 117–18, 188–9, 190,
212, 221, 258, 261, 263–5, 281–4,
286, 288, 310–11
celosías 84
ceramics 71, 73, 86–7, 99–100, 345
Cerdaña (Cerdanya/Cerdagne) 95–6,
125, 210
Cervantes Saavedra, Miguel de 166, 183,
185, 209
Chana, Manuel Catalán 352
Chapel of Santiago (Burgos) 110
Charles V *see* Carlos I
Churriguera family 216
Cid, El (Rodrigo Díaz de Vivar) 51, 61–
6, 70
cinema 336–7
Ciudad Rodrigo 149
Civil War 106, 290–317, 366
Cluny 35
Coca 92–3
Coín 100
collectives, anarchist 298–308
Columbus, Christopher 121–4, 151, 262
Colunga 128
Comares palace 104
Comillas 344
comuneros 131–2
Condestable chapel (Burgos) 112
conquistadors, origins of 148–51
conversos 115–16, 147, 162
Corbera 316–17
Córdoba 11–17, 19–25, 34, 57, 58, 75
Cordobés, El (Manuel Benítez) 332–3,
334–5
Cortés, Luis 144–5
Costa Blanca 350–52
Costa Brava 347–8
Costa del Sol 348, 352
costumbrista school 265
Covadonga 2–5, 6
Coy, Javier 136–45

INDEX

Cross of the Angels 6
Cross of Victory 6
Cuba, loss of 258, 277, 282

Dalí, Salvador 310–11
death, theme of 145, 208
Descent into Limbo (Cano) 201
desornamentado style 156
Díaz de Vivar, Rodrigo *see* Cid, El
'Disasters of War' (Goya) 240–41
Divino, El (Luis de Morales) 171–2
Domènech i Montaner, Lluís 266–70
Domingo, Xavier 363–4
Don Juan legend, source of 208
Doncel, El 126
Donoso Cortés, Juan 251–2
'Dream and Lie of Franco' (Picasso) 311
Dream of Philip (El Greco) 174

Elliott, J. H. 158, 189
emigration, rural 319–20, 336
Empúries 347–8
Enlightenment 220–21, 224–5, 228, 233
Enrique II, King 91–2
Enrique IV, King 93–4
Escorial, El 153–7, 164–5, 174, 228
Espolón (Burgos) 52
Estella 46
ETA 370–77
Evocation (Picasso) 280
Extremadura 148–51, 202

Fable of Arachne (Velázquez) 195
Family, The (Velázquez) 196–7, 198
Fayon 316
Felipe II (Philip II), King 106, 138, 153–65, 170–71, 174–5, 180
Felipe III, King 181–2
Felipe IV, King 187–91, 205, 210
Felipe V, King 211–15
Fernández, Gregorio 198, 199
Fernando I, King 34, 35, 37
Fernando III, King (Fernando el Santo) 75, 84, 85, 98, 110–11

Fernando V, King (Fernando of Aragón) 62, 85, 88–126 *passim*, 130, 133
Fernando VII, King 239–42, 246
flamenco 328–31, 355–6
Fletcher, Richard 62, 70
football 336
Ford, Richard 193, 243
Forment, Damián 170
Franco y Bahamonde, General Francisco 5, 53, 62, 85, 106, 113, 139, 140, 244, 289, 290–323
Fuendetodos 223–4, 240

Galicia 17–18, 26, 50–51, 237, 345–7
Gandesa 316
Garrote Vil (Casas) 275–6, 277
Gaudí, Antoni 265, 270–73, 344
Generalife gardens 119–20
germanías 132–3
Gijón 341
Gil de Siloé 111–12, 113–14
Giner, Salvador 367–9
Giralda 72, 81–2
Gomera, La 123
González, Felipe 325, 327
Gonzalo de Córdoba 125
Goya y Lucientes, Francisco de 166, 222–42 *passim*, 340, 368
Gran Via (Madrid) 249
Granada 35, 97–105, 118–21, 125–6, 199–200, 201
Granja, La 211–15, 256
Great Mosque (Mezquita) of Córdoba 14–17, 24–5, 26, 134
Greco, El (Domenikos Theotokopoulos) 76, 77, 166, 171, 172–7
Guadalajara 113, 134, 292
Guadalupe 151, 203
Guanches 123
Guas, Juan 113–14
Guernica (Gernika) 295, 309, 343
Guernica (Picasso) 68, 309–13
gypsies 119–21

Hermida, gorge of 31
Herrera, Juan de 155, 178
Hispanidad 151
honour 366–7
hórreos 344, 346
hospitality 364–5, 368–9
huerta 302
   at Valencia 66, 69, 96
Huesca 43
hunger, culture of 331–2

Ibañez, Antonio Raimundo 345
Iglesia, Daniel de la 53–4
ikastolas 321
Ildefonso, St 79–81
Illuminists 147–8
Immaculate Conception, Doctrine of
   137
individualismo 364
Infantado (Mendoza) palace 113, 134,
   292
Inquisition 115–17, 138, 146, 147, 162,
   220
Isabel I, Queen (Isabel of Castile/Isabel
   the Catholic) 62, 85, 88–126
   passim, 133, 171, 335
Isabel II, Queen 246, 248, 255–6
Isabel of Portugal (mother to Isabel of
   Castile) 88, 111–12
Isla Cristina 353–9

Jaca 33, 41, 42–3
Jaén 75
James, St 18, 41, 74
Játiva 70
Jerez de los Caballeros 151
Jerez de la Frontera 150
Jews 13, 73, 74, 91, 115–16, 121
John of the Cross, St 162
José I, King 235
José Antonio (Primo de Rivera) 295–6,
   323
José de Sigüenza, Fray 155, 156, 175
Jovellanos, Gaspar Melchor de 220–21,
   229, 230

Juan II of Castile, King 88, 111–12
Juan Carlos, King 85, 323–7, 366–7, 369
Juan de Juanes 135
Juana la Beltraneja 93–4, 97
Juana la Loca 125, 129, 130, 131–2
Jujol, Josep Maria 273

Kamen, Henry 162
Koklova, Olga 310
Kubler, George 153, 156

La Alberca 149
La Rábida 122–3
La Rúa 39
Labours of Hercules (Zurbarán) 203,
   205
language 21, 31, 264–5, 372–3, 374
Lanzarote 339–41
Laredo 344
Las Casas, Bartolomé de 148, 165
Las Dueñas, Convent of 145
Las Huelgas, monastery of 109–11, 297
Las Meninas (Velázquez) 196–7, 198
Lebeña 31–2
Leodegarius 44
León 27–30, 31, 32, 33–40, 76
Lepe 354
Libro de Buen Amor 139
limpieza de sangre 147
Llanes 128
Lleó Morera house 267–9
Llerena 202
Llull, Ramón 263
Logroño 46
Lorca, Federico García 82, 120
Luis de León, Fray 90, 137–8, 172

McCully, Marilyn 311
Machuca, Pedro 135
Madinat al-Zahra 22–4
Madrid 180–85, 221–2, 245–60
   see also individual buildings
Madrigal de las Altas Torres 88–90, 108,
   115

INDEX

Málaga 97

Man and Woman in Front of a Pile of Excrement (Miró) 311

Mañara Vicentelo, Miguel 207–8

Manises 71, 99–100

Mannerism 171, 172, 173

Manrique, César 338–41

Manzana de la Discòrdia 267

Marañon, Gregorio 158

Marbella 348

María Cristina (wife to Fernando VII) 246–8

María Luisa (wife to Carlos IV) 230, 231

María Luisa park (Seville) 81, 356

Marsans, Enrique 295

Martyrdom of St Maurice and the Theban Legion (El Greco) 174–5

Masip, Vicente Juan 135

May 2 and *May 3* (Goya) 239

Medellín 150

Medina del Campo 89, 93, 116, 131

Melía, José 348

Mendoza palace *see* Infantado palace

Menédez Pidal, Ramón 5, 62

Mengs, Antón Rafael 222, 225

Mequinenza 316

Mezquita *see* Great Mosque

Minotauromachie (Picasso) 312

Mir, Joaquim 281

Miraflores, Charterhouse of 111–12

Miró, Joan 310, 311, 337–8

Modernista movement 261, 265–76, 277, 344

Montañés, Juan Martínez 198–200

Morales, Luis de (El Divino) 171–2

Moriscos, 161, 162, 182

Morocco 283, 284, 286, 290–91

Mota, La 93

Movida, La 39–40

Mozarabs 31, 55, 73–4, 78–9

Mudéjars 75–6

Mulhacén (Granada) 97

Muñoz, Luis 299, 300, 301, 314

Murcia 75, 349

Murillo, Bartolomé Esteban 135, 166, 206–9, 238

Naranco, Monte del 7–10

Niño de La Guardia 116

Nonell, Isidre 281

Noucentisme style 310

Old Woman Cooking (Velázquez) 179

Opus Dei 320

Oratory of San Felipe Neri (Cádiz) 236, 238

Orgaz 175

Orwell, George 260, 299

Oviedo 5–11, 289, 337

Pacheco, Francisco 177–8, 179

Palacio de Oriente 222

Palau de la Música Catalana 266–7

Palau Güell 272

Palos 122

Pantheon of León 33, 36–8

Pantoja de la Cruz 165, 171

Parc Güell 273

Pareja, Juan de 191

Paterna 99–100

Patio de los Naranjos 15

Payne, S. G. 158, 239

Pedrera, La (Barcelona) 273

Pedro I, King (Pedro the Cruel) 85, 91, 133

Pelayo 3–5, 6

Peña de Francia 149

Philip II *see* Felipe II

Philip the Handsome 125, 130

Picasso, Pablo 68, 278–81, 309–13, 334

Pico Veleta (Granada) 98

Picos de Europa (Asturias) 1–5, 10, 31–2, 127

Pilar, El (Zaragoza) 225

Pilgrims' Way to Santiago 35, 38–9, 41–50

plateresque style 113–14, 135, 143

Plaza Mayor (Madrid) 182–3, 335–6
Plaza Mayor (Salamanca) 216–17
Poema del mío Cid 74
poetry 19–20, 58, 73
police computer centre 322
Portico of Glory (Santiago de
    Compostela) 42, 50, 346
Prado gallery (Madrid) 183, 185–6,
    221–2, 248
Premonition of Civil War (Dalí) 310–11
Priego de Córdoba 217–18
Primo de Rivera, José Antonio 295–6,
    323
Primo de Rivera, Miguel 106, 284–6
Pseudo-Dionysius the Areopagite 173
Puente del Arzobispo 100
Puente la Reina 45
Puerto Banus (Costa del Sol) 348
Puerto del Carmen (Lanzarote) 341
Puerto de la Cruz (Tenerife) 339
Puerta del Perdón (Córdoba) 15
Puerta del Sol (Madrid) 182, 235, 239
Puig i Cadafalch, Josep 267, 273–4, 278,
    286

Quatre Gats, Els (Barcelona) 278, 281
Quevedo 27–8
Quinta del Sordo (Madrid) 241

Ramblas 261–2
Ramirez, Pepín 340–41
rauxa 367
Reconquista 4, 72, 75, 365–6
reflejo metálico 71, 87
Renaissance 134–5, 142–4
retablo(s) 78, 80, 112, 167–70
rías, Galician 346–7
Ribadeo 345
Ribadesella 128
Ribalta, Francisco 166, 192–3
Ribera, Jusepe 163, 166, 193
Rioja, La 46, 47, 56
Rokeby Venus (Veláquez) 191
Romanesque style 273–4

Roncesvalles 14, 45
Rosellón (Roussillon) 95–6, 125, 210
Royal Chapel (Granada) 125–6, 171
Rubens, Pieter Paul 194, 313
Rusiñol, Santiago 274–5, 278

Sabartés, Jaime 278, 280
Sagrada Familia 265, 270–71
Sagrado, Monte 9
Sagunto 70
Sahagún 48
*St Peter Nolasco's Vision of the
    Crucified St Peter* (Zurbarán) 203
Salamanca 136–45, 216–17
Salamanca Sky 142–3
San Benito (Valladolid) 167–70
San Esteban (Salamanca) 136
San Gregorio, College of (Valladolid)
    113–14
San Isidoro (León) 36
San Juan de los Reyes (Toledo) 112–13
San Julián de los Prados (Oviedo) 7
San Marcos (León) 27–8, 35–6, 39
San Miguel (Estella) 46
San Miguel de Escalada (León) 31
San Nicolás (Granada) 101
San Pablo el Real, monastery of 202
San Pedro de Cardeña, monastery of
    (Burgos) 65
San Sebastián 341–2
Sancha, Doña (wife to Fernando I) 34,
    35, 37
Sánchez-Albornoz, Claudio 32, 63
Sánchez Coello 165, 171
Sánchez Cotán, Juan 204
Sangüesa 44–5
Sant Pau, hospital of (Barcelona) 269–
    70
Santa Cristina de Leña (Asturias) 30–31
Santa Cruz (Seville) 84
Santa Cruz (Tenerife) 290
Santa Fe 120–21
Santa Gadea (Burgos) 64
Santa Hermandad 115

Santa María de Gracia, Convent of (Madrigal) 89, 90
Santa María del Naranco (Asturias) 8–10
Santa María la Real (Sangüesa) 44
Santiago, church of (Logroño) 46
Santiago de Compostela 18, 26, 42, 50, 345–6
Santillana del Mar 344
Santo Domingo de la Calzada 47, 170
Santo Domingo de Silos 48–50
Santo Tomás Cantuariensis (Salamanca) 136
Santo Tomé (Toledo) 175
Santullano (Oviedo) 7
Science and Charity (Picasso) 279
Sebastián, Santiago 68–9, 144–5, 313
Segovia 107, 131
seny 367
Seville 35, 58, 72, 75, 81–7, 117–18, 356
  alcázar at 85–7, 91, 133
  'golden age' in 177–9
  La Caridad at 207–8
Sigüenza, cathedral of 126
'Silver Philip' (Velázquez) 195–6
Simancas, castle of 132
Simón, Francisco Jerónimo 192–3
Sitges 275
slavery 21, 178, 191
socialist government 327, 362, 375
Soft Construction with Boiled Beans (Dalí) 310–11
Sorolla, Joaquín 259
Sorozábal, Pablo 371–7
Sos del Rey Católico 94–5
Still Life with Oranges (Zurbarán) 205
Suárez, Adolfo 324–5, 326
Surrender of Breda (Velázquez) 188

taifas 35, 56, 58–9, 65, 72
Talavera de la Reina 100
tapestries 222, 227–8
Tàpies, Antonio 338
Tazones 127–8

Teide, Mount (Tenerife) 123
Tejero, Antonio 325–7, 363
Tenerife 123, 290, 339
Teresa of Avila, St 116, 162–4
terrorism, Basque 370–77
tertulia 332
Teruel 76, 95, 100, 315
Theotokopoulos, Domenikos *see* Greco, El
Tioda (architect) 6, 7
Tobacco Factory (Seville) 84
Toledo 50–51, 57–8, 65, 76–81, 112–13
  cathedral of 76, 77–81, 119, 124, 131, 170, 173–4
  El Greco and 172–7
Tordesillas 129–30, 131
Toro 42
Torre del Oro (Seville) 72
Torremolinos 348
tourism 320, 340–52, 358
Transparency, The (Toledo) 78
Triana 82
Trueta, Josep 263
Trujillo 150–51

Unamuno, Miguel de 138
Utopia of Filarete 144
Utrillo, Miquel 278

Valdediós (Asturias) 30
Valencia, Rafael 86–7
Valencia 66–72, 75, 96, 132–3, 134–5, 182, 212
Valladolid 113–14, 181
Valley of the Fallen 322–3
Vázquez de Arce, Martín (El Doncel) 126
Velázquez, Diego Rodríguez de Silva y 166, 179–200 *passim*, 209, 210, 368
venta ambulante 121
Vergara, Ignacio 216
View and Plan of Toledo (El Greco) 175
Vigarny, Felipe 170

Villaviciosa 128
Vincent Ferrer, St 69
Visagra gate (Toledo) 57, 175
Viti, El 335
Vivar 64
Vulcan's Forge (Velázquez) 195, 368

Wass, Hans
    see Guas, Juan
Wellington, Duke of 236
Weyden, Rogier van der 185
women 83–4, 141, 365

writing
    Arabic 19–20, 58, 73, 84–5
    Spanish 183, 265

Yáñez, Fernando 134–5
Yuste 152–3, 157

Zahara 118
Zamora 42
Zapater, Martín 224
Zaragoza 17, 43, 59–61, 72, 224–5
Ziryab 19
Zurbarán, Francisco de 166, 202–6, 208–9

READ MORE IN PENGUIN

In every corner of the world, on every subject under the sun, Penguin represents quality and variety – the very best in publishing today.

For complete information about books available from Penguin – including Puffins, Penguin Classics and Arkana – and how to order them, write to us at the appropriate address below. Please note that for copyright reasons the selection of books varies from country to country.

In the United Kingdom: Please write to *Dept. EP, Penguin Books Ltd, Bath Road, Harmondsworth, West Drayton, Middlesex UB7 ODA*

In the United States: Please write to *Consumer Sales, Penguin USA, P.O. Box 999, Dept. 17109, Bergenfield, New Jersey 07621-0120.* VISA and MasterCard holders call 1-800-253-6476 to order Penguin titles

In Canada: Please write to *Penguin Books Canada Ltd, 10 Alcorn Avenue, Suite 300, Toronto, Ontario M4V 3B2*

In Australia: Please write to *Penguin Books Australia Ltd, P.O. Box 257, Ringwood, Victoria 3134*

In New Zealand: Please write to *Penguin Books (NZ) Ltd, Private Bag 102902, North Shore Mail Centre, Auckland 10*

In India: Please write to *Penguin Books India Pvt Ltd, 706 Eros Apartments, 56 Nehru Place, New Delhi 110 019*

In the Netherlands: Please write to *Penguin Books Netherlands bv, Postbus 3507, NL-1001 AH Amsterdam*

In Germany: Please write to *Penguin Books Deutschland GmbH, Metzlerstrasse 26, 60594 Frankfurt am Main*

In Spain: Please write to *Penguin Books S. A., Bravo Murillo 19, 1° B, 28015 Madrid*

In Italy: Please write to *Penguin Italia s.r.l., Via Felice Casati 20, I–20124 Milano*

In France: Please write to *Penguin France S. A., 17 rue Lejeune, F–31000 Toulouse*

In Japan: Please write to *Penguin Books Japan, Ishikiribashi Building, 2–5–4, Suido, Bunkyo-ku, Tokyo 112*

In South Africa: Please write to *Longman Penguin Southern Africa (Pty) Ltd, Private Bag X08, Bertsham 2013*

READ MORE IN PENGUIN

A SELECTION OF TRAVEL BOOKS

Hindoo Holiday	J. R. Ackerley
The Innocent Anthropologist	Nigel Barley
South from Granada	Gerald Brenan
The Road to Oxiana	Robert Byron
An Indian Summer	James Cameron
Granite Island	Dorothy Carrington
The Hill of Devi	E. M. Forster
Journey to Kars	Philip Glazebrook
Journey Without Maps	Graham Greene
South of Haunted Dreams	Eddy L. Harris
Mornings in Mexico	D. H. Lawrence
Between the Woods and the Water	Patrick Leigh Fermor
Mani	Patrick Leigh Fermor
A Time of Gifts	Patrick Leigh Fermor
The Stones of Florence *and* Venice Observed	Mary McCarthy
Calcutta	Geoffrey Moorhouse
Among the Cities	Jan Morris
Spain	Jan Morris
Sydney	Jan Morris
Travels in Nepal	Charlie Pye-Smith
The Kindgom by the Sea	Paul Theroux
The Pillars of Hercules	Paul Theroux
The Marsh Arabs	Wilfred Thesiger
Behind the Wall	Colin Thubron
Journey into Cyprus	Colin Thubron
The Lost Heart of Asia	Colin Thubron
Ninety-Two Days	Evelyn Waugh
Third-Class Ticket	Heather Wood
The Smile of Murugan	Michael Wood
From Sea to Shining Sea	Gavin Young